Advance Praise for *Raw Life*:

"Patrick Boyer's well-known respect for the intelligence of others is on display here. He lets us, in effect, see the raw documents of raw life. The cases here are often troubling but sometimes heartwarming."

— Honourable R. Roy McMurtry, Q.C.

"Bracebridge, before 1900, was so wild that it required fourteen magistrates or JPs to keep the peace. The bench book of James Boyer, one of few legally trained magistrates in the province pre-1900, provides the focus for this book. The result is a rare glimpse of frontier Muskoka. Introductory chapters by magistrate Boyer's great-grandson Patrick, himself learned in the law and steeped in Muskoka history, make the lively stories in *Raw Life* especially informative for anyone interested in Ontario's justice system."

— Honourable D.C. Thomas, Muskoka District Judge

"Boyer's skills as a writer and careful historian are on full display here. We learn about the people of the era as if the author had somehow observed them personally."

— Edward L. Greenspan, Q.C.

Boyer, J.
Raw life.

PRICE: $39.99

JAN 2013

ALSO BY J. PATRICK BOYER

Solitary Courage: Mona Winberg and the Triumph over Disability (2010)

Local Library, Global Passport: The Evolution of a Carnegie Library (2008)

A Passion for Justice: How "Vinegar Jim" McRuer Became Canada's Greatest Law Reformer (revised paperback edition, 2008)

A Man & His Words (2003)

Leading in an Upside-Down Word (contributing editor, 2003)

"Just Trust Us": The Erosion of Accountability in Canada (2003)

The Leadership Challenge in the 21st Century (2002)

Accountability and Canadian Government (2000)

Boyer's Ontario Election Law (1996)

A Passion for Justice: The Life and Legacy of J.C. McRuer (hardcover edition, 1994)

Direct Democracy in Canada: The History and Future of Referendums (1992)

The People's Mandate: Referendums and a More Democratic Canada (1992)

Hands-On Democracy: How You Can Take Part in Canada's Renewal (1993)

La Democratie pour tous: Le citoyen ... artisan du renouveau Canadien (1993)

Local Elections in Canada: The Law Governing Elections of Municipal Councils, School Boards and Other Local Authorities (1988)

Election Law in Canada: The Law and Procedure of Federal, Provincial and Territorial Elections — Vol. I (1987)

Election Law in Canada: The Law and Procedure of Federal, Provincial and Territorial Elections — Vol. II (1987)

Money and Message: The Law Governing Election Financing, Advertising, Broadcasting and Campaigning in Canada (1983)

Lawmaking by the People: Referendums and Plebiscites in Canada (1981)

RAW LIFE

Cameos of 1890s Justice from
a Magistrate's Bench Book

J. PATRICK BOYER

DUNDURN
TORONTO

Project Editor: Michael Carroll
Editor: Domenic Farrell
Design: Courtney Horner
Printer: Webcom

Library and Archives Canada Cataloguing in Publication

Boyer, J. Patrick
     Raw life : cameos of 1890s justice from a magistrate's bench book / by J. Patrick Boyer ; forewords by Edward L. Greenspan and Roy McMurtry.

Includes bibliographical references and index.
Issued also in electronic formats.
ISBN 978-0-9781600-4-3

     1. Crime--Ontario--Muskoka (District municipality)--History--19th century. 2. Law enforcement--Ontario--Muskoka (District municipality)--History--19th century. 3. Criminal justice, Administration of--Ontario--Muskoka (District municipality)--History--19th century. I. Title.

HV6810.M87B69 2012   364.9713'16   C2012-900120-1

1 2 3 4 5   16 15 14 13 12

We acknowledge the support of the **Canada Council for the Arts** and the **Ontario Arts Council** for our publishing program. We also acknowledge the financial support of the **Government of Canada** through the **Canada Book Fund** and **Livres Canada Books**, and the **Government of Ontario** through the **Ontario Book Publishing Tax Credit** and the **Ontario Media Development Corporation**.

Care has been taken to trace the ownership of copyright material used in this book. The author and the publisher welcome any information enabling them to rectify any references or credits in subsequent editions.

J. Kirk Howard, President

Printed and bound in Canada.
www.dundurn.com

Dundurn	Gazelle Book Services Limited	Dundurn
3 Church Street, Suite 500	White Cross Mills	2250 Military Road
Toronto, Ontario, Canada	High Town, Lancaster, England	Tonawanda, NY
M5E 1M2	LA1 4XS	U.S.A. 14150

In memory of James and Hannah Boyer
and the feisty resolve
of all whose lives are in turmoil

CONTENTS

COMMON HUMANITY

Raw Life shows the experience of our pioneer ancestors on those often challenging days when the rule of law and the rough tumble of life intersected with raw honesty in Magistrate's Court.

The "raw life" of earlier times is not diluted or glossed over here by extracting its essence or generalizing its features; instead, the book presents these original moments in time in the actual words of the people involved, providing those reading them in our present times with both astonishment and amusement. We get the straight goods as they appeared on the record.

These cases from more than a century ago offer a unique way to glimpse life and learn history. For although each case on its own may be a very small snapshot indeed, this book resembles a composite photo album. It imparts an overall impression of how social and economic conditions refract through the justice system, and in doing so it portrays the culture of a community, the legal framework of a country, and the timeless face of humanity.

The diverse scenes are grouped according to themes, ranging from "early road rage" to "women's fears and women's fates," from "hard love for the indigent" to "the high price of stolen goods." Reproducing the proceedings in their original form gives a contemporary reader an opportunity to sense the rhythms of small-town life and low-life action, without mediation or "interpretation." The cases are often troubling, but sometimes heartwarming. Overall, they show in the administration of justice how individuals on the bench seek to provide even-handed treatment for a most uneven assortment of claims and prosecutions.

Law and the administration of justice are not abstract phenomena. To be understood and appreciated, they must always be seen in context. Patrick Boyer sets the scene for these cases by first providing that historical setting: portraits of those who served as justices of the peace; and background history about the community in which these vignettes of crime and justice unfolded. We see the evolution of the office of justice of the peace, but we also glimpse in the lives of JPs themselves that the rawness of the times was often as much a part of their own experience as of the men and women arraigned before them in the courtroom.

Although I have known Patrick as a friend for over four decades, it was a revelation to learn more about his ancestor magistrate in the chapters describing James Boyer and his times. It is clear that "raw

life" was what everyone in Magistrate's Court experienced, including the justice of the peace himself. In the lesson of that man's life, we are reminded that all of us are human, even when we occupy a public office. Despite many differences that demarcate us, one from another, as individuals, our common humanity is the greater link uniting us all.

R. Roy McMurtry: "common humanity uniting us all." (Photo: David Batten, Toronto)

It is rightly said that justice delayed is justice denied, but it is equally true that justice delayed is the undoing of a healthy social order. That is why the lowly justice of the peace occupies a high rank, or deserves to, in a country where they serve to quickly address individual grievances and misdemeanours with front-line justice, so that these are not allowed to fester during delay, or go unanswered and grow over time into bigger crimes or deeper social injustices.

The human stories embedded in these episodes that Patrick refers to as "the small change of history" — in comparison to more historic or noteworthy cases from higher courts — put a personal face on an earlier Canadian society that, though vastly different in culture and technology, is eerily like our own in its humanity. *Raw Life* offers a rare dose of realism, one that demolishes false nostalgia for "the good old days" even as it fosters a sense of optimism about humanity's enduring resilience.

In the book's final chapters, Patrick draws out many of the parallels between the 1890s and our present era, while also noting what has changed. The land of Canada is much the same, even though our way of living on it has altered dramatically. The laws of Canada still engage the same challenges, even though they have been reformed and expanded to meet new conditions. What we see in *Raw Life*, through the workings of the Canadian justice system at its lower reaches, is how we share in common with our ancestors the reality of human character being tested in a variety of difficult circumstances.

Patrick Boyer previously made a contribution to preserving our legal heritage with *A Passion for Justice,* his masterly biography of Canada's remarkable jurist and law reformer, J.C. McRuer. Now, with *Raw Life,* Patrick displays his continuing commitment to this field, and once more displays his writer's skills by integrating solid research, important history, and direct evidence from the courtroom itself. Most astonishingly, he also provides a compelling, and unusual, tribute to his ancestors.

Honourable R. Roy McMurtry, O.C., O.O., Q.C.

THIS UNIQUE AFTERTASTE
OF HISTORY

Patrick Boyer made an incredible discovery when he found his great-grandfather James Boyer's bench book. James, who served as a justice of the peace in Bracebridge, Ontario, in the 1870s, 1880s, and 1890s, used the bench book to record his own notes of the facts and evidence of the trials he heard, along with the rulings in those cases. It is our good fortune that Patrick has decided not just to share the bench book with us, but to provide it to us with an illuminating description of life in Northern Ontario at the end of the nineteenth century.

The Magistrate's Court described in *Raw Life* was truly the people's court. You will not find any trials of the century here. But while the trials were brief and justice swift, these cases clearly had the potential to have a major impact on the lives of those involved. Charges such as theft, assault, and drunk and disorderly conduct were common, and we can still sense the tension that must have existed between neighbours, spouses, and other aggrieved parties before the court. Family members take sides against family members, witnesses contradict one another, and we are left to wonder — as Justice Boyer was left to decide — who to believe. Bracebridge was still being settled in the 1890s, and we can sense in these disputes that the justice of the peace may have been the linchpin who kept the developing community from anarchy.

In Part I, Patrick takes us back to his great-grandfather's time. Patrick's skills as a writer and careful historian are on full display here. We learn about the people of the era as if the author had somehow observed them personally. The early chapters of this book vividly provide the important history and context for what is to come. Anyone who cares about our great history will be fascinated by the richness of the description of small-town northern Ontario in the 1890s.

You may be tempted to jump ahead to the bench book chapters. Resist this temptation. The chapters that precede Part II are not mere *surplusage*. If James Boyer had never taken a single note in court, Part I of *Raw Life* would still be a fascinating story of the time. Patrick's discovery of the bench book was like finding a rough mineral, and we can see it as the gem that it is thanks to his polishing in Part I.

All judges inevitably bring the experiences of their formative years to the judgment they employ on the bench. James Boyer's formative years, leading

up to his years as a justice of the peace were truly remarkable. The tale of his life's journey would not be out of place in a Charles Dickens novel, except that James's story is not fictitious. No doubt his wife's compelling personal history must have also influenced and guided James's temperament as a justice of the peace. The chapters on James's life are essential to this book. Had the bench book of an otherwise

Edward L. Greenspan: "human experience … a timeless bond." (Photo: Al Gilbert, C.M.)

anonymous justice of the peace been discovered, it would be a far more generic experience to read the cases. Patrick gives us a personal introduction to his fascinating great-grandfather so that we can picture him hearing the cases, and bringing his life experience into the decisions he renders.

It would have been easy for the author to have simply written a brief introduction and published the bench book with no further context. Instead, throughout Part I Patrick paints a canvas of Bracebridge and its inhabitants in the 1890s. In Part II, Patrick lets James provide the details that complete the picture. The bench book entries are the heart of this book. Consider that Justice of the Peace Boyer's bench book is likely the only surviving record of the cases described. Undoubtedly, in most of the cases, the bench book entries may be the only remaining written record of the participants' very existence.

The bench book entries are presented unedited, in their original form, as they should be. As you read the cases, take note of the dates. In some instances, the case is heard the very same day as the alleged offence. Take your time as you explore the cases. Read them slowly and let the settings and descriptions of Part I fuel your imagination to fill in the blanks.

These are indeed stories of raw life, but do not forget these are real life too. It is fascinating to use these stories to contemplate how different life was then, little more than a century ago. But it is also intriguing to examine whether the conflicts from back then are really much different from the disputes and conflicts that we continue to see within our own lives and communities. That thought, and others springing from this unique taste of history, are handily woven together by Patrick in Part III.

As James Boyer heard cases, he had no idea that his notes would one day provide a unique insight into life in Ontario at the turn of the last century to an audience of readers in the next millennium. With a sense of awe, we can try to wonder what our great-grandchildren's lives may be like. But as this book reminds us, while we may progress with our technology and civilization, the human experience from generation to generation remains a timeless bond.

Edward L. Greenspan, Q.C., LL.D., D.C.L

Prelude

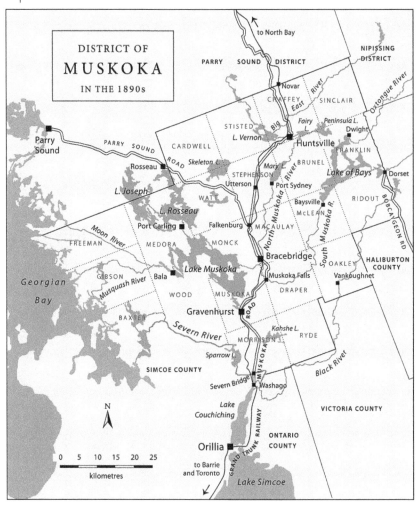

DISTRICT OF
MUSKOKA
IN THE 1890s

to North Bay

PARRY   SOUND   DISTRICT

NIPISSING
DISTRICT

Novar

CHAFFEY   SINCLAIR

East River

Big

Fairy
L.

Peninsula L.
Dwight

STISTED

L. Vernon

Huntsville

FRANKLIN

Parry
Sound

PARRY   SOUND

CARDWELL

ROAD

Skeleton L.

Mary L.

BRUNEL

Lake of Bays

Dorset

Rosseau

STEPHENSON

North Muskoka River

L. Joseph

Utterson

Port Sydney

Baysville

RIDOUT

BOBCAYGEON RD

WATT

McLEAN

South Muskoka R.

L. Rosseau

Port Carling

Falkenburg

MACAULAY

Moon River

FREEMAN

MEDORA

MONCK

Bracebridge

OAKLEY

HALIBURTON
COUNTY

Georgian

GIBSON

Musquash River

Bala

Lake Muskoka

Muskoka Falls

Vankoughnet

Bay

MUSKOKA

DRAPER

WOOD

BAXTER

Gravenhurst

ROAD

Kahshe L.

Severn River

MORRISON

RYDE

SIMCOE COUNTY

Sparrow L.

MUSKOKA

Black River

Severn Bridge

Washago

VICTORIA COUNTY

N

Lake
Couchiching

GRAND TRUNK RAILWAY

0   5   10   15   20   25

kilometres

Orillia

to Barrie
and Toronto

ONTARIO
COUNTY

Lake Simcoe

Oxtongue River

Theme of the Drama: Justice, and the Small Change of History

Sexual favours for sale, feisty street brawls outside taverns, women stalked, wives beaten, potato diggers and bricklayers suing flinty employers for unpaid wages: if this is 1890s Bracebridge theatre brought to the courtroom stage, what else can be happening in this hub of Muskoka's celebrated tourist district?

Along the town's main street, a butcher has maggot-infested meat in his cellar. Down by the river, a local slaughterhouse owner, undeterred by earlier fines, dumps offal into the waters. All the while, a quack Scottish "doctor" authoritatively prescribes ineffectual medicines, the town's Chinese laundryman surreptitiously contaminates the street by discharging used chemical fluids at night, and Yankee bushlot distillers apprehensively hide their backwoods operations from prowling revenue inspectors. Farm boys ride horses furiously through the muddy principal thoroughfare. Stray cows graze on homeowners' flower gardens and vegetable patches.

Wily men trap muskrat above the legal limit, and desperate men feed their hungry families with deer killed out of season.

Men and women wrestled with themselves, primitive conditions, discordant possibilities, and their neighbours. Their unfolding dramas were held in check and covered over, whenever possible, by a thin veneer of civilization. And where that civilization's vaunted "rule of law" intersected with these actors was in Magistrate's Court.

For this book's presentation of those cases, I've chosen a theatrical motif because trials are morality plays, a form of theatre. Besides resolving disputes and meting out punishment to specific offenders, courts present drama for the wider community, dispatching general messages about right conduct. As further inspiration for the motif, James Boyer's own formative years in Stratford and his lifelong devotion to the works of William Shakespeare likewise invite theatrical awareness for the story of justice in his 1890s Magistrate's Court. Like a play by Shakespeare, the numerous scenes comprising *Raw Life* display in full range the human condition: pathetic, comedic, heroic, ironic, and tragic.

Part I serves as a prelude to the cases: its chapters set the context, sketching the character of the times, and introducing Magistrate James Boyer. Part II presents previously unpublished glimpses of Muskoka life as seen from a unique, behind-the-stage-sets vantage point: the magistrate's bench. Part III views through the lens of time — looking from the twenty-first century back to the late nineteenth — how these "morality plays" reveal both continuity and change in society's standards and Canadian justice.

Life's crazy jumble was presented in Magistrate's Court according to its own sequence and harmonies of organization, and that is how it was recorded by James Boyer. Instead of reproducing ten years' worth of cases as they occurred day after day, however, I've grouped them into twenty-six thematic "acts" for a more comprehensive sense of the way justice was dispensed. But categories impose artificial barriers between the elements of life as it actually occurs, and the trade-off for orderly comparison of similar events can limit understanding at a higher level. I fear my quest for a suitable category in which to place an episode parallels a constable's 1890s challenge in deciding which of several possible charges to lay in a complex situation. For instance, in one case a settler brought his neighbour before the magistrate on a charge of unlawfully killing ducks on Sunday, and collected half the fine. Is that best placed with the cases of (a) illegal hunting of game, (b) breaching observance of The Lord's Day Act, (c) those ongoing feuds between neighbours that intermittently escalate to laying charges, or (d) how the justice system awarded private citizens a portion of the fine for bringing a lawbreaker to court? Because that real 1897 event incorporated all four, placing the case in the "Ill-Gotten Game" chapter rather than in the "Saving the Sabbath" chapter was, like the labelling in several other cases, as artfully arbitrary as a director deciding where on stage certain performers should stand.

Some further choices had to be made, too, when translating five hundred handwritten pages of 1890s cases into a contemporary book. Some similar cases have been dropped from the chapters on fighting, drinking, and suing for unpaid wages; after a while, one gets the point, and space is limited. Likewise, a few cases that involved only an arraignment, guilty plea, and sentencing, with no interesting evidence about what transpired, have been excluded. Yet, most cases, including many similarly sparse on detail, have been reproduced because they portray life in its rawer varieties and provide a cumulative impression of life behind the picturesque postcard images of Muskoka.

You will not encounter Muskoka's leading lights or major characters here. If not for a brief entry in James Boyer's bench book, there would be no remembrance, in many cases, that the people who do appear in these pages ever lived. These are the walk-on players, the small folk whose limited action gives counterpoint to the leaders acting out grander roles on the town's stage and in our country's history. Rarely did the prominent or prosperous, the pious or polite, get dragged into "police court." The only churches mentioned in these 1890s cases are the Salvation Army and the Free Methodists, which ministered religion to the same threadbare congregation whose members on weekdays found themselves variously reassembled in Magistrate's Court.

Individuals hauled before the local justices of the peace were not charged for high crimes, but for low-life enjoyment of a Bracebridge brothel; not for capital murder, but for running their knife across the guy wire of a tent at an evangelical prayer meeting, or for threatening to slash his wife's throat "from ear to ear"; not for defrauding the government of thousands of dollars, but for lifting a silk scarf or stealing a dog.

James Boyer's bench book, in furnishing the contents for Part II, adds colour to that grey zone of society where good manners end and the rule of law must begin. His Magistrate's Courtroom, becoming once again an illuminated stage in a long-darkened playhouse, highlights an intrinsic theme of justice: *How small people at its margins are treated reveals big truths about a society.*

This book is about the meaning of justice in places so out of the way they cannot be identified by local historic site markers, involving lives so minor they cannot be found in the town's official histories. It was precisely for those hard-pressed individuals, in those twilight places, that civil rights and the possibility of justice meant everything. If the rule of law is not real at ground level, then lofty pronouncements about "justice" can only ring hollow in the ears of struggling citizens.

I believe resurrecting these cases from Canadian history and viewing its fuller picture allows us to interpret human progress better, and more sympathetically. While inadvertent omission is a passive fault, neglect is usually a purposeful one. So, while reprising these brief courtroom appearances of earlier Canadians may entertain and enthrall with the emotions they evoke, perhaps they can also educate and enlighten through their embrace of everyday experience.

Many of these Muskoka Magistrate's Court cases never made it into the news columns of Bracebridge's weekly newspapers. When they did, the entries were usually brief: "Chas. Grimes of the township of Watt was before Justice Boyer last Thursday and committed for trial on a charge of stealing saw logs"; "On Tuesday before Justice Boyer, Joshua Earnshaw, a young man of Watt, was charged with having criminally assaulted Eliza Emerson, a 12-year-old girl living in the same township"; "Tuesday afternoon, H.A. Piper was fined $1 and costs, in all $4.50, for using obscene and irritating language on the street towards Annie Hay."

There is much to ruminate about and reflect upon in this engaging, human, realistic, sometimes funny, and often disturbing view of a rugged and lively small town. Bracebridge in the 1890s is a place and time that is foreign to us now, but the people we encounter may not seem so dissimilar to Canadians today, at their own edges of emotion and in their engagement with raw life.

In the end, the dramatic theme emerging from this seemingly inconsequential tableau of "small-change" cases is nothing less than the most fundamental imperative in all societies: the quality of justice.

The small change of history does add up. The morality of a nation is not confined to pious people in the pews, but is equally on display in the hallowed sanctity of its squat stone jails.

Part I: Setting the Stage

Chapter One

THE VENUE: FROM DIRT FLOORS TO THE GAY NINETIES

Muskoka District, land of First Nations peoples for over five thousand years when Canada's incomparable explorer David Thompson mapped the place in 1837, was traversed by fur traders and surveyors in the early to mid-1800s, but only felt the hard edge of intrusion with logging along its southern perimeter in the 1850s and land settlement a decade later. Construction of crude colonization roads opened the way for early arrivals. Then the trickle of settlers turned into a flood after Ontario's legislature, wanting to entice more newcomers to fill and farm the empty tract, enacted The Free Grant Lands and Homestead Act in 1868. The result was a land boom.

The exhilarating promise of a fresh start in life drew many improbable settlers to this wilderness frontier. An anxious jumble of characters abandoned their problems and set out for Muskoka to start anew on their hundred acres of "free" land, hoping to cash in on a promise Ontario's government and its immigration agents were aggressively promoting through advertisements in American and British newspapers and in the booklet *Emigration to Canada: The Province of Ontario*, circulated widely in 1869 to publicize Muskoka's glowing agricultural prospects for new settlers.

Few heading to Muskoka sought a transformation more complete than a desperate thirty-five-year-old lawyer who, early one September morning in 1869, boarded the train in New York as Isaac Jelfs, but stepped off in Toronto as James Boyer. Accompanying him was a pregnant woman, their little girl, a curly-haired teenager, and another woman in her early twenties. Nobody could have mistaken this formally dressed family group for pioneer settlers heading into Muskoka's wilds to hack a homestead out of dense forest. Yet, such was their intent.

Not only was Jelfs abandoning his name. He was forfeiting a long-craved legal career with the politically influential Broadway Avenue firm of Brown, Hall & Vanderpoel. He was relinquishing his recording secretary's role with the Episcopalian Methodist Church in Brooklyn. He was abandoning the vice-presidency of the Brooklyn Britannia Benevolent Association, an office to which he'd been glowingly elected in May that year, being presented with a copy of Byron's poetical works and making, as the *Brooklyn Daily Eagle* reported, "one of his happy speeches on the occasion."

The real kicker was that he had closed the front door of the Jelfs's 18th Street family home in Brooklyn for the last time. Overnight Isaac vanished from the life of his wife, Eliza, and their young daughter, Elizabeth. The pregnant woman on the train, Hannah Boyer, was not his wife in law, but had become a second wife in reality after she'd captured Isaac's heart at a Britannia Benevolent Association Saturday night dance several years before. The two-year-old girl on the train was their first love child, Annie, whose birth the couple had discreetly left unrecorded in New York's registries. Equally absent from official documents was any record of their marriage, since neither in New York nor later in Canada would they ever have a legal wedding. James and Hannah and their affiliated family travelled by train, boat, stagecoach, and boat again to at last reach the village wharf in Bracebridge and their new life.

"Mr. and Mrs. James Boyer" had quit a bustling, overcrowded, foul city to enter a pristine wilderness, whose thick silence was punctuated only by bird songs, the hollow rushing of quiet breezes in tall pines, and the steadily comforting sound of crashing waterfalls. Muskoka's pure air had special buoyancy, its dampness releasing the pungent earthy muskiness of fresh wood and mossy rock, a swilling mixture with heady evergreen scents made even fresher by breezes crossing the district's rocky expanses and crystalline lakes. Bracebridge itself, a stark settlement barely a decade old, was a tiny scattering of shacks, tree stumps, and rough, muddy pathways, isolated, primitive, and much further from New York than all the miles the Boyers had journeyed to get here.

Hannah and James Boyer settled in Macaulay Township, east of Bracebridge, where he soon set about clearing land for farming. James cherished the remoteness, as did other settlers resolved on escaping their pasts. His New York years had simply been the latest chapter in a life buffeted by fate so poignantly that Edward Greenspan remarked, "The tale of his life's journey would not be out of place in a Charles Dickens novel, except that James's story is not fictitious." Greenspan believes "the chapters on James's life are essential to this book." Yet the telling of his story and of the equally stirring, entwined saga of Hannah Boyer would require more space, to do their story justice, than can be accommodated here. So it will appear as a separate volume entitled *Another Country, Another Life*.

In 1868 Bracebridge was designated district capital because of its geographic centrality, and soon several provincial government offices opened to serve the entire Muskoka territory, which not only contributed to the settlement's growth, but also helped establish the community's character as the centre for Muskoka government and administration of justice. Muskokans, irregularly scattered across a large and rugged landscape with poor transportation and rudimentary communication, recognized the emergence of a central hub. In Bracebridge itself, these officials and courts faced plenty of work sorting out the human and economic hodgepodge emerging from Muskoka's raw opening phase.

In the larger picture, the provincial policy of building colonization roads and offering free land had served its intended purpose. The district was being populated and settlements were growing.

Clear-cut logging created drab open space for the emerging settlement of Bracebridge, seen here in 1871, two years after the Boyers arrived from New York. The Muskoka Colonization Road enters this picture from the right, just after crossing the Muskoka River, then turns north to become the village's main street. The Northern Advocate *newspaper, which James Boyer edited, was the first publication in Ontario's northern districts.*

As the settlement grew, the usual aspects of civil society developed. Protestants in early 1870s Bracebridge had the choice of salvation through Methodist, Presbyterian, or Anglican churches. By mid-decade a Roman Catholic priest took up residence in town for the first time — the beginning of another flock. Adherents not only headed to worship services segregated into their respective denominations, but enjoyed community entertainments sponsored by their particular churches.

More broadly, social life was becoming organized: members of the Orange Lodge had a meeting hall; the children, a school; and adults, the Mechanics' Institute library and its reading room with newspapers and periodicals from Toronto, New York, and London. This Mechanics' Institute, which began to operate the community's first library service in 1874, was a worthy institution for Bracebridge. A Mechanics' Institute was the best available structure for organizing a community library in those days, since free public libraries had yet to emerge. The first Mechanics' Institute in Ontario was formed at Kingston in 1834, and other larger centres in southern Ontario had since created community libraries this way as well.

The Muskokans of the 1860s and 1870s were different from the immigrants arriving in southern Ontario in the 1820s. The earlier settlers, recalled by historian Robert McDougall, were often "the bungs and dregs of English society," characterized by their poverty and illiteracy. Those reaching Muskoka a half-century later were, in much greater proportion, educated and entrepreneurial. Just as McDougall recognized in the former their "sterling qualities of character" that made them "the muscle and sinew of the new civilization" emerging in the province, he saw how a smaller number of educated and literate immigrants amongst them gave the emerging community "its mind, its taste, and its voice."

The fact that Muskoka remained closed to settlement until the 1860s meant it had been held in reserve for later waves of settlers, whose social and economic status and levels of education gave the district strong minds, decided tastes, and outspoken voices. This historical sequence contributed to differentiating Muskokans from others in earlier-settled southern Ontario. Many of those coming to settle Muskoka between the late 1860s and 1880s were more accustomed to modern ways and had higher expectations for themselves than did the earlier settlers, but their fresh start in life required more of them: not just a pioneering encounter with raw land, but also a struggle with the rude conditions on the Canadian Shield. The exchange was bound to produce a particular character.

Bracebridge itself is a river town, and the waterfalls have played a central role in its development, not only powering its early grist, lumber, and shingle mills, but forcing into existence a local economy based on transshipment of goods: moving cargoes from steamboats to horse-drawn wagons, and vice versa, because the falls were a barrier to water-borne transport further upstream into the Muskoka interior. The waterfalls and river also inspired construction of facilities to accommodate travellers and their needs, because the natural setting of the town attracted visitors who enjoyed its scenery despite the stumps and mud. Soon the town site was dotted with hotels and taverns, on both sides of the river.

During Muskoka's navigation season, which could stretch to eight months, steamboats from Gravenhurst brought freight, mail, and passengers to Bracebridge Wharf. The Muskoka River's falls at Bracebridge marked the upper reach of Muskoka River navigation and made the town the main transshipment centre between boats and wagons for Muskoka's north-central interior, a local advantage that lasted until the railway came through in 1885, continuing to Huntsville and beyond.

As its economic activity and commercial trade hummed, Bracebridge emerged as a central hub, not only for government offices and legal administration, but also for the movement of people and cargoes by river, by road, and, after the Grand Trunk Railway reached the place in 1885, by rail.

Agricultural settlement in the townships around Bracebridge, in the spots it could flourish, added a farming economy to this mix, advanced by the early presence in Bracebridge of a grist mill. Next, businesses selling farm equipment and supplies emerged, followed by the formation of an agricultural society and the holding of fall fairs to inspire improved farming methods and better animal husbandry.

General economic development created a demand for labourers, millwrights, woodsmen, factory-hands, and teamsters. Several more tradesmen were arriving in Bracebridge each year. All the while, the forestry economy in Muskoka was keeping several thousand hard at work logging, droving, and milling. In the process, Muskoka was achieving a diverse mixture of peoples

Pioneer William Spreadborough's wife stands behind the fence while he and their four boys are out in front. The family's hard work and pursuit of quality are displayed in their cabin: logs squared and interlocked at the corners, a sloping and shingled roof, framed windows with curtained glass panes, and the fence built of split rail.

with a wide range of skills and aptitudes, many with strong backs, a large number with intelligent minds, all propelled by stubborn determination.

Although people enjoyed robust life in a natural setting, fitting their activities rhythmically with the district's alternating seasons, the ever-present hardships and toil made Muskoka an inhospitable and unnatural home for malingerers. People did not come to the frontier to claim land or work in a mill expecting a frivolous escapade. A few were able to get by doing little work; these were rich rascals, the "remittance men" sent to Muskoka by socially prominent British families to remove their embarrassing presence from respectable society, but at least the money sent out, or remitted, to them in the distant colony helped Muskoka's cash-short economy. Another plus was how a number of these dandy misfits added lustre to the community's arts and letters clubs and early drama societies.

England also contributed to Muskoka's population mix from its poorest classes. Here again the British adopted an out-of-sight, out-of-mind approach, "solving" their social problems by merely shipping them overseas: prisoners to the penal colony of distant Australia, orphans and street urchins to the farms of Canada. Thousands of "orphans, waifs, and strays" were shipped to rough and rural pioneering Canada where struggle awaited them. Muskoka had the highest concentration of these "home children" child labourers — so named because they came from homes for orphans — thanks to the district's settlement and development between 1870 and 1930 coinciding exactly with the duration of a deportation program emptying out the orphanages, poor houses, and slums of the "Mother Country" into Britain's colonies. Many fetched up as indentured child labourers on the farms of Muskoka's townships, most badly exploited, unschooled and unsupervised, overworked and underfed, melding into the economic underclass that was forming in rural Muskoka on farms that barely sustained those living and working on them.

Decades later, William E. Taylor, himself the son of an eleven-year-old orphan who laboured as an indentured home boy on a Canadian farm, explained that these youngsters were sent "in a mixture of intense confusion, terror, child courage and, occasionally, optimism. They absorbed the shock of early Canada, cultural and geographic; lived a grinding pioneer life we can now barely comprehend; fought, died, or somehow survived the holocaust of trench warfare; struggled through the Depression and in turn, watched their own children enter another war." Taylor noted how greatly "their lives and thinking contrasts with the current Canadian mood of self-pity and dependence." These world-wise and stoic children, who grew into adulthood and in most cases formed Muskoka families of their own, constituted another component of the human wave that reached the district during its settlement years and melded into the hard-love sentiment typifying Muskokans.

Wherever or however they lived, Muskokans needed goods and services, and enterprising settlers were establishing a supply to meet demand. By the early 1870s, services available to people in Bracebridge and its surrounding townships included those of a doctor, notary public, conveyancer, druggist, music teacher, and several land surveyors. Among the community's tradesmen could be found a house builder, carpenter, window glazier, butcher, and baker. There was the post office, a newspaper, a blacksmith, the stage coach service, and hoteliers, each in their way helping people communicate and travel.

This rutted mud roadway had pole fences to keep cows out of gardens and people walking in the darkness of night on the path. The log barn at right would have been damp and dark, with its flat un-drained roof, tiny window, and dirt floor. The cabin, with chimney, sloped roof, and boards covering the dormers, was a typical dwelling of Muskoka homesteaders.

A number of retailers had also opened their doors to offer specialty lines of furniture, musical instruments, boots and shoes, leather supplies, groceries, dry goods, and clothing. In the heavier end of things, still others offered threshing and separating machinery, shingle making, lime and lathe sales, grist milling, and the services of a sawmill. For those who suddenly packed it in, coffins were available in Bracebridge, "made of the latest style and on short notice."

Such enterprises and services were also emerging in Huntsville, Gravenhurst, and other comparable Ontario towns of the day. Something rarer in Bracebridge was its woollen mill, established at the falls by Henry Bird in 1872. It rapidly became an important part of the town, helping to guarantee the progress of Bracebridge and the success of the many hard-pressed Muskoka farmers who'd discovered with chagrin that their patch on the Canadian Shield was too rocky and swampy, with soils too thin, to serve for traditional farming.

Some other towns had woollen mills too, but two things that gave Bird's Woollen Mill a unique place in Muskoka's development were its added impacts on agriculture and resort vacations. The booming mill needed huge supplies of wool. Rocky Muskoka farms, unsuitable for crops, were ideal for grazing sheep.

Bracebridge industry soared when Henry Bird built this woollen mill by the falls in the early 1870s, giving a lift to Muskoka farming in the process. Sheep on the district's rugged lands produced wool for his mill and famous "Muskoka Lamb" for the dining rooms of summer resorts and big city hotels.

Henry Bird made generous arrangements with financially strapped Muskoka farmers to raise sheep, provided they sold their wool only to his Bracebridge mill. At the same time, Muskoka was experiencing the emergence of hotels and lodges for visitors. Distinctive and handy, "Muskoka Spring Lamb" became a menu specialty in their dining rooms. Muskoka's new sheep farmers made lucrative arrangements with the district's enterprising hoteliers to supply both fresh lamb and mutton. As soon as train service connected the district to the country's larger centres, these born-again farmers began meeting the demand for Muskoka's now-famous spring lamb in major hotels across Canada too.

Bird's Woollen Mill also became a major manufacturer of woollen products, selling its famous "Bird Blanket" across the country and abroad. The mill's substantial stone facilities would be expanded a number of times, the company remaining a large employer and economic mainstay of Bracebridge for the next eighty years.

An equally crucial industry that came to both Bracebridge and Huntsville was leather tanning. Once Bracebridge became incorporated, elected representatives began exercising their new ability to speak officially for the village with interested businessmen about establishing new factories and manufacturing arrangements. As a result, within just three years the Beardmore tannery was up and running, giving Bracebridge a still larger base on which to continue building up its substantial economy.

Once again, Muskoka's farmers benefited enormously. Companies operating Muskoka's tanning businesses became major buyers for their animal hides and an equally ready market for the vast quantities of tanning bark they stripped from hemlock trees and shipped by wagon and barge to the riverside facilities in Bracebridge. As with those now raising sheep, the fact many of these hardscrabble farmers lacked rich soil or flat fields was beside the point for this kind of "agricultural harvest."

Economic development, with parallel growth of community services and facilities for the people, had, like Muskoka itself, many ups and downs and rocky patches. One early setback came with a blighting economic downturn in the mid-1870s, a by-product of the significant recession that gripped the U.S. during those years. In 1874 the council of Macaulay Township (in which Bracebridge was located) attempted to overcome the stagnation by granting a five-year exemption from municipal taxes to sawmills, flour mills, woollen factories, and foundries. Such extraordinary measures were needed as incentive for economic development in Bracebridge, for, as author W. E. Hamilton, taking stock of the community in March 1875 said, circumstances had "knocked the bottom out of the institution of Bracebridge." This activist response by local government leaders showed that Muskokans were not content to be passive. They believed the new society they were creating in the district would be what they made it, and that its success depended on their resiliency.

It had only taken a few years of the government's settlement policy for Muskoka, effectively promoted by Thomas McMurray and James Boyer through the *Northern Advocate*, to fill the district with pioneer

Cutting white pine and "clearing the land" challenged even the most determined Muskoka homesteaders, who sometimes had to plant in patches around the stumps until they could remove them. Muskoka's soil was often just a thin overlay on bedrock; where deeper, it could be ploughed, but the blade often caught in roots of the felled pines.

farmers. By 1877 the whole of Macaulay Township east of Bracebridge was taken up. All but five of the most marginal lots in the township were occupied. Generally, this was the pattern in most Muskoka townships accessible by colonization road or boat. Once free-grant lands were no longer available, a new settler could only get a farm by buying it from an original homesteader, or from the Crown if an original claim had not resulted in a patent of land.

Many homesteaders found Muskoka farming more than they'd bargained for. If asked what crops they had, they'd reply "growing stones." Cramped farm fields, first cleared of the forest, then freed of their stumps, next began sprouting rocks, which were forced to the surface by frost and by ploughing. The Boyers, in common with most settlers on the Canadian Shield, found that much of their farming time was spent harvesting not vegetables but boulders, using their horse to pull, not a wagon loaded with hay to the livery stables in town, but a stoneboat loaded with rocks to the edge of their field.

Often too many large stones made the effort of hauling them to the edge of the field unbearable. Weary farm families simply formed additional mounds throughout their fields. After several years, these painstakingly piled stones resembled taunting grave markers in a burial ground of their owners' aspirations.

In 1875, when the settlement of Bracebridge was incorporated as a village separate from lots in the surrounding townships, the newly elected council voted to appoint James Boyer first clerk of the new municipality. Being in the village, rather than near it, would benefit all concerned. After six harsh yet memorable years as Macaulay homesteaders, the Boyers looked forward to modest comfort, closer to others. They were slightly less concerned now, after the passage of time, about being unmasked. The community had come to accept them as a married couple.

In May 1876, using money from selling "the homestead farm," Hannah purchased a small frame house at the north end of town. The Boyer house at 2 Manitoba Street was on the west side, about fifty yards from where, seventeen years earlier, the lone pioneer John Beal had built a humble squatter's shanty as the settlement's first dwelling. The colonization road, which subsequently passed Beal's front door, causing the loner to relocate to more remote Rosseau, had been named Manitoba Street, just as other principal thoroughfares had been renamed Dominion, Ontario, and Quebec streets, to express Bracebridge's soaring patriotism.

The land at the rear of the Boyers' house, sloping gently to the west, was soon filled up with garden vegetables in summer and snow in winter. Two blocks east, a gurgling spring formed a pond, from which Hannah and the children harvested watercress in summer and fetched buckets of cold clear water year-round. They bought raw milk fresh from a farm nearby.

They would live in this house for the rest of their lives. In all, Hannah and James produced seven children. After Annie, born in New York, and Nellie, William, and Charles, who first saw the light of day in Macaulay Township, came another son, George, born on July 21, 1878. He was followed by Bertha, who arrived on October 20, 1880. The last child, a son named Frederick, was born May 5, 1883. William died when only nineteen

In this 1890s scene outside the Boyer's modest frame house on Manitoba Street at the north end of Bracebridge, James disappears into a book while Hannah shows daughters Annie and Nellie, in white blouses, a detail about her stitching. Of the Boyers' three sons, George stands, Fred holds "Spot," and Charlie is absent. Sometimes a town constable or an aggrieved party would appear at this front door at night or during a holiday and "speedy justice" would be dispensed by Muskoka's justice of the peace.

months, in November 1875. Bertha lived just eight weeks before disease carried her away on December 17, 1880.

The Boyer family attended the Bracebridge Methodist church, which James had joined on moving to Muskoka, seeing it as a reasonable alternative to the Episcopalian Methodist Church he'd belonged to in Brooklyn, and the best choice, given his views and character, among the limited options available. He soon became secretary of the Methodist's cemetery board, and served as a church trustee. Hannah was similarly active in the Methodist church and its women's organizations, living "a consistent Christian life," as her son George put it, "doing her duty to her family and neighbours and to her church faithfully and well."

Church was not all about duty, though. The real magnet of Sunday service was the music. James loved singing in the choir. His ever-expanding collection of books included many volumes of church music. James also played clarinet and flute, sang bass, and delighted in having his family sing Handel's *Messiah*. The rest of the family was equally musical. Son Charles was especially gifted, and a great dancer as well. Son George, who would begin teaching barefoot pupils at a rural one-room Macaulay school by age sixteen, was leading the Methodist church choir in Bracebridge by nineteen, and singing the soprano parts, or at least the air, until his voice changed.

Bracebridge was filling up with families who, like the Boyers, were leaving their outlying bushlots. Having given it a good shot, and putting in enough time to qualify for their free land grant, they now sought something better than scratch farming. So, many now came to town, hoping to improve their fortunes there.

However, a number of those who abandoned their bushlots wanted out of Muskoka altogether, hoping never to return. Those who caught "Manitoba Fever" went west, where they hoped for better Prairie farms. A decade later, others would head deeper into northeastern Ontario to farm "the clay belt" around Cochrane, where millions of acres of fertile flat soil had been discovered: a farmer's paradise hidden within a seemingly endless landscape of muskeg and exposed bedrock. Over the same period, many more departed for the always-beckoning United States, either returning to New England or the Midwest from which they'd come, or heading west, drawn to the coast by California's allure.

One such man was Robert Dollar. He had been one of the Boyers' neighbours while they lived on the farm. He had prospered in Muskoka's lumber business, and had risen to a position of influence in the community, serving on Bracebridge council, where he worked closely with his neighbour, the village clerk. In one outing to the polls, however, Councillor Dollar suffered electoral defeat, losing by three votes. In the face of such voter ingratitude, he quit Muskoka for California, where he developed the ocean-going Dollar Steamships Line and became a millionaire.

James engaged in conveyancing work at the Land Titles Office, and in January 1871 had been appointed first clerk of Macaulay Township. But just six months after starting this municipal work, a human dynamo blew into his life — Thomas McMurray, who had started the *Northern Advocate*, the first

Finding six men to pose for a photo in the mid-1880s was as easy as setting up the camera outside Bracebridge's busy Crown Lands office, hub of real estate transactions and property registrations, where James Boyer conducted his active land conveyancing practice.

newspaper in the northern districts. He wanted James to edit the publication. James accepted McMurray's offer, and from 1871 to 1873 the *Northern Advocate* became James's main focus. His job as editor was one that he was ideally suited to, because a primary mission of the weekly was to promote settlement under the free-grant lands system. He'd learned of the program in New York, was now benefiting from it, and was keen to promote it to others. He gathered reports from successful Muskoka farmers and published, at McMurray's behest, a great deal of "practical information" to help new homesteaders. The *Northern Advocate* was sold in Muskoka, but also distributed widely in parts of the United States and Britain. The same information was also published in book form, *The Free Grant Lands of Canada,* giving McMurray another "first": the first book published in the north country. The start of a competitor newspaper in Bracebridge, the *Free Grant Gazette,* and McMurray's overextension of his financial resources in building offices for the town's main street at the time of the mid-1870s recession, led to the demise of the *Northern Advocate*. With its closure, James Boyer returned to his position as Macaulay Township clerk.

Whatever their impact on individual fortunes, the recurring boom and bust cycles of capitalist economies eventually created an economic upswing that pulled Bracebridge into recovery. By the end of the 1870s, William Hamilton was able to report: "There was as a general thing much of bustle and life in the village, owing to the lumber traffic and the large number of immigrants on their way to locate on free grants or to purchase farms."

The bleak irony in this good news was that many newcomers had learned of these opportunities through the promotional book *The Free Grant Lands of Canada* and the widely circulated *Northern Advocate*, but by incurring the financial outlay of building stores and offices in anticipation of the prosperity the settlers would bring to town, the visionary entrepreneur Thomas McMurray had been unable to hold on long enough to take advantage of the newcomers' arrival and the return of good times.

By the end of the 1870s, Bracebridge's population had climbed to a thousand inhabitants, and the village hummed with its many small factories, most financed by the Bracebridge bank owned locally by Alfred Hunt. The town's citizens were kept up to date and politically aroused by two rival local newspapers, the Liberal *Gazette* and the new *Muskoka Herald,* which upheld Conservative interests.

Bracebridge continued to benefit from the fact that it was a natural home for mills of all types, which were operated by the waterpower of the falls, and for factories that were dependent upon large supplies of freshly running water. The town's early industry — the flour mill, lumber mills, and shingle factory, later joined by the woollen mill and leather tanneries — was now augmented by a match factory, a furniture factory, brickworks, a cheese factory, a buggy shop, blacksmith shops, and livery stables.

The initial Beardmore tannery, reorganized as the Muskoka Leather Company, was now flanked along the riverbank below Bracebridge Bay by the sprawling Anglo-Canadian Leather Company's tanning facilities. Local tanning would continue to expand until the companies combined production made Bracebridge part of the largest leather-producing operation in the British Empire, using hides imported from as far away as Argentina. All that was required for this pre-eminence in the leather economy, apart from hard work by tannery labourers and continuous harvesting of tanning bark by local farmers, was acceptance by all concerned that the Muskoka River downstream from the facilities would be outrageously polluted, filled with dead fish and the bodies of shoreline creatures that had perished — all killed by the stinking vats of fouled tannic acid emptied into the river's waters.

Despite "Manitoba Fever" and the exodus of a number of farming homesteaders, the district continued to receive new arrivals. Employers were attracting tradesmen for jobs in mills and manufactories. As the population grew, Muskoka began to acquire more in the way of enriching cultural and social institutions.

Amongst the latter were the many local chapters of loyalist societies and fraternal lodges, bodies set up to reinforce the adherence of their members to familiar causes in this unfamiliar setting, and to provide mutual support for one another in difficult times. These various societies and orders, lodges and associations, were not service clubs of the kind that carry out helpful community-building projects; their focus was looking to the well-being and support of their own members.

It was that attribute, in an era without government welfare or social assistance programs, that helps account for the presence of so large a number of these entities in places like Bracebridge, and why most enjoyed large memberships, quite apart from the grand causes they ostensibly stood for. Such rudimentary "welfare" as was available in Muskoka was mostly provided through local chapters of these non-governmental organizations, and by local congregations of churches, which likewise looked to the well-being of their own adherents, thanks to the unspoken pioneers' pact of mutual self-help.

James Boyer became secretary of the Sons of England Lancaster Lodge, secretary of the Loyal Orange Lodge, and secretary of the Loyal True Blue Association. Besides carrying his note-taking supplies to these meetings, he seemed to bring positive energy, too. Accounts of his involvement with the Orangemen, whom he joined through Bracebridge Lodge No. 218 in 1876, refer to his "enthusiasm."

The existence in this small town of so many loyalist societies, as well as the several parallel ones for women, in many of which Hannah participated, gave testimony to just how British-minded the Bracebridge community was. Increasingly embodying its identity as a dynamic frontier town on the rugged Canadian Shield, the town was still an inseparable piece of Canada, which, in turn, was an integral part of the British Empire. In the cities, towns, and villages across Canada, just as across the Empire's numerous British countries and territorial possessions, the red-white-and-blue Union Jack waved from a thousand flagpoles. Pupils in small and scattered schoolhouses gazed in respectful awe at the red-coloured areas on the wall map that identified so much of the world as the British Empire "on which the sun never set."

Bracebridge's loyalist societies esteemed visible patriotism. James never wore a flower, except a rose in his lapel on St. George's Day to honour the patron saint of England. Intermittently, as municipal clerk he included on Bracebridge council's agenda the purchase of a flag for the use of the town. And while he knowledgeably addressed loyalist clubs on the Battle of Waterloo and generally displayed a scholar's interest in British affairs, James also took his family to "the Glorious Twelfth" celebrations of the Orange Lodge where, after the parades, more palpable displays occurred as sun-leathered men circled drums in a field, beating them with such intense rhythmic frenzy the corners of their Protestant mouths foamed. That raw intensity, too, was part of the "patriotic" reality. When elections rolled around, the Orange Lodge could be sure to deliver voters, who invariably cast their ballots in support of the Conservative candidate.

Over the years James not only rose to senior ranks in all these societies, but also participated actively in other fraternal associations, like the Independent Order of Odd Fellows and the Independent Order of Foresters, as secretary and in other top offices. All these entities served to knit together the social fabric of Muskokans. They also served to create a bellicose culture that would militantly commemorate the Protestant victory at the Battle of the Boyne every July 12, embrace without hesitation the armed suppression of the Riel Rebellion, enthusiastically send young

Muskoka settlers to their deaths in Britain's war against Dutch settlers in distant South Africa, and raise an entire battalion, the 122nd, with district-wide support, for the four-year massacre in Europe that would come in 1914 with The Great War.

The culture and economy of Muskoka that had taken shape was not a stagnating one, however. The Boyers and the other early homesteaders and tradespeople who first settled the region were joined by visitors. Ontario government's homesteading project, which simply aimed to open up Muskoka for farming, began to take an unusual turn. The arrival of adventuresome folk who made their way up the colonization road and around the lakes by small boats in the 1860s helped to transform the culture of the region and add an unanticipated aspect to the local economy.

Permanent settlers were joined by people who came to Muskoka not to start a new life but to refresh the one they already had. They did not want to clear the land and farm it but to hunt its woods for game and gaze upon its scenic splendour. They sought not to use the lakes and rivers to transport logs but to fish and boat for pleasure. The magic in it was that they came, not to try to make money, but to spend it.

Because Muskoka offered people the experience of being in a natural northern setting — one conveniently close to the cities of the south — the district found itself welcoming people who wanted "a Muskoka vacation." Without the interaction of summer visitors and permanent residents, this new way of life could not have emerged, but the commingling of the two types of people added a dynamic new element to the character of Muskokans above and beyond the mixture formed from the interaction of lumbering, farming, and manufacturing activities. Henceforth, the term *Muskokans* necessarily embraced seasonal vacationers and permanent residents, because you could not have one without the other. The symbiosis of the two became a nuanced mixture of mutual dependence, friendship, and antipathy.

Alex Cockburn would be called "the father of Muskoka tourism" because his steamboats, operating out of Gravenhurst, made vacationing at summer places on three of the district's major lakes, whose shorelines often could not be reached by road, possible. Yet the men who created

As the farthest place that steamboats could come up the Muskoka River before encountering waterfalls, Bracebridge and its wharf provided a major transshipment facility for central Muskoka. Wagons and coaches ran the steep slopes of Dominion Street, seen beyond the steamers, connecting passengers and cargoes with boat transport around Lake Muskoka and Gravenhurst.

those lakeside lodges could also claim paternity, as could the settlers who opened the roads and built up the settlements with their stores and services, because tourists could not have visited the district unless settlers had already colonized it, even if just for a few short years. The two phases were not far apart in time. Muskoka's first adventure visitors arrived in July 1860 and summer vacationing began soon after, incrementally becoming a more and more important part of the district's development.

The vacation economy was not created from a single blueprint, but constructed piece by piece by the district's permanent residents and their visitor guests. Homesteaders with disappointing crops found that if their rocky fields backed onto a major lake, they could make an alternative livelihood by opening their log homes to parties of fishermen. The transition of these homes from rustic homestead to summer resort was a product of a mutual exchange between the cabin dwellers and the wealthy sportsmen who came to stay in their accommodation. Families would vacate their beds, put fresh straw ticks on them for the guests, and move into a shed to sleep. The small parties of sportsmen were content with a couple of square meals a day at the family table. Each adjusted to the other, and learned from each other, as their standards and expectations evolved. If the initial experience was a happy one, the following year an entrepreneurial homesteader might advertise space available for sportsmen, and when the anglers or hunters arrived, typically from the United States, they would discover an addition had been made to the cabin since last season, which now offered more space.

The names of these evolving early lodges epitomized their essential domestic character: "Cleveland's House," "Windermere House," Francis and Ann Judd's cabin, "Juddhaven," and John Montieth's place, "Montieth House," all proclaim their true status in their names.

Over several decades a continuously upgraded range of accommodations emerged. Modest cabins became rustic lodges. Then purpose-built structures replaced cabins. Stuffed deer heads on lobby walls were replaced by oil paintings of Muskoka steamboats. Those at the vanguard created palatial lakeside homes and summer resorts with sloping lawns to the waters' edge.

Such summer places were being replicated around all Muskoka's main lakes, as farmers throughout the district learned to use their homes as resorts and their unpromising lakeside fields for tennis courts, lawn bowling greens, and golf courses. John Aitkin, who built up elegant Windermere House with his wife Lizzy Boyer — one of Hannah's sisters who'd come from Brooklyn and lived four years in the Boyers' Manitoba Street house before snaring the widower Aitkin — created Muskoka's very first golf course.

Roads remained a challenge but the waterways offered convenient alternative transportation routes. The various types of watercraft that plied the lakes of the region offered a variety of benefits to guests, from elegant transportation to the pleasures of waterborne adventure. Once railways reached Muskoka, making connections to the growing fleets of steamboats, the district's robust vacation economy became part of the Muskoka way of life. In vacation accommodation, just as in land settlement, the democratic district

Arrival of the Grand Trunk Railway in Bracebridge would boost and transform the local economy. Here the road gang blasts through rock in 1884 to create a level approach to the river, before bridging over the falls' chasm.

was open to anyone who came, offering humble cabins, easy accommodation for families wanting leisure, and elegant spaces of luxury for plutocrats.

As Muskoka grew and evolved, James Boyer continued as steady pilot of municipal affairs in Bracebridge. Depending on the mayor and council, some years were better than others. Bracebridge's local government was generally progressive, providing electrical services and clean water, subsidies to attract new industries, and pushing for new and better public buildings.

By the late 1880s, the village had grown enough to qualify as a town. In 1889, when his private-member's bill to incorporate Bracebridge as a town was passed by Ontario's legislature, Muskoka MPP George Marter sent a telegram to the town office. Clerk Boyer relayed word of the new

In 1894 Bracebridge became the first municipality to own and operate its own electricity system, buying out a private power plant and propelling the town's economic surge with clean, cheap hydro-electricity for the motors of industry and better lights for homes, shops, and factories. By the end of the 1890s, demand for electricity in town led to construction of Bracebridge No. 2 generating station at the foot of the falls, completed in 1902.

municipal milestone being reached to town constable Robert Armstrong, who rang the town bell for a full hour as the community celebrated their new municipal status and their law officer's stamina.

Another major milestone in the development of Bracebridge was the creation of an electricity system for the town. Bracebridge became the first municipality in Ontario to own and operate its own electricity generating station. In conducting these developments, council took a leading role. Clerk Boyer, among other related duties, conducted the plebiscite by which ratepayers voted to raise funds for the municipal hydro-electric system. The electric works greatly benefited townsfolk and existing business operations: the installation of thirteen streetlights transformed the main streets downtown, allowing shops to extend their shopping hours into the evening, and increasing safety in the streets at night. Stores and workplaces

Major leather tanning facilities in Bracebridge and Huntsville helped Muskoka emerge as part of the largest tannery facility in the British Empire, with cow hides imported from as far as Argentina. In addition to creating many (often dangerous) jobs, the tanneries also provided Muskoka farmers with a new lease on life, buying hemlock bark from them to brew the tannic acid they needed to cure the leather. The money was a boon to the farmers, but the tanneries' effluvia resulted in the two towns' rivers becoming outrageously polluted.

acquired electric lights, then electric motors. A competitive advantage had been gained with the town's ownership of the electricity supply. Bracebridge offered electric power at low cost to sweeten the deal for new industries it was competing with other Ontario municipalities to attract.

On October 12, 1890, James wrote Hannah, who was visiting her sisters in New Jersey, "There is talk of another very large Tannery in Bracebridge. I have written to the parties to meet the council tomorrow night."

The town's ensuing success in landing yet another leather tanning operation illustrates how the tight interaction of government and industry in Bracebridge helped municipal development. First, town council, when negotiating with David W. Alexander of Toronto to establish the tannery, offered a two-thousand dollar bonus as further enticement beyond the advantage of low-cost electricity.

Second, James, as clerk, drafted a bylaw for voters to approve the incentive payment, which they did in the plebiscite that he conducted. Third, it was decided that the new tannery should be on the south side of the river. But the piece of land, although increasingly a part of the town socially and economically, with the J.D. Shier lumber mills and Singleton Brown's shingle mill in that same section, as well as a growing number of homes, was still legally part of Macaulay Township. So the town council and its residents immediately set to work to ensure that the necessary changes were made to bring that land within the town's borders. On cue, residents in the affected area applied to Bracebridge for this section to be annexed by the town, council voted money to get the necessary private bill passed through Ontario's legislature, and also offered $150 to Macaulay Township council if its members would help lobby to get the act passed, which they did. The act passed, allowing the town to expand further both in industry and territory.

It was a fine example of a working democracy, with the local council advancing interests that benefited the town and its people, the citizens being involved by appealing for annexation and by voting in a plebiscite, and the legislature holding a vote on its interest in the matter. Time and again, across Muskoka, this thoroughgoing democratic nature was on display, a direct product of the time of the district's political formation and the kind of people who had come to build a new society for themselves.

Fortunate settlers, winners at land-grant roulette, discovered pockets of truly fine farmland in Muskoka's intermittent valleys and flats. They prided themselves on good animal husbandry and crop practices. Their produce was shown for prizes in Muskoka's many fall fairs. It compared well to the best in Ontario at other agricultural fairs in populous parts of the province.

Whether as the secretary, a director, or, by 1888, president of the Bracebridge Agricultural Society, and later as president of the Parry Sound and Muskoka Agricultural Society, James enthusiastically travelled, usually in the company of a fellow officer, to display Muskoka's prize-winning produce. In successive years he appeared with bushels and baskets at the Canadian National Exhibition in Toronto, the Central Canada Exhibition in Ottawa, and the fall fairs at Owen Sound and Barrie, to put Muskoka farmers' best products on show. This became increasingly important, he knew, because Muskoka was getting a lot of bad press as a stony nightmare for luckless farmers.

A good harvest of Muskoka hay required storing it from rain, wind, and animals; these men used ladders and pitchforks and piled it high outdoors to dry. For this impressive 1890s photograph, women donned Sunday clothes while men posed with a yoked team and atop a stack. The barn's well-selected logs were squared at the corners, though not all were debarked; a fine shingle roof, and boards nailed up until the supply ran out, helped keep the interior dry.

In one letter home to Hannah from Owen Sound, James described himself as "terrifically bound up in fall fair work." When a reporter favourably looked over the exhibit of Muskoka produce, he offered a proposition: "Good exhibit. If you pay me, I'll write it up in the paper." James was indignant, and "did not pay."

It was no different in Toronto. In 1887 the Bracebridge Agricultural Society sent its president, Peter Shannon, and secretary, James Boyer, to exhibit produce at Toronto's Exhibition. Both men were keen to show that Muskoka could be an agricultural contender despite what the district's critics said. James, in a September 12 letter home to Hannah from Toronto, described the CNE praise Muskoka's produce received. People discovered "a splendid exhibit" of prized entries from farms in all sections of Muskoka. "It was difficult," James wrote, "to make some of the visitors believe that grapes (Lindley or Rogers No. 9), some bunches of which weighed 1¼ pounds each, were grown in the open air of

Livestock, baked goods, and farm produce were on proud display each September at the Bracebridge Fall Fair, as were townsfolk. The spacious agricultural hall housed prize-winning entries from kitchen and field, and offered a balcony view of the race track. The buildings at left and right are on Victoria Street, the house at left, atop the rocky hill, is on Church Street. James Boyer, proud booster of Muskoka farming, was for decades an officer of the Agricultural Society, including serving as president.

Muskoka." One of the samples of wheat grown on light, sandy soil in Macaulay sold at the close of the Exhibition to an American for one dollar, a notable amount in that time. "Our Duchess apples are not beaten by any that are exhibited prizes. Both the *Globe* and the *Mail* wanted to be paid to puff our exhibit," he concluded, "but Shannon and myself refused to pay them one cent." Muskoka's valiant farmers faced hardened newspapermen as well as hard land.

The district was, of course, a mixture of topography and soils, and not everyone had located on good land. Some with marginal lands but an entrepreneurial nature successfully shifted to sheep rearing and wool production, others harvested lucrative tanbark and maple syrup from their

Bracebridge Public School, as it appeared in the 1890s. The windowsills and other stonework were made by James Boyer's brother-in-law, Harry Boyer. The school bell at the top came loose one day, while being rung to call children in, tumbling heavily to the ground, missing James and Hannah Boyer's son George by two feet.

trees, while still others shifted their land use to the cash crop of Muskoka's vacation economy. Just as Muskoka as a whole had a mixed economy, most of its homesteaders operated mixed farms.

For many would-be farmers, though, the dream that first brought them into the district, when Muskoka was being promoted to immigrants for farming, had been shattered by their inability to fulfill even the minimum conditions of the free-grant system for acquiring title to their land. In 1886, although 133 persons were newly located on lots in the district's townships that year, there were also 99 cancellations of grants for non-fulfillment of settlement duties.

Although many poor farms were abandoned, some families stayed on in unfavourable locations and sank to subsistence-level living. In this way, the agricultural experience in Muskoka over the decades of free-grant settlement was gradually producing, in addition to its success stories, an economic underclass. These people were living on poor farms but were too poor to go anywhere else. Quite a few homesteaders had

Trains running south through Bracebridge from Ontario's northern hinterland or the Canadian West were so long and heavy they required two locomotives. At right, Bird's Woollen Mill increases production for Canada-wide and British Empire markets.

burned their bridges behind them, in the manner of James and Hannah, so could not "return home," but they could not afford to relocate to anything better, either. Looking beyond the front verandahs of the Muskoka lakeside resorts and tennis courts where genteel city ladies in long dresses laughed while tapping balls, Canada's 1891 census takers found two-thirds of Muskoka's people dwelling in rural areas, many of them destitute.

By the close of the 1800s, Muskoka, and its towns, villages, small settlements, and random, scattered farms at the southern edge of the Canadian Shield, had each assumed distinctive characteristics, attributes which contributed, as social historian G.P. de T. Glazebrook expressed it, to "the great variety that was Ontario." Bracebridge in the 1890s was, like most of the province's villages and small towns, intact with its own commercial and social life.

This view of Bracebridge, taken about 1902, shows the centre of town as it was by the end of the 1890s. The short-lived Hess Furniture factory, five-storeys high, on the left, is adjacent to a sawmill and lumber yard; the river is spanned by a wooden bridge to Hunts Hill; the train station (centre right) is busy with freight traffic; across the street from it is the Albion Hotel, which stood until 2011.

Manufacturing and commerce sparked life in Bracebridge as the dawn of the twentieth century approached. Here, Henry Bird's Woollen Mill dominates the foreground, and the central business section of town stretches up Manitoba Street beyond.

Workmen and workhorses in early 1890s Bracebridge pause at a busy mill and lumberyard in the centre of town, above the falls. Log booms in the river await their fast-moving saw blades.

During the decade, the town's population more than doubled, from 1,020 residents counted in the 1891 census to 2,480 recorded in 1901. By the end of the decade, tax assessment of town properties topped more than half a million dollars, at $504,633. The town had also incurred a debt of $44,000, with plebiscite support from Bracebridge taxpayers, to create Ontario's first municipally-owned electricity generating and distribution system, and to lay pipes beneath the town's streets for clean drinking water to reduce water-borne illness in the municipality. The yearly receipts of the town from taxes and fees added up to about $36,000.

Within three decades of the town's pioneer John Beal arriving by canoe, Bracebridge had grown to become an economic centre despite the number of marginal farms in its surrounding townships. In 1890 the building of another vast leather tannery and the creation of a major park within the town exemplified the town's twin pillars of economic development and vital cultural life. Both reinforced the robust sense townsfolk had of Bracebridge as a go-ahead community.

The possibilities continued to dazzle. By the 1890s James Boyer was secretary and a director of the Bracebridge & Trading Lake Railway Company, which aimed to build a railroad from Bracebridge east to Baysville and Lake of Bays, and west to Beaumaris and Lake Muskoka. Railways, including the transcontinental that passed through Muskoka, had become an exciting physical link with the wider world.

Canada counted for the biggest expanse of British red on the world map, and thanks to common political institutions and language, shared laws and legal principles, and even derivative English judicial offices such as the justice of the peace, Canada's "British subjects" experienced what historian Carl Berger called "a sense of Empire." Despite this conscious connection to grandeur on a global scale, the country as a whole consisted of fewer than five million people sprinkled over a seemingly endless territory. Ontario styled itself Canada's "Empire Province," and, at the start of the 1890s, boasted a population of 2,100,000. The population of Muskoka, which in 1891 was 15,666 and rose some 5,000 more by the turn of the century, was still a far cry from the *millions* of people promoters like Thomas McMurray had boasted would by now be prospering on their free-grant farms.

Despite this fact, life in Bracebridge, reflected week by week on the rival pages of the Grit *Gazette* and the Tory *Herald*, unfolded within a confident sense people had of being part of something larger than themselves. News and advertisements from the United States, reports of global developments, and accounts of national political events, all meshed seamlessly with local births and deaths, weddings and hockey matches, updates on crop prices, and advertisements seeking able-bodied harvesters to go west by train and bring Prairie wheat in from the field.

Queen Victoria, who had ascended the throne in 1837, the same year David Thompson first mapped Muskoka, was well into the longest reign of any British monarch, having herself become as much an institution as the Crown itself. Bracebridge had its Victoria Hotel, Victoria Street, and like most every municipality in Ontario, its Queen Street. In 1897 the agricultural society's show grounds were renamed "Jubilee Park" to commemorate Victoria's diamond jubilee.

The long political reign of the Liberal-Conservative Party in Canada under its wise and wily leader Sir John A. Macdonald, who helped form the country in 1867 with the creation of a new federal constitution, and then oversee its development with bold new national policies and the addition of Prince Edward Island, Manitoba, and British Columbia as provinces, was spluttering to its end. After Sir John A.'s death in 1891, which shocked the country not because he was an old man but because it seemed a Canadian institution had vanished, a succession of Tory prime ministers — John Abbott, John Thompson, Mackenzie Bowell, and Charles Tupper — held office before the Liberal leader, Sir Wilfrid Laurier, was elected in 1896. Laurier's leadership in re-fashioning the Liberal Party of Canada and forming a "cabinet of all the talents" by bringing to Ottawa such illustrious provincial leaders as Ontario's Premier Oliver Mowat began an historic shift in the country's political alignments. All these events were fully reported in the local newspapers and discussed avidly in Bracebridge, a highly political town.

The 1890s stood as a high water mark for the British Empire. By the turn of the new century, Queen Victoria would be gone, another human institution vanished. Britain's seemingly invincible military was bogged down in a war in South Africa that would extract a high price, as a relatively small number of resolute fighters in a faraway land stalled the world's greatest military power in its tracks. Young Bracebridge men were transported to fight and die in South Africa because Canada was an integral part of the British Empire. For London this war was important, and in Muskoka emotions ran high in support of the blood-letting. Market Street in central Bracebridge would be renamed "Kimberley" Avenue after the South African city, and a triangle of land in the centre of town was designated "Memorial Park" for the sons of Muskoka settlers who died while killing Dutch settlers on their farmlands half a world away. The British proved as adept in drawing from their colonies healthy young men to die in their wars as they had been in dispatching to the colonies their troublesome dandies, convicted felons, and orphaned children — a two-way flow of traffic orchestrated by the benignly misnamed "Mother Country."

Despite the carnage of the Boer War, the last decade of the 1800s would be popularly dubbed "The Gay Nineties," capturing the open gaiety in society exuded by those able to enjoy life's pleasures. Beneath the surface glitter of the Victorian era at its zenith loomed rawer reality.

With the arrival of another economic downturn as the final decade of the century began, doubts about the country's viability resurfaced. In Toronto, Goldwyn Smith, journalist and renowned professor of economics, elevated such misgivings to hard-ribbed analysis in his book *Canada and the Canadian Question,* in which he marshalled economic, geographic, and political reasons for folding Canada's brief experiment with nationhood into union with the United States.

In its celebration of life, the revels of the "Gay Nineties" offered a popular way to defy and transcend these social, economic, political, and military strains. Celebration was in the atmosphere of Bracebridge. Embattled individuals, who struggled in their circumstances and from time to time found themselves before Magistrate James Boyer, were otherwise at the band concerts, in the parades, and on the sports fields. Individuals experiencing rougher social conditions and the raw edges of life might not themselves have chosen the moniker "Gay Nineties" for their times, but then people in a position to name eras are seldom the threadbare folk living on hard energy at society's margins.

In the predictable boom-bust cycle of a capitalist economy, the decade advanced from economic depression into a recovery. With general prosperity returning, many Muskokans did have a good time. Bracebridge newspapers ran accounts of local sporting matches, outdoor church services, visiting circuses, fabulous touring bands, fall fairs, community picnics, theatrical performances, and festive excursions across the lakes by boat, down the roads by buggy, and along the tracks by train.

In the struggle to overcome all of these ups and downs, Muskoka's incomparable character emerged. From the opening of the settlement the district was a place of natural beauty, physical hardship, dashed hopes, sudden profits, irreconcilable conflicts, and new starts. The diverse peoples flocking from distant places to claim land were, year by year, increasingly re-formed by the land's claim on them. It made them democrats and stoics.

Families had become homesteaders in a localized Ontario economy of mixed farming and wage labour in forestry, mills, tanneries, and manufacturing workplaces, integrated with facilities for transportation, accommodation, and services for vacationers. They dwelt on their rural acreages or in Muskoka's main towns of Gravenhurst, Bracebridge, and Huntsville; the larger villages of Bala, MacTier, Port Carling, Rosseau, Baysville, Dorset, and Port Sydney; or the smaller settlements such as Walker's Point, Windermere, Milford Bay, Utterson, Dwight, Falkenburg. These people lived amid rugged conditions and scenic splendour in the Canadian Shield's northern hinterland but still close to the southern cities, witnessing changes for which they were both designer and creator, and of which they were sometimes beneficiary and other times victim. They were interacting alike with well-to-do folk trekking into the district for vacations, and edgy neighbours who were scrounging year-round just to get by.

Out of the rawness of this cauldron emerged a distinctive new variety of people, the "Muskokans."

Chapter Two

THE COURT: CANADIAN JPS BY THE LATE NINETEENTH CENTURY

Bracebridge was a political hotbed. Dominion and provincial elections were frequent, council elections rolled around every New Year's Day, and townsfolk voted on contentious plebiscite questions frequently: all helped stoke the fires of political intensity. Rare was the Muskokan who hesitated to state his opinions on anything, from the fence-sitting leaders of the country to the location of his neighbour's line fence. Nobody could escape taking sides, in this era before the secret ballot, when each man's vote was openly cast amidst spirited townsfolk thronging at public polling stations, where the voter's spoken declaration was, in fact, usually a proud or defiant shout, naming his chosen candidate. Everybody knew where a fellow stood, and whom he supported.

Fitting in so as not to stand out, James Boyer identified himself as "an Independent Liberal" shortly after arriving in the district. He was not an active partisan. His position as town clerk restrained him from being outspoken, and conducting municipal elections and plebiscites required him to be neutral. He used this as a shield, content to be a quiet Liberal bystander to controversy. James still feared that partisan animosity could trigger closer scrutiny by adversaries and betray his identity. As a participant-observer (someone directly engaged in the affairs of his community through a variety of roles, who simultaneously had to stand apart from them as recording secretary, municipal clerk, or newspaperman, etc.), he exuded a balanced quality; he was a calmly reticent man whose nature suggested to others he could keep confidences. Many consulted James for his informed view on things, and he steadily rose in local stature because he was not seen as a threat to anyone.

Someone who frequently sought him out was Alexander Cockburn, the first Muskokan James encountered — the two had shared the same rough coach ride into the district in September 1869. The influential steamboat owner and timber entrepreneur had run in federal and provincial elections, was a catalyst in district politics, and by 1878 was the Liberal MP representing Muskoka. Cockburn kept interested in Boyer's career, partly for sentiment as the man who "introduced" him to Muskoka when they crossed the Severn River together, but also out of shrewdness because his rising political career required good relations with someone who, at turns a newspaper editor, school teacher, municipal clerk, and officer of more than a half-dozen church, fraternal, loyalist, and agricultural societies, could influence so many others. The two men enjoyed booting about information and ideas, since both shared a wily outlook about the workings of government and politics. Although both were Liberals, each was also his own man. James voted for Conservative candidates if he agreed with their stands more, while Alexander voted with the Conservatives in Parliament or the legislature if it helped install locks on the Indian River for his steamboats, get Crown timber concessions to log Muskoka's forests, or win government grants for his pioneering steamboat program.

Cockburn would be of great help to James in his bid to become a justice of the peace. Boyer was unable to practise law because becoming a member of The Law Society of Upper Canada would mean establishing his professional qualifications, which in turn meant reference to New York, where he was known by a different name, was an American citizen, and had left a wife and daughter behind. But he was still in love with the law. Boyer's lack of standing as a lawyer, however, was the very qualification needed to make him a candidate for justice of the peace in Muskoka. The rules, Cockburn noted to him, stipulated that a JP could not be a lawyer. All the same, the provincial government liked to appoint a person of standing in the community, and James, after a decade in Muskoka, clearly had achieved that. If the prospective nominee was steeped in the law, but not active in its practise, even better. If a Liberal, even an "Independent" one, better still.

Cockburn could recommend, but the decision would be made by Oliver Mowat, provincial Liberal leader and head of Ontario's government as premier and attorney general. This wily, mutton-chopped premier with poor eyesight and thick glasses would remain in office a record number of years until 1896, only departing Queen's Park in order to become Canada's minister of justice in the new Laurier government in Ottawa. Premier Mowat's long-running success was underpinned by his continuous attention to political patronage, including whom he appointed as local magistrates. In 1878 he named his fellow Liberal "James Isaac Boyer" of Bracebridge as Magistrate for Muskoka District.

In early Ontario justices of the peace held courts designed to meet the minimum standards of justice, rough-hewn for a rough land. They lacked the firm foundation upon which the English system of JPs was based, and became increasingly ineffective in the face of the developing complexities of Canadian life. By the 1870s James Boyer found himself occupying a judicial office so evolved in Canada that it only loosely approximated the English original.

He'd become familiar as a boy with the role of county magistrates in his Moreton-in-Marsh village, where effective local government was principally in their hands, then in Stratford-upon-Avon, through his years law-clerking there. In that English setting, he could never have imagined himself in such a role, given the social standing of British JPs. But he was now in the New World, where everything was possible for those looking to get ahead.

Not only did men change in Canada, but so did institutions. James's new front-line judicial office in 1878 was certainly not the model originally exported with Britain's imperial extension of the Old World into the New.

In fact, it had been a long stretch of seven centuries since King Richard I first gave knights power "to preserve the peace in specified areas." The JP's role had grown and changed dramatically in England even before reaching the stage of development exported to Britain's North American colonies in the 1700s.

In the mid-1300s, for instance, several statutes clarified and expanded the powers of JPs. A 1327 act provided that "good men and lawful" should be appointed "for the better maintaining and keeping of the peace" in each English county. In 1344 these keepers of the peace were granted extended authority, jointly "with others wise and learned in the law," to hear and determine felonies and trespasses. After a while these "keepers" of the peace commonly became known as "justices" of the peace, and this popular way of referring to them was officially adopted in a 1361 statute that specifically formalized their powers over the restraint, pursuit, arrest, and punishment of offenders. Under this act, Parliament assigned to every county in England "one Lord and with him three or four of the most worthy in the county with some learning in the law" to keep the peace, arrest and imprison offenders, and hear and determine felonies and trespasses. The following year, these "most worthy" persons became justices of the peace in their own right, when another statute established that commissions of the peace would meet four times a year, eventually giving rise to what became known as "Quarter Sessions." This enactment also provided that JPs, independently of others learned in the law but with a jury, could try criminal offenders.

Successive statutes then extended the criminal jurisdiction of the Court of General Quarter Sessions, beginning in the fifteenth century when JPs were empowered to try certain offences *outside* of quarter sessions, *without* a jury. These proceedings, conducted by JPs exercising their summary offence jurisdiction, became known as "Petit Sessions," a term continued in England until 1949, when they were renamed "Magistrate's Courts."

However, it was their non-judicial duties that increasingly made justices of the peace a central part of local government. Today, when judicial functions and government operations are distinctly separate, it is hard to imagine the two combined; however, in 1890s Bracebridge James Boyer was justice of the peace and town clerk at the same time, a combination consistent with the role played by JPs in England, where they had steadily acquired substantial administrative powers in local government in addition to their judicial duties. During the 1400s, for example, justices of the peace in England gained so many regulatory and supervisory duties that soon their responsibilities, notes legal historian James Wilson, "blurred the fine distinction between judicial and administrative duties or criminal and civil jurisdictions." This "double jurisdiction allowed the justices to confirm themselves as more or less self-contained local oligarchies which doled out administrative and judicial pronouncements with almost absolute and unfettered control."

After four centuries of piecemeal development, a new 1590 enactment by Parliament focused the JPs powers by restating them and clarifying that justices of the peace could "proceed in three separate ways according to the matter at hand: they could sit alone, they could sit jointly with one or more of their fellow justices, or they could sit collectively as they had been doing since the 1360s as a general sessions of the whole county." Through the next century, notes Wilson, most civil administration in the counties came to be performed by these Courts of Quarter Sessions. In addition to resolving disputes and meting out punishments to lawbreakers, JPs were increasingly confirmed in statutes as administrators conducting local government. The cumulative effect was staggering. By 1689 a JP's government administrative duties ran the gamut from overseeing bridge repairs and the building and maintaining of jails, to issuing alcohol licences, and sanctioning taxes for parish needs. These were tasks that, in time, with pressure for more accountability and democratic control, would become the responsibility of elected municipal councils. Until that happened, however, this steadily growing roster of administrative powers meant that, as scholar David Phillips observes, "for most people, the justices, rather than the central government, represented public authority as they would experience it in their daily lives."

Because they wielded such significant powers, the qualifications of justices of the peace mattered. One of those 1300s statutes required that justices of the peace be "the most sufficient knights, esquires, and gentlemen of the land." Fifty years later a 1439 act stipulated that JPs must own land valued at twenty pounds a year, meaning they had to be to a modest extent members of England's propertied class. Despite the power JPs wielded, and perhaps to some degree because of it, finding qualified men willing to perform the role was difficult. The time consumed and the potential to make enemies tended to repel men possessing the requisite social and economic standing. Still, those prominent men who did agree to become JPs were often landed gentry. Throughout England's countryside these propertied and educated individuals often played a catalyst's role in public affairs. Their independence neither required, nor much tolerated, directions from a distant, all-powerful authority.

The English jurist Maitland wryly observed, in an 1888 essay entitled "The Shallows and Silences of Real Life," how the most learned stipendiary magistrates "will find it hard to get so high a reputation among country folk for speaking with the voice of the law, as that which has been enjoyed by many a country squire whose only juristic attainment was the possession of a clerk who could find the appropriate page in *Burn's Justice*." Canadian jurist and law reformer James C. McRuer added that England's justices of the peace were "persons who felt the responsibilities of their position, who acted out of a deeply developed sense of stewardship, and who were respected and relied on by their poorer neighbours, to whom they were the embodiment of 'the law.'"

In short, respect for JPs had steadily grown as a consequence of who they were socially, how effectively they functioned in office, their growing powers in local governance, and their independence. Increases in their statutory powers propelled them into ever-greater prominence, right into modern times when the vast majority of criminal prosecutions in England are disposed of by justices of the peace in the exercise of their summary jurisdiction. They proved indispensable in resolving petty local frictions that were neither so trivial they could be ignored, not so severe as to land a culprit in a higher court on a heavy criminal charge.

As created in England, this institution represented ground floor, walk-in justice. The fact JPs had emerged from the solid foundations of an existing social order, one they both understood and helped to perpetuate, would be one of countless differences when the office of JP was exported to fledgling colonies.

The practice of introducing this institution into the rudimentary social order in overseas territories began in North America with England's first overseas colony, Newfoundland, continued in new colonies like Virginia and Nova Scotia along the coast of New England, and in 1760 extended to New France, once Britain gained these colonies. Three years after Quebec's capitulation, King George III issued a royal proclamation giving Governor Murray, among other things, full authority to constitute justices of the peace and appoint men of his choosing to the positions. So began the process that would eventually produce justices of the peace in Ontario, and, specifically, in Muskoka, a century later.

It was one thing to have the authority to create JPs, quite another to have the right handle on how to do so. After all, the JP's functions in England had developed over time as a distinctive component of a most particular society, evolving to suit English needs in ways appropriate for English conditions, in ways only possible within that setting. Such uniqueness meant replicating justices of the peace, in short order and in a different society, was difficult.

The quest to adapt British institutions and practices within North America's fledgling communities took unexpected turns. It seemed probable that grafting English laws and judicial procedures onto an existing French society, in the wake of centuries of French–English warfare and mutual hatred, would create a toxic reaction leading to rejection of the transplant. Yet, the relationship between magistrates, police, and people in Quebec and Lower Canada did not seem overly difficult. With evidence from Quebec records following 1764, historian Donald Fyson has now corrected many earlier misinterpretations about this "British" institution in a largely French-speaking community, documenting, from "banal cases involving no particularly interesting judicial principles," substantial continuity between the old French regime and the new British order that replaced it. The transplant was taking root, at least where JPs were appointed in the established communities of Quebec.

Reaching beyond those established Quebec settlements, however, the situation was quite different as the colony expanded into the unsettled territory to the west that would in time become Ontario. The year after Murray created the first justices of the peace in 1764, new districts were created in Quebec's sprawling regions of wilderness. "Provisions for administration at the local level were provided for each of the newly created districts at this time by the granting of commissions as justices of the peace," explains Wilson, "with three justices empowered to hold quarter sessions in each of their appointed districts." The principal problem with these districts serving as the primary judicial units was that their much larger size and sparsely settled population, compared to their corresponding county unit in England, made it hard to find qualified men to serve as JPs. The problem was further exacerbated because Roman Catholics were now barred by law from being appointed and few Protestants lived in Quebec.

The result was predictable. Relationships of power and authority became strained, laws went unenforced, procedures remained unfamiliar, and the different outlooks of English-speaking and French-speaking colonists clouded the picture — problems that were compounded by the fact that the vast areas of the new districts made control and administration difficult and slow. Dissatisfaction was mounting. Inhabitants, demanding a say in government, agitated in part because of the problems that arose from an administrative and legal system operated by justices of the peace. The British government responded with a new constitution, embodied in the Quebec Act of 1774. Despite other changes, it maintained the institution of a local magistrate in the French-speaking territories and extended this judicial-administrative position to settlements in the inland territory that would, in time, become Ontario.

After the 1770s this inland Quebec territory began filling in with settlers. In just a decade and a half, colonial development in this sector advanced so much that it required its own local structure for governance, rather than depending on its distant capital down the St. Lawrence. A separate government system soon became necessary for this westerly region because its new settlers, unlike those in old Quebec, were mostly English-speaking, non-Catholic, and, also, were militant supporters of the British Crown. Many had fought on the losing side in the American Revolution, when thirteen of England's colonies had rebelled against the Crown and fought to create a new republic, the United States of America. Those on the losing side, fleeing with their lives from torched homes and confiscated farms, were dubbed "United Empire Loyalists." They started life anew in the remaining British North American territories, some settling in Nova Scotia, others crossing into this empty inland territory to live on the north shore of Lake Ontario and in the Niagara Peninsula. They brought with them loyalty to the Crown, an aggrieved sense of injustice that would long endure in Ontario's political culture as anti-Americanism, and familiarity with such British institutions as the local justice of the peace as it had evolved it in a North American setting.

To accommodate this altered reality, the British Parliament again revamped constitutional arrangements, this time in the Constitutional Act of 1790, changing Quebec's governance structure by dividing the colony, renaming its successor parts Lower Canada and Upper Canada (in relation to their lower and upper elevations on the St. Lawrence River.) Besides dividing and renaming territory, the act also established a constitution for the new Province of Upper Canada.

By this date English-style justices of the peace had already been exercising jurisdiction in this extended segment of Quebec territory, as thinly populated as it had been, for over two decades. Under this 1790 reconstitution, the Court of the General Quarter Sessions of the Peace was left untouched, so the structure of local government remained basically as it had been, with JPs wielding significant roles in local government as well as administering justice. A landmark 1790 development, creation of a legislature, opened colonial life in the province to something more democratic than before. Election of representatives to Upper Canada's first legislative assembly followed in 1791.

This legislature in the early years of Upper Canada was, as Wilson notes, "confined largely to provincial matters, and the actual maintenance of local affairs and justice in Upper Canada was controlled by the men appointed justices of the peace sitting in the Court of General Quarter Sessions of the Peace for each district." This arrangement replicated the pattern in England familiar to the MPs at Westminster who debated and enacted the Constitution Act of 1790. It was also favoured by Britain's Colonial Office, which sought, in as many ways as it could, to control political life in its remaining North American colonies, having just lost many of its most prosperous and populous ones along the Atlantic seaboard. JPs, given pivotal roles in local government across the province, were appointed with the approval of the British governor in Upper Canada.

The British regime was still shaken by the French and American revolutions, and feared "mob rule" and "democracy"; these two were, in fact, identified as the same thing, an apprehension that worked itself into many controls the British instituted in Upper Canada to restrain North America's yeasty democratic tendencies. Where citizens of the new American republic swore allegiance to the Constitution, Upper Canada's residents were "British subjects," whose loyalty was to the Crown. These were two fundamentally different foundations upon which to erect the "rule of law." The 1791 election of an assembly of representatives in Upper Canada was a timid step in the direction of democracy. This legislative body remained ineffectual because real power still resided with the legislative council, a second chamber with greater powers and whose regime-supporting members were not elected but appointed by the governor.

Within this configuration designed to constrain democratic tendencies, the province's justices of the peace played major roles, thanks to their powerhouse combination of judicial and governmental functions in local affairs. Until the 1830s, as historian James Aitchison notes, "No town meeting could legally be held without a warrant for the purpose signed by two justices." In other words, freedom of assembly existed only if the regime, represented by its justices of the peace, approved of who was going to gather, and for what purpose.

The "rule of law" supported the established order by keeping democracy at bay in other ways, too. When a provincial statute in 1793 empowered Upper Canada's townships to select officials who would handle minor local matters, not only was the authority of these men limited, they were subject to supervision by justices of the peace even in handling their minor tasks. That was not an aberration. It was a local microcosm of the provincial scene itself, where elected representatives in the assembly were severely limited in their roles and subject to being overridden by the appointed legislative council and governor.

The next noteworthy development for the province's justices of the peace came in 1800 when Upper Canada's legislature adopted in its entirety the criminal law of England as it stood in 1792. This established that JPs in the province possessed the same extensive powers as their English counterparts. Several decades of developments in the colony were thus now confirmed and clarified by statutory authority and renewed legitimacy. That, at least, was the theory.

In practice, a chronic shortage of justices of the peace had been hobbling the province for years. This fact, long ignored in the relevant historical literature, came to light in the early 1950s when James Aitchison, researching his doctoral thesis, "The Development of Local Government in Upper Canada, 1783–1850," uncovered the rawer realities of the province's pioneer communities. He discovered what settlers in Upper

Canada knew only too well: the local JPs wielded great power and were part of the colonial province's problems, not its solutions. Many men named in the Commission of the Peace did not take their qualifying oath. Others, once qualified, refused to act. These problems were compounded because the government was reluctant to replace justices of the peace who had died or been removed from their districts. On top of that, Aitchison found, many townships were simply not represented at the district Quarter Sessions, or even at the township level. Public administration in the province was, in a word, chaotic.

If justices of the peace had been peripheral officials with little responsibility, their contribution to the chaos would have been negligible. But such a staggering array of responsibilities fell to them that their failure to perform created bottlenecks in local governance. First, there was policing. Before the rise of professional police forces, JPs worked alongside local constables enforcing the law. For anybody wanting to start legal proceedings against a person, a justice of the peace was the first point of contact. Because a victim had to swear out a complaint before a JP to start a prosecution, it was required that he or she name the offender. If the identity of the offender was unknown, for instance, in the case of a thief who'd disappeared, it became the victim's responsibility to do the detective work needed to produce a name. Given the harshness of this requirement in some circumstances, justices of the peace would sometimes shoulder this responsibility themselves, bending the rules and doing, as legal historian Susan Lewthwaite put it in 2001, "what they could to help the victim track down the offender."

Secondly, in the routine course of their duties, as Lewthwaite summarized, justices of the peace "took depositions of witnesses, examined defendants, issued warrants and summonses, bailed or jailed defendants, bound witnesses in recognizance to attend trial, and organized the paperwork for trials."

A third responsibility arose in the absence of a local coroner, when a justice of the peace would preside at the inquest. As legal historian David Murray noted in 2002, JPs occasionally even had a direct role in examining the body. For an 1840 inquest in Chippewa, the justice of the peace later recounted how "the body was in such a state of decomposition I could scarcely get a person to touch it and it was 11 o'clock at night before we got it into the coffin."

Fourth, justices of the peace had courtroom roles deciding cases. A JP could try a number of minor offences summarily, meaning without a jury, in the same manner as a lower court judge. When it came time for more serious offences, district magistrates would sit with JPs on the bench at Quarter Sessions, an intermediate level of courts. "Only the most serious cases," as Lewthwaite notes, went to the Court of King's Bench at the assizes.

In hearing cases, JPs sometimes acted alone, in other cases not. As Murray reminds us, ancient English law "empowered justices of the peace to act alone on some issues, to act with one or more fellow magistrates on others, and to act collectively as the Court of General Quarter Sessions on still others." This was also the situation in Upper Canada. In practice, this system was rough and ready. The Court of Quarter Sessions met four times a year, more frequently in special sessions if necessary, but the number of JPs who attended varied because with distance and weather not everyone always showed up.

Fifth, justices of the peace exercised extensive powers of government, integrating matters of public administration with their duties in the administration of justice. The Court of Quarter Sessions's jurisdiction extended far beyond civil and criminal matters for its district to include responsibility for local administration. In fact, prior to creation of municipal corporations in 1832, as Aitchison stresses, "this court was in complete charge of district finance." Upper Canada justices of the peace prepared spending estimates of the district for the year ahead, determined local taxation levels needed to raise that amount of money, raised loans for courthouses and jails, oversaw their construction, appointed the district treasurer, approved all non-statutory expenditures, examined the treasurer's books, could remove the treasurer at will, and heard assessment appeals. Yet, that was hardly the end of it. They also regulated ferries, had responsibility for roads and bridges, determined who got liquor licences, and exercised numerous powers with respect to township officers. In short, until 1832, with no municipal corporations and without any town meetings in surveyed townships, the Court of Quarter Sessions "received all the authority granted by the legislature to deal with the special needs of villages and towns."

Sixth, because the act of governing requires interpretation and enforcement of laws, justices of the peace shouldered numerous additional duties of adjudication in their governance role, as Aitchison itemized. They imposed penalties for infractions of laws, and heard civil actions for small debt recovery. They exercised these powers either alone or in pairs, depending on the seriousness of the infraction. Acting alone, JPs could order overseers to do roadwork within their districts, receive overseers' books, lay out commutation money, and administer oaths to township officials to perform their duties. Acting in pairs, they could consider and allow tax assessors' returns, issue warrants to debt collectors, and approve the apprenticeship of orphaned children by a town warden.

Seventh, King George III's proclamation in 1763 handed JPs a further, even higher, responsibility: they were expected to uphold and enforce a Christian moral order. The king directed Governor Murray and his justices of the peace to "cause all laws already made against blasphemy, profaneness, adultery, fornication, polygamy, incest, profanation of the Lord's Day, swearing, and drunkenness, to be vigorously put in execution in every part of your government," taking "due care for the Punishment of these, and every other Vice and Immorality." This "morality movement" drew its strength from England, where by the late eighteenth century a resurgence of Christian moral values, particularly from Methodist and Anglican quarters, spread out to the colonies through directives to those in the highest levels of government. This duty to enforce morality among the people posed a problem for justices of the peace operating in a setting and culture different from that of England. In Niagara District, at the time the most populated section of the province, the views of many did not align with the moralistic pattern being urged on the colonials. Niagara magistrates faced conflicting pressures enforcing a Christian moral order in a district, as Murray noted, "where some inhabitants were not shy in demanding they do just that, while others were equally determined to lead their own lives, free of unwelcome judicial interference."

JPs became real players in the province's opening decades, even if they played their roles overseeing local administrative, financial, and basic judicial services unevenly. As historian Frederick Armstrong aptly notes, justices of the peace had emerged as "the hinge between the people and the provincial government."

With so many roles, and with a shortage of justices of the peace to carry them out, the cascading consequences of neglect meant many vital aspects of local government went unaddressed, raising the rebellious ire of townsfolk, villagers, and rural settlers, who, during the 1830s, had a growing list of other unheeded complaints, too, from arbitrary government to impassable roads.

What townspeople demanded, Aitchison explains, were efficient and zealous magistrates who would attend to their duties within the township. "Consequently we find them complaining that for want of magistrates town meetings were not held, township officers could not be sworn in, statute labour was unsupervised and unperformed, certificates for the performance of settlement duties were not issued, lawbreakers went unpunished, the public peace unpreserved, and, since without magistrates the courts of requests could not be held, trifling disputes went unsettled."

By 1837 these pressures erupted into armed rebellion. That insurgency, combined with simultaneous rebellion in Lower Canada, got the attention of the Colonial Office in London. Was Britain at risk of losing more of its North American colonies?

Although Upper Canada had *representative* government, in the form of its popularly elected provincial legislature, an inquiry into the uprisings and grievances by Lord Durham, dispatched from England to investigate, produced a report calling for *responsible* government, which entailed something new in colonial development: accountability. Once more a new constitution was enacted. In 1840 a new single entity named Canada, consisting of two parts, Canada East and Canada West (the new names for Lower Canada and Upper Canada, respectively) was created, with its two parts more closely integrated. Especially important was the advent of "responsible government," with more accountability of government and a greater role for the elected legislative assembly.

While these major constitutional developments did provide a clearer legal framework for JPs, reality at ground level still required more than proclamations, constitutional authority, statutes, and appointments. For an extended period, the province continued to suffer a real shortage of JPs, which Aitchison attributes to the government believing "that only a small proportion of the population constituted suitable magisterial timber." With rapid population increase from the 1820s, the ratio of justices of the peace to society as a whole became extremely imbalanced. By the late 1830s this shortage of JPs contributed to mounting dissatisfaction, not just on the part of those who openly rebelled in 1837, but by the provincial government itself, which responded by overcompensating, appointing numerous JPs and making many hundreds more office holders, from mayors and reeves to game wardens, justices of the peace *ex officio*.

Another ground-level complication was caused by the fact that, because justices of the peace fulfilled far-reaching duties and wielded many powers, a lot turned on who got appointed. One class of qualified candidates were actually disqualified: following the pattern from England, practising lawyers could not act as justices of the peace. British authority Clive Emsley notes that while justices of the peace in England were judicial officials, "they had only the most tenuous links with the legal world," an observation equally applicable to JPs in Upper Canada, although at least in 1840, explains Murray, the provincial government "moved to appoint professional lawyers as district judges to oversee the magistrates." The district court judge, who did have to be a qualified lawyer, served as chairman of the Court of Quarter Sessions, "ensuring continuity and greater professionalism in that court."

An explicit qualification was property ownership, a prospective appointee having to own property worth at least one hundred pounds per year, clear of deductions. As Lewthwaite explains, "the idea was that men who owned property had a stake in the community and were its natural leaders." This property requirement in England meant potential justices of the peace were often members of the landed aristocracy, while in Upper Canada they were mostly farmers, mill owners, and merchants.

Beyond that property requirement, it is unclear what other criteria guided the province's British-appointed governor in choosing justices of the peace. Because he could not personally know potential candidates in every district, he took advice from circuit judges who traveled the districts and from local officials. Factors recommending candidates would have included proximity of the candidate's residence to important towns in the district, the candidate's character, his local knowledge and experience, competency, and expected acceptability within the local community, although, as Lewthwaite notes about this last point, opinions of ordinary settlers were not sought directly. Once the governor decided on a set of candidates, he issued a Commission of the Peace naming them to the bench of the district in question.

Historian Margaret Banks noted, after reviewing development of courts in Ontario, that it was not hard to identify a suitable candidate for justice of the peace: he would simply be the individual with more training or education than anyone else, which often was relatively little. Along the Canadian frontier, the justice of the peace would be credible so long as, compared to others in the same settlement, he was *relatively* the most authoritative and qualified person. In this aspect at least, one could say the Canadian JP resembled his English counterpart: in both communities, the administration of justice rose, or settled, to its own level of possibilities.

Whatever their other qualifications, justices of the peace, like judges themselves, were appointed under the political patronage system. Magistrate's Court was seen, at least by those behind the scenes, as much an extension of party government as it was an independent citadel for equity and justice.

Absence of merit-based appointments undercut the ostensible effort to establish the rule of law, but what else could one do? Training might have helped, but no training was provided for those appointed justices of the peace. Men receiving the nod often had no connection to legal affairs whatsoever. Individuals who had come to Ontario from England may have had an appreciation for the JP's function there, but unless connected with the legal world as James Boyer had been, they would not know its actual operations.

As a result of all this, in 1842 the powers-that-be sought to improve the standards and qualifications of justices of the peace, a sensible move given all the power JPs wielded. Observing that it was "of the utmost consequence to all classes of Her Majesty's Subjects that none but persons well qualified should be permitted to act as justices of the peace," the legislature stipulated that "all justices of the peace to be appointed in the several districts of this province shall be of the most sufficient persons, dwelling in the said districts, respectively."

One reason these initiatives over several decades did not work out was the mindset of colonists, many of whom thought practices in Britain were transportable. For them, exporting the English justice of the peace to a North American setting was integral to the larger aspiration of replicating British ways wholesale. Efforts to recreate vast "clergy reserves" on choice land in Upper Canada for exclusive benefit of the established state religions of England and Scotland, was another bizarre and inequitable demonstration of this colonial predilection. This colonial-minded outlook was still on display in the 1930s when the new Bank of Canada was modelled directly on the Bank of England with no adjustment for the essential structural difference in which Britain's and Canada's respective central banks handle monetary policy, such as one being a unitary, the other a federal, state. Other examples of this propensity to look at Canada and see Britain abound. The institution of justice of the peace would need to be recognized for what it was *in Canada,* and undergo major adjustments, if it was to fit in at all.

A related difficulty was the simple historical reality that the office of JP did not get established in a single bounded territory at one point in time. Quite the opposite. The development was most uneven, in time and in space. The places early Canadian magistrates found themselves varied considerably, depending on the period, and on decisions about how to carve out territorial jurisdictions for governmental and judicial administration.

Historian Hilda Neatby studied the administration of justice under the Quebec Act and discovered "the civil authority of justices of the peace did not extend even to all the newer areas of the province." Even within areas that were covered, added Margaret Banks in *Evolution of the Ontario Courts, 1788–1981,* it was left up to the justices of the peace to declare their territorial divisions themselves, a stark contrast to the situation in Britain where Parliament dealt authoritatively with such matters, using county boundaries that were firmly fixed and routinely resorted to as a basis for judicial and governmental organization. In what would become Ontario, JPs "were not required to follow county or township boundary lines," explained Banks, "and there was no uniformity in the matter. Sometimes the county was used as a basis for division. A single township might contain two divisions and contiguous parts of two or more adjacent townships might constitute a single division. Divisions could be adapted to the actual state of settlement." Seen in a positive light, such flexibility could at least be considered a useful attribute for a developing colonial territory in early stages of development.

By 1867 a further round of constitutional change ushered in the federation of four colonial provinces under the name Canada. The British North America Act divided jurisdiction between federal and provincial levels of government, an innovative two-tiered system of government that first emerged in a North American First Nations federation, was further developed in the Constitution of the United States, and then used for Canada, initially in 1840 and now more fully in 1867, as the best way to unify British colonies in North America under a common government while accommodating their cultural and regional differences. In the process, Upper Canada's name was changed to Ontario, and its upper house, an elected body since 1840, was abolished. Section 92(14) of the British North America Act gave the province power to set the qualifications for justices of the peace, and to appoint them.

Although justices of the peace in Britain steadily gained power, in Upper Canada the great powers and authority of the justices of the peace had by degrees been taken over by legally trained magistrates and judges as growth of cities and larger towns made a central and stable court system possible. For instance, by 1832, as Wilson notes, "municipal corporations began to erode what some historians have termed the 'autocratic' powers of the justices of the peace." One way JPs' powers were curbed was by town charters providing for elected boards of police who, rather than the justices of the peace, would be responsible for policing. After the Baldwin Act in 1852 laid the foundations for modern municipal government in Ontario, elected municipal councils began taking over local government administration from the JPs. The trend continued following Confederation in 1867, as Ontario's legislature changed the local power structure, stipulating that no justice of the peace other than a police magistrate "shall adjudicate upon, admit to bail, discharge prisoners, or otherwise act, except at the Courts of General Sessions of the Peace, in any case for any town or city where there is a police magistrate, except in case of the illness or absence, or at the request, in writing, of the police magistrate."

The project of curtailing JP power in Ontario was understandable, if bizarre. The provincial government, seeking to compensate for the earlier lack of such officials, had appointed so many JPs in the mid-1800s that nobody knew how many existed. No central system kept track of justices of the peace. Those who relocated from one jurisdiction to another within the province, or even moved out of the country altogether, or died, often did so without the provincial attorney-general's department, responsible for administration of justice in the province, ever being aware. At no time could anybody say, due to woefully incomplete records, how many JPs Ontario had, let alone much else about them.

In this context, the move to shoulder out or constrain the JPs' powers continued. For instance, the bench for the Court of General Sessions of the Peace, Ontario's equivalent of Quarter Sessions in England, was composed of the county court judge as chairman sitting with justices of the peace, but after 1873 county court judges could preside alone, with justices of the peace no longer needing to be present for this court to be properly constituted. Gradually, the jurisdiction of an Ontario justice of the peace was becoming limited.

Because JPs possessed tremendous powers in the opening decades of life in the province, they potentially faced corrupting influences, especially given their combined judicial and administrative duties at the local level. In contrast to the American institutionalization of "checks and balances," Canada's British-inherited institutions handed a lot of unfettered power to early justices of the peace. The challenge to the "Family Compact" oligarchy that controlled Upper Canada by Mackenzie and other reformers in the 1830s was based on both the theory and their evidence that where there was such a concentration of power, there would also be partiality and corruption. Whether that kind of corruption existed to the extent critics of the magistracy suggest remains an open topic for research and debate.

But *systemic* corruption, which allows an institution to be subverted even as it honourably and effectively carries out its work, because of its structure and operations, was built right into the machinery for administration of justice in Upper Canada. Whether it was through the manner of appointments, the role of JPs in policing, their political roles in local governance, their administrative tasks in connection with prosecuting alleged lawbreakers, or the income they obtained from the fines they levied against those they found guilty, the institution came with fundamental flaws.

A lot turned on how justices of the peace earned their money. Generally, JPs were poorly remunerated, which created a number of problems. Modest pay was supposed to ensure that those who opted to serve as JPs were "respectable," meaning they didn't do it for the money because they didn't need the income, but that reasoning had shortfalls in practice. For openers, in the early decades of the province, while justices of the peace had some remuneration for the transaction of judicial business, this provided little incentive for them, as Aitchison noted, "to carry out their purely local government functions, for which they were not paid at all, or to attend Quarter Sessions." Some JPs in the province were "stipendiary," meaning they received a stipend of money from the government, but most were not. Many were remunerated out of the fines they themselves assessed against the persons they convicted. Without convictions, such justices of the peace got no pay.

Was absence of proper records about who even occupied the uncounted offices of justice of the peace a reason for such an off-handed remuneration policy? Or was this low-budget enterprise with its implicit problems simply overlooked by the provincial government on the basis that what is not seen as a problem does not exist as one? How officials get paid shapes the way the institution they serve will operate. In countries where police officers, customs inspectors, permit issuers, and judges are paid little money, their government may expect them, while it turns a blind eye, to make up the shortfall through "indirect taxation" of bribes extracted from the citizens forced to interact with these officials. James McRuer, when examining the office of justice of the peace in Ontario, concluded without much difficulty that the fee system for justice of the peace was "subversive to the administration of justice."

It produced an incentive that gave rise around the province to some justices of the peace being truly ardent in executing their duties, actually travelling with constables helping them find infractions to prosecute. While speedy justice required that a JP be handy when needed to decide a matter, such front-line enforcement was as inappropriate for judicial officers as champerty and maintenance was for lawyers. Sometimes a municipality filled the breach, paying its local magistrate. In Bracebridge this practice was an on-again, off-again arrangement, fluctuating with changes in the town council's attitude, the level of municipal revenues, and the council agenda that James Boyer, wearing his hat as town clerk, helped set. Boyer strongly advocated the principle that a public official should be paid from public funds, not from the fines he himself levied.

Chapter Three

THE STAGE: MAGISTRATE'S COURT IN 1890S BRACEBRIDGE

In 1892 during the same decade as the cases in this book, Parliament brought new order to Canada's criminal law and procedure by codifying countless separate statutory provisions into a single, comprehensive Criminal Code. Codification, a sensible approach long used by other legal systems but not the English, made Canada the first country in the British Empire to consolidate, integrate, and harmonize its legal regime governing criminal behaviour.

The landmark codification work was done by Judge Sir James Robert Gowan of Barrie, who had already become known to the public as one of the commissioners investigating the Pacific Scandal after it helped bring down the government of Sir John A. Macdonald. Now, for the intricate and profound challenge of thinking through the possibilities and implications when combining all existing criminal law and harmonizing all criminal procedure into a single statute, Judge Gowan carried out much of his demanding task in the pleasant surroundings of Lake Muskoka.

Gowan summered on a large island near the mouth of the Muskoka River named Hogg Island, which he renamed *Eileen Gowan* after his own family, using a Gaelic version of the word for island. The same island would also accommodate far-reaching discussions and decisions affecting law and justice later in the twentieth century as summer home to Honourable R. Roy McMurtry, who served over several decades as Ontario's attorney general, solicitor general, and chief justice.

In clearing away the tangled legal underbrush and bringing rationality to the system as a whole, Gowan's recommendations, when enacted by Parliament as the Criminal Code of Canada, helped clarify the long-standing practice of having many local justices of the peace available who could punish petty offenders, filter out frivolous or vexatious cases, and evaluate more serious charges.

In shoring up the power of JPs, the 1892 changes also removed from jurors the right to initiate an investigation if they suspected an offence had been committed, vesting that power instead in justices of the peace and other magistrates. That change was made by Section 557 of the Code, which also authorized JPs to be the ones to summon potential witnesses and examine them under oath.

The "rule of law" at ground level required that justices of the peace be readily available to dispense speedy justice. By quickly cooling hot disputes between neighbours or within families, resolving petty conflicts erupting along society's outer edges, and meting out punishments to relatively minor offenders hauled before him by a local constable, game warden, or aggrieved neighbour, the front-line JP could thwart community lawlessness that otherwise would prevail.

Yet, while a JP could do this for many infractions, he could not do it for all. More serious offences were beyond the magistrate's jurisdiction. Both before and after codification in 1892, graver matters were either heard by a judge or by a panel of several JPs. This concept had first emerged in England and was part of the system exported to Canada, as noted in the preceding chapter, and while the office of JP had evolved significantly in Canada, this requirement remained unaltered.

A pragmatic reason for JPs to sit in a panel of two or three for more serious charges was that these first-responders of the judicial system lacked legal background or special training for adjudication. Prudent public policy thus favoured a collective approach with shared responsibility, reducing the risk that a lone magistrate might run too far off the rails. Having a panel could be a safeguard for the rule of law.

A second practical reason for empowering several JPs to hear a matter that otherwise required a judge could easily be understood in places like Muskoka. Small towns, frontier settlements, and rural locales did not have nearby judges with jurisdiction to try these graver offences. In Bracebridge's early years, when travel was arduous and took a long time, he was to be found sixty miles to the south, in Barrie.

Often the panel of JPs was authorized to make a judgment and impose a sentence itself, although in some instances their work amounted to a preliminary hearing after which they ordered that the case proceed to the nearest judge. Although James Boyer tried many cases alone, often one or two other JPs had to join him on the bench because of these rules. The more justices of the peace available, the easier it was to assemble a duo or trio, and the speedier justice could be.

Muskoka District, like the rest of Ontario, was actually awash in justices of the peace. During the 1890s no fewer than fifteen other men assisted James Boyer on the bench: Harry S. Bowyer, Singleton Brown, Robert M. Browning, Alfred Hunt, John Inglis, Charles W. Lount, John McDermott, E. Josiah Pratt, Peter M. Shannon, William H. Spencer, William G. Stimpson, William Sword, John Thomson, Isaac White, and John H. Willmott. A few were regulars, some served infrequently.

One reason for the overpopulation of JPs was patronage. A party in control of the provincial government used the "spoils of office" to reward its political friends, many being appointed justices of the peace. Premier Mowat enjoyed this exercise and used it to his continuing advantage. Naming magistrates and grand juries was, as historian Desmond Brown notes about Nova Scotia but which was as true for Ontario, "a prime source of patronage."

Today the term *patronage* carries the negative connotation of paying off a party supporter with a job, but in the past this practice of hiring and appointing political supporters entailed more. Beyond the partisan benefits derived from filling positions with government loyalists, patronage was a means to maintain the established order, by ensuring the regime's laws would be enforced and its values upheld. People in power had a point of view about the importance of this and wanted, at ground level, to ensure continuance of the conditions in which they operated.

If patronage had a defensible place in this scheme of things, a second factor contributing to a "higher than expected" number of JPs was the absence of any directing mind for the process of creating and keeping them. While the power to appoint was real, coordination was absent, control a chimera. Government was limited, and the modern public service had yet to emerge. With the government lacking an administrative system to oversee such matters, nobody had a clue how many JPs were even alive, let alone reporting for duty across Ontario.

The provincial government, unable to keep an accurate record of its uncounted JPs, threw up its hands and just kept appointing more, a loose precautionary measure to ensure that public policy and party requirements alike were being broadly served. Intermittently, Ontario's government not only made a further wave of new appointments, but for good measure renewed all the appointed JPs believed to be in office at the time. This loose practice was of a piece with that era of approximation in record keeping. Voters' lists, too, continued to carry names of people who had moved away or moved on.

Looking back, it is easy to believe this haphazard system might have been better. Yet, an early Muskoka justice of the peace, W.E. Foot, shows why it was hard for the attorney general's office in Toronto to know where, across Ontario's sprawling hinterland, all its JPs were scattered. Foot hustled to Canada from Ireland in 1872 to claim free land in Muskoka's Medora Township, locating his property at an indentation of Lake Muskoka that he named "Foot's Bay." However, like many other free-grant settlers, he later moved into Bracebridge, leaving behind his original name on that lakeside locale.

In Bracebridge Mr. Foot became active as a justice of the peace, among other things, but in the early 1880s the aptly named man again took foot, shipping out this time for the Northwest Territory. There he stayed until relocating to Toronto in 1886. Then he quit the provincial capital for Parry Sound, where he became deputy registrar and justice of the peace for the next twenty years. Clearly, being a JP did not hold one down. As Foot in fact showed, it was a ticket to ride in Canada's mobile and developing society during the country's dynamic decades of settlement. He became part of society's free-floating supply of JPs. His story was far from unique.

Beyond death and mobility, something else made it hard to keep an accurate central record in Toronto of who, at any given time, might be presiding in Ontario's far-flung Magistrate's Courts. Justices of the peace included everyone elected as mayors and reeves, plus all those appointed game wardens. By virtue of holding their office or position, they were empowered *ex officio* (emanating from office) to act as JPs in addition to their other duties. This component of the system not only ensured a well-grounded local element, but reinforced the local power structure, the crossover or combination of roles oddly echoing the magistrates' earlier all-embracing role in local governance. The fact that municipal elections were held every New Year's Day meant that across the province a reasonably frequent turnover occurred among those who held these offices. This annual change in elected officials contributed to the confusion over who was sitting as a justice of the peace. The number of game wardens was equally uncertain, for similar reasons of appointment and continuance in office.

Sometimes the only person available to hear a case was one of these *ex officio* municipal officials. Huntsville, twenty-five miles north of Bracebridge, was incorporated as a village in 1886, so, from that date, Huntsville's first reeve, L.E. Kinton, could have acted as a JP, giving swifter justice and avoiding the cost and inconvenience of travel to Bracebridge. Life must have been peaceful in Huntsville's opening days, however, because the first recorded dispute only came several years later when Dr. F.L. Howland, Kinton's successor as reeve, presided in a makeshift courtroom. The case involved two Chaffey Township neighbours who got into a fight over a contested line fence between their properties.

The complainant, with one blackened eye swollen shut and the other side of his face puffed up, sat in court by himself, looking dejected, seeking justice for his black eye and redress for his removed fence. The defendant, a much smaller man, recounted local historian Joe Cookson, sat beside his wife, "a very hefty and capable looking woman," "looking equally as glum."

As a lone justice of the peace, Reeve Howland was to review the case and, if he found the complaint justified, send it for trial in Bracebridge. Howland questioned the complainant about the reason for the dispute, asked about the location of the attack, then inquired, "How many times did this man hit you?"

"Oh! He never hit me, your honour. No siree, it was her. That woman's a regular devil, your honour. She's a menace to the countryside."

"You're sure the defendant himself never struck you?"

"Quite sure, your honour. He's a kindly sort of man. But her, I sure could tell you plenty."

"Never mind," coughed Dr. Howland, as he cleared his throat, looked down, and shuffled some papers on his desk. He then looked up again to pronounce: "I'm going to dismiss this case and bind all three of you over to keep the peace. In regards to the fence, next time I see the reeve of Chaffey I'll get him to send his 'fence viewers' over to look the situation over. We'll abide by their decision. Case dismissed."

Whether as a medical man, or head of a council, or the newspaper editor he also was, Dr. Howland as an *ex officio* justice of the peace had clearly acquired practical ways to resolve contentious matters.

A small town's watchful eyes and active tongues usually meant that culprits and perpetrators were promptly arraigned.

One day some men were brought up for tossing attention-getting candies at girls during a Salvation Army church service. Then next, a sly trapper appeared after getting caught with 176 muskrat pelts out of season. Plenty of heavier action was served up, too: men fighting in the woods with axes, men fighting along the roads with shovels and buggy whips, a husband threatening to slit his wife's throat from ear to ear with his straight razor.

A constant flow of assault and battery cases moved through Magistrate's Court in 1890s Bracebridge, too, as men settled scores and the town danced to its steady rhythm of street brawls.

The slosh of alcohol showed up everywhere, from harmless drunks sitting in the street to instruct enthralled school children, to spiteful ones slipping insinuations about a man's wife into barroom talk and provoking a bare-knuckled, knockdown fistfight. Life was raw in many ways. Shooting a neighbour's dog did not go unpunished. Those who destroyed other men's fences, whether through burning, stealing, or vandalizing, were brought to justice.

The town was a theatre that never closed, and the justice of the peace was always standing by, ready to perform his leading role with the ever-shifting cast of characters.

A variety of conflicts to be adjudicated were spawned by disagreements over money and commerce, such as financial struggles over unpaid wages and broken contracts. Logs, because they were valuable, were often the object of money-based conflicts, as men struggled to acquire these assets through illegal cutting, outright theft, bushlot battles over the location of property lines and the logs within them, and skirmishes over unmarked logs allegedly found in the public domain along the roadside.

Captains charged for operating boats without a licence for commercial purposes, for transporting more paying passengers across Muskoka's lakes than their boats were authorized to carry, or for selling fresh garden produce to summer cottagers (including a judge) at the end of their docks without being licensed to do so, presented another face of Muskoka's ongoing conflicts: local officials sought to regulate commerce by challenging enterprising individuals who, for their part, helpfully sought to provide important services in a district dependant on tourism. It was a defining conflict for "the rule of law."

Joining this steady parade of criminal and financial cases, another procession through the Magistrate's Courtroom emanated from the community's social and cultural impulses. On this stage the magistrate's performance was to enforce laws that satisfied community norms when lack of respect, absence of courtesy, cutting corners, dodging blame, creating mischief, making mistakes, expressing rude resentments, or indulging in escapades went beyond accepted standards of propriety. In this, James Boyer had to contend with the double standards of humans who celebrate virtue but look to find it in others more than in themselves.

Brothels, whether operating in town or at a discreet buggy ride's distance into the countryside, generated courtroom sensations, and in doing so, epitomized the conflicts created by the community's double standard. Less serious but in like vein was a honeymoon charivari in Bracebridge that amused many townsfolk who chuckled to think that the groom was not the only young man to have fun on his wedding night, but which predictably offended a few. The event became a cause of mild consternation after its youthful perpetrators were dragged by the town's stern chief constable, "Old Man Dodd," before a bemused magistrate as the community sought to find its markers for moral probity.

Other cases, whether arising from misbehaviour at church meetings and theatrical performances, or other unmannerly outbreaks, seem petty by almost any standard. Yet, they do serve to underscore how some law or other against public mischief is always handy and awaiting invocation by public authorities wanting to constrain unruly or high-spirited humans.

Whether a case was grave or trivial, the Bracebridge Magistrate's Court in the 1890s generally served as a fast, convenient, and reliable arena of justice.

A prosecution begun on March 11, 1895, by Chief Constable Robert Armstrong against Elizabeth Weston for running a brothel was adjourned by Justice of the Peace Boyer so the chief could procure evidence, and when court resumed just two days later, the charge against her was "dismissed for want of evidence." Constable Armstrong, having learned *his* lesson in court, subsequently stepped forward much better prepared to bring charges against "Queenie" Dufresne, calling a parade of witnesses who described the late-night comings and goings at her house of ill-fame, and got her convicted.

Muskoka Magistrate's Court was the ever-ready venue to resolve conflicts between private parties and to enforce public laws. The former included fighting spouses, employees suing for unpaid wages, and owners seeking the recovery of stolen dogs and chickens. The latter ranged from municipal bylaw infractions detected by the town constable or the local hygiene inspector, to breaches of the statutes of the Province of Ontario and the Dominion of Canada dealing with licensing of vessels, prostitution, firearms, hunting, trapping, fishing, distilling liquor, and gambling.

The court was generally convened in the town hall on Dominion Street in Bracebridge. Prominent in the centre of the community, it sat adjacent to the *Muskoka Herald* building, whose stone-walled basement was rented out as a convenient lock-up for accused persons awaiting their appearance in court until the number of attempted breakouts did such damage to the structure that the newspaper proprietors cancelled the arrangement.

Bracebridge Town Hall on Dominion Street, where James Boyer was municipal clerk, also conveniently housed Magistrate's Court, over which he presided. The Muskoka Herald *building is to the left; its cellar was used as the town jail for a period until many attempted breakouts by prisoners did such damage the arrangement was cancelled.*

Depending on the number of people attending court, sessions took place either in the council chamber, or the larger second-floor entertainment hall, a proscenium theatre otherwise alive with community plays, touring concerts, or library-sponsored readings by such popular visiting notables as First Nations poet Pauline Johnson. Although such arrangements may seem slightly improvised, they were formality itself compared to the series of makeshift courtrooms used by the Muskoka magistrate in the Orange Lodge hall and elsewhere around town prior to erection of the capacious town hall in 1881.

The tall, redbrick Bracebridge municipal hall was not only the most prominent building on the most prestigious street in town, but was also a highly convenient venue for James Boyer, because he could fulfill his duties as justice of the peace, attend to his functions as municipal clerk, conduct his conveyancing practice, and receive calligraphy orders for memorial addresses, all within the same precincts, or just next door at the adjacent

Land Registry Office. Such convenience facilitated speedy justice, because court could be immediately convened whenever the need arose.

The adage "justice delayed is justice denied" was taken to heart. Justice of the Peace James Boyer was never off duty. His court was a continuously open stage for ready justice. He heard cases on Saturday. If it was after hours, aggrieved parties went to his modest wood-frame residence at the north end of the town's main street. If he was home ill, as he once was when the town constable brought in boys he'd caught stealing chickens, James rose from his sick bed and dealt with such urgent matters anyway. Even on Christmas Day, justice in Bracebridge did not rest: he opened his door to deal with a constable who'd brought in a couple men intoxicated from celebrating the Christ child's birth. For nighttime emergencies, he could reliably be reached at his home. If he was out of town on municipal business, it was "next man up"; the town had other JPs who could fill the breach.

In good weather the JPs sometimes were disposed to "balance the convenience of the parties" by taking themselves to other locales in Muskoka. Thus, James Boyer and John McDermott went to Port Carling to hear a case in mid-August 1897, a time of year when the inescapable necessity of a scenic boat trip down the river from Bracebridge and up Lake Muskoka to picturesque Port Carling happily served the ends of justice, although apparently no occasion presented itself requiring them to travel to Port Carling by sleigh in January. Another time, the court was held in the village of Uffington. These travelling courts were rare.

Magistrate's Court in Bracebridge was, of course, just one stage in a larger theatre for the administration of justice. At the same time that James Boyer was presiding in it, higher courts were offering Muskokans more enthralling lessons about the harsher climes of civil litigation and criminal law.

One of the most dramatic civil cases arose from the burning of steamboat *Flora Barnes*. The "*Flora Barnes* trouble" began in 1883, when Bracebridge was still a village and James Boyer was already conducting Magistrate's Court, but a decade before his cases reported in this book took place.

The *Flora Barnes* had been tied up for some time at the town wharf below the falls in Bracebridge Bay. Under instruction from town council to follow a strict line in collecting taxes, particularly for non-residents of the municipality, the town constable seized the steamer and offered her for sale to cover the owner's unpaid taxes. The worst thing that could have happened then did: destruction of the craft by fire.

Following the fire, the ship's owner, Thomas Barnes, filed suit claiming some $3,500 in damages from the village, alleging illegal seizure. On March 20, 1883, Bracebridge clerk James Boyer brought before council the fateful letter from Barnes's Toronto lawyers, Malone & Malone, advising of the claim. In response, village council retained the services of a Barrie firm, Lount & Lount. When the case first came before the Barrie assizes it was adjourned. The day of reckoning would be postponed for as long as Samuel and George Lount could use legal delaying tactics.

A year and one week passed before the case came up again for hearing, on March 27, 1884. The trial at Barrie was a disaster for the village. The expense of providing witnesses mounted, as a parade of those giving evidence made their way to the stand day after day. In total, there were more than a dozen men (including James Boyer), a combination of Bracebridge officials or men with particular knowledge of the matter, as well as experts retained by the Lount firm. All this evidence, and the cost to adduce it, was to no avail. The village of Bracebridge was ordered to pay Thomas Barnes his claim for damages, and costs as well.

Still in a state of shock, Bracebridge councillors met in June, almost instinctively deciding not to let the matter rest. The village's appeal would be taken by a different Barrie firm, Strathy & Ault. A month later, council met again to consider a letter received from the new barristers about Bracebridge's dim prospects in the matter. Reeve Alfred Hunt was instructed by council to go to Barrie and consult with Strathy and Ault. The upshot was that on August 12, the village council solemnly decided to withdraw its appeal, pay Barnes $3,671, and relinquish its claim for $310 in unpaid taxes, with the village given ninety days to raise the money.

A bylaw was prepared by Clerk Boyer, approved by council, and submitted to Bracebridge ratepayers in a plebiscite that he conducted. A reluctant citizenry voted its approval to raise four thousand dollars by debenture to liquidate the debt to Barnes. A sum of six hundred dollars was paid, as well, to Lount & Lount for their services at trial.

The major setback cast a pale of doubt over the villagers and injury to their councillors' confidence that endured well into the 1890s. The heavy financial burden weighed on the community for years as people's taxes paid down the four thousand dollar debenture and its stubbornly accruing interest. It would be decades in Bracebridge before any mother again named her newborn daughter Flora.

The 1890s' most memorable criminal case involved the charge that William J. Hammond had murdered his wife. After Hammond met a girl named Katie Tough in Gravenhurst, he married her across the U.S. border in Buffalo, then placed an insurance policy on her life. When she was found dead in a snowbank back in Gravenhurst, the coroner deduced she had been poisoned. Hammond's trial opened at Muskoka court of assizes on February 15, 1897. After hearing the evidence, however, the jury in Bracebridge disagreed with the coroner's conclusion. Seven voted for acquittal, five for conviction. With a hung jury, a new trial was ordered.

At the fall assizes that year, a different jury returned a verdict of guilty. Hammond's death sentence was set for February 18, 1898, but with an appeal pending, the case continued to excite wide interest across Muskoka and in Toronto's daily newspapers. A month before his pending execution, the *Muskoka Herald* ran the following, penned though not signed by James Boyer: "Upon the decision of the Chancery Divisional Court in regards to two points of law hangs the life of William J. Hammond, who is now in the condemned cell in the Bracebridge jail awaiting his doom on February 18th. A jury of his peers disagreed at his first trial, but when the case was heard a second time a verdict of guilty was returned and he was sentenced to the gallows. The crime was committed, according to the Crown, so that Hammond could profit by the insurance policies placed upon the life of his wife."

With the clock running down toward his execution, the Court of Appeal decided the evidence given by Hammond at the inquest after his wife's death should not have been allowed at the second trial. So another new trial was ordered. Hammond's third trial for the same crime opened at the Muskoka assizes on June 2, 1898. The case had now become so notorious that Ontario's chief justice, Sir William R. Meredith, a former leader of the Ontario Conservative Party in the legislature, travelled from Toronto to Bracebridge in Muskoka's pleasant early summer season to conduct the trial himself.

No new witnesses were called. Very little new evidence was introduced, and that which was adduced was found immaterial. The essential story remained the same. Katie had been found in the snow in Gravenhurst March 6, 1896, in a dying condition said to be caused by swallowing poison. Constable Archie Sloan investigated and told of prussic acid purchases in Gravenhurst the same day. The jury retired for an hour and evidently found the chain of evidence about as strong and complete as circumstantial evidence could make a case. They returned to the courtroom, bringing in a verdict of guilty.

Chief Justice Meredith, seizing the opportunity, delivered a tongue-lashing to William Hammond while sending a moral message to the general public. In pronouncing, yet again, the sentence of death on Hammond, Meredith stated: "For your poor and aged father there is profound sympathy: had you been as faithful to your wife as he has been to you, the death and misery you have caused would not have taken place and you would not be standing where you are, a convicted murderer."

Because Bracebridge's jail was notorious for the ease prisoners had in escaping it, Hammond was imprisoned in the Simcoe County Gaol at Barrie until September 8, when he was delivered back to Bracebridge, securely shackled. Ontario's official executioner came to town as well, and began building a scaffold in the yard of the Muskoka District Gaol on Dominion Street. The sound and sight of its construction attracted onlookers. Drama in the community mounted. Hammond himself could hear the sawing and hammering as his gallows took shape in the days before he was to die.

On the appointed day, as the eerie grey light of dawn broke over the staged spectacle, the town bell began to toll. Its hollow tone echoed ominously across the small community's rooftops, the mood of solemn expectation thickening. In a further theatrical flourish, a black flag was run up the pole at the town hall, adjacent to the gallows, heightening the bleak moment's macabre drama.

Up the fresh wooden steps to the hangman's platform climbed young William Hammond. Townspeople had risen early to witness the spectacle as best they could through or over the walled-off jail yard. Performing their grim roles behind the whitewashed wooden fence were the sheriff, constables, a clergyman, and the hangman. The assembly looked on in stony silence. The convicted murderer was directed to stand on the hinged trap door. The coarse rope noose was secured around his neck. The door beneath his feet was released. The rope snapped taught as he plummeted down. The noose accomplished its crude purpose, ending William Hammond's life early that September morning.

Public executions continued into the 1890s because conventional wisdom held that the value of such an exercise, to be a truly instructive lesson, demanded a strong closing scene, like a mutinous shipmate being flogged on deck or keelhauled in the forced presence of the crew. Public execution was believed to deliver an educational punch for the populace by being both enthralling and revolting. Hammond's 1898 hanging took place behind a high wooden fence and out of direct sight for many people, but the event remained the talk of the town for years to come. Crime did not pay. The bleak finality of Hammond's quest for cash and his execution set a mood that reached everywhere crimes were being tried and punished in Bracebridge, including Magistrate's Court.

To the chagrin of public authorities, however, not every crime resulted in a criminal being brought to justice, rather counteracting the moral impact of Hammond's ghoulish execution. Muskoka's share of mysterious murders and unsolved thefts included, for instance, the infamous Bracebridge bank robbery of 1897.

Begun in the early 1880s, Alfred Hunt's private bank in Bracebridge, prominent in a redbrick building on the main street of town, was the very first bank to operate in Muskoka. It provided excellent service and valued convenience to its customers, who no longer had to bank at distant centres. On Thursday morning, May 27, bank clerk T.H. Pringle arrived at his usual hour to open up, only to be greeted by the strong odour of gunpowder. He was astounded to discover the building had been entered during the night. Making his way directly to the vault, he found a hole had been drilled through the door and the combination lock blown off.

Across town, Thomas Magee, who had earlier reported to police several tools missing from his blacksmithy and wagon shop, soon learned that his brace, sledgehammer, and crowbar were now at Hunt's Bank, being held as exhibits for a trial if a culprit could be apprehended. Although his tools were in the bank, gone missing from it were some one thousand dollars in cash, several gold watches, some notes of exchange, Mickle Lumber Company orders, and nine thousand dollars in the town's most recent waterworks debentures, issued to Richard Lance of Beatrice, who had left them with Mr. Hunt for safekeeping. Magee got his tools back, in time, but no one was ever brought to justice for this well-planned robbery. The lesson from that one, to those who sought to believe it, was that crime did pay

As the twentieth century arrived, Muskoka District's prestigious new Court House opened at the corner of Dominion and Ontario streets in Bracebridge, just as James Boyer retired after a quarter-century as district magistrate. His successors would hold court here.

Within the year the Hunt Bank closed. Its crash shook Bracebridge and the large surrounding area of Muskoka. The bank's collapse wiped out Alfred Hunt's own extensive fortune, but the depositors at his bank received the return of nearly all their money. Hunt, whom townspeople had earlier elected mayor in the mid-1890s, continued to be held in high local esteem. "The bank should not have busted," asserted the bank's solicitor, Arthur A. Mahaffy, who believed the Hunt Bank to still be fundamentally sound. But Alfred Hunt, focused on the bank's sizeable problems rather than its basic soundness, and still shaken by the bank robbery the year before, persisted in assigning his assets for the benefit of the bank's creditors. That was the end of independent local banking in Muskoka. The national banks promptly moved in.

These three cases and many other higher court proceedings in Bracebridge added to the local judicial culture of the 1890s, theatre that was rounded out by the all-too-human vignettes unfolding, at the same time, on the stage of Magistrate's Court.

Chapter Four

THE CONSTABULARY: PRODUCERS
OF POLICE COURT DRAMA

Without Police Chief Robert Armstrong and other law officers apprehending miscreants and hauling them into court, James Boyer and his fellow justices of the peace would have been much freer to engage in the other pursuits by which they earned their livelihoods. Yet constables were resolutely on duty, maintaining the peace and enforcing the law in and around Bracebridge, essential cast members in the town's dramas of justice, their pivotal role in the process contributing the popular term *police court* to the place where justices of the peace presided.

In establishing the rule of law and producing the raw material for more trials, they were joined by other actors in the role of enforcer. For in 1890s Canada, the constabulary was not the only arm of the law. Private citizens also appeared in Magistrate's Court in a prosecutorial role, not for some private grievance but for the share of fines they were entitled to collect from the conviction of someone caught breaking a public law. The ancient law of *moieties*, still part of Canada's Criminal Code in the days James Boyer tried these cases, was a reward system that greatly multiplied the available eyes and ears of enforcement. *Moieties* lengthened the arm of the law by, potentially, making all citizens throughout the district into private constables.

The most reliable producers of drama in the courtroom, however, were the regular police officers who brought charges as a result of trolling known hotspots. The starring role that the magistrate played in upholding the rule of law depended on solid supporting performances by those policing the town and its environs as constables, revenue agents, health and sanitation inspectors, bylaw-enforcement officers, game wardens, and fence inspectors. These prowling constables arrested drunks at street level and poachers in the backwoods, to maintain peace and order, and to establish the rule of law. They showed up in court, accompanied by the sullen or surly individuals they'd taken into custody, where they pressed charges, gave evidence, and completed their prosecutions.

It was all of one piece, a common theatre of justice. To the police officer, the morning Magistrate's Court was as important a stage on which to perform his role as the back alleys he patrolled in the evening and the troubled taverns he kept subdued late at night.

It was not always easy for the police to carry out their duties. Two cases from 1894, found later in the chapter "A Constable's Unhappy Lot," suggest that establishing the rule of law in Canada's scattered clearings and growing towns involved a contest of wills. While Canadians are raised on tales of how heroic Mounties rose to this challenge along the northwest frontier, the same feat was equally required in the small towns of Ontario, though by a force neither so well trained nor as renowned as the Royal Canadian Mounted Police.

Indeed, it was an odd assortment of constables and officials in Bracebridge and Muskoka who sought, quite unevenly, to provide some civilizing context for the raw disputes that constantly erupted as people jostled with neighbours, contended with nature, and boiled over with annoyances and frustrations.

Bracebridge's chief constable in the 1890s was Robert E. Armstrong, who'd first arrived in 1883 to head the town's police department, and subsequently served as Muskoka District constable as well. In 1889, when the Ontario legislature passed the bill incorporating Bracebridge as a town, the chief honoured this historic moment by ringing the town bell for a full hour of jubilant celebration, proving both his fine sense of occasion and his formidable physical strength.

With a name starting the alphabet, Armstrong appeared first on the list of dozens of Bracebridge proprietors, entrepreneurs, and office holders in an 1891 directory published by the *Muskoka Herald,* which identified him as "Chief Constable." Armstrong's brass-buttoned uniform and full moustache reinforced the reassuring impression he gave townsfolk as a well-maintained and authoritative figure.

Just as the JPs performed other roles in town, police officers often had extra callings as well. In addition to police work, Chief Armstrong was a liveryman, who operated his business and stables from a large wooden structure on property in the centre of town, just off Dominion Street. When the building was destroyed by fire in 1909, he built a substantial replacement brick building for the livery business, which his widow carried on after he died in 1911 until selling out to Ernest E. Boyd in 1913.

Constables did their best to stay equal to their challenging task, for instance by carrying a "nightstick," or club. In the mid-1890s a controversial escalation of police power stirred Bracebridge. On October 21, 1895, James Boyer, operating in his role as town clerk, prepared an application under Section 105 of the Criminal Code of 1892, which empowered a justice of the peace to authorize what would otherwise constitute an offence: carrying a firearm. Then, as JP, he granted Thomas Dodd, newly hired by the municipality as Bracebridge's "night watchman," permission to carry a revolver for one year.

Following Armstrong's retirement from police work in 1903, the town council, choosing from many applicants, selected William McConnell and John Miller as the new arms of the law in Bracebridge, with McConnell as chief.

In the frontier's contest of wills, it was not only the police constables who required courage. On occasion, so did the justices of the peace. In the mid-1870s, for instance, following failed efforts by intimidated constables to bring in dangerous men on outstanding arrest warrants, a frustrated Magistrate Charles Lount went himself into the townships to arrest two shantymen at their lumber camp, taking them from the daunting midst of their roughneck companions. A decade later, in June 1885, courage was still a prerequisite of office when James Boyer, accompanied by Justice of the Peace Alfred Hunt and Constables Johnson and Young, walked steadily down the middle of Bracebridge's main street to confront an angry mob of Italian railway construction workers who were mounting a strike and protest for their hard-earned but unpaid wages. Boyer read the Riot Act to them, commanding them on pain of arrest to disperse, which they did.

Constables in Bracebridge did not usually leave hard matters to others, however. In the late 1870s and 1880s, when William J. Hill was police chief and J.H. Tomlin his assistant constable, the pair had not only to deal with small crimes of delinquent boys and horse thieves, but also take on boisterous forces of loggers. As the heyday of lumbering swept a new wave of men into town, such occurrences became more frequent. With the population rising from thirteen hundred in 1880 to over three thousand by 1889, this economic expansion produced a new kind of raw reality.

One characteristic of the district's lumber economy was its role in "vastly increasing alcohol consumption," concluded Larry D. Cotton after reviewing Muskoka newspaper accounts from this era. Competing lumber companies, he explains in *Whiskey and Wickedness*, "would sometimes attract shantymen into their employment by holding 'open house' at a hotel," where "free whiskey would be part of the incentive offered to sign on for the winter." Because the isolated, rugged, and dangerous work in lumbering was better remunerated than many jobs, it attracted vigorous younger men. The lumber camps themselves were strictly booze-free, so loggers, "who naturally wanted to have a few drinks and some fun after they were paid," could hardly wait to hit town in the spring once they drew their winter's earnings. The growing number of hotels in Bracebridge and other Muskoka towns "would be filled with shantymen every fall and spring, looking for a good time."

Orillia's two newspapers, the *Packet* and the *Times,* reported in June 1883 an example of the kind of incident such situations could produce. In Bracebridge, a gang of some twenty men had arrived in town, their dangerous work of driving logs completed and their pockets filled with wages. One of the lumbermen, who'd been directing obscene and insulting language at several Bracebridge women, was hauled before Magistrate Boyer on a charge of drunkenness. The man refused to pay his fine and escaped from the courtroom with the help of his logger buddies. Gathering even more shantymen together, they defiantly prepared to resist the constables whom the magistrate had promptly sent after them. A "terrible fight" between the two sides did not settle matters. With reinforcements needed to make arrests, special constables were then deputized and sent into battle, when "much hard fighting took place before the lawless woodsmen were brought under control."

Five shantymen were taken into custody, but the others escaped arrest. After nightfall they went back into Bracebridge to raid the jail and free their companions. Rather than slinking into the bush, they then went en masse to a local hotel to celebrate the day's events, a brazen display of just how secure these roughnecks felt in this pioneer town.

If this challenge to the rule of law and Bracebridge's constabulary went unchallenged, it would reveal just how thin civilization's veneer really was, and perhaps encourage the town's descent into anarchy under rule of the mob. So, returning with yet more reinforcements, a strengthened posse of constables surprised the celebrating fugitives, recapturing the five lumbermen and returning them to jail. Later their undaunted comrades, who'd again successfully escaped during the melee at the hotel, "returned in the middle of the night and conveyed whiskey to their locked-up friends to lighten their burden."

Two river drovers who'd escaped the Bracebridge constables were arrested several days later at the Albion Hotel in Gravenhurst, but the ringleader of the shantymen, eighteen-year-old Joseph Rule, eluded capture and made his way home to Peterborough. Arrested there, he was brought in chains back to Bracebridge Magistrate's Court, where he boldly threatened everyone in sight with retribution. Undeterred, however, James Boyer "sent Rule and his other jailed companions to Peterborough to serve out their sentences."

This episode, noteworthy for its drama but not exceptional for its character, typified the era when liquor flowed freely at Bracebridge's five prospering hotels. Barrie's *Northern Advance* would report on March 5, 1885, that, "howling drunks are common in Bracebridge."

The community had in fact been awash from its inception in a perfect sea of booze, its hotels, many with names grander than their premises, driving alcohol consumption. In 1861, when it still had only two log buildings to its credit, the embryonic village opened its first tavern in one of them, Hiram James McDonald's "Royal Hotel." By 1864 Alexander Bailey opened his establishment, the "Victoria Hotel," to honour the reigning monarch, at the foot of the falls on the north side of the river. The following year James Cooper also constructed a log building on the north side of the river, which he christened the "North Falls Hotel" after the original name of the settlement. Hotel guests and nearby settlers found liquor readily available in all of them at any hour.

Life was roughened by more than consumption of raw whiskey. In May 1869 Muskoka pioneer Seymour Penson arrived in Bracebridge and checked out the Royal and Dominion hotels, finding both "very small and primitive." The former had about ten rooms, the latter double that number, both overcrowded. He stayed at the Dominion, in which the only available accommodation was on the sitting-room floor, where half the hotel's paying guests slept before an open fireplace.

At the start of the 1870s, Bracebridge's population numbered 375 but by the end of the decade stood at 1,300. To handle growing accommodation requirements, two more hotels, the British Lion and the North American, were built in 1870 at the corners of Dominion and Ontario streets, facing one another across the roadway. Although the village now had six hotels, they still could not keep up with demand, and guests slept in rows on the floors of the North American, Victoria, Royal, Dominion, British Lion, and Queen's hotels. The patrons placed great demand on the billiard tables, dining rooms, and especially the bars of these establishments. In addition to housing arriving settlers and travellers, Bracebridge's hotels competed for the local workingman's dollar in their bars, a situation that frequently required the services of the constable in order to deal with the brawls that erupted inside and the street fights that occurred outside the premises of the hotels as a result of the their brisk sales of intoxicants. The hoteliers also hosted events to curry favour with powerful local interests, important if they hoped to stay in business in the wide-open way they had become accustomed to.

Temperance forces, which some in Bracebridge saw as aligned with the work of the constables, began to rise in response to the challenges of too much alcohol, and became as active politically as the hoteliers and pro-liquor interests, gaining control of municipal government in 1868. The new council passed bylaws restricting liquor licences in the Bracebridge settlement and imposing stringent regulations, requiring the hotels to become more than glorified drinking holes. The limit was to be five "places of public entertainment," and new tavern fees were set at twenty-five dollars yearly.

Other measures of restraint were imposed, though in these early days these measures were still controls rather than prohibitions. For instance, after 1868 Bracebridge businesses such as general stores, blacksmith shops, and hardware stores that sought and got shop licences for liquor could only sell whiskey in a minimum of one-quart containers, and could no longer allow customers to drink on the premises. Until then, notes Cotton, "customers could buy small samples such as a dipper full of whiskey (called a 'grunt') taken from a barrel at the back of the store" and down it on the spot. Because it was harder to get tavern licences, and because it cost more to build and operate a tavern, he adds, it was much cheaper and easier to obtain a shop licence. "Prospective whiskey merchants could simply buy one hundred dollars' worth of household and foodstuff articles, rent a commercial space, and roll in the whiskey barrels."

In the early 1870s, two of Bracebridge's many hoteliers, George Gow of the Dominion Hotel and Hiram McDonald of the Royal, got themselves elected to municipal council and saw to it that the temperance forces were kept at bay and that those wanting liquor licences got them. In response, temperance crusader Thomas McMurray stepped up his campaign through the *Northern Advocate* to "End the Traffic in Strong Drink." The community's temperance movement would also be shored up during the 1870s by voters from Bracebridge's increasing number of Protestant churches. Their struggle against Gow and McDonald was aided when, in 1876, a new provincial statute was enacted that sought to cleanse practices in local government by taking tavern and shop licensing away from municipal councils, giving the responsibility to a district licensing commission instead.

Of course, as every constable knew, those who could not buy liquor at a local hotel or tavern might resort to the timeless expedient of stealing it. In June 1885 a man broke into Brasher's liquor store in Bracebridge and removed a quantity of brandy. Catching the thief was not too hard. He was later found by constables Johnson and Dennison, according to the June 11 edition of Barrie's *Northern Advance,* lying beside the railway track in a state of helpless intoxication.

The battles over booze ebbed and flowed but never came to a standstill. All the while, hapless police faced the conundrum of having to work the middle ground of law enforcement in a deeply divided community. Public drunkenness was a problem, but the temperance movement aim of tighter liquor control would only increase the constabulary's challenges, and the workload in Magistrate James Boyer's court.

Temperance seemed ascendant. By 1886 the Scott Act so restricted licensing of liquor that many hotels were forced to close. By 1890 temperance was increasingly accepted in many quarters as the new standard for right living. The call for temperance had now ominously escalated into the more autocratic and austere policy of prohibition. Driving this zero-tolerance policy were zealous hard-liners, of whom Thomas McMurray, by this time engaged in a Canada-wide tour preaching prohibition, was one of the most ardent.

In response, the work of distilling and distributing alcohol went underground. "Stills appeared everywhere in Muskoka's backwoods," reports Cotton, "and 'blind pigs' or bootlegging became a growth industry." One such operation in Oakley Township, east of Bracebridge, came to light when charges laid in Magistrate's Court in September 1898.

Not all distilling operations were hidden in the back woods, though. When a 1902 fire destroyed many buildings in Bracebridge's downtown business core on a cold February night, the oldest structure to fall was the Brown Estate building, which had a frame made from heavy timbers hewn in the bush back in the days when first-class pine could be had for the cutting within a few hundred yards of where the building stood. In the attic of this early Bracebridge structure firemen discovered a large tank, which licence inspector E.F. Stephenson and the liquor commissioners examined, pronouncing it part of a still. How it came to be there, nobody in Bracebridge volunteered.

Despite local initiatives by Bracebridge's formidable temperance forces and newly enacted provincial measures that gave their cause the force of law, alcohol continued to flow through the veins of many Muskokans in the 1890s. In turn, cases arising from the exploits and conundrums of individuals "under the influence" continued to pass, just as steadily, through Muskoka Magistrate's Court, until 1911, when a majority of Bracebridge citizens finally voted the municipality "dry" in a prohibition plebiscite.

Throughout the bench book, one can find many cases where booze served as a contributing factor in the charges laid. Alcohol also extracted costs from others in Muskoka, particularly the family members of society's underside — the hungry children and beaten wives — who experienced much pain and suffering. The plight of most may never have made it into the pages of James Boyer's bench book or the Bracebridge newspapers, but would certainly have tallied negatively in the integrity ledgers of the town's tavern owners.

Conditions of social rawness became aggravated, as already described, with the presence of logging crews in Muskoka. The next assault wave arrived with the roughneck construction gangs building the railways. From the 1870s into the 1890s, railway construction stimulated a booming regional economy, drawing into central Muskoka "thousands of tough railway navvies." Fighting between them and the shantymen of the lumber camps followed as night the day, and, as Cotton documents in *Whiskey and Wickedness*, "use of firearms and knives became quite commonplace in the 1870s and 1880s, resulting in a number of deaths." By 1900, with completion of Muskoka's major railway construction projects, many of these rowdy men had moved on, and, combined with more stringent control over the liquor situation, the raw life of Bracebridge seemed to be ebbing into a more genteel social order.

The sex trade, however, remained a constant. No amount of Victorian hypocrisy or supposed social gentility could mask matters that constables had to address in a country where the law, in criminalizing such commerce, created the brothels of Bracebridge. "Wherever there is plenty of money and lots of young single men," observed Cotton of this phenomenon in Muskoka's capital, "houses of ill-repute seemed to flourish."

From the early 1870s through the 1880s, bordellos, often operating as boarding houses and inns, required steady attention from the Bracebridge law enforcers. Two such establishments were closed down in March 1880 when the women who acted as the "proprietors" of each were convicted by Magistrate James Boyer of keeping houses of prostitution. As Orillia's *Packet* reported on March 31 that year, these women were given heavy fines, but also made to know that the fines would not be enforced if they left Bracebridge within three days. That was James Boyer's preferred way of addressing the problem: in effect, moving it to some other municipality.

Not only Orillia's newspapers, but also businessmen from that town thirty-five miles to the south, took attentive interest in the red lights of Bracebridge. Orillia's Sam Smith, for instance, operated a prospering Bracebridge house with four female hostesses during the winter of 1885. "The business became so popular," reports Cotton, that Bracebridge police "could no longer ignore it." Constables Ouderkirk and Binyan organized a team of special constables for a raid on Smith's premises.

News of the episode not only titillated readers of Orillia's ever gossipy *Packet,* but also those of Barrie's high-minded *Northern Advance*, both of which reported on March 5 that year how Sam Smith had been arrested outside the house, another man chased without capture because he knew a road down a hill better than the pursuing constables, and how charges and convictions quickly followed. Smith, as owner of the establishment, was fined seventy dollars and told to get out of town. Four females were given thirty-six hours to do likewise.

Bracebridge police could not rest for long, however. Two months later, constables Howard, Ouderkirk, and Johnson raided another house, arresting two inmates and "a regular customer" by the name of Jack Beaudry.

Nudity of a more public variety occurred down at the river, where swimming was popular, especially among those too poor to afford bathing costumes. No one much cared about this perfect human encounter with nature, other than some older church-goers and their smooth-faced ministers, who mistook the muddy banks of the Muskoka River for a slippery slope to degenerate living. In time council came to put that point of view into Bracebridge Bylaw Number 128, dealing with morals. It stipulated that bathers in the river could no longer be naked.

Despite this quest for moral uplift, it took time for this bylaw on bathing attire to take hold within Bracebridge town limits. In 1911 during the intense heat of summer, after police chief McConnell received several complaints that boys swimming in the river had neglected to clothe themselves sufficiently, if at all, he loudly announced through the newspapers that he was "going to lay charges." McConnell was popular with the boys of the town, who gave him his nickname of "Pink" after the famous Pinkerton detectives, their short and cryptic name facilitating urgent warnings of "Here comes Pink!" Probably all the advance warning McConnell circulated helped ensure that no charges were ever laid, allowing some great swims to occur in Bracebridge that year.

A mixture of fear and pride accompanied these men who, usually with little or no training for the job, donned uniforms and enforced the law across Canada's uneven frontier terrain. With "peace and order" two cornerstones of the country's constitution, it fell to local law enforcers to make this conceptual attribute a reality where it counted: on the streets of the country's towns, especially after nightfall. The local justice of the peace enabled prompt, close-at-hand resolution of conflicts, while the constable was equally a stabilizing influence in an instable society. That influence derived its power from being able to bring lawbreakers to face a range of punishments.

Chapter Five

THE PUNISHMENTS: COMMON GAOL, FINES, AND SOCIAL IGNOMINY

A wide variety of outcomes were possible in Magistrate's Court.

Occasionally, charges were dismissed. This happened when there was a lack of sufficient evidence to convict the madam running a Bracebridge brothel, or when a township council prosecuted a hapless farmer for unlicensed selling of his vegetables by boat to summer cottagers at their docks and breaching an anti-hawking bylaw council had only enacted a few days earlier. Sometimes an untrained police constable or overly zealous prosecutor brought cases before James Boyer that seemed to be in the nuisance category. Some cases were excessively trivial. As a justice of the peace, he needed to be discerning and compassionate in dismissing them.

But most often the charges stuck. Typically, a guilty party was ordered to pay a fine. Some had to post a bond or surety. On rare occasions, even though the accused was found guilty, the punishment was suspended. When the case demanded it, the nearby Bracebridge lock-up was a major part of the magistrate's arsenal of punishments. A number of those convicted served time in jail as an immediate sentence, or as a result of being unable to pay their fine.

The days when a thief or arsonist could be sentenced to suffer social humiliation, and perhaps physical injury, in public stocks, were gone. With his head, hands, and feet protruding through imprisoning boards, locals could formerly insult and harass the exposed convict at will. In this way the culprit's punishment was made palpable by citizens of the community ventilating their rage and mockery — a midpoint in the transition from mob rule to the rule of law. Even though stocks were never in use on the Bracebridge commons, there were a number of other ways private citizens still performed an activist role in the justice system, for instance arraigning individuals they caught breaking a law and collecting half the fine as a reward. Nor was use of public shaming as punishment entirely foreign to Bracebridge Magistrate's Court in the 1890s; convicted prostitutes were ordered to either serve time with hard labour or get out of town.

In relative terms, some of the 1890s jail sentences that Bracebridge justices of the peace imposed seem as draconian by today's standards as public execution was for murder: weeks in the lock-up for seemingly minor transgressions.

Those at the lower edge of Muskoka society often paid their fines not with money but with their time, because in sentencing, jail time was always a backup, the stipulated default punishment for those unable to pay cash. For a number of the poor, going behind bars was the only option.

Some stiff sentences seem outrageously unfair: weeks or months in detention for simple vagrancy. But could these sentences have been charitable acts? As the days shortened and temperatures fell, Bracebridge constables found derelict men and brought them to the justice of the peace. James Boyer, hearing evidence that their crime was having no visible means of support nor any place to go, ordered them to a period of incarceration long enough to carry them through the harshest of the winter months in sheltered and dry quarters with adequate food.

In the 1890s common vagrancy was an offence under Canada's Criminal Code, partly to protect communities, partly to protect vagrants.

No welfare programs existed to support the indigent. This expedient of putting homeless, unemployed poor people in the local lock-up improvised a primitive charity. Local police and magistrates preferred that those with no means of support not freeze or starve to death during winter in the streets or abandoned sheds of their community. In Bracebridge, in such cases, the jail door was seldom locked on these inmates.

If time in jail was possibly a blessing for the homeless man sentenced to food and shelter for the winter, it was definitely a setback for the prostitute removed from society and unable to earn her money. The same punishment did not fit everyone equally.

Across Canada jails were as different as the places in which they stood. Some were adequate but others not, most showing in common simply that those who built them wanted to create rudimentary facilities for the least amount of money. With limited funds for schools and none for a hospital, Bracebridge council's impulse to frugality blended with a common belief that criminals needed nothing more than the bare minimum. Jail was a place where they were placed to be kept away from society, on a par with the bleak asylums with barred windows and locked doors where "crazy people" were incarcerated.

The first Bracebridge jail was built of logs. It sat in the centre of the settlement, at the corner of Dominion and Ontario streets. Like most early structures in the community, the jail featured natural elements, from its sturdy log walls right down to its bare dirt floor. No sooner had the facility been built, in anticipation of crime to come, than a collection was taken up to pay bail for its first occupant. Enthusiastic locals chipped in a total of twenty-five dollars. This relatively large amount was then held in trust for the benefit of the lock-up's first customer. It was a whimsical Bracebridge concept for celebrating the jail's inauguration with its prisoner's immediate release, an inventive equivalent to an official opening ceremony for the new facility.

This log jail still exists today. It is not a heritage attraction for a town dependent on tourism, as one might expect, but a storage building at a private home along Santa's Village Road on the west side of town. Its ancient log walls are now covered with board-and-batten. Geraniums in planters decorate its exterior to complete the disguise.

The first Bracebridge jail, shown as it exists today — its log walls covered with siding, decorated with flowers, serving as a storage shed.

The structure was hauled to this location more than a century ago from its original site, to make way for a large, wooden, provincial government office building. That, in turn, gave way in 1900 to Muskoka's red-brick district courthouse on the same location.

As life in town became testier and occupants in the jail more frequent, feeding the inmates became an item of business. Robert White, who operated a grocery store and bakery in a block of brick buildings at the corner of Manitoba and Mary streets where St. Thomas's Anglican Church stands today, bid on and won the contract to be "keeper of the gaol," which primarily meant providing prisoners their food.

White sometimes sent his young employee, Gerard Simmons, with these meals. On one occasion Simmons took the tray of food to two inmates, finding the door locked and the windows secure but the prisoners gone. "Just as he was turning away to take the food back," recounted local historian and magistrate Redmond Thomas of this episode, "he heard loud yells of 'Wait! Wait!' and saw two men run from the British Lion Hotel which was just across the street."

The day before, this same pair, workers building the railroad through town, had received their pay "and in the evening had invested freely in alcoholic beverages and become so riotously drunk that they had been run in." The next morning in the jail they "had an awful thirst and still some cash left. Right across the street they could see an oasis, the barroom of the British Lion Hotel," explained Thomas. "The more they gazed at the British Lion, the thirstier they got." Their inspection revealed the prison door was strong, and the windows securely barred. "But the floor! Ah, the floor! It was only earth! If a little chipmunk can dig a hole in the earth surely two husky men could dig one, too. They burrowed out of the jail and adjourned to the British Lion to slake their thirst."

Yet, as Thomas also noted, "hard-working construction men need food too. Why buy a meal at a hotel when the public purse furnishes one for free at the jail? Why, indeed!" So, as the escapees monitored the time they should remain at large, sipping their drinks while watching through the barroom window to make sure they did not miss a free meal, they spotted young Simmons arrive, "gulped down the last of their drinks and hied themselves back to the jail for victuals!"

The inadequacy of this simple jail was on a par with other facilities forming part of the Bracebridge institutions for the administration of justice, matching for example the equally rudimentary nature of the inaugural courtroom established in Bracebridge in 1877.

Yet, the growing town was all for progress, especially when a senior level of government could pay for new facilities. Bracebridge not only needed a local lock-up, as any town might, but in addition required, as capital town of the District of Muskoka, a district jail. Because that was a responsibility of the provincial government, as part of its constitutional jurisdiction over administration of justice, the Ontario government of Premier John Sandfield Macdonald came under increasing pressure from Muskoka councils and Muskoka's representative in the legislature, J.C. Miller, to act. In 1879 a new building housing five cells was built under a contract let by the Ontario Department of Public Works by low bidder Neil Livingstone of Gravenhurst.

This new structure was made of brick, the construction material of choice in Bracebridge after the Gibbs & Griffin brickworks had begun manufacturing locally in 1871. Solid brick walls would not only be more resistant to fire, but harder for escapees to work through than the earlier log walls and dirt floor. Erected on property reserved for the provincial government near the Land Registry Office on Dominion Street, this new lock-up inaugurated a district jail serving all Muskoka.

As part of Muskoka's emerging facilities for the administration of justice, the jail was an improvement for incarceration of prisoners, but the district was still minimally served. A decade later, in November 1888, a grand jury in Bracebridge inspected the place and the jury's foreman, Thomas Myers, reported to Sheriff James Whitney Bettes how "they found the gaol scrupulously clean and well aired" but recommended "a larger building, more sanitary appliances, and a safer enclosure for the yard to prevent the escape of prisoners when out for exercise." The jurors were also concerned that the district had no provision "for insane persons awaiting the pleasure of the lieutenant governor for their removal to an institution." In short, mentally ill persons were being kept in the jail alongside other prisoners.

James Boyer was acutely aware of the problems with the Bracebridge jail, both as magistrate and town clerk, and in 1889 helped persuade council to take the recommendations of the grand jury to heart. Council voted to send Mayor Armstrong and Councillor Hunt to Toronto as a two-man deputation authorized to discuss with Ontario's premier the need to build a new jail for Muskoka District, the existing building "being altogether too small, insecure, and unsanitary."

Still, another decade later, this situation had changed little. Despite recommended improvements, no further public money had been directed to these facilities. The authorities clearly knew how inadequate the district jail was, as is shown by their action in 1898 at the conclusion of the sensational murder trial of William Hammond from Gravenhurst when the prisoner was removed to Barrie for incarceration because it had a stronger jail. Hammond was securely held there, until brought back to Bracebridge for execution.

Harshness handling outsiders and misfits was an outcome of the era's view of human character, but it was also a measure of the society's lack of institutions and absence of procedures to cope with broken people. A bleak episode occurred during the winter of 1904, revealing a continuation of the same institutional conditions and outlooks as when the 1890s cases in this book arose. In February that year, John Eastall, an elderly man, had been sent from Huntsville to the jail in Bracebridge because he had no place to go and no one to care for him. Shortly thereafter he died. The old man, an early and respected pioneer in north Muskoka's Sinclair Township, had been admitted

The log-cabin jail was replaced by a brick jail, which in turn was supplanted by this 1904 stone jail, which stood behind Bracebridge Town Hall, a half-block from the new District Court House. Six decades later it was torn down to put up a parking lot.

to hospital in Huntsville when his neighbours found him with hands and feet frozen. At the hospital, he was found to be mentally unstable and could not be kept there. Without facilities to keep him, lamented the Huntsville *Forester,* the old man "was placed in the hands of police, carried off to Bracebridge jail, suffered premature death within its dingy walls and buried, we suppose, with all the honours which belong to an old, friendless vagrant."

The Huntsville newspaper focused its dismay on Bracebridge and its jail facilities, not its own hometown hospital and medical staff who had washed their hands of responsibility for the local man with a convenient diagnosis of mental instability and sent him away to another municipality and its rudimentary facilities. Still, even given that fact, it was true that the jail in which John Eastall died did not meet expectations. Bracebridge, after all, was not just a neighbouring municipality; it was the capital town of Muskoka, and, as such, had, or might be expected to have, public facilities commensurate with its role.

Whether in Huntsville, Bracebridge, or elsewhere across Muskoka District, the absence of adequate facilities made a mockery of the rule of law, and rendered hollow even the minimal sense of compassion in that day. Muskoka historian Susan Pryke relates how cases like John Eastall's "haunted" Huntsville's police chief, William Selkirk, causing him to recommend in March 1906 that town council petition the legislature to build a house of refuge. Muskoka's member of the legislature, A.A. Mahaffy, became champion of the cause, calling a meeting of reeves, mayors, and other interested parties in Bracebridge to discuss establishing a home for the aged and infirm in the district.

"It was not as easy as Mahaffy hoped," Pryke concluded. Even by 1921 nothing had changed. That year, at the inaugural banquet of the Muskoka Municipal Association, Mahaffy again urged Muskoka's elected representatives to secure a house of refuge. But no home for the aged would be built in Muskoka for almost a half-century more, when one of Mahaffy's successors as MPP for Muskoka, Robert J. Boyer, a grandson of James Boyer, spearheaded the creation of The Pines Home for the Aged in the early 1960s, facing defiant opposition from two township councils. Muskoka was last of all Ontario's counties and districts to have such a facility. For a very long time, tough love and self-reliance endured as Muskoka's way, the remorseless culture of people who had themselves struggled in harsh settings to make their own way.

Spending money on convicts and "lunatics" was seen as unnecessary, and referring to people who might occupy such facilities in derogatory terms seemed to make it easier to discount the need. Even after Muskoka's imposing new district courthouse opened for business on Bracebridge's prestigious Dominion Street in 1900, improvement of jail facilities still languished on the public agenda. Instead, the government simply leased the conveniently close stone-walled basement of the Muskoka Herald Building on Dominion Street from the newspaper's proprietor, Edgar Bastedo, for use as a lock-up. The building, though constructed only for a newspaper and printing operation, was at least considered more secure than the earlier jail. Yet repeated damage to the newspaper's premises by prisoners trying to break out, as earlier noted, led Bastedo to end the arrangement. Helping the community in its time of need had been instinctive for public-minded Bastedo, but his building was suffering physical damage and the reputation of the premises as a place co-occupied by feisty criminals was not helping Herald business.

This turn of events propelled Bracebridge council to get a better local lock-up. It secured a patch of land for sixty dollars from S.H. Armstrong at the rear of the town hall, where in 1904 local contractor John Baker constructed a more secure facility. It was massively built, with thick walls of stone, a sturdy door with heavy hinges and a strong lock, three cells inside, plus a stove, toilet, and small washbasin. Its few small windows, on the south side, were closely barred.

The town's constables used these cells to detain individuals charged with an offence until they could appear before the magistrate the next morning, to house prisoners convicted and sentenced to serve jail time, and to shelter vagrants and sometimes others who were mentally ill. Beside the structure stood a stable for the town's team of horses, which stood until 1934 when trucks replaced horses and the building was demolished. In 1967 the stone jail itself was purchased by Bracebridge lawyer H.E.S. "Bert" Sugg and razed to make way for a parking lot behind his law office. Asphalt then covered over both the space where prisoners had once paced out their days and the hollyhocks beyond their windows that had grown tall and bloomed in summer.

Whatever causes people to employ euphemistic phrases for reality, it was certainly at play in Bracebridge to describe the various lock-ups over the years. At first, to some the local jail was "the Bastille," a humorous pretense that the town's lock-up was on a par with the infamous stone prison in Paris. In the long era of Queen Victoria's reign, another name for the place housing criminals, charged and convicted and sentenced to be confined in the name of the Crown, was "Her Majesty's Cottage." After the queen's death, and with construction in 1904 of a new jail from local-cut stone, the popular name became, more simply, the "Stone Cottage." Once Duncan McDonald was appointed in 1909 as warden of the district jail in Bracebridge, that centre for incarceration would become known by yet another euphemism, "Dunc's Castle." Adding humour or using euphemisms may have assisted to diminish reality in the minds of some.

Prisoners in Bracebridge were not always behind bars. Sometimes they were outside working, sometimes they simply escaped, and occasionally they were brought out for execution.

The new district jail was to the north of the courthouse, built at the corner of Dominion and Ontario streets in 1900. Behind the courthouse the land sloped away and a vegetable garden was created to help supply food for prisoners. Prisoners themselves tended the garden. They did more, too, recalled Magistrate Redmond Thomas, as part of their sentence of hard labour, "mowing the lawn and shovelling the snow and doing all the janitor work."

The record of Bracebridge jails serving their intended purpose of retaining prisoners in confinement was not outstanding. One of the reasons for this poor record was the inventive determination of the prisoners, of course, but one also has to wonder about the implicit complicity of Bracebridgites themselves. The villagers had created a fund to pay the bail of the first prisoner, the authorities had dragged their feet in upgrading facilities, and if a prisoner escaped, the townsfolk would not have to pay for his food. It can be safely said that secure incarceration was never a big deal locally.

In addition to the notorious escapes of shantymen sprung by their logger buddies and railway labourers slipping out of jail for a drink at a hotel bar across the street and then returning to their cell at meal time, a long succession of impatient prisoners attempted to escape, many succeeding. In 1889, as noted, Bracebridge council sent a deputation to Premier Mowat asking for increased jail and court accommodation for Muskoka, a need officially crystallized as "urgent necessity" when on March 11 that year district jailer Robinson found one of his prisoners had escaped during the night.

Short of building stronger retaining facilities, one local expedient for curtailing a successful getaway was issuing prisoners with a highly visible combination of pants and jackets that were part bright yellow and part black. Even this measure was foiled, however: a couple of artful Bracebridge prisoners, who had been whitewashing the high prison yard fence, cleverly painted their telltale trousers white, making a getaway over the fence in mid-summer and walking out of town masquerading as tourists.

After the First World War, when Redmond Thomas was articling as a law clerk at the Bracebridge courthouse, he and Crown Attorney Johnson returned to the office to complete some work. They had made very little noise on their arrival that night, because it was raining and they wore rubbers. The two were working silently in adjoining offices, neither of them talking or moving around. Right below them was the so-called "dungeon," a row of extra-strong cells serving as an annex to the district jail, whose windows faced eastward across the garden, an ideal escape route. Suddenly, clanking noises came from the dungeon. Johnson came softly through the connecting door, and in a low tone said to Thomas, "Go quietly and tell Dunc."

Leaving the courthouse through it north-side door, the law student crossed the lawn and informed Warden Duncan McDonald, whose residence was attached to the front of the district jail, that a breakout appeared to be in progress. The warden got his revolver and the two went to the dungeon, entering, McDonald first, through a door in the back wall of the courthouse. The only inmates were two prisoners who had been caught in Muskoka after escaping from Kingston Penitentiary. Having decided to bust out of the Bracebridge institution next, they had smashed the iron cots in their cells and were using pieces of them to force the cell doors. The arrival of the no-nonsense warden and his six-shooter ended the shenanigans. The prisoners stayed in their cells. Redmond Thomas went back to his "prosaic work."

In 1937 two prisoners succeeded in breaking out of the district jail in Bracebridge by springing a bar on an upper window and fleeing over the wall. One was found in Parkhill, the other recaptured in Stratford. That same year, a breakout from the dungeon in the basement of the courthouse — by the similar means of wrenching the bars off a window — resulted in Warden Cornie Reynolds, the night watchman, Dave Matheson, and Night Constable Cudmore chasing the escaped convict.

In 1941 Bracebridge youths Clarence Boyes and Alvin Hives got into the local sport of pursuing escapees. That November the two won certificates from "Red" Foster's Young Canada Club for spotting and reporting to police the location of an escaped prisoner from the Bracebridge jail.

The yard of this jail, enclosed by a high board fence that stretched along Chancery Lane and ran behind the residence of the district jailer and the jail itself, was the site of execution for two convicted murderers: Will Hammond, in 1898, for the poisoning death of his wife; and George Cyr, in 1922, for the double murder of farmers Lena Solave and her husband, Andrew, in the course of attempting a robbery. On February 15, 1946, the grim Bracebridge District Gaol, its yard containing the lime-filled coffin of George Cyr, who was buried there in an unmarked location, was closed. The official reason was that the brick, iron, and concrete structure had supposedly become a fire hazard. The jail at Parry Sound would henceforth be used for Muskoka prisoners, which helped to significantly reduce the embarrassing statistics on the number of breakouts in Bracebridge.

Many in jail were people who had appeared in James Boyer's court and been sentenced to pay a fine, but could not. Fines ranged from one dollar to fifty dollars, but were mostly in the four-dollar to seven-dollar bracket. For those with little means of support, often part of the problem that contributed to them being before the magistrate in the first place, paying a fine was often the true punishment. Whenever James levied a fine, he also indicated how many days or weeks would need to be served in equivalency. Sometimes, being forced to forfeit scarce money simply led the convicted person to opt instead to serve the time. In other cases, the sheer inability of those convicted to pay even the relatively small amounts levied resulted in them automatically going into the lock-up. Wage rates fell below the level many workers found necessary just to purchase their basic needs, quite apart from what many squandered on drink as they temporarily escaped their plight.

The financial penalty Boyer imposed in some cases seems surprisingly disproportionate to the value of the item stolen or the seriousness of the crime committed, something perhaps explained by the different values, both social and economic, of that era compared to our own.

Evaluating the impact of a twenty-dollar fine in the 1890s can, to some extent, be done by comparing it with prices charged in Bracebridge stores at that time. In 1891 ladies felt-and-beaver hats could be found selling for 25 cents and up. A barrel of flour went for $4.25. Hood's "Sarsaparilla" could be obtained "100 doses, one dollar." The Great South American Nervine Tonic (for all nervous disorders, as well as serving as a stomach and liver cure) could be had for $1.00 for a large sixteen-ounce bottle, "every bottle warranted." Fifty-two issues of the *Muskoka Herald* came for a subscription price of $1.00. Mr. Perry, general railway and steamship ticket agent at Bracebridge, was selling passage from New York to Glasgow at prices starting from $35.00, which was the same price as a trip from Bracebridge to Calgary and back by train. In the farm equipment department, mowers and rakes in 1893 ranged from $40.00 to $58.00. Thos. Magee & Co. Carriage Shop in 1897 sold one-horse long sleighs with box and seat for $20.00, while cutters ran $30.00 to $50.00. Rolls of wallpaper could be had from 5 cents to 12 cents and up, per roll. Lafayette cigars cost 5 cents, Royal Turkish cigars, 15 cents. A Winchester rifle could be purchased from G.R. Simmons's store in 1897 for $13.50 with round barrel or $14.50 in the octagonal barrel model. J.W. Ney & Co., "Muskoka's Great Departmental Store," advertised the following in March 1897: ladies winter vests, 25 cents; men's German-mink caps, $1.50; five cans of good corn, 25 cents; twenty-five pounds of dried apples, $1.00; four pounds of good black tea or mixed tea, $1.00; thirty-two pounds of sugar, $1.00; men's all-wool, heavy étoffe pants, $1.25. In such a marketplace, a $20.00 fine precluded a lot of buying.

There are two aspects of fines found in the Ontario's justice system in the 1890s that many today would find surprising. One feature of the system of fines was that private prosecutors — the self-selecting citizen-constable making a "citizen's arrest" — stood to gain a portion of the fine levied against the culprit he'd brought to justice, in keeping with the custom of paying moieties. Another remarkable aspect of the system was that Ontario's many non-stipendiary magistrates got their fees out of the fines collected in their courts.

That was their only source of income from the job, their financial reward for the work, time, and effort spent. This practice helped keep down the public's cost in the administration of justice, allowing the municipal and provincial governments to give themselves a free ride by not paying justices of the peace other than the "stipendiary magistrates" receiving remuneration or a stipend from the provincial government. Of course, today such a practice would be considered an intrinsic conflict of interest: the more fines a JP levied, and the higher he set them, the more fees he could earn.

Although the cases found in this book were tried when the Victorian Age was at its height and pressures of its well-defined public morality had a massive impact on private conduct, not everybody honoured the code. The degree to which those having to appear as an accused or defendant in court felt humiliated depended on their sensibilities and social standing, the reach of religion in their lives, and their personal character. It was also, of course, a function of what one was charged with.

Erstwhile worshippers in Bracebridge's many churches sought to adhere to the norms promulgated by the local clergy. The wealthier citizens could indulge in social hypocrisy, while the poor were free to live a rawer life, but for all of them the size of the Muskoka stage on which one's ignominy played out was a factor. Bracebridge was still small enough that people pretty well knew everyone else, so a person's reputation became well-handled public property, something that was far less of a restraint in larger centres such as Toronto.

Such "small town justice" permitted a blending of humiliation and psychology with James Boyer's harsh sentences of high fines and long jail terms for convicted prostitutes: these penalties, he informed them, would be suspended if they got out of town within three days and never came back. Again, because no reasons were ever given by JPs for their decisions, we can only surmise what he may have been thinking. As a churchman, James knew that community morals frowned on "fallen women," whether they trolled through the streets of town or waited for customers in "houses of ill-repute." He also knew, as clerk of a spending-conscious municipality, that forcing prostitutes to leave town would save the cost of keeping them fed and supervised in jail. Finally, he also would have understood that a cumulative impact of enough stiff sentences against prostitutes could earn for Bracebridge the reputation among those plying the sex trade as a place to avoid.

Another facet of public morality was that some citizens did not fear the consequences for their soul of doing a nefarious deed; rather, they feared the consequences of getting caught. This, too, was influenced in part by one's social standing or public position, which could act as a check on wrongdoing if a person feared damage to their reputation if hauled into police court. Such restraint was summed up in the urgent caution: "Don't do it or the police might catch you!" However, someone else could actually rise in his own eyes and in his buddies' esteem by the very same process. In 1883 the rowdy toughs from Muskoka's lumber camps, led by eighteen-year-old Joseph Rule of Peterborough, acted brazenly in town and defiantly in court. When Rule boldly threatened Magistrate Boyer and everyone else if he was not immediately freed, the wild man probably rose in his own self-esteem as somebody not to be meddled with, but he likely also gained admiration from his fellow rioters arrested at the same time. No doubt, while subsequently serving time, Rule's attitude also generated respect from his fellow prisoners as well.

Displays ranging from haughty defiance to personal shame in Bracebridge Magistrate's Court underscore why humiliation, though often an important component of punishment, had unpredictable value in maintaining either the social order or the rule of law.

Public shaming as a form of punishment spelled ruin for the distinguished "doctor" from Scotland, who, until his trial, was prominently ensconced in a Bracebridge hotel, advertising his cures in the local newspapers, and visiting his "patients" in their homes around town. His confidence game depended on people believing his qualifications and trusting his remedies. Faced with charges that he was a quack, even before Magistrate Boyer found him guilty and levied a fine of twenty-five dollars plus costs, "Dr." Malcolm McLeod could be shamed right out of the doctoring business and shortly thereafter, right out of town, too.

The enterprising businessman from Orillia convicted for operating a brothel in Bracebridge possibly felt stung when Magistrate Boyer's order that he "stay out of town" was prominently published in the Orillia and Bracebridge newspapers, although he probably slyly welcomed the publicity gained among the sort who were his prospective sex-trade workers and customers. One man's social ignominy may be another man's calling card.

The power of shame as a force in restraining people from acting badly is, however, difficult to measure. A building contractor sued by a bricklayer in Bracebridge Magistrate's Court for unpaid wages may have feared getting a reputation that would make it hard for him to hire other workers in the future. Or, he may have welcomed the court appearance as a means to bolster his renown for hardness, and thereby keep wild and wily workers in line. The contractor's attitude about appearing before the justice of the peace and what that might do to, or for, his reputation could also depend on whether the economy was in a boom or bust cycle, with workers scarce or plentiful. It could even be that he had no money to pay because he was going broke and would soon be a bankrupt failure, in which case an even larger social ignominy was looming for him than being called for not paying a working man his due.

That example of the unpaid bricklayer, typical of numerous unpaid wage claims in 1890s Bracebridge, underscores that many variables, including each individual's character, can influence how personal honour and public humiliation meld in a given case. Punishment may produce shame in one person and pride in another.

In the complex steps danced between an accused person and those operating the justice system, the impact of a psychological gambit may be trivial or significant. Yet, it had a real role.

One of the masters of human psychology in this era was the renowned Toronto police magistrate George T. Denison, who not only set an illustrious example for James Boyer, but for all magistrates across Ontario and beyond. Colonel Denison tried more indictable offences over his forty-year career than any judge or magistrate in Canada or Britain. He was widely renowned for his savvy and his entertaining courtroom manner. Reports of his decisions spread swiftly through the legal community's grapevine, and were featured in Toronto's daily newspapers, which were also read in Bracebridge. To those involved in the administration of justice in Muskoka, Denison was legendary and much discussed. A commonplace saying among them was that in Denison's court there was little law but a lot of justice.

Recollections of a Police Magistrate, published in 1920, is his rich compendium of cases, methods, and philosophies. A sampler case among the many hundreds, helping show how Denison's reputation was earned, involved a horse trader, an important occupation in an era when horsepower was at its height and the buying and selling of horses a common practice.

A man not knowing much about horses had bought a steed from a trader who said the horse was sound and a good worker. Then the purchaser found the horse to be neither. The victim got the trader charged with defrauding him, by making false pretences, out of the price of the horse: one hundred dollars.

"The facts came out before me," recalled Denison, "and evidence of veterinary surgeons would prove that the horse was worthless. I would then ask the trader, 'What have you to say?'

"He would then reply, 'The horse is alright.'

"I would say, 'Are you sure of that?'

"'Yes.'

"'Are you sure?'

"'Yes.'

"'Then there is no difficulty. You take your horse back, and give the complainant the $100.'

"The man would object. I would remand the case for a few days and say, 'If you don't do that, then I will know that you intended to cheat him from the beginning, and I will know what to do.' This scheme generally put things right and no one was wronged."

Denison's logic illustrated the refinement of sentencing possible from a shrewd man wise to human ways.

How a magistrate might use psychology was also on display in late 1800s Bracebridge when Magistrate William Spencer, as noted by Redmond Thomas, had to sort out a charge of forgery. The "very serious crime of forgery was always punished by a term (minimum two years) in the Kingston Penitentiary or even more severely by a slightly shorter term in the very much tougher old Central Prison."

A colourful local character, "whom everyone considered pretty wacky," had wandered into the Northern Crown Bank and possessed himself of a couple of blank cheques, which he filled in with the sum of two dollars, himself as payee, and the "signature" of a wealthy man. When the cheques bounced, the people who cashed them complained to Police Chief William McConnell.

On the official record of the case, Magistrate Spencer noted one day's imprisonment, "a mere bookkeeping entry as no such sentence is ever served," wrote Thomas, "but the sentence he announced was 100 year's imprisonment, to be suspended as long as the defendant refrained from writing any more cheques. The wacky character gave no further trouble; he did not want to spend a century in Kingston Penitentiary."

Magistrate George Denison's fabulous Toronto police court was not only a model for James Boyer and William Spencer doing similar work in Bracebridge. It also yielded lessons about attitudes of people charged with violating the law and their expectations about the process of trial and punishment. Col. Denison often found himself on the butt end of haughty distain from society's wealthy and well-placed citizens when they found themselves charged with minor infractions of laws they did not believe should apply to them. Such a reaction by privileged people indicates how embarrassment at being caught can be transformed into aggressive criticism, especially if they consider themselves superior beings. Their talk about the importance of "the rule of law" over polished dinner tables was, in their mind, always meant to apply to the rabble, not them.

For his part, George Denison, an old military veteran, preferred dealing with seasoned criminals who, as he put it, only wanted "a fair trial the way the game should be played."

Chapter Six

THE SCRIPT: MAGISTRATE BOYER'S BENCH BOOK

Judges or magistrates keep hand-written notes of evidence heard, impressions made, and relevant points of law while ensconced "on the bench," the most elevated place in the chamber over which they preside. Not surprisingly, these notebooks of personal records have been dubbed "bench books."

These scribbled notes have no official status as court records. Bench books are often destroyed when a judge retires, sometimes even immediately after the trial to which they relate has been concluded, because the judge's publicly released "reasons for judgment" — not the work-in-progress jottings — constitute the official outcome of that case. Some entries in his or her bench book, for instance a personal aside or a sequence of notes revealing how a judge's thinking shifts over the course of a trial, may undermine or even be at odds with the final verdict. If they are not dispatched at the end of a trial, then they often are at the end of a career: "I ordered all my bench books burned," confided Honourable R. Roy McMurtry after he retired as Ontario's chief justice in 2007.

In 1871 James Boyer became editor of the Northern Advocate, *in 1873 municipal clerk, and in 1878 magistrate of Muskoka District, a position he held until 1900. He also served in senior positions in the Agricultural Society, the Methodist church, fraternal organizations, and loyalist associations. This photo was used in an 1886 photo-montage of Muskoka Agricultural Society officers, and for his 1891 biography in* Men of Canada. *(Photo: Ellison & Company, Bracebridge)*

While such prudence causes many of these records to be intentionally destroyed by their creators, other bench books, though never willingly consigned to oblivion, are lost over time due to poor storage. Archival records in the dank cellars of the Owen Sound town hall, it was reported, were so damp and decayed they sprouted a crop of mushrooms. Some equally dismal fate likely befell James Boyer's bench books covering his cases between 1878 and 1890. Only his volume for the final decade of the century survives.

The five hundred numbered and fine-lined glossy pages of his leather-bound volume, purchased for $1.25 from Eaton's Department Store, preserve to this day his copperplate handwriting. The spine and corners of the 8½ by 13 inch book are covered in tawny suede. Durable black faux-leather over most of the front and back covers has served its protective role well through time. A crimson leather patch near the top of the spine is imprinted with the gold-lettered words, "Minute Book," and is adorned with solid bars and flourishes above and below.

James Boyer was adept at getting down all important points, and recording a telling phrase, thanks to his years as a law clerk in England, note-taking lawyer interviewing clients in New York, municipal clerk keeping official minutes of hundreds of council meetings, and recording secretary for proceedings of Bracebridge societies and Muskoka associations. His acquired knack for summarizing events had been further honed writing up succinct accounts of lengthy community meetings for the *Northern Advocate*. For James, making a good record was an ingrained skill and a valued exercise in its own right.

James's sense of presentation extended beyond handwriting to layout and design, so his bench book entries were also artistic works of graphic composition. His natural eye for symmetry and balance, already well developed through crafting countless wills and affidavits, had become further refined at the *Advocate* print shop, where he had a hand in the design of display ads, printed handbills, and posters for public events. As for his record of these court cases, he wrote them up as they were unfolding, swiftly yet with attention to form of presentation. The typeset cases in Part II replace his handwriting, but overleaf is a specimen of the original. Beyond visual clarity and charm of form was the all-important content captured in the bench book: the record of charges laid, testimony heard, and verdict reached.

Some charges characteristically used that awkward grammar of court proceedings when a prosecuting constable looks up an offence in the Criminal Code or a provincial statute or town bylaw, then folds its stilted terminology around an alleged wrongdoing. For instance, when Alexander Bolton was found in mid-November 1894 by Constable Robert E. Armstrong to be a vagrant in town, wording from the Code that made vagrancy a crime was matched to the facts as follows: "For that defendant on the 15th of November was at Bracebridge not having any visible means

Magistrates Court — May 6th 1896.

Before James Boyer JP.

Thomas Dodd ⎫ For having on the 2nd day of May inst
   v Thrift ⎪ at the Town of Bracebridge in said
Thomas Thrift & ⎬ District did unlawfully throw stumps
Edmund Arbie ⎭ roots and other waste wood in the
              waters of the Muskoka River.

  The charge having been read to Defendants they severally pleaded not guilty.

Thomas Dodd sworn

         I am Constable of the Town of Bracebridge. On the 2nd May inst. I was standing near the British Lion I heard something plunge in the River. I went down and stood on the end of the Iron Bridge. I saw Thrift dump a barrow load of roots stumps and brush in the river. Arbie was digging up the roots near by. I asked if they knew they were breaking the law. They said they didnt. The river abounds with pickerel trout and other fish

XXd by Mr Bird

         I saw some of the roots sink as soon as they were put in, some of the stuff floated across the river towards the rack at the power house.

        Defendants convicted and fined $1 each and $2.10 each to be paid forthwith and in default to be levied by distress and in default to be imprisoned in the Common Gaol at Bracebridge for 30 days.

                      James Boyer JP.

Paid

Convns retd

of maintaining himself did live without employment." In Part II this cumbersome grammar in a constable's charge, when he sought to combine statutory wording with a miscreant's behaviour, has been tweaked just enough to ensure a reader at least understands what offence the accused was being tried for. By the same token, some uncommon abbreviations have been replaced by the full word for ease of comprehension.

After the charge had been read to an accused, James recorded the person's plea of "guilty" or "not guilty." If the trial was a civil action, the nature of the plaintiff's accusation against the defendant was established at the start and likewise inscribed in the bench book.

In criminal cases, if guilt was admitted, what followed directly was a sentence (usually a fine or time in the lock-up), with no evidence recorded or reasons given. If the plea was not guilty, however, evidence was taken, witnesses called, and clarification sought through cross-examination or questions from the bench. For most trials, James only recorded bare-bones information, which can be disappointing when trying to understand the larger context. When charges were contested, however, the results were usually more illuminating, because, to establish what happened, information was revealed and recorded about people's plights and community conditions.

Sometimes a case was simply dismissed, mostly for lack of good evidence. There were also cases brought before the justice of the peace that probably could have been dismissed for their triviality, instances that hardly required legal redress at all but rather wise understanding. The dilemma then facing the JP was to determine a way to dispose satisfactorily of the contentious struggle that brought the inflamed parties before him. One method James Boyer resorted to was to allow for the effluxion of time, a well-known contributor of "solutions." For instance, when two men appeared in his court because of a heated exchange of intemperate words at an election meeting, or when a boy was followed home by a dog whose owner then became upset because he thought the lad was luring the animal away, the JP faced a small Solomon-like moment. James's solution was

Bracebridge Constable Thomas Dodd, continuously on patrol for people throwing garbage into the streets, ravines, or the river, in the spring of 1896 brought charges before Magistrate James Boyer against two men who had flung stumps and other refuse into the water. This bench book entry is the record Boyer made of their trial as it progressed.

to convict the defendant, but then add: "and judgment suspended and defendant to be brought up for judgment when called upon." That was the last ever heard of the case. As weeks passed without the "guilty" party being called back for sentencing, tempers cooled and the trivial incident was overtaken by greater concerns in the lives of the aggrieved individuals.

The language in the bench book is also revealing of the times. In 1890s Muskoka, "arse" was apparently considered less risqué than "ass," for James Boyer's written record of one witness who told her neighbour to "kiss her ass" was later overwritten by him as "arse." Either way, the intended sentiment seemed to have been adequately enough conveyed between the two families living next to one another to have resulted in a good fight followed by a day of reckoning in court. James Boyer's own ambivalence, reflected in some entries written "b---h" and others as "bitch," and "G-d d----d" elsewhere written as "God-damned," is resolved by printing the words as spoken in testimony, not as occasionally sanitized in their transcription, thus more accurately recording the "raw life" that Magistrate's Court embraced.

If the magistrate-scribe himself altered words, should some of his other text also be edited for this book? Some older or different spellings conveying the character of the era have been retained, such as "gaol," pronounced jail but spelled that arcane way. Others, changed for clarity, include "shewed" to showed, "segar" to cigar, and "halloring" to hollering. A witness who "heard the dogs giving tongue" did not, however, have his poetic manner of speech truncated to "barking."

Muskoka from the outset was a colourful place and the names of some larger-than-life characters making their appearances on the magistrate's stage and in his bench book evoke those times: Napoleon Duval, Washington Bigelow, Gustavus A. Binyon, Osceola Gladiator, Murtaugh McCoubray, Montford Manaril, Burton B. Wendover, Asa Harps, Lorenzo McHenry, and William Eneas Toshack. Generations were present, as with "Patrick Carleton the Younger," and "William Hannon the Elder." Some were known to the court by their monikers: Joseph Fisher was mostly identified as "Fish"; the woman who was monarch of a Bracebridge bordello was universally called "Queenie" Dufresne; and prostitute Lucy Rickard traded around town as "Spot," and that is also how she was known to the law. Lillian Rowbottom, another prostitute, saw less need for a nickname since her real surname already seemed appropriate for a person in her profession.

As for the second oldest profession, Bracebridge had several lawyers in practice during these years, and occasionally parties appearing before Magistrate Boyer were represented by counsel, which is evident in the bench book. Mainly, however, those appearing in court represented themselves, money being one factor, feelings of intimidation another.

A few cases ended inconclusively, as far as entries in the bench book are concerned. Such mysteries are likely explained by the fact an indigent person may have been unable to meet his obligation to pay a fine, which normally meant serving time instead, or the possibility that the person in question had absconded from the jurisdiction. While most cases were neatly tied up, both as to outcome and the written record, the fact that a few were not is a reminder that even proceedings in a court of law may simply fizzle out, or that an overly busy magistrate, being human, may have intended to later return to finish off an entry but just never got it done.

Sometimes several weeks passed between cases. Other times a flurry of prosecutions erupted, usually when a particular town constable felt public pressure to crack down, a newly hired hygiene inspector was out to prove his mettle, or a hard-up individual learned he could earn some income through moieties and bestirred himself to lay private prosecutions for public offences against his friends and neighbours. If the prosecutor did not get a conviction, however, he paid the court costs. In a hunting case, James Boyer "paid informant half the fine, $20, less $6 costs for 2 cases dismissed."

Magistrate Boyer's rescued volume contains more information than one would typically find in a bench book today. Having no court clerk to record the proceedings, register the verdicts, or administer the fines, James did it all. Yet handling court administration was not a stretch for this man, who was a seasoned municipal clerk and the recording secretary of many community organizations.

For the Muskoka court over which he presided, his leather-bound book became the official, and only, record of what transpired. It therefore had to be complete. Including more than just the style of cause, names of the parties, and record of testimony, James used his bench book to keep track of most everything concerning his work as magistrate. Notations at the end of cases record the disposition of the matter (convicted, dismissed, decision appealed). If the guilty party was sentenced to serve time, that fact and confirmation of his committal to jail were recorded. Entries were also made when a convicted person, unable to pay his fine, was put in jail on default.

The bench book also became James's ledger for payment of fines and costs, noting the amount of fine levied and the payment received, any money paid to constables and witnesses, or allocated to court expenses, and the amount given as financial reward to a person laying the charge. Receipts are glued in. Where amounts were paid off in installments, a series of entries tracked the gradual reduction of a convicted person's debt.

Such financial and administrative entries were jotted directly in the bench book at the bottom of the case report in question, because there was no separate journal for recording the amounts and because 1890s efficiency dictated keeping things simple and together. To keep his records of decided cases complete, James would usually turn back several pages to the relevant case and add a notation, sometimes weeks or months later: for instance, when a garnishee had finally produced money for a fine; or when a convicted person who'd absconded had been tracked down and arrested by the sheriff. Yet he was a busy man and sometimes just made a cluster of entries for several different cases, all at one time and on a later page, when catching up on his work. Even then, the key information was all in the same volume.

Justices of the peace exercising summary conviction powers did not give reasons for judgment, so none appear in James Boyer's bench book. In the absence of reasons for judgment, it is hard to know what he or his fellow JPs really thought about these cases.

Even in cases when witnesses gave evidence and were cross-examined, the bench book offers, not a transcript, but only a synopsis of what was said. Yet even a verbatim record, were it available, could never disclose all that a judge sees and senses in a courtroom. Synoptic reports, like minutes of any meeting, are just one person's written account of a phenomenon. Ontario Chief Justice James McRuer "placed great weight on the decisions of a trial judge who was able to see the witnesses' body language, sense the character of the accused, appraise the honesty of the parties, and handle and inspect any physical evidence to evaluate its worth." McRuer contrasted that to an appeal court reviewing the case with nothing more than a written record to go by, something akin to us now being able only to read the printed page of these cases from Bracebridge in the 1890s rather than being there in person. We get the textual record, but not the smells and sounds, the squirming and sweating, the bravado or contrition.

Still, one can extrapolate.

A number of cases brought before Magistrate Boyer by unpaid labourers suggest his sympathies lay with the workingman, though he also lived in the community and knew the difference between a malingering worker and a struggling contractor trying to make ends meet while providing local employment.

Likewise, the plight of pitiable wretches brought into court by the town constable for being unemployed vagrants loitering about town with no visible means of support might indicate that, in the department of "hard love," Boyer was generous to a fault. Yet that interpretation might need to be considered in the context of the realities of his times. The 1890s had no programs of public support for indigent people, and Canada's small towns lacked institutions to house them in wintertime, so being ordered into jail was a crude form of social welfare for the homeless. A cold and hungry man got a place to stay that was safe, heated, dry, and clean, with a couple of meals a day in the bargain.

Overall, these cases offer more an uncompromising portrait of community life itself than they do the thinking of those who decided them.

Because James Boyer played many roles at the same time, they sometimes combined or overlapped to guide his decision-making. As clerk of the municipality, he was abreast of the council's agenda for getting a better jail, covering the costs of policing, and handling public complaints about derelicts around town and prostitutes in Bracebridge brothels. As both JP and clerk, his first-hand knowledge of the town's administrative and legal affairs helped the community find satisfactory balance, even in such small practical details as council contemplating issuing a revolver to the town's night constable but being concerned about the cost. Boyer, as clerk, pointed out that, as justice of the peace, he had recently confiscated a handgun that could either be sold to raise five or ten dollars for the court, or acquired with next to no payment by the municipality.

The increasing presence in Muskoka of cottagers and summer resorts meant supplying their needs in a convenient manner had become a new pillar of the local economy. In the 1890s James had to decide several cases arising from a municipality charging provisioners selling produce and other food items to summer cottagers from supply boats. Their boats, although licensed for navigation and passed for safety inspection, appeared to have run aground on the hidden shoals of a municipality's licensing requirement, thanks to a freshly enacted bylaw. Although the restrictive law against hawkers and peddlers was so new that the reeve had only signed it moments before court opened, the township council had already begun to enforce it against boat operators who had been in the summer supply business for some time.

With summer tourism a key part of Muskoka's economic lifeblood, Boyer appreciated that these enterprising farmers and supply-boat operators were doing their best to cater to visitors' needs by bringing fresh produce from their field directly to the docks of summer homes and tourist resorts around central Muskoka lakes. They brought in supplies of bananas and canned goods to supplement what they could grow locally, thus providing even greater benefit and more convenience to summer residents, at least one of whom, according to evidence in his bench book, was a judge. Where was justice to be balanced? James weighed the matter in light of his own experience as a municipal clerk of one of Muskoka's largest municipalities, his ongoing efforts through the Muskoka Agricultural Society to encourage local farming, and boyhood remembrance of Moreton-in-Marsh, where farmers brought their fresh produce to weekly market for the convenience and benefit of all. He then dismissed the cases and required the municipality to pay all costs.

Illegible handwriting in archival documents created before advent of the typewriter may never be properly deciphered, but this is not a problem with the bench book script. James had earned his livelihood since boyhood writing with painstaking clarity in law offices at Moreton-in-Marsh, Stratford, and New York; in Bracebridge he even supplemented his income as a professional calligrapher.

For the journeyman task of recording trials, he wrote with pen and ink, quickly and cleanly, taking down basic details and essential evidence as it was given. Short forms and abbreviations he'd first learned as a law clerk in England helped him keep up with the rapid flow of testimony before him in Bracebridge. For non-lawyer readers, the following are explanations of his sometimes cryptic bench book entries and several legal terms:

Cross-examination: As a party to an action or a witness gives their testimony, they can be "examined" or questioned by their lawyer if they have one, or by the judge to clarify a fact. Next they may be subject to "cross-examination" by the other side to challenge those facts or their credibility. In the bench book, the questions asked in cross-examination are not recorded, only the answers. Boyer's abbreviation for cross-examined was "XXd."

Produced: This single word in the midst of testimony refers to a witness having produced, or presented to the court as an exhibit, some item of evidence. Often these were documents, such as a doctor's prescription or a municipal bylaw, but in one case the proffered evidence was a distiller's illegal bushlot still; in another, several fowl that had been stolen; in still others, confiscated guns and animal parts.

Depositions taken on paper: A deposition is the giving of sworn evidence, and in a dozen or so cases that seemed to involve sensitive business or personal matters or awkward marital situations, the testimony of the parties was written down in a document separate from the bench book and, frustratingly, not incorporated in it. In effect, this was like holding an *in camera,* or closed, session of Magistrate's Court, since nothing appears on the record. It was unlikely the depositions were read aloud in court either, where the public had a right to be present. No explanation is given about the conditions under which this method of getting the facts of the case before the JP was appropriate. Whether such testimony given under oath and in writing would have been recorded by James Boyer, or prepared as an affidavit by a solicitor for his client appearing in court, and then handed to the magistrate, is also unclear. It could have been either, and given the various cases where this was done, was probably a bit of both.

Settled between the parties: This notation means that in a civil action, such as one person suing another over a fight they'd had, the plaintiff and defendant reached a compromise without the court having to make an order. That was not a pre-trial settlement, because the case had already begun to be heard in court when this entry was made in the bench book to record the disposition of the matter. This did not mean the magistrate played no role in the matter, because this settlement only happened in court after proceedings got underway and some resolution of the issue, perhaps by an apology, maybe with a payment, was achieved. James Boyer was a man who could remain calm in the midst of hot feelings and anger, and gave off a formidable impression when he wanted to look sternly upon, say, a clutch of inebriated street brawlers appearing before him. A pointed question from him, in that context, was no doubt conducive, on more than one occasion, to avoiding a public trial for a private dispute.

Cross-suit: Some fights continued off the street and into the courtroom because the combative individuals sued one another, private prosecutions that were different from the cases of a police constable laying Criminal Code charges for assault and battery or disturbance of the peace. Such private litigation often entailed the person being sued responding in kind against the other combatant: a cross-suit. In these cases, evidence taken in the trial of one would then be used as the same evidence for a faster trial of the other.

Conviction returned: This entry appeared in James Boyer's bench book at the conclusion of most cases, and meant, first, that there had been a conviction of the accused (rather than, say, a dismissal of the charge), and second, that this "return," or report by an officer of the court, indicated on the record the manner in which he had performed the duty imposed upon him as a magistrate. A conviction, which is the result when a person is found guilty of an offence, can be either ordinary or summary. An ordinary conviction takes place in a criminal prosecution by indictment, and may flow from an accused person's plea of guilty, or from a jury's verdict of guilty. Most cases within the jurisdiction of justices of the peace, however, and therefore recorded by James Boyer in his bench book, were summary conviction matters. The judgment was pronounced by one or more justices of the peace under the authority given them by the relevant statute, such as the Criminal Code, The Fish and Game Act, The Lord's Day Act, or any other of the several dozen provincial and federal enactments that gave them criminal or penal jurisdiction.

Paid: A notation to confirm that the convicted person's fine had been paid into court.

Paid constable $4.80: The record of an amount the JP paid, out of the fine received by the court, to reimburse a law enforcement officer for expenses incurred and as a fee for his police work on the case in question.

Court $2.20: A payment ordered by the JP to be paid from the fine to cover administration of justice costs for Muskoka Magistrate's Court.

Paid witness $2.15: Sometimes witnesses were paid, for example in the 1894 domestic violence case *McBride v. McBride*. In one case, a witness who'd shown up at court was paid even though the trial had to be postponed because the accused had failed to materialize. The witness had done his duty in appearing and was not to be penalized by losing a day's pay.

Entered into a recognizance: When an accused was found guilty of such offences as disturbing the peace or beating his wife, one of the penalties in the magistrate's arsenal was to require the offender to make an obligation, or bond, known in common law as a "recognizance," that would secure his performance of some act such as keeping the peace and being of good behaviour for a specified time, such as a year. A recognizance could also be to guarantee the offender's performance of something else, such as payment of a debt or appearance at the assizes. Usually, a sizeable amount of money formed part of this bond, which would be forfeited if the offender failed to abide by his recognizance. If the convicted party could not raise the money himself, he tapped friends and relatives to make up the amount, and their names were then recorded in the bench book. Because they would forfeit their money if the offender failed to keep the peace, their financial interest acted as a further continuous and present force for compliance.

Committed: This single word recorded the fact that the convicted person had been locked up to serve a prisoner's sentence in the Bracebridge jail.

Costs to follow the event: The simple word *costs* comes with a complex array of meanings in courtroom proceedings. It can cover the charges a solicitor is entitled to recover from a client for professional services and disbursements. It can denote the expenses a person is entitled to recover from the other side by reason of being a party to legal proceedings. In criminal cases, a general rule is that the Crown neither receives nor pays costs. Generally, in a civil action, the decision by a judge or magistrate to "award costs" to one side or the other is discretionary, although some statutes or procedural rules may specifically provide for allocating this benefit (or penalty, depending on whether one receives, or pays, the costs.) When James Boyer wrote "costs to follow the event," he meant the losing side had to pay the costs incurred by the winning side.

In default of sufficient distress: This phrase meant that, if the convicted person did not have enough money to pay the fine, nor enough goods to be seized by the sheriff and sold to cover the fine, then the consequence of such a "default" would be for him to pay, instead, by serving time for a stipulated number of days in jail. The word *distress,* from the Latin *distringere* meaning "to bind fast," means an authorized taking of personal property from the possession of a wrongdoer as a pledge to redress an injury, perform a duty, or satisfy a demand — such as paying a court-ordered fine.

Distress to issue: This notation meant a distress warrant would be issued by the magistrate to the sheriff, empowering him to seize property of the person named in the warrant, then sell it or otherwise use the asset to cover payment of a fine.

Cost of distress: The sheriff would incur expenses in realizing on the property of a person ordered by the court to pay, and these costs would be reimbursed by the court. The "cost of distress" entry was accompanied by the amount so paid.

Garnishee summons: When a person was sentenced to pay an amount but could not immediately do so, one remedy was for the magistrate to issue a court order to garnishee, or divert, money due to that person, for instance from an employee for wages earned, to the sheriff, thence to the court in turn, where it was used to pay the fine or debt.

Hard labour: While some sentences of incarceration entailed being locked away in the town jail for a specified number of days, meaning that punishment was a temporary loss of one's freedom, the sentence sometimes was more severe. One such sentence involved being "imprisoned in the common gaol at Bracebridge and kept there *at hard labour* for 6 weeks." Hard labour conjures an image of a prisoner in chains and leg-clamp wielding a heavy sledgehammer to break rocks. In fact, sentences of "hard labour" usually required prisoners to work separated from other prisoners, and sleep on the floor without a mattress. If a convicted person was being locked up because they could not pay their fine, hard labour could not be imposed. Hard labour was never a punishment under common law as developed by judges. It was established under statute law in the early 1700s in Britain, and was later imported into Canada. It has since been abolished. In 1890s Bracebridge the work, if actually imposed at all, consisted mostly of such labouring chores for the municipality as shovelling sand or coal, sawing and splitting firewood, digging ditches or weeds, or removing snow or ice.

Fine refunded: In special situations, where a fine was levied by the magistrate and paid by the convicted individual, the amount was then refunded to him. This occurred, for instance, in an 1895 case against Ling Lee, who operated the town laundry. Although no explanation for this refund was given, one may surmise that JPs Robert Browning and James Boyer felt this "Chinaman," who on other occasions had been the victim of provocation by Bracebridge youths, and, further, who may not have understood the prior warnings given him about pouring the toxic fluids used in his laundry onto the ground to drain over neighbours' properties (having no drain in his laundry premises), now got the message and should not have to forfeit his hard-earned five dollars — an amount that represented washing and ironing 250 shirts. Another example was the fine paid by Albert Mortimer in 1897 for operating a grocery boat without a licence, which five weeks later was remitted to him by the Government of Canada.

Convicted but no penalty imposed: A rare and happy outcome for an accused: this entry meant the law had been breached, but that in the magistrate's view the matter was so inconsequential or technical, or that the accused had already somehow "paid the price," that enough was enough. In one such case, however, the defendant was at least required to pay costs.

Discharged with a caution: Only slightly less desirable was this outcome, which occurred when an accused, though found guilty, was given a discharge, meaning he could walk free without a fine or jail time, receiving only a cautionary warning from the magistrate not to do it again.

Defendant absconded: This entry recorded that a person, rather than submitting to the jurisdiction of the court or to serving jail time, had taken off. If the matter warranted it, the sheriff would then try to find him and bring him back.

Defendant constricted: The term used when a violent person was placed in manacles or chains, as in the 1895 case of Frederick Donald.

Adverse possession: This doctrine in property law, applicable to lands in the Registry system of landholding, which was the regime in Muskoka, holds that if a person visibly occupies and uses the property of another, to that person's knowledge, for a period of ten years, and does so without legal challenge from the owner of the occupier's right to be there, then his "adverse possession" of the property makes that land his own in law. Among cases in the bench book where this doctrine was germane was an 1895 battle over a fence in Stephenson Township involving Norman Wallace and a host of others.

Squatter's rights: A squatter is somebody who settles without legal authority on another's land, particularly on public lands, which formed most of Muskoka before the Crown had granted parcels to individuals. Such a person can actually acquire title to a piece of land so occupied by enclosing it, building a dwelling place, and openly living on it. A number of early Muskoka properties were acquired this way, including the one James Boyer bought from a squatter for his first home in the district.

Moieties: Canadian lawmakers imported a practice long known to English courts as the "moiety," an incentive to encourage individuals to prosecute offences. Such private prosecutors were known in law as "common informers," individuals who took proceedings for breaches of the law for no other reason than to get the penalty or a share of it. Their role was part and parcel of the system that included a "citizen's arrest," which authorizes a person, though he or she is not a law enforcement officer, to arrest anyone caught in the act of committing a crime or an offence. A "moiety" is like a finder's fee, the term itself being an English make-over of the French word *moitié,* meaning half, because a judge or justice of the peace could pay half the fine levied against a convicted party to whoever had prosecuted him. In Canadian courtroom practice, "moieties" came to mean *any* fractional part of the fine. This payment, which cost the public treasury nothing, was an expedient to increase law enforcement far beyond the limited number of constables and game wardens in service. Both moieties and common informers have since been abolished in Canadian law, although the possibility of a citizen making an arrest endures. For more on the practical impacts of paying moieties, see the introduction to Chapter 14: Ill-Gotten Game in Part II.

Reg ex rel: This abbreviation, which appears for instance in the 1896 case styled *Reg ex rel John A. Ross v Charles Roach,* is the abbreviation for *Regina,* Latin for queen, in whose name Crown prosecutions were taken during the time Victoria was monarch (it would be Rex, Latin for king, during the reign of a male monarch), and for *ex relatione*, again Latin, meaning "from a narrative or information." In the 1890s informations could be partly at the suit of the sovereign and partly at the suit of a subject, a common informer who was also known in law as "the relator" because he related the information about the illegal or unlawful activity giving rise to a court case.

Once the courtroom cleared, silence and calm descended as James would wait for the ink to dry on the page of his bench book.

It was a brief moment to organize papers and gather thoughts. No doubt he reflected upon how, one by one, the cases before him revealed the rough and ready life that people who'd come to Muskoka with soaring hopes now found themselves living during the 1890s. James was privy to many things most others were not. His courtroom sessions, illuminating the social conditions and hard culture of Muskoka, dramatized the infinite but understandable predicaments people got themselves into.

Then he'd close his bench book, ready for the next case.

Part II: The Dramas, in Twenty-Six Acts with Numerous Scenes

Robert E. Armstrong }   For having on the 3d May
          v   }   1894 at Bracebridge been
Elizabeth Dempsey   }   an inmate of a certain
house of ill fame.

  Plea not guilty
Robert E. Armstrong sworn
                              I am a Constable for
the District of Muskoka. About one o'clock this
morning I went to the house kept by Dufresne
in Bracebridge and I found the Prisoner
and the woman Dufresne and two men in the
house at that time and arrested the whole of
them.
Prisoner convicted and fined $50 and
costs $5.55 to be paid forthwith and in
default to be imprisoned in the Common
Gaol at Bracebridge and there kept at
hard labour for the space of six calendar
months.
                          Alfred Hunt J.P.
                          James Boyer J.P.

Comm'n ret'd   Committed

Chapter One

A Constable's Unhappy Lot

Many of these cases would never have materialized if not for the work of the constabulary, so it seems fitting to begin with a couple that centre on law enforcement officers themselves.

Police officers in the 1890s got no training for their work. They simply started green, then educated themselves about policing as time passed and they gained experience in keeping the peace. Muskoka boasted resolute men who were often quite courageous in law enforcement. In addition to policemen, those who played roles establishing the law amidst rough and ready conditions included public health officials, hygiene inspectors, fence inspectors, and tax collectors. Despite moments of valour, sometimes awkward moments of truth underscored the refrain, from a popular Gilbert and Sullivan opera of the era, that "A policeman's lot is not a happy one!"

Magistrate's Court — April 30th, 1894
Before Justices Boyer and Browning
Jackson Foster v Arthur Bridgman

For having on April 24th, 1894 wilfully obstructed the said informant as collector of taxes for the Township of Draper in making a lawful seizure of property for unpaid taxes.

Defendant pleaded not guilty.

Jackson Foster sworn

I am the collector of taxes for the Township of Draper, and have been for the last five years. On the 14th day of April I went to the residence of William Bridgman in said township to make a seizure for unpaid taxes. I had made a demand upon Bridgman more than 14 days before I went to make the seizure.

I saw defendant who lives with his brother William Bridgman. I told him what my business was and asked if his brother was home. He said he wasn't. I told him I was going to seize. He said, "Go and do it, my brother could have paid his taxes six months ago." I started to go to the stable to take a cow.

Defendant called me back and said I was "not to take the cow." I went back to the house and he asked me to come in as he wanted to show me something. I went in. Defendant had a gun in his hand, and had his thumb on the lock. He put his finger on the cap and said, "Do you see that." I said, "Yes, I see it." He said, "If you touch that cow, that cap will be the means of blowing your brains out." Defendant said the gun was loaded. I asked defendant if he was going to shoot and he said, "Yes." I said, "Don't shoot for I will not take your cow."

I was unable to make the seizure on account of defendant's threat. I have not seized the cow yet. I was at the house four times to demand the taxes.

Defendant convicted and fined $100 and $5 costs, and in default of immediate payment, to be imprisoned in the common gaol at Bracebridge and there to be kept at hard labour for the space of six calendar months.

James Boyer, J.P.
R.M. Browning, J.P.

Magistrate's Court — April 30th, 1894
Before James Boyer, J.P.
WILFORD *G. Hill* v George Bray

Assault and battery at Huntsville on April 18th, 1894.

The charge having been read to defendant, he pleaded not guilty.

W. Mahaffy for complainant

W.G. Hill sworn

I am a member of Bracebridge Fire Co. On the 18th of April I went with the Fire Co. to a fire in Huntsville and assisted at the fire. About 10 o'clock that night myself and 9 others were waiting for the train to bring us home. We went up the street. We were singing. It was nothing wrong or obscene. Some Salvation Army tunes. Some men came up. We stopped singing. Defendant was one of them. Another man caught me by the arm and said, "Come with me." He let me go.

Defendant then caught me and said, "Come with me." I went with him. He put me in the lock-up. On the way I asked him what charge there was against me. He said nothing. He had hold of me. He put me in the gaol. I was there about an hour. Gladhill let me out afterwards. I was not brought before a magistrate. I told defendant I had come up to the fire and had my fireman's hat and boots on. There were three others put in the gaol with me.

We had not been breaking the law. I am a constable myself. The singing was not as loud as the Salvation Army sing on the street. Defendant did not say he was a constable. Defendant did not make any charge against me or say what I was to go to the gaol for.

Cross-examined

I did not use any profane language. I refused to go till I knew what I had to go for. I hadn't seen defendant till he came up to me. It was not light enough to distinguish one man from another.

Alfred Hillman

I went to Huntsville the day of the fire. Hill, myself and 7 others were going to the Salvation Army barracks. None of us were using bad language or creating a disturbance, 3 or 4 men came up and arrested me. Hill went a little way and asked what they wanted him for. Defendant said you are my prisoner but didn't say on what charge. Defendant put Hill in the gaol. I saw Defendant catch hold of Hill. I asked defendant what he arrested him for. He said never mind. I did not go in the gaol. I got away.

William Ridley sworn

I live in Gravenhurst. Was at Huntsville fire. Belong to Gravenhurst Fire Co. I know Hill. Saw defendant when he arrested Hill. It was about 10 o'clock p.m. Came up with Hill from Cook's Hotel. We walked up by twos and was singing a song. We then changed to sing 'Whiter than Snow' and asked a small boy where the Salvation Army barracks was. I saw a scramble and saw defendant arrest Hill and say you are my prisoner. He didn't say anything else. He afterwards said he had been using bad language. I was with Hill and didn't hear him use any bad language or do anything wrong.

Alfred Woodruff sworn

I went with Bracebridge Fire Co. to Huntsville. I was one of the party singing. There was no bad language used. Defendant went up to Hill and said you are my prisoner. That was all I heard. If Hill had been using bad language I must have heard it.

Philip Sharp sworn

I went to Huntsville with the Gravenhurst Fire Co. I was arrested with the others. I didn't hear any bad language used.

Victor Guinet sworn

Am a member of Bracebridge Fire Co. Was at Huntsville and was with the party singing on the street. There was no bad language used.

Cross-examined

I did not use any bad language.

For the Defence

Defendant sworn

I heard a noise and heard some parties cursing and swearing. I went up and told them it was against the law. They said they knew what they were doing and they would do as they liked. I don't know which one was making the racket but Hill was among them. I was appointed a special constable by the reeve alone.

Cross-examined

It was about 10 p.m., a dark night and no street lamps on the street. They were making more noise than the Salvation Army ordinarily does. Hill was a stranger to me. Hill said, "Jesus Christ we'll do as we like." A man was standing between me and him.

I was sworn in as constable by the reeve. No other magistrate present. I laid my hand on his shoulder and said I arrested him for using profane language. The reeve let them out without consulting me.

Defendant convicted and fined $5 and $11.80 costs, to be paid forthwith, and in default of immediate payment, to be imprisoned in the common gaol at Bracebridge and there kept at hard labour for 6 weeks.

James Boyer, J.P.

Constable $6.80
P. Sharp $1.35
W. Ridley $1.35
Court $2.30
Total $11.80

Chapter Two

PROVOCATION

In 1893 Vancouver council passed a bylaw designating areas of the city for Chinese laundries, nibbling at the edge of the larger controversy that saw windows smashed and buildings burned in Chinatown by whites, who didn't like Chinese laundries because they did the work for less, taking jobs as well as business.

In that decade Bracebridge had few Chinese residents, and nobody else was much interested in the laundry business. Women in the community were as happy to see a Chinese laundry open as they were to see a qualified midwife move to town. While the issues in a small settlement were thus not the same as in the west coast city, in Canada's communities of all sizes some people acted as if racial minorities occupied a lower rung on the social ladder.

The struggle for human rights has been waged over many years in countless settings, sometimes with memorable cases and historic turning points, but more frequently through uncounted episodes that contributed bit by bit to creating a pluralistic society. In 1890s Bracebridge one of those seemingly minor episodes involved a Chinese Canadian named Sing Lee, and a ten-day jail sentence.

MAGISTRATE'S COURT — APRIL 12TH, 1898
BEFORE JAMES BOYER, J.P.
SING LEE V WALTER POST

For having, on April 6th, at the Town of Bracebridge, unlawfully damaged and injured certain property of the said Sing Lee.
Defendant pleaded not guilty.

Raymond Simmons sworn
I was in Sing Lee's laundry in Bracebridge on last Wednesday night the 6th of April. I saw defendant there about 7:30 to 9:30. I saw defendant throw some water on some shirts. Defendant was showing the boys how to play a trick and had a cup of water up to the wall. One of the boys struck his elbow and then ran up some steps past the shirts. Defendant threw water at him and it went on the shirts. Defendant had been told by Sing Lee to go out but took no notice. None of us had any business there that night. Two or three shirts were damaged. The boys will not stay out even though Sing Lee tells them.

William O'Hare sworn
I saw defendant in the laundry on Wednesday night. Defendant was playing a trick with water in a cup. A boy struck him, he threw the water but it went on the shirts. The shirts would have to be re-laundered. There were three or four white shirts damaged. I have heard the proprietor order the boys out but they would not go.

Edward Dodd sworn

Defendant was in the laundry on Wednesday night when I went in. Defendant had a cup of water in his hand; he was playing a trick, when his brother struck his elbow. He threw the water at his brother and some water went on the shirts. The shirts were plainly to be seen. I have, more than once, heard proprietor tell the boys to go but they wouldn't go. Proprietor has to keep his door locked to keep the boys out.

Herbert Post sworn

I work at Sing Lee's laundry. Corroborated others' statements. The charge for washing and laundering shirts is ten cents.

Lee Gee Ton sworn

Every night after tea the boys come to my place and spoil my business. On Wednesday Walter Post threw water on the shirts and spoiled four. I had to wash four. Defendant calls me "son of a "bitch" when I order him out. The boys refuse to go when I tell them.

Defendant fined $1.40 damages and costs of $4.45, to be paid forthwith, and in default, to be imprisoned in the common gaol at Bracebridge for the space of ten days.

James Boyer, J.P.

Committed to gaol.
Conviction returned.

Chapter Three

CONTENDING WITH DISEASE

Public health officials respond to alarmed communities facing a potential contagion of some dangerous disease by forcing individuals into quarantine as a rudimentary way of protecting against the spread of deadly peril. The practice is not new. After 1888 when cases of diphtheria caused the death of several children in Bracebridge, including all three youngsters in the Galliard household, Muskokans remained vigilant. In 1894, for example, Bracebridge Magistrate's Court heard three cases brought by Cardwell Township Board of Health arising from an incidence of diphtheria near the village of Rosseau, where a quarantine was in force.

Another, quite different, medical episode in that same decade centred on "Doctor" McLeod and the reputed therapeutic value of certain herbal treatments and substances he prescribed. This case, which involved two trials on the same day on charges brought by Constable Thomas Wasson, illustrates how residents of a community, then as today, can often be lost in the twilight zone between the contending health claims of naturopathy and prescription drugs.

MAGISTRATE'S COURT — APRIL 2ND, 1894

BEFORE MESSRS. BOYER AND BROWNING, J.P.S

THE LOCAL BOARD OF HEALTH OF TOWNSHIP OF CARDWELL V JEREMIAH CROWDER

For neglect to notify Board of Health of diphtheria in his house at Cardwell in November last.

The charge having been read to defendant, he pleaded not guilty.

John Wilson sworn

I live in Cardwell. I know defendant. He lives in Cardwell. I saw him on 8th of November last. I asked him how his children were; he said he thought they had a touch of quinsy. I advised him to get a doctor.

Cross-examined

Defendant was going towards Rosseau.

Richard Barteger sworn

I live in Cardwell. I know defendant. On the 7th or 8th of November I took a bag of flour to his house. I saw defendant in front of his house. I laid the flour on the fence, as defendant told me not to go in the house, that they had diphtheria and I had better not go in. There was no placard on the house at the time.

Cross-examined

I saw defendant on the road about two miles from Rosseau. He was going to see a doctor.

Joseph Paisley sworn

I know defendant. I saw him last November at his house and was talking to him. He said to pass on as they had the diphtheria. He said the doctor had pronounced it diphtheria. There was a placard on a stump near the house.

Samuel Simpson sworn

I live with defendant and have since the 15th or 20th of October. My family came on Wednesday the 1st November, and defendant's boy got sick on the next Saturday. He had been sick before the 1st November. The little girl was taken sick on the 4th but was out till Monday night. The boy was not out after the 4th. Defendant went Thursday noon to get the doctor and did not get back till night. Doctor came on Wednesday noon, on the 8th. Both children died on the 11th. My children had been sick with the diphtheria before this.

Matthew Wilson sworn

I am the secretary of the Local Board of Health of the Township of Cardwell. I know defendant. On the 9th of November I put up a placard on defendant's house at the instance of Dr. Waddy, a physician at Rosseau. Defendant had not reported any disease in his house to me before this. It was about nine o'clock in the morning I got notice from the doctor.

Case dismissed.

James Boyer, J.P.
R.M. Browning, J.P.

Magistrate's Court — April 2nd, 1894
Before Messrs. Boyer and Browning, J.P.s
Local Board of Health of Cardwell v George Crowder

For having, on December 29th, 1893, exposed himself, in violation of Section 85 of the Public Health Act.

Charge having been read, the prisoner pleaded not guilty.

Matthew Wilson sworn

I know the defendant. He lives with his father Douglas Crowder on the Cardwell road. The house was placarded for diphtheria on the 9th of November. I put up the placard at the instance of Dr. Waddy. It remained there till February 1894. I frequently saw defendant from November till February.

Joseph Discon sworn

I know defendant. I saw him on December 29th on the road about three miles from his home. It was the south Cardwell road. He was going home. He was alone. There was another party on the road a short distance from him.

For the Defence

A. Douglas Crowder sworn

I am the father of the defendant. Defendant went to Mr. Matthew Wilson's house to get some food. At this time we were forbidden to go out.

Cross-examined

I got a bag of flour on the 28th. I told them the articles I wanted.

Melinda Crowder sworn

I am the mother of the defendant. My son was sent over to Mr. Matthew Wilson to get some groceries on or about the 28th or 29th of December. Before the 29th Mr. Wilson told me to send defendant to his house by a footpath.

Matthew Wilson (recalled to the stand)

I supplied Crowders with groceries:

- December 18th: $5.87 in goods, consisting of 1 bag flour, rice 25 cents, rolled oats 25 cents, sugar 25 cents, fluid beef 35 cents, pepper 13 cents, tobacco 50 cents.
- December 20th: Goods amounting to $1.65, consisting of 6 ½ lbs bacon, extract beef 70 cents, lemons 10 cents.
- December 23rd: amount $1.18. One lb tea, sugar 25 cents, raisins 25 cents, apples 25 cents.
- December 28th: amount $1.75, 1 lb bag flour.

Defendant convicted and fined $5 and costs $7, to be paid forthwith, and in default, to be levied by distress, and in default of distress, to be imprisoned in the common gaol at Bracebridge for 14 days.

James Boyer, J.P.
R.M. Browning, J.P.

Paid constable $4.80
Court $2.20
Conviction returned.
Paid.

MAGISTRATE'S COURT — OCTOBER 20TH, 1898
BEFORE JAMES BOYER, J.P.
THOMAS WASSON V MALCOLM MCLEOD

For that defendant, not being a person registered pursuant to the provisions of the Ontario Medical Act (R.S.O. 1897, Chapter 176) within the space of one year last past, to wit in or about the month of October 1898, at the Town of Bracebridge, did take and use a name, title or description viz., "Dr. McLeod, Scottish Herbalist," implying and calculated to lead people to infer that defendant was registered under the provisions of the R.S.O. 1897, Chap. 176. and was recognized by law as a Physician and Licentiate in medicine, contrary to the statute in that case made and provided.

Defendant pleaded not guilty.

Mr. Ashworth for prosecution
Mr. O.M. Arnold for defendant

Alfred E. Stephenson sworn
I am the Publisher of the *Free Grant Gazette*, a newspaper published weekly in Bracebridge. I know defendant. He came to me to publish an advertisement as a Scottish Herbalist. I produce a copy of the paper of October 13th containing an advertisement of defendant. (Entered as Exhibit A.) It was ordered to be put in paper and was paid for by defendant. Defendant inserted a similar advertisement about a month ago.

Cross-examined
I don't know who wrote the ad. I got it through the mail. When defendant paid for the advertisement I didn't show it him in the paper.

Re-direct

Defendant asked me what was the amount of the bill. I told him and he paid me.

Alexander Foster sworn

I keep the Dominion Hotel in Bracebridge. Defendant has been staying at my hotel. I have called him Doctor McLeod. He is registered as such. He has been commonly known as Doctor McLeod. Parties inquiring for him asked for Doctor McLeod.

Cross-examined

He didn't tell me he was a doctor. I never saw him with his name.

John Gibson sworn

I live in Bracebridge. I know defendant. I first saw him at a boarding house. He called at my house.

Alexander Taylor sworn

I live in Bracebridge. I saw an ad in the *Free Grant Gazette* similar to the one produced, and defendant came to my house in consequence of what my wife said. He wrote me a prescription. The prescription now produced is the handwriting of defendant. I saw him write it (entered as Exhibit B) and he handed it to me. I got it filled. I sent my wife for it. I used the medicine. At the time I got the medicine I believe defendant was a qualified physician from reading the advertisement.

Cross-examined

I suppose Dr. means Doctor. It also stands for Debtor. Exhibit B is what I call a medical recipe. He didn't say he was a Doctor.

John Thomson sworn

I am a druggist in Bracebridge. I know defendant. I have filled several prescriptions signed Dr. McLeod. I filled one for Mrs. Taylor of the same ingredients as the one produced and from the signature Dr. McLeod. I inferred defendant was a duly qualified physician.

Cross-examined

I will not swear Mrs. Taylor produced the paper marked Exhibit B but she produced a paper having the same ingredients as the one produced. I would not infer from the words Scottish Herbalist that defendant was a doctor but a man who sold herbs. That's the way it was understood in Scotland. The Dr. on the Exhibit B did not lead me to think he was a doctor. The exhibit produced is a recipe. I call it a prescription. Recipes like the one produced are commonly sold by others than registered practitioners. I don't know if the one produced is a patent recipe or not. All the ingredients are herbs. They are compounded in the same manner as patent medicines.

Re-direct

If I did not know defendant, the recipe produced would impress me that defendant was a duly qualified physician. The paper produced by Mrs. Taylor was signed Dr. McLeod.

For the Defence

Thomas Wasson sworn (Mr. Arnold then having decided to call him.)

Defendant convicted and fined $25 and $5.50 costs, to be paid forthwith, and in default, to be imprisoned in the common gaol at Bracebridge for the space of one month.

James Boyer, J.P.

Fine and costs paid.

Paid constable.

Conviction returned.

MAGISTRATE'S COURT — OCTOBER 20TH, 1898
BEFORE JAMES BOYER, J.P.
THOMAS WASSON v MALCOLM McLEOD

Information amended as follows: **For that defendant, not being a person registered pursuant to the provisions of the Ontario Medical Act (R.S.O. 1897, Chapter 176), within the space of one year last past, to wit in or about the month of October 1898, at the Town of Bracebridge in said District, did for hire gain or hope of reward practice medicine by prescribing and attending on John Gibson and Alexander Taylor of the Town of Bracebridge and others contrary to the statute in that case made and provided.** Defendant pleaded not guilty.

Mr. Ashworth for prosecution

Mr. Arnold for the defendant

Alexander Taylor sworn

I live in Bracebridge. I know defendant. I first met him 2 or 3 months ago. I saw him in my house. He didn't ask me any questions but wrote out the prescription produced as "Exhibit B" and handed it to me. I was suffering from inability to hold my urine. I told him how I was affected, and he then wrote out the prescription and handed it to me, and I then gave him $5.00. I knew that from defendant, as to the cost, and I paid him the $5.00.

About 2 weeks after, defendant came to my house and asked me how I was getting along. I told him I was not much better. He said it would take time. He visited me the same as an ordinary physician. I understood he was a regular doctor. He came to my house 2 or 3 times since to see how I was getting along. He hasn't given me any other prescriptions.

Cross-examined

I treated the last visits as friendly calls. He didn't give me any medicine on either of these occasions and didn't charge me. I knew what ailed me the first time. I understood I paid him $5 for the recipe. He did not tell me he was a doctor and I didn't ask him.

Re-direct

I got the first lot of medicine from the defendant. He said it was all herbs he dealt in.

Malcolm McLeod sworn

I am the defendant. I know Mrs. Amos White of Bracebridge. I saw her over a month ago. I don't remember where. I had supplied her with medicine. I prescribed for her all of 3 months since. She was weak and got some medicine from me. She partly told me her symptoms and asked me if I could give her something. She had a lump in the neck. I gave her a prescription for a cough the last time I saw her. I didn't charge her for that.

I know Alexander Taylor. His wife came to me to go and see her husband who was sick. I don't think I asked many questions. Mrs. Taylor told me some of the symptoms. I diagnosed the case and gave him suitable medicine. Exhibit B is in my handwriting. I charged Taylor $5 and he was to get the prescription filled at the druggist's. I had the advertisement now produced (Exhibit A) inserted in the *Free Grant Gazette*. I had a similar advertisement in the same paper in September.

I have sold prescriptions to other people in town. One to a lady the other day for her little boy. I gave suitable herbs for the disease. I generally give the first lot free and charge for the prescription. The circular now produced is my circular (Exhibit C). The Exhibits D and E and F are prescriptions given by me.

Cross-examined

The compound described here as Exhibit B I claim to be of my own discovery. Compounds D and E also I claim as my own discovery. I told Taylor I didn't sell medicine. I don't ask parties their symptoms. I do not prescribe for any person and it is not my custom to ask questions about symptoms. I am the proprietor of the recipes. Exhibit F is a stimulant.

Defendant convicted and fined $25 and $4.25 costs, to be paid forthwith, and in default, to be imprisoned in the common gaol at Bracebridge for the space of one month.

James Boyer, J.P.

Fine and costs paid.
Paid constable.
Conviction returned.

Chapter Four

Property Fights and
Property Rights

Contrary claims and competing interests over property fuelled disputes between pioneers that sometimes only the local magistrate could resolve. Some cases arose because of confusion over whose property it really was; two involved vandalism (but were not contested and are not reproduced here); and one drama produced a suit and counter-suit.

These fights are a clear reminder that the real issue was never the quiescent land itself, but rather the rawness of people's provoked relations with one another when contesting their right to the same piece of real estate.

Magistrate's Court — April 12th, 1895
Before James Boyer, J.P.
Christopher Thrift v Albert Rowley

Assault and battery at the Township of Macaulay on April 5th, 1895.
The defendant pleaded not guilty.

Christopher Thrift sworn

I live in Macaulay Township with my brother. I found Defendant on Lot 22, Con 3, Macaulay with a young man named George Trewin. He was tapping trees there. I went and told him he had no business there. He said, "Is this not the lot Mrs. Scott lives on?" I told him it made no difference whose lot it was, as I had agreed to buy the lots from the Canada Permanent Company and the agreement was accepted. Mr. Mason, the company's inspector, told me to let him know if anyone interfered with their property.

After speaking to him I turned to come away. He threatened to run me out of the bush. He came after me, caught up to me. I was afraid that he would strike me, so I grabbed him by the throat. He tried to throw me backwards twice. He tried to pull me round to throw me down and I tripped over a log and fell on my back. While I was down he struck me four times. After defendant had struck me George Trewin said to him, "Albert, you had better let him alone or you will get into trouble."

For the Defence

Albert Rowley sworn

On 5th April I was in the sugar bush on Lot 22, Con 3, Macaulay. George Trewin was there with me. Complainant came in the bush and said to me, "If you don't get off here you will get into trouble." He said he had an agreement with the company and owned Lots 21 and 22. I asked him what he'd take to let me go on in the bush. He said he wouldn't take a cent. "I want you to take your things and get off here."

He got hold of me by the throat with one hand and had the axe in the other hand. I caught hold of him and jerked the axe out of his hand. He jerked me on my knees. I got up and he tried to throw me but I put him down. He tried to roll me off him. He had hold of my throat and I struck him 3 times to make him let go. When he let go I got up and he let me get up. He then struck me on the left shoulder with his fist.

Cross-examined by complainant
You walked away about a rod.

George Trewin sworn
I was present when this affair took place. Complainant caught defendant by the collar. Defendant held axe out full length behind him. Defendant told him to drop the axe. Complainant jerked defendant on his knees. Defendant got up and threw complainant on his back and struck him four or five times. When they fell I was about a rod away. I went up to them. I did not see complainant strike defendant.

Cross-examined by complainant
You called to me to take him off. I didn't do so, but told him to let you up.

Rosilla Maria Thrift
Complainant lives with me. Defendant came in. I asked him what he had been doing. He said he had a scuffle with Rowley.

Robert M. Browning sworn
I am the agent of Canada Permanent Loans & Savings Company here. Lot 22, Concession 3 is at present in my hands for sale. There is at present no agreement with complainant regarding this lot. I had no notice from the

Company as to any agreement with complainant, as I should have had, had there been an agreement.

Complaint dismissed with costs to complainant.

James Boyer, J.P.

Paid constable $1.85

Court $1.50

Magistrate's Court — December 14th, 1898
Before James Boyer, J.P.
Frederick Stimpson v Robert Horning

Assault and battery at the Township of Stephenson on December 9th, 1898. Defendant pleaded not guilty.

Frederick Stimpson sworn

Sarah Stimpson is my mother. Defendant assaulted my mother at Henry Horning's place in Stephenson. I was in possession of Horning's place, under a warrant issued by Mrs. Annie Brown under a chattel mortgage. Defendant drove up to the door about 1 p.m. of the 9th instant. He threw down the fence and ran towards the door, forced it partly open and grabbed my mother. I had got there at that time. He had hold of her by the throat and said, "I'll show you buggers if you are going to lock me out."

Cross-examined

I got the warrant 2 or 3 days before the assault. It may have been on the 8th, the day before the assault. I was then in possession. I had authority to look after the place and take possession from Horning just before he left to go to hospital. He gave me the keys of the house and told me to look after the place and the cattle. No amount was fixed as to remuneration. Mrs. Brown told me to keep possession of the place till she further instructed me.

Prisoner, Mrs. Smalley, and a woman reputed to be Mrs. Horning came on the 9th instant. Smalley and Horning ran towards the door. Mother had stepped inside and closed the door. Defendant took Mother by the throat. She didn't strike at him. He was choking her badly. I pulled him away. She appeared to be hurt. Defendant stated what he came for. Afterwards they asked me what authority I had. I didn't pick up a knife. They stayed about three-quarters of an hour and then left. Both Henry Horning and Mrs. Brown has told me that she (Mrs. Brown) was Henry Horning's daughter.

Sarah Stimpson sworn

On the 9th December instant, I was at Horning's place with my son. I went to the door to empty some slops after dinner. I heard my son say "Mother, shut the door." He was running towards the house. I shut the door. I found someone pushing the door. He grabbed me by the throat, and as he pushed the door open he struck me on the shoulder. My son pulled defendant away from me and pushed Smalley away. Mrs. Smalley came up and said that it was her house. My throat was swollen and my shoulder was sore. I didn't strike defendant or strike at him. I had orders from Mrs. Brown to clean up the place for the funeral. I did not see my son take up a knife.

William G. Stimpson sworn

I was present on the day in question. I saw the assault take place by defendant on my wife. I saw the defendant drive up, throw down the fence and made a quick move for the door. My son told his mother to shut the door. She did so. Defendant ran at and forced the door sufficient to get his left arm in. I was then at the door. Defendant had hold of my wife by the throat with the left hand. My son pulled him away. Defendant said, "Would you hit me?" My son said, "A man should be hit who will strike a woman." I said to defendant, "What kind of work is this to strike a woman?" He said, "To let you buggers see you can't do as you like round here." I didn't see my son pick up a knife.

Annie Braun sworn
I was in Horning's house on the day in question but in another part of the house. I didn't see what took place.

For the Defence

Defendant sworn
When we drove up, the door was partly open. Fred Stimpson said, "Mother, shut the door." I pushed it open. Mrs. Stimpson grabbed hold of me and said, "Where are you going?" I was authorized to go by Mrs. Horning. Mrs. Stimpson struck at me. I put up my hand to protect my face. I didn't take her by the throat. Mrs. Horning asked complainant who gave him authority to go. He said he had authority and he was going to keep it.

Cross-examined
There was some resistance when I tried to get in at the door. I didn't put my hand on Mrs. Stimpson at all. She was fighting at me when Fred Stimpson came up.

Annie Horning sworn
I am the widow of Mr. Henry Horning. I was with defendant at my late husband's place on 9th instant. I went to search for a will and to take an inventory of things on the place so that I could take out Letters of Administration. When I got in, Mr. Stimpson had his hand on Horning's shoulder. Fred Stimpson said he would put me out. Defendant didn't have Mrs. Stimpson by the throat. Fred Stimpson wouldn't allow me to make the search, and put some papers in his pocket.

Cross-examined
When I got in, defendant had his arm up, and Mrs. Stimpson was fighting at him. Fred Stimpson pushed me against the wall.

Henry Smalley sworn

I was with defendant and my daughter on the day in question. The door was partly open. Horning went in. I followed. I didn't see what happened between defendant and Mrs. Stimpson. He crowded against her going in but I didn't see defendant catch Mrs. Stimpson by the throat. I didn't see any blows struck. Mrs. Stimpson first accused me of taking her by the throat.

Cross-examined

I heard the Wednesday before that Fred Stimpson was in possession under Mr. Horning's authority.

Defendant convicted and fined $2 and costs $5.45, to be paid forthwith, and in default, to be imprisoned and kept at hard labour in the common gaol at Bracebridge for one month.

James Boyer, J.P.

> Court $2.45
> Constable $3.00
> Fine and costs paid.

MAGISTRATE'S COURT — DECEMBER 14TH, 1898
BEFORE JAMES BOYER, J.P.
ANNIE HORNING V FREDERICK STIMPSON

Assault and battery at Stephenson on December 9th, 1898.
Defendant pleaded not guilty.

Annie Horning sworn
On the afternoon of 9th instant I saw defendant at my late husband's house.

He took me by the shoulder, shook me twice and jammed me against the wall and said he would put me out as I had no business there. I told him to take his hands off me. He wouldn't. Mr. Horning then told him to take his hands off. He did so and caught hold of him. He got a knife out of the drawer and came towards me with it in his hand. He was 4 or 5 feet from me. He didn't attempt to strike me with it.

Cross-examined
I was just behind Fred Stimpson when he came in.

Robert Horning sworn
I was present on the occasion referred to. Defendant caught hold of Mrs. Horning, shook her and jammed her against the wall. I told him to take his hands off her. He did so and took hold of me. I didn't see defendant with a knife in his hand.

Defence

Sarah Stimpson sworn
I was present on the occasion. I didn't see my son touch Mrs. Horning, and must have done so if he had as I was close to them.

Cross-examined
My son grabbed Mr. Horning to protect me.

William George Stimpson sworn
I was present on the occasion. I followed Mrs. Horning in. My son didn't touch Mrs. Horning at all. I could see what happened.

Cross-examined

I was in the kitchen. Mrs. Horning went into the front room as soon as she came in.

Defendant fined $2 and costs $2.50, to be paid forthwith, and in default, to be imprisoned in the common gaol at Bracebridge and there kept at hard labour for one month. Paid in full.

James Boyer, J.P.

Chapter Five

RAW NEIGHBOURLY RELATIONS

Just because people live side by side or near one another is no guarantee they will be a "neighbour" in the dictionary sense of being "one who should be friendly or as having claim on others' friendliness." On the contrary, as the following four glimpses of unfriendly life in 1890s Muskoka suggest, having human beings live close together may expose mismatched traits and rougher tendencies.

Worthy of special reflection, in considering how people may fight, is the May 1895 case against Frances E. Piper. It resulted in a nominal fine, yet a year in jail. Perhaps this sentence embodied a tacit understanding between Frances's husband, Henry Piper, and Magistrate James Boyer that such an expedient could be a convenient if low-grade form of institutionalization for a woman with mental illness, allowing her to remain in custody in Bracebridge, where Henry could more readily visit his wife than if she were removed from the community to a distant asylum for the insane.

Magistrate's Court — October 11th, 1893
Before James Boyer, J.P.
Frederick Trethewey v Robert Orr the Younger

Assault and battery at Stephenson on October 6th, 1893 on one Elizabeth Winters.

The charge having been read to defendant, he pleaded not guilty.

Elizabeth Winters sworn

I live with Mr. Trethewey in the Township of Stephenson. Last Friday, the 6th, about 11:00 a.m. I was in a field getting potatoes. Defendant came along, stood on the fence and threw a stone and struck me on the arm. He threw 2 or 3 stones but only one struck me. It was a stone of the size of the one produced. Defendant was using bad language and calling me names. I didn't answer him. My brother Robert about 9 years old was with me.

Robert Winters 9 years of age (not sworn) says

Last Friday I was in the field with my sister digging potatoes. Defendant got up on the fence and threw a stone and hit my sister. He threw several stones but only struck her once. I saw the mark where the stone struck her.

For the Defence

Defendant sworn

On Friday last I went to the field where the other witnesses were working to see if there were any chickens there. I went back to the house without speaking to anyone. The field is opposite where we live. I threw a stone but it didn't hit the witness. The little boy threw a potato at me.

Defendant convicted but no penalty imposed. Defendant paid costs of $3.05.

James Boyer, J.P.

Constable paid $1.85

Magistrate's Court — May 14th, 1895
Before James Boyer, J.P.
Sarah Hey v Frances E. Piper

For using threatening language and threatening to poison complainant and all her family, at Bracebridge, on 8th May 1895.
Defendant pleaded not guilty.

Mr. Johnson for prosecution

Sarah Hey sworn
I live in Bracebridge. I know defendant who lives on the lot west of me. On the 8th day of May I sent my two little girls for the cow. They came back and said Mrs. Piper was chasing them.

I went with the children afterwards and asked her why she did not leave my children alone. She said my children hit her cow over the eye. She called me a housebreaker, a hen thief, and a dog poisoner. She also said we wouldn't have the cow long to hurt. She would poison it and all of us too and we hadn't long to live. "Mind you, you haven't long to live." My two children were with me.

Mr. Piper was across the street. He crossed the street, whispered to his wife, and she didn't say any more. I was in fear she would do as she said.

Anna Hey sworn
I am the daughter of the last witness. I remember the 8th May last. I saw Mrs. Piper in the afternoon when my sister and I went to hunt the cow.

Mrs. Piper came out with a stick and chased us home. My mother, sister and I went out again to hunt the cow. My mother asked why she didn't leave us alone. She, Mrs. Piper, said we hit her cow across the eye. We didn't touch the cow. She called my sister and I housebreaker's daughters. She called my mother a housebreaker, hen thief, and a dog poisoner.

Later in the evening we saw Mrs. Piper on the street. She again called us a housebreaker's hen thief and dog poisoner and said, "I'll poison you all before long, and the cow too." Mr. Piper came and spoke to her and then she went away. She is in the habit of calling us names and using threatening language to us. I am very much afraid of her.

Rachel Hey sworn

I am a sister of the last witness. Mrs. Piper lives next to us. I saw Mrs. Piper on the 8th of May last. We were going after the cow when she came out with a stick and chased us back. We did not say anything to her. She called us housebreaker's daughters. I hadn't touched anything of hers. We then went and got the cow home.

Afterwards when we turned the cow out Mrs. Piper brought her cow in front of her place and stayed beside it. She called mother a housebreaker, a hen thief, and a dog poisoner. She said she would poison us and the cow too and that before very long, and that we hadn't long to live. We were all very afraid of her. Mrs. Piper calls us names every time we pass.

For the Defence

Henry A. Piper sworn

I was working in the garden. My wife was working near the house. I told her the Hey children were going up the road. Mrs. Piper went up after them. I saw one of the children hit the heifer across the face. They then ran back to the house. Mrs. Piper came right back to the house.

Mrs. Hey then came back with the children and said that she would also hit the cow if she saw it. Mrs. Piper asked Mrs. Hey to make her children leave the cow alone. Mrs. Hey called her a liar and told her to kiss her arse. In the evening Mrs. Piper did not say anything to Mrs. Hey.

Cross-examined

Mrs. Piper said to me that perhaps Mrs. Hey would have something of her own poisoned and then she would know something about it. Mrs. Piper did not say anything else.

Mrs. Hey recalled

Mrs. Piper started to talk to me first in the evening. I didn't say anything to her about poisoning a dog. Mrs. Piper said "she would poison us all" to me and not to Mr. Piper.

Defendant sworn

I went to see if my cows were alright and saw one of the girls hit my heifer on the face. Mrs. Hey came back with a stick and said she would also hit the cow. She called me a liar. I didn't say the words Mrs. Hey said I did.

Defendant ordered to enter into recognizance herself in $2 and two sureties of $1 each to keep the peace and be of good behaviour, and to pay the costs of $2.75, and in default, to be imprisoned in the common gaol for the space of 12 months.

James Boyer, J.P.

Committed.

MAGISTRATE'S COURT — SEPTEMBER 10TH, 1895
BEFORE JAMES BOYER, J.P.
ELIZA BOND, WIFE OF ROBERT BOND
v CHARLES EVERITT THE ELDER

Assault and battery at the Township of Macaulay on September 6th, 1895 on one Arthur Bond.

Defendant pleaded not guilty.

Arthur Bond sworn

I am 12 years of age and live with my father in Township of Macaulay. On the 6th September, just as it was getting dark, defendant's cow was in our turnips. I went and drove it out and was driving it along the road towards defendant's house. Defendant came up just as I turned to go home, and struck me with his clenched fist on the side of the head. It hurt me some. The blow knocked me down. Defendant did not speak to me or I to him. I had no stick. I did not beat the cow. I went home and told my mother what had happened. I did not see any one around there.

Cross-examined

You struck me. I didn't have a stick in my hand.

Eliza Bond sworn

I am the mother of the last witness. Defendant is a neighbour of ours. Last Friday evening I sent the boy to drive the cow out of our turnips. The boy came back in about 15 minutes. I could see that something had happened. I asked him what was the matter. He told me. He had a swelling on the side of the head apparently from a blow.

Cross-examined

My husband was not standing at the gate when it happened.

For the Defence

Defendant sworn

The cow was standing on the hill near me. His father sent the boy with a stick to drive the cow away. He struck the cow several times. I took hold of the stick and told him not to strike the cow. He screamed. I said, "Don't be afraid, nothing will hurt you but don't abuse the cow." The boy went home.

Defendant convicted and fined $1 and $5.45 costs, to be paid forthwith, and in default, to be imprisoned in the lock-up at Bracebridge for one calendar month with hard labour.

James Boyer, J.P.

Fine paid.
Constable $3.95
Court $ $1.50
Total $5.45
Paid constable.

Magistrate's Court — September 3rd, 1898
Before James Boyer, J.P.
Henry Chamberlain v Elias H. Traves

For that defendant on August 27th, 1898, at the Township of Oakley, did unlawfully assault and beat the said informant.
Defendant pleaded not guilty.

Henry Chamberlain sworn
I live in Oakley near to defendant. Last Saturday I saw defendant on his place which is opposite mine. It was in the morning. My wife was going to the well on her mother's lot.

Defendant said if she went he would knock her down and kick her guts out, or anyone else that took water out of that well for our house. My wife went to the well. I followed her.

Defendant got there first and sat on the well top. He said to my wife, "You could have some water if it wasn't for that rotten gutted liar at the fence." He said everybody knew I thrashed my wife. He said, "Come to me and I'll knock your face off."

I said, "That's the kind of man you are, to fight a sick man, or try to throw your mother out of doors." He said he would come over and finish me.

My wife told him not to hurt me, as I was a sick man, and said, "He can't help himself so don't you touch him."

He shook his fist in her face and told her to stand back, too, or he'd knock her down. He said he was going to finish me. He came over the fence.

I had no coat on. He caught hold of my vest and shook me, tearing the buttons off. My wife and sister-in-law interfered to prevent him hitting me. While he held me there, he tried to make me say he didn't drive the cows through the pasture.

We were in the habit of getting water from this well, and had permission to do so. This all took place on the concession road. I am suffering from heart trouble.

Susanna Chamberlain sworn

I am the wife of the last witness and I live in the Township of Oakley. On Saturday, August 27th I saw defendant on his place nearly opposite my place on the concession. I went over to defendant's place to get a pail of water. We had permission from Mr. Thomas Traves to get water there. My boy went to get water, and Elias Traves ordered him back.

I went out and asked him what I had done that he wouldn't give me a pail of water, and said that if Tom Traves said I couldn't have it I would go without.

He said if I came he'd kick my guts out. My husband was on the concession. Defendant said if it wasn't for my husband I could have some water.

I said, "You are worse than the cannibals in Africa."

Defendant said he would knock my husband down. My husband said all he could do was thrash a sick man or a boy, or put his mother out. Defendant put his fist up to knock me. I got over the fence and my sister and I and Tom got hold of him to put him off. My husband had three fainting spells after this and was in bed all Sunday. The buttons were torn off the waistcoat.

George Chamberlain sworn

I live in the Township of Draper, and am a brother of Henry Chamberlain. On Saturday morning I saw defendant in his own place. My brother was on the road. I was in my brother's house. I saw my brother after he came back.

He was sick after it.

For the Defence

Defendant sworn
On the morning in question I stopped the boy going to get the water. Mrs. Chamberlain came out and insisted on having the water. Chamberlain came to the fence and said I was a liar. His vest was not buttoned. I did not shake him. Those standing around took hold of me to pull me off.

Thomas Traves sworn
I told my brother to keep them from getting water. He did so twice. Chamberlain was calling him a liar.

Fanny Chamberlain sworn
I was there and saw defendant take hold of Chamberlain. Defendant said he didn't intend to strike him. I took hold of Traves to prevent him from fighting.

Defendant convicted and fined $1 and costs $6.36, to be paid forthwith, and in default, to be imprisoned in the common gaol at Bracebridge for the term of one month.

James Boyer, J.P. for Muskoka

Fine and costs paid.

Chapter Six

WOMEN'S FEARS AND WOMEN'S FATES

If human aggression and pettiness could be displayed by families living near one another, turbulence in personal relationships really escalated when those fighting did not even have to leave home to do it.

Yet, no matter how blighting their domestic battles nor how bitter a family's feelings, blood clans divided against themselves could also swiftly unite against outsiders. These cases, almost certainly just a fraction of the incidences of domestic violence and spousal abuse in Bracebridge and around Muskoka's townships, vividly portray feuding families. The catalogue of perils did not end there. Additional plights included a wife and children failing to get financial support, and a wife being forced to cook for crews of labourers. Muskoka women sought redress in Bracebridge Magistrate's Court, where the justice of the peace, in the absence of social services, had to come to terms with life's unmediated rawness as best he could.

With his wife and daughters in their good dresses, this Muskokan ensures his primitive homestead with its front yard of stumps is on best display. He wears his top hat, while also displaying his saw, axe, chair, and dog. Hollow logs were split and interlocked for the roof; his barn at right is near the lake; panes of glass are in most windows; washed clothes dry on the line. Whatever they'd known before, these female pioneers now faced raw simplicity incarnate.

Advances in Muskoka's townships are evident in the sawn-board walls and framed glass windows of this rural general store, with its display of brooms, shovels, hoes, rakes, buckets, and yokes. The upturned barrels might have held anything from crackers to apples. The woman carrying a metal pail, typically used for milk, may have used it in barter, trade being key to Muskoka's dollar-scarce economy.

In other cases decided by James Boyer but which are not reproduced below, four women charged men with assault and battery; in one case, the defendant paid the plaintiff and she dropped her charges; in the others, defendants pleaded guilty and paid the penalty.

Rounding out a woman's view of daily life in 1890s Muskoka, still other cases involved women pursued by aspiring lovers, women adrift in society, women protecting other women and looking after children, and women (including one whose real name, interestingly, was Mrs. Hussey) seeking escape from the house for pleasure and adventure.

MAGISTRATE'S COURT — APRIL 27TH, 1893
BEFORE MESSRS. BOYER AND SHANNON, J.P.s
ELLEN RUSSELL v AUGUSTINE RUSSELL

For having, on or about April 18th, 1893, at Monck, being able to work and thereby or by other means able to maintain complainant, his wife, did wilfully neglect so to do.
The charge, by law, having been read to defendant, he pleaded not guilty.

Ellen Russell sworn
I am the wife of the defendant and have been married to him about 23 years. About a month since, we had two children sick in the house. Defendant struck me in the face and gave me 2 black eyes and caught me by the hair of the head, beating my head against the door several times. It was about giving one of the children some medicine. Defendant has several times since then told me to get away. I left him on the 18th in consequence of his bad treatment.

One of my sons was going river driving, and defendant told him to take me with him, or to take me to hell out of there. I left there with my son and went to his father's place in Bracebridge, and stayed there Tuesday night. Defendant came there on the Wednesday night and wanted me to go home. I declined to go back, as the place is too small for such a large family.

Defendant took me to the Queen's Hotel and got a room for me. I stayed there two nights. The hotelkeeper said I had better go up to his father's and see what they were going to do with me as he only had permission to keep me one night. My husband promised Higgins to pay for my board. My husband and myself have parted several times. He has told me to go away. He uses very bad language and told me to get to hell out of there. I have 10 children living and the youngest is 4 months old. The house is 14 x 18 on the ground floor.

Henry Russell sworn
I am a son of the parties. I saw father beat my mother about the time she speaks of. I told him he had not ought to have done it. The two quarrel often enough. I have heard him tell Mother to leave on two occasions. I was sick at the time he struck mother. She told him Mrs. Piper would come and run the house. Mrs. Piper had been to the house on one occasion about 4 years ago.

Defendant convicted and sentenced to be imprisoned in the gaol at Bracebridge, and there kept at hard labour for 3 months, but judgment not to be enforced if defendant pays costs of $4.50 and promises to behave better in future and enters into his own bond in $100 to keep the peace for one year.

James Boyer, J.P.
Peter W. Shannon, J.P.

Paid costs $4.50 and entered into recognizance as above.
Paid constable $2.00.

Magistrate's Court — June 2nd, 1893
Before James Boyer, J.P.
Phoebe Ann Baxter v Harry Law

For assault and battery at Bracebridge on May 15th, 1893.
The charge having been read to defendant, he pleaded not guilty.

W. Palmer for defendant

Phoebe Ann Baxter sworn

I live with my father in Bracebridge near Perry's Mill. I have known defendant for about a month. On Monday the 15th May last, between 9 and 10 o'clock, I was coming from the Salvation Army. Defendant came from Foster's (Dominion Hotel) across the road to me, and asked to see me home. It was late and I said, "I guess so." He went with me.

We went along the railroad track, as the road was flooded. We turned along the road past William Story's house. Near the tool house on the railroad, defendant took hold of my hand. I told my younger sister who was with me to take the baby. I told him to go home. He wouldn't.

When near William Story's, he tried to throw me down, and said he was going to have it anyway. I cried to Mrs. Walls. Defendant held me. I told my sister to call Mrs. Story. He had hold of me round the waist. I screamed. He caught hold of me by the thigh.

Both Mr. and Mrs. Story came out. Defendant said I was only a damned whore anyway. Mrs. Story spoke to the defendant. I am quite sure defendant is the man. I had walked with him from the Dominion and saw him under the lamplight.

Cross-examined

Defendant used to keep company with my sister. I had the baby in my hands all the time.

Elizabeth Baxter

I am between 11 and 12 (made statement not under oath).

W.H. Story sworn

One night, near 3 weeks since, I heard some female voices calling Mrs. Story and Mrs. Walls. We were about to go to bed. It was about 10 o'clock. We both went out. I saw two girls, and heard a man's voice, but didn't see who it was.

For the Defence

Alfred Hunt sworn
Produced order cashed 31st May for 13¾ days, order dated 27th May.[1]

Alexander Foster sworn
    Am hotel keeper. Defendant boarded with me.

William H. Dodds sworn
I have been working for Wilbert Love at Port Sandfield, commenced 1st July. Defendant came with Mr. Love on 12th May instant to the mill. He worked there till last Tuesday night the 30th instant. I worked with him there on the 15th.

Complaint dismissed.

James Boyer, J.P.

---

[1]This evidence for the defence appears directed to establishing the character of defendant Harry Law as a well-grounded working man with a watertight alibi. Witness Alfred Hunt owned and operated Muskoka's first bank, and the "order" he cashed was for defendant Harry Law's wages, paid by Wilbert Love, owner of Elgin House resort near Port Sandfield, for work many miles from Bracebridge at the time he was alleged to be in Bracebridge. William Dodds corroborates that. Other witnesses could not positively identify Law as the man in question.

MAGISTRATE'S COURT — JANUARY 2ND, 1894
BEFORE MESSRS. BROWNING, SPENCER AND BOYER, J.P.s
ELLEN RUSSELL V AUGUSTINE RUSSELL

For deserting of wife and neglecting to maintain family at Monck on December 28th, 1893.

Defendant pleaded not guilty.

Ellen Russell sworn

I am the wife of the defendant. I have been living with my son since last haymaking. My son had been supporting me. I went on Wednesday last to the store where I had been in the habit of getting goods on my husband's account. She refused to give me any more goods. I have not received any money from my husband to support the family since my youngest child was born about a year since. My husband has not been living with me since July last. Neither my husband nor son has provided me with necessary clothing for myself or the children. I have 5 children not able to earn their own living.

Cross-examined

I have lived on the farm during the time. I went back to the farm to help the boys. We have had flour and meal brought in by my son.

Order refused.

James Boyer, J.P.
R.M. Browning, J.P.
William H. Spencer, J.P.

Magistrate's Court — March 19th, 1894
Before James Boyer, J.P.
and Singleton Brown, Reeve
Robert E. Armstrong v Hugh L. Dickson

For that he, the said Hugh L. Dickson, being a person able to work and thereby or by other means able to maintain his family, did wilfully neglect so to do.

The charge having been read to prisoner, he pleaded not guilty.

Anne Kirk sworn

I am the wife of George Kirk, living in Bracebridge. On the 24th of October last, prisoner brought three children to my place to board. He agreed to pay ten dollars a month for their board. He has only paid $11.30. I asked him for money last week, he gave me 30 cents and said that was all he had. He has had money lately. Last Friday night I made complaint to the mayor of the town. Last week another child of the prisoner came to the house. Last Wednesday the father took this child away and the child came back to my place again at night.

Alfred Hunt sworn

I am the Mayor of Bracebridge. Mrs. Kirk came to me last Friday and stated that she had four children of Dickson's to keep, that she had kept three of them five months and had only received $11.30 for their board. I brought the matter before the council, who granted an order for $10.00 for Mrs. Kirk to assist in supporting the children.

Prisoner convicted and sentenced to be imprisoned in the common gaol at Bracebridge, and there kept at hard labour for the term of one calendar month.

James Boyer, J.P.
Singleton Brown, Reeve

Conviction returned.

MAGISTRATE'S COURT — SEPTEMBER 24TH, 1894
BEFORE JAMES BOYER, J.P.
MARGARET JANE MCBRIDE V ROBERT MCBRIDE

Assault and battery at Township of Draper on September 17th, 1894.
The charge having been read to defendant, he pleaded not guilty.

Margaret Jane McBride sworn
I am the wife of defendant and live in Draper. On the afternoon of 17th I was washing. My husband came in and asked me if it was true I was to meet a certain young man on the road. I said, "No, I didn't meet the young man." He called me vile names. I took my hand to give him a slap in the mouth. He took hold of me by the hair and one arm and pushed my head down and tried to break my neck. He pulled a quantity of hair out of my head. I got down on the floor. He then sat on me, on my body, and threatened to finish me unless I answered a question.

He sent the little girl for Mr. Cairns. He held me on the floor for about an hour, and still had hold of my hair. Mr. and Mrs. Cairns came over. He let me go. Mrs. Cairns took me away with her. He made me spit blood. He has threatened my life on several occasions. My arms were bruised and my shoulder also in trying to get away from him. I am afraid to live with him.

Cross-examined
I did strike him and took a pipe out of his mouth. We struggled for 10 or 15 minutes before he got me down on the floor. I never threatened him or assaulted him before.

David Cairns sworn
I live in Draper, about a mile from the defendant. I was sent to defendant's place. I went there. I saw defendant and his wife sitting on the floor. She had a child at the breast. Defendant had hold of her by the hair of her head. I said,

"Robert what is this? I thought you promised me you would never strike her again." He said, "Neither have I. If I had, that would be the last of it." I said, "Let go of her head and let her get up." He did so. She went to my house with my wife. I have heard defendant threaten his wife about a year ago.

For the Defence

Robert McBride, defendant, sworn

Last Monday I had heard something about my wife. I asked her about it. I was sitting on the log in the house near where she was washing. I said, "Did Mrs. Cairns not tell you so and so (alluding to the report)?" She said, "No, it's some of your lies." She said she would tear the liver out of me. She scratched my nose, pushed me back against the wall. I caught her by the wrist. She hit me on the hand. I didn't strike her. She tore my shirt and I put my hand in her hair and she pulled me down.

Defendant convicted and fined $5 and $11.30 costs, to be paid forthwith, and in default, to be imprisoned in the common gaol at Bracebridge and there kept at hard labour for 2 calendar months and to enter into his own bond in $200 and 2 sureties in $100 each to keep the peace towards his wife for 12 months.

James Boyer, J.P.

Fine $5.00
Constable $2.95 Paid
Witness John P. $2.15 Paid
James P. $2.15 Paid
David C. $2.15 Paid
Court $1.90
Total $16.30

Paid October 1st, 1894

Recognizance entered into by defendant in amount of $200 (Angus McLeod, Bracebridge, lumberman, $100; John McLeod, $100).

September 29th, 1894
Filed recognizance with Clerk of the Peace.
    Conviction returned.

Magistrate's Court — October 29th, 1894
Before James Boyer, J.P.
Martha Fennell v Gustavus A. Binyon

Assault and battery at Bracebridge on October 26th, 1894.
The charge having been read to defendant he pleaded not guilty.

Martha Fennell sworn
I live in Bracebridge. On the 26th October instant, shortly after 9 o'clock
p.m., I was at defendant's house. Defendant's wife asked me to go to the
Free Methodist Church. I consented to go. Defendant asked what time we
would be back. His wife said soon after 9 o'clock.

It was after going to the Free Methodist Church we went to defendant's
house. I went in there with his wife after coming from the church. Defendant
told me he wanted to speak to me. He asked me to sit down in the shop.
He accused his wife and myself of having boys follow us. I said no one had
followed us. He said he had watched them. Defendant's wife and myself
went in the kitchen and he made the same charge. He said he didn't want
Mr. Fennell to think he was coaxing me there.

In consequence of what defendant's daughter said to me, I intended to
stay there that night. I told defendant if he didn't want me to stay there were
other places I could go to. I said I would take my things and go. He said
there was a bed there and I was welcome to stay. I picked up my things to go.
Defendant then grabbed his wife by the back of the neck and struck me on
the face, on the jaw. I told him I would call the constable. I then went away.

Cross-examined

My face was not bruised. Defendant unlocked the door and I went out. The blow was struck in the kitchen. He had not told me twice that evening to leave his house. I started to leave as soon as he told me. I was going when he told me. I was hurt a little.

For the Defence

Gustavus A. Binyon sworn

My daughter asked me on Thursday afternoon if Mrs. Fennell could stay at my place from Thursday to Sunday. I said I didn't want her to stay to create trouble between herself and husband. I told her to go out on Thursday evening, as herself and my wife came in about 20 minutes past 9. I put my hands on her to put her out. The first time she didn't go. I didn't strike her. She said if you don't want me here I can go. It was in the kitchen I pushed her.

Cross-examined

I took you by the shoulder to put you out. I was sober at the time.[2]

Elizabeth Binyon sworn

I am wife of defendant. Complainant came on Thursday afternoon with my husband's daughter. I didn't invite her to stay. On Friday she stayed at our place till evening. After we came back from the church my husband said to complainant he was not going to harbour another man's wife. He asked her twice to leave.

She had some things there which she wanted before she went. I was doing some sewing for her. It was not finished. My husband took hold of

---

[2] That Gustavus Binyon had to testify about his sobriety on cross-examination relates to the fact he had a companion in the bottle. In a case produced in Chapter 11: Worse for the Liquor, James Boyer convicted him on charges of being drunk and disorderly in public.

me by the back of the neck and then took hold of complainant by the back of the neck. She was not struck at all.

Complaint dismissed.

James Boyer, J.P.

MAGISTRATE'S COURT — MAY 31ST, 1895
BEFORE JAMES BOYER, J.P.
CATHERINE WATSON V JOHN WATSON

For having on May 30th, 1895, at the Town of Bracebridge, threatened his wife, the complainant, as follows: "If you go home I'll put these scissors through you."
Defendant pleaded guilty. Defendant required to find sureties, himself in $200 and two sureties in $100 each, to keep the peace and be of good behaviour towards his wife for 12 months, and to pay the costs of the proceedings $4.30 or to be committed in default.

Defendant, and Neil Livingston and Peter Hutchison, entered into recognizances as above.

James Boyer, J.P.

Paid.
Returned.

Magistrate's Court — June 25th, 1895
Before James Boyer, J.P.
Margaret Donald v Frederick Donald

Assault and battery at the Township of Monck on April 23rd, 1895.
Defendant pleaded not guilty.

Margaret Donald sworn

I am the wife of the defendant, and live in the Township of Monck. On the 23rd of April last I told my son Norman to give the pigs some feed. This was in the morning. My husband was present in the house. He gave me a blow in the face with his closed hand. The blow made a bruise on my brow.

He had not spoken to me or I to him when he struck me. I ran into another room out of his way. He followed me, took the frying pan off the stove and struck me with it on the left side, and said if the boys left me he would murder me. He has threatened many times to murder me. My side was injured from the blow and is not well yet. Defendant is of very violent temper and has several times beaten me.

Norman Donald sworn

I am the son of the parties and live with them. I remember on the 23rd of April last, Mother told me to give the pigs some feed. He said to me to take the peas. He then got up and struck Ma on the forehead. Mother then scratched his face. She then went into another room. Defendant had the frying pan. He threw it at Mother's head and struck her on the side. He said if my brothers went out he would knock her down and cut her throat. Mother went out into the garden. I have on many occasions seen my father strike my mother.

Cross-examined

I saw you throw the frying pan at my mother. I was in the room.

For the Defence

Defendant sworn

On the day in question a man came to castrate the pigs. I said the pigs should have the peas so as to catch them. My wife said they shouldn't have any. I put my hand to push her aside. She scratched my face. I went to take hold of her. My oldest son got between us, pushed me back, and said you are at it again. She struck me on the head with a lifter. I went to shut the door.

The boys tried to keep me in. I showed Mason my face. He said, "It's very pretty." I then went in. She was in the bedroom. The oldest son was in the room. I admit taking the frying pan in my passion and I admit having thrown it, but I had no intention of striking her. It didn't strike her but struck between her and the bed.

Norman Donald recalled

It was a blow with the clenched fist my father struck her. I saw the frying pan strike my mother on the left side.

Defendant constricted and fined $10 and costs $5.95, and in default of immediate payment, to be imprisoned in the common gaol at Bracebridge and there kept at hard labour for the space of two months, and also to enter into recognizance himself in $200 with two sureties in $100 each, to keep the peace toward his wife for one year or be committed in default.

Constable $3.70
Court $2.25
Total $5.95

Defendant paid the fine and costs, and entered into recognizance himself in $200 and Charles Donald of Monck, farmer, in $200 to keep the peace for 12 months.

Filed recognizance

James Boyer, J.P.

Receipt attached:

Bracebridge June 29th, 1895

Received from J. Boyer Esq., J.P., the sum of ten dollars, being fine imposed in the case of Donald v Donald.

William H. Spencer
Treasurer of Monck

Magistrate's Court — December 28th, 1895
Before James Boyer, J.P.
Charles Devall v Ignatius Elf

Assault and battery at Bracebridge on December 27th, 1895.

The charge having been read to prisoner, he pleaded not guilty.

Ida Jane Devall sworn

I am the wife of Chas. Devall of this township. About 8:30 last night, in the absence of my husband, defendant came in and brought a picture of my husband's first wife and put it on the table. I said my husband was at the lodge. He told me to tell my husband to come down to the British Lion Hotel next morning.

I was sitting at the table combing my hair when prisoner caught me by the hair and took hold of my chin. He said I would take a very nice picture and he hoped he would have it to do.

I had my hand on the table and prisoner caught hold of it and rubbed it on the table. He went away but came back about half past nine and wanted me to take a ride with him in the rig. He was under the influence of liquor.

Cross-examined by Mr. Mahaffy

Thomas Longhery sworn

I was at Mr. Devall's house when defendant came in the first time. He caught Mrs. Devall by the hair, and after he had taken hold of her hand he said she would take a nice picture. She laughed at him and then left the room and did not come back.

Cross-examined by Mr. Mahaffy

Mrs. Devall was half-crying and half-laughing.

John Devall

Mr. Devall is my father. I was at home when defendant came to the house last night, about half past nine. Defendant said he came back the second time to see if my father was home.

Defendant sworn

I had to deliver a picture of Mr. Devall's first wife to Mr. Devall.

Case dismissed.

James Boyer, J.P.

MAGISTRATE'S COURT — FEBRUARY 24TH, 1896
BEFORE JAMES BOYER, J.P.
ELIZABETH BINYON V GUSTAVUS A. BINYON

Assault and battery at the Town of Bracebridge on or about January 20th, 1896.

Defendant entered into recognizance in $2.00, to keep the peace and be of good behaviour towards the said Elizabeth Binyon for one year from date.[3]

James Boyer, J.P.

Paid costs.

Paid constable 50 cents.

Magistrate's Court — July 6th, 1896
Before James Boyer, J.P.
Martha Nichols v Charles Everitt the Elder

Assault and battery at the Township of McLean on June 3rd, 1896.
Defendant pleaded not guilty.

Martha Nicholls sworn

I live in the Township of McLean near to prisoner. On the 3rd June last, about 11 o'clock a.m., I saw prisoner on the road near my house. I went out to him to ask him for some money he owed me. I asked him when he was going to pay it. He said, "Never." I said, "Give me up the goods you got." He said, "Go to hell, you damned old slut." I said, "Don't call me such names."

He dropped a milk pail he had in his hand and caught hold of the barrel of his gun with both hands and struck at me with the butt end. I think I stepped back. The gun just missed striking me on the head. He again called me a damned old slut.

Cross-examined

I never grabbed you by the neck.

Samuel Nicholls sworn

---

[3]Five months later, Gustavus Binyon would again be convicted by James Boyer for assaulting his wife, Elizabeth — an event reported in a following case.

I am the son of the last witness and live with her. On a Wednesday in the early part of June I saw prisoner coming along the road. I told mother. She went and asked him when he intended to pay the money. He said, "Never," and said, "Go to hell, you damned old slut."

My mother didn't take hold of prisoner or touch him. He struck at her with the butt of the gun which went within a few inches of her head. I was about 12 feet off. He went off a little way and turned round and again called her a damned old slut.

For the Defence

Prisoner sworn
I didn't raise the gun to strike her but only to push her hand away when she grabbed me by the neck. I said she needn't think she would thrash me, same as she did Powers.

Prisoner convicted and fined $10 and $7.88 costs, to be paid forthwith, and in default, to be imprisoned in the common gaol at Bracebridge and there kept at hard labour for 2 calendar months.

James Boyer, J.P.

Constable $6.38 Paid
Court $1.50 Paid

MAGISTRATE'S COURT — JULY 17TH, 1896
BEFORE JAMES BOYER, J.P.
SARAH KENNEDY V GUSTAVUS A. BINYON

Assault and battery on his wife, Elizabeth Binyon, at Bracebridge, on July 16th, 1896.

The charge having been read to defendant, he pleaded not guilty.

Mr. Palmer for the defendant.

Elizabeth Binyon sworn
I am the wife of the defendant. Yesterday evening defendant came in and asked for his dinner. It was ready for him. He swore at me, called me bad names and struck me on the nose with his clenched fist. I went out in the kitchen. He followed me and caught hold of me by the back of the neck and hurt me.

Cross-examined by Mr. Palmer.
He swore at me and called me names as soon as he came in.

Sarah Kennedy sworn
I am the wife of Samuel Kennedy and live in part of the same house as defendant. I rent part of the house from defendant.

Yesterday between 3 and 4 p.m. defendant came home. He was cursing and swearing about his dinner. His wife had the dinner on the table. He came over to where she was standing and slapped her in the face with his fist. She said, "You aren't going to do it again." He followed her into the kitchen and grabbed her by the back of the neck. She cried. I went for the constable.

Cross-examined
I didn't have any conversation with defendant about his wife. She didn't ask me to lay the information. I laid it because she was afraid.

Samuel Kennedy sworn
I live in the same house with defendant. I was at home yesterday afternoon when this occurred. Binyon was swearing as he came in. I heard his wife tell him not to do that again as I came in at the door. Mrs. Binyon went

into the kitchen. Defendant followed her, took her by the back of the neck, made her cry out and pushed her into his own room.

For the Defence

Defendant sworn

Yesterday afternoon I went home to get my dinner. I had taken some provisions home previous to that. I went in. My wife and Mrs. Kennedy were in the room. I complained that flies were on the food on the table. I didn't strike her but took her by the back of the neck and told her to get my dinner.

Defendant convicted and fined $10 and $5.30 costs, to be paid forthwith, and in default, to be imprisoned and kept at hard labour in the common gaol at Bracebridge for the space of six weeks.

James Boyer, J.P.

Court $1.80
Constable $3.50
Total $5.30
Paid.
Paid constable.
Conviction returned.

Magistrate's Court — October 24th, 1896
Before James Boyer, J.P.
Mary Jane Yeoman v John Yeoman

Assault and battery on complainant (his wife), at Bracebridge, on October 17th, 1896.

The charge having been read to defendant, he pleaded not guilty.

Mary Jane Yeoman sworn

I am the wife of the defendant. Last Saturday night, the 17th, defendant came home drunk and said, "Is that all there is to eat in the house?" I had not much in the house as defendant had not given me any money lately. I told him there was a bill for $13 rent. Defendant struck me across the mouth and ordered me out of the house, and said it would be my life next. I then went for a constable.

For the Defence

John Yeoman sworn

I came home on Saturday last, after being at work 3½ weeks up the lake. Some people in town was owing me money and had promised to pay it while I was away. I left $4 at home before I went away. I do not remember about the trouble at home and how it began.

Defendant fined $1 and $5.41 costs, to be paid forthwith, and in default, to be imprisoned in the common gaol at Bracebridge for 21 days with hard labour and to enter into his own recognizance in $100 to keep the peace for one year.

James Boyer, J.P.

Conviction returned.

Defendant entered into recognizance to keep the peace for one year. He was given one week to pay the fine and costs. On November 2, he paid $5 on account. Account later paid in full, and constable was paid by the justice of the peace $3.31.

Contemporaneously, John Yeoman was busy bringing an action against his employer, John Baird, for eight dollars unpaid wages. See Chapter 17: Bartering for Work, Fighting for Wages.

MAGISTRATE'S COURT — MARCH 2ND, 1898
BEFORE JAMES BOYER, J.P.
SAMUEL A. SPENCER V MARY ANN BICKFORD

Charge: Insanity and dangerous to be at large.

Defendant, who had been arrested and remanded so that further inquiries could be made, was brought before me and discharged.

James Boyer, J.P.

Costs in above case $1.25.

MAGISTRATE'S COURT — JULY 2ND, 1898
BEFORE JAMES BOYER, J.P.
AND SINGLETON BROWN, J.P.
GEORGE WILSON V CHARLOTTE WILSON

For having, on June 30th, 1898, at the Township of Muskoka, unlawfully assaulted and beaten the said George Wilson.

Defendant pleaded not guilty.

George Wilson sworn

I live in the Township of Muskoka. Defendant is my wife. On the 29th of June, a man came to hire with me to cut cordwood. Another man was leaving. I engaged the man. Defendant refused to have any man any longer around the place. I had been boarding the men who worked for me. Taylor Marsland has been working for me and boarding with me.

She told Marsland she would make him go. If he didn't go she would throw his clothes out. I said I wanted him to stay. She then began breaking the crockery and the window and sash, and threw some of the crockery at me. She said she wasn't able to work for the men, and I told her I would do the work and pay for her board somewhere else. I had got the dinner nearly ready when the men began to come. She said she would not let them come and went to meet them with the well pole. She threatened to level them with this if they set foot in the garden. I took the well pole away from her. I caught and held her until the men went into the house.

Defendant went and lay down on the bed part of the time and part of the time on the doorstep between the rooms. This was on the 30th that we came up to dinner as aforesaid. After dinner we went out under a shade tree. Defendant came out and asked for the sugar bowl and butter dish, about which I knew nothing. She declared she would smash every dish in the house if I didn't fetch them. She began to do so and broke some of them. I ran in and stopped her. I picked her up and threw her on the bed and asked her to behave herself. She said, "No, she would die first." She then bit me. The mark on my thigh was caused by her biting me.

Taylor Marsland sworn

I have been working for complainant and boarding in his house. There had been two men working and boarding there. She threatened to throw my clothes out on the 29th. On the 30th, when we came up to dinner, she said she wouldn't let the men come in the house. She said that if I ever put my foot inside the fence she would knock me down with the well pole. I saw her throw some saucers at me. I heard crockery breaking when defendant was alone in the house. I heard Mr. Wilson, when he and defendant were alone in the house, tell her not to bite him, and I saw the wound in his thigh. She threatened to destroy the clothes belonging to me and the other man. I saw her strike at Mr. Wilson with a stone. He did not throw defendant out of the house. She asked Jack Wilson to help her.

John Wilson sworn

I am not any relation to the parties concerned. I work at Mrs. Wilson's and get my meals there but do not sleep there. I heard a disturbance between the parties on both days. I saw a hat thrown out.

Thomas McLachlan sworn

I went to work for Mr. Wilson on Wednesday the 29th. I was going to live in the house. I saw defendant on the 30th pick up a stone as if to throw at him but he rushed in and took it away. I heard complainant tell defendant she could go and board out and he would do the work and pay her board.

Defendant convicted and fined $1 and $3.57 costs, and in default of immediate payment, to be imprisoned in the common gaol at Bracebridge for the space of one calendar month and to be bound over to keep the peace for one year.

Recognizance entered into by herself in $100.

James Boyer, J.P.

> Paid constable.
> Conviction returned.

MAGISTRATE'S COURT — AUGUST 8TH, 1898
BEFORE JAMES BOYER, J.P.
JENNIE HUSSEY V FRANK HUSSEY

For having, on August 7th, 1898, at the Town of Bracebridge, unlawfully assaulted and beaten the said Jennie Hussey.

Defendant pleaded not guilty.

Jennie Hussey sworn

I am defendant's wife. About 8 o'clock last night Father Collins asked me to go up the lakes to sell tickets today at the regatta. My husband seemed willing I should go. I was getting my lunch ready. He said, "Put up enough lunch, I'm going too. I'll tag you all around and see what you'll do." I said he could go to the devil. I was going but he was not going with me. He said,

"You damned bitch, I'll show you if you'll go without me." He said he knew what I was going up for. I was going "to have a high old time." I picked up a stick and went towards him when he struck me in the mouth. I then hit him with the stick. This was not the first time he struck me.

Annie Gore sworn

I am living with my aunt Mrs. Hussey at present. I was there last night. Mrs. Hussey was putting up lunch. He said, "Put up more lunch, I am going too." She took no notice the first time but the second time she said, "You can go yourself then. You're not going with me. You can go to the devil. I won't have you tagging after me." He said, "You damned bitch, I'll show you whether I'll go or not." She picked up the top of a box and then I ran out.

Francis Martin sworn

I was at Hussey's last night. Mrs. Hussey was doing up lunch to go on the excursion today. Defendant told her to put up more lunch. She said, "You go to the devil, you are not going to tag round after me all day." He said, "You damned bitch." He then went to the drawer to get the purse and shoved her back out of the way. She then picked up a board and I ran out. I came back with Annie Gore and he said, "None of your sneaking around here, there's nobody killed."

Defendant convicted and fined $1.00 and $4.75 costs, and to enter into his own bond in $100 to keep the peace for one year and in default of immediate payment, be imprisoned in the common gaol at Bracebridge for the space of one month.

James Boyer, J.P.

Fine and costs paid and recognizance entered into.

Paid constable $3.

Conviction returned.

MAGISTRATE'S COURT — AUGUST 9TH, 1898
BEFORE JAMES BOYER, J.P.
ALFRED STUNDEN v WILLIAM E. FLEMING

For having, on or about August 5th, 1898, at the Village of Huntsville, threatened to kill one Blanche Royal.

Defendant pleaded not guilty.

Blanche Royal sworn

I live in the Township of Stisted. I went there last Thursday. I know the defendant. I saw him about four or five o'clock at Stisted on Friday evening the 5th. I said nothing to him. He stayed around the place an hour or two.

On Saturday the 6th I went to Huntsville. About 1 o'clock p.m. Dan McCarthy drove me to Huntsville. He was with me, and we tried to avoid defendant, who was following us. Defendant handed me the note produced, marked "A." He had another letter which he let me see. It consisted of about four sheets. I read one sheet when he snatched it away again. In it he said he intended following me around and making my life a perfect hell even if he had to follow me on foot. He said that I caused all this trouble and could avoid it by marrying him. He said he didn't intend to harm me then, but when he did he'd let me know, and no matter where I went a pistol shot would reach a long way.

I was standing alone when he came up and asked me to send him a note saying whether I would marry him or would he follow me all around. I said I would send the note to get rid of him.

On Sunday morning he sent the note produced, marked "B," by the little boy, and said he would wait on the hill for an answer. I knew defendant in Washington, D.C. He wanted to keep company with me. Before leaving Washington I told him I didn't want anything more to do with him. We went to Toronto about the 17th of May. He followed about 2 weeks after. I wrote to him before he came to Toronto but gave him no encouragement. He went back to Washington but returned about the latter part of June.

He threatened that if I didn't renew my former promises with him that he would kill me. He frightened me, so I said I would. A week ago Sunday, in Toronto, he sent me a note by a boy. It said that he intended to kill me that night at eight o'clock so I'd better say my prayers. When going out the door he renewed his threat and also threatened to cut my throat from ear to ear with a razor. From the threats made by defendant I am in fear that he will take my life.

Dan McCarthy sworn
I live in the Township of Stisted. I know last witness and am working for her father. I have seen defendant at Royal's farm on Friday. On Saturday I saw him in Huntsville. I was sent in by Mr. Royal on business. Mrs. Royal went with me.

Defendant followed her about different places in Huntsville. He met us at last and put his hand in his pocket. She stepped back and he handed her the piece of paper produced. He said she needn't be afraid of him. She said she didn't want to have anything to do with him. He said, "You know what I want you to do. Be careful or I'll carry out what I said in Toronto." He said, "It's no use you running away from me, for a pistol shot will reach a long way." He followed her about wherever she went. She had read part of the second letter when he snatched it away from her.

For the Defence

Defendant sworn
I never intended to harm the girl, Blanche Royal, at all. I never did her any harm. I am selling nursery stock for Stone & Wellington. My object in going up to Stisted was to get introductions through Mr. Royal to the farmers up there which would assist me in my business. She stepped back and we talked for quite a while.

Defendant ordered to enter into bond to keep the peace, for $200 and one surety $200, and to pay the costs of this enquiry $11.64 and in default, to be imprisoned in the common gaol at Bracebridge for the space of twelve months.

James Boyer, J.P.

Committed to gaol.
Constable $9.99
Court $1.65
Total $11.64

Chapter Seven

Hard Love for the Indigent

In late nineteenth century Muskoka, poverty was deemed the fault of those suffering it. Little help for the indigent came from government, except when a municipal council in a dire circumstance might intermittently make a compassionate gesture, a modest, one-time payment. Churches and fraternal organizations assisted their impoverished members in practical ways, but, often, poor people were neither adherents nor members so did not benefit.

Alcohol was a cause of downfall for many living in poverty. Local chapters of provincial organizations for temperance and "moral uplift" sought to improve the lot of distressed and disadvantaged Muskokans by persuading them to forsake booze and embrace God.

It would only be once a sense of *collective* responsibility developed that the welfare state became possible, providing "universal coverage" for all members of a disadvantaged class. In the twentieth century, the social welfare movement in Ontario, supported province-wide by reformers in local communities such as Bracebridge, would spawn government programs, social agencies, administrative structures, and a range of entitlements aimed at improving the conditions of people struggling with the rawness of life.

That sea change first required a reordering of society's view of itself. In the late nineteenth century, there were few social agencies to step in. Life was still austere. Justices of the peace had to address the plight of poor people *individually*, a man or a woman arraigned in court whose problem was real in that moment.

The following ten cases display "hard love" for the indigent. The town constable arrested the homeless under the Criminal Code's vagrancy prohibitions, Magistrate Boyer tried them summarily, and the men were put in the town jail where regular meals, dry bedding, and warm shelter came free. Unemployed homeless men who had no visible means of support were incarcerated in Bracebridge in the 1890s for periods of varying length: twenty-one days, thirty days, ten weeks, three calendar months, three calendar months with hard labour, and six months with hard labour. Often their "punishment" coincided with onset of chill winter weather. The town paid the cost of feeding the incarcerated men. Simple and crude, this rudimentary welfare program seemed the most practical expedient in the circumstances.

Even so, in several cases, the punishment of vagrants seemed unduly harsh, as if James Boyer, who was also clerk of the municipality and aware of council's sentiments and limited resources, intended to send a signal through the grapevine to drifting hobos that Bracebridge was a place to steer clear of.

Most vagrants were men who welcomed a safe place to sleep, but not one. Elizabeth Jackson pleaded guilty and chose to pay her fine and court costs, rather than serve time. Indeed, of all these 1890s vagrancy cases, hers was the only sentence with that choice. James Boyer evidently understood that Elizabeth Jackson had an option unavailable to male vagrants of that era, a theme returned to in Chapter 16: Pressures on the Sex Trade. Presumably, they both considered it better for her to be free to circulate in the community instead of being fed and housed at the expense of the municipality. There was, moreover, no separate jail facility for females.

In one other of these cases, something more than meets the eye was also probably happening. In mid-November 1894, Harry Catlin and George Earle, two homeless men with nothing to eat and no shelter except the town fire hall into which they'd crawled late at night, were convicted for vagrancy by James Boyer, who then suspended their sentences. They could walk free and had no fine to pay.

No explanation for that decision is given in the bench book, but the JP would have known that levying a fine against impoverished men would only have resulted in locking them up for failure to pay. Since it was November, with harsh winter conditions a few weeks off, and since Catlin and Earle were likely not local men but two drifters travelling as a pair, this freedom sentence was their ticket to move on. Because the two were not heard from again, presumably they kept right on drifting, "riding the rails" on freight trains that since 1885 connected Bracebridge to a wider world, to try their luck in another community, as James likely surmised they would.

Unemployed drifters who settled into the Bracebridge fire hall to sleep for the night, rather than sneaking unobserved into a farmer's barn as others who were loners often did, knew they would be detected by local authorities and, in the bargain, hopefully get sentenced to a period of being housed and fed in Her Majesty's Hotel. That was not to be the "hard love" fate of Catlin and Earle in 1894 Bracebridge.

MAGISTRATE'S COURT — DECEMBER 11TH, 1893
BEFORE MESSRS. PRATT AND BOYER, J.P.s
ROBERT E. ARMSTRONG V JONATHAN FERGUSON

For having no visible means of subsistence at Bracebridge on December 10th, 1893.
The charge having been read to prisoner, he pleaded guilty.

Prisoner committed to the gaol at Bracebridge for 10 weeks.

James Boyer J.P.
Josiah Pratt J.P.

Conviction returned.

MAGISTRATE'S COURT — NOVEMBER 15TH, 1894
BEFORE JAMES BOYER, J.P.
ROBERT E. ARMSTRONG V ALEXANDER BOLTON

For that defendant, on November 15th, 1894, was at Bracebridge not having any visible means of maintaining himself and did live without employment.

Robert E. Armstrong sworn
I am a constable for the District of Muskoka. I found the prisoner lying down in the fire hall at Bracebridge. He had no authority to be there. Prisoner has been begging in the town.

Prisoner convicted and sentenced to be imprisoned in the common gaol at Bracebridge and there kept at hard labour for 6 months.

James Boyer, J.P.

Conviction returned.

MAGISTRATE'S COURT — NOVEMBER 15TH, 1894
BEFORE JAMES BOYER, J.P.
ROBERT E. ARMSTRONG V HARRY CATLIN,
GEORGE EARLE

For that defendants, on November 14th, 1894, at Bracebridge not having any visible means of maintaining themselves did live without employment.

Robert E. Armstrong sworn
I found the prisoners in the fire hall Bracebridge last night about midnight.

Prisoners said they were resting themselves. I locked them up. They said they had nothing to eat.

Prisoners convicted and judgment suspended.

James Boyer, J.P.

Magistrate's Court — January 5th, 1895
Before James Boyer, J.P.
Robert E. Armstrong v William Kirby

For that defendant, at Bracebridge, on January 5th, 1895, being a person not having any visible means of maintaining himself did live without employment.

Prisoner committed to common gaol at Bracebridge for 21 days.

James Boyer, J.P.

Conviction returned.

Magistrate's Court — January 19th, 1895
Before James Boyer, J.P.
Robert E. Armstrong v James Harvie

For that defendant, at Bracebridge, on January 19th, 1895, being a person not having any visible means of maintaining himself did live without employment.

Prisoner pleaded guilty.

Prisoner committed to common gaol at Bracebridge for 30 days.

James Boyer, J.P.

Conviction returned.

Magistrate's Court — December 3rd, 1895
Before James Boyer, J.P.
Thomas Dodd v William Fraser

For that defendant, on December 2nd, 1895, at the Town of Bracebridge, being a loose, idle or disorderly person, not having any visible means of maintaining himself, did live without employment.

The charge having been read to prisoner, he pleaded not guilty.

Thomas Dodd sworn

I am constable and night watchman of Bracebridge. On Sunday morning, at 10 minutes past 12 a.m., I saw prisoner pushed out of Binyon's. Binyon asked me to take him away. I was going to meet the train and couldn't do so. As I returned from the station I saw a man on the sidewalk opposite Thomas Street. He fell down. I watched him awhile. He went as far as Hidds Hotel and tried to get in, and then went towards the British Lion Hotel. He fell two or three times towards the sheriff's office. I took hold of him. I took him to the lock-up but as the gaoler wouldn't take him without a warrant, I put him in the fire hall to keep him from freezing.

The night before last I again found prisoner in the fire hall — about a quarter past 10 — very much under the influence of liquor. He fell against a ladder. I let him remain there that night. Last night, shortly after 10 o'clock, I again found him in the fire hall sleeping. The reeve told me to have him arrested. Prisoner told me he had no money nor no home.

Prisoner convicted and sentenced to be imprisoned in the common gaol at Bracebridge and there kept at hard labour for 3 calendar months.

James Boyer, J.P.

Conviction returned.

MAGISTRATE'S COURT — DECEMBER 26TH, 1895
BEFORE JAMES BOYER, J.P.
ROBERT E. ARMSTRONG V HENRY ALEXANDER EVANS

For that prisoner, on December 25th, 1895, at Bracebridge, being a loose, idle or disorderly person not having any visible means of maintaining himself, did live without employment.

Prisoner committed to the common gaol at Bracebridge and kept there at hard labour for 3 calendar months.

James Boyer, J.P.

Conviction returned.

MAGISTRATE'S COURT — JUNE 22ND, 1896
BEFORE JAMES BOYER, J.P.
THOMAS DODD V C. WILLIAM INMAN

For that defendant, on June 16th, 1896, at Bracebridge, being a loose, idle or disorderly person and not having any visible means of maintaining himself, did live without employment.

Defendant pleaded not guilty.

Thomas Dodd sworn

I am a constable for the Town of Bracebridge. On Tuesday the 22nd I arrested the defendant about 7 a.m. He was throwing his hat up in the air, running across the street and shouting. The man acted as if he was insane. I locked him up as he was not safe to be at large.

Defendant convicted and committed to the common gaol at Bracebridge for 30 days.

James Boyer, J.P.

Conviction returned.

MAGISTRATE'S COURT — JUNE 25TH, 1898
BEFORE JAMES BOYER, J.P.
JAMES ARNOTT V ELIZABETH JACKSON

For that defendant, on June 19th, 1898, at Bracebridge, being a person not having any visible means of maintaining herself, did live without employment.

Defendant pleaded guilty.

Fined $2 and $3.50 costs, to be paid forthwith, and in default, to be imprisoned and kept at hard labour in the common gaol at Bracebridge for 21 days.

James Boyer, J.P.

Fine paid.
Conviction returned.

Magistrate's Court — December 14th, 1898
Before James Boyer, J.P.
James Arnott v William Elliott

For that defendant, on December 13th, 1898, at Bracebridge, being a loose, idle or disorderly person not having any means of maintaining himself, did live without employment.

Prisoner pleaded guilty.

Committed to common gaol at Bracebridge for 3 months.

James Boyer, J.P.

Chapter Eight

UNSANITARY CONDITIONS AND PUBLIC HEALTH FEVERS

Today food products are "recalled" for health and safety reasons, often after a number of deaths have occurred. Such recalls are usually accompanied by anxious voices chorusing for "security of the food supply," as if measures could exist to ensure no harm would ever again befall eaters. What was it like in the good old days?

In Bracebridge in the 1890s, cases came before Magistrate's Court because of maggots in the butcher's corned beef, blue mould on the beef, uncooked offal in the pig swill, dead horses partly buried in the ground, toxic cleaner's fluid poured out a laundry shop window to drain away beneath adjacent buildings, garbage thrown into the streets and town ravines, and raw sewage dumped onto open land within the town boundaries. Sooner or later, each proved hard to hide from the nostrils of townsfolk and the patrols of the public health inspector.

Residents' eyes in the small community proved to be as sharp as their

By end of the 1890s, Bracebridge's logged-over town site remains treeless, log booms dominate the river, mills and office buildings jostle for space, and wooden walks in varying states of repair line the muddy streets. The town's water reservoir, the whitewashed low stone structure with flat roof at the bridge's right, was part of the municipality's piped-water system. Constructed to curtail waterborne disease by improving hygiene, the system was built after an 1891 analysis of water from the town well declared it very bad "and on no account to be used for drinking purposes."

noses were acute, spotting improperly buried carcasses and detecting a slaughterhouse operating with no regard for basic hygiene. The perpetrators of these offences, too, were soon caught in the dragnet of ground-level justice, and faced their day of reckoning in Magistrate's Court.

One such defendant was Sing Lee, owner and operator of the laundry in Bracebridge, but this time as an accused rather than plaintiff. He was the culprit whose cleaning fluid contaminated the vicinity. James Boyer evidently took pains to ensure Sing Lee was being dealt with fairly. His is the only case where the charge, having been read to an accused, was then also explained, to be sure he understood what he was in court for. Apart from dealing with the linguistic and cultural barrier, James also seemed to feel, the point about pollution having been made, a further step was needed to ensure justice in his court and harmony in the community: this is also the only case in which a fine was levied, paid by the accused, then *refunded* to him.

MAGISTRATE'S COURT — AUGUST 15TH, 1893
BEFORE MESSRS. PRATT AND BOYER, J.P.s
SAMUEL SPENCER, SANITARY INSPECTOR
v JONATHAN LEADER

For that the defendant, on or about August 8th, 1893, at the Town of Bracebridge, did unlawfully keep and use a slaughter house in said Town without having first obtained the consent of the local Board of Health authorizing him so to do.

Defendant pleaded guilty and fined $5.00 and $3.75 costs, to be paid forthwith, and in default, to be levied by distress, and in default of distress, to be imprisoned in common gaol at Bracebridge for 14 days.

Josiah Pratt, J.P.
James Boyer, J.P.

Paid.
Conviction returned.

MAGISTRATE'S COURT — OCTOBER 5TH, 1895
BEFORE MESSRS. BROWNING AND BOYER, J.P.s
THOMAS DODD, SANITARY INSPECTOR OF THE TOWN OF
BRACEBRIDGE v SING LEE

For having, on October 4th, 1895, at Bracebridge, unlawfully deposited upon the lot occupied by him refuse and other filth injurious to the public health.

The charge having been read and explained to defendant, who is a Chinaman, he pleaded not guilty.

Thomas Dodd sworn

I am Sanitary Inspector of this town. I served defendant with a written notice on September 23rd to desist from putting slop water out on his premises. It was slop water from washing. Defendant is in the washing business. Part of the slop water runs under the house on the next lot, some part of it runs and forms a pool at the rear of the lot. It is very offensive to smell and dangerous to the public health.

I went to defendant's place on October 4th. Defendant admitted he had put the water there that day and every day since I served him with the notice. There is no drain from defendant's premises. The water and filth run under his own place and under the buildings on each side.

Charles I. Hunt sworn

I occupy a barber's shop next building to defendant. Sometimes I am not able to open the back window of my premises on account of the offensive smell. I believe it is dangerous to health. I have been annoyed by the smell for about a month.

Prisoner convicted and fined $5 and $3.75 costs, to be paid forthwith, and in default, to be levied by distress, and in default of sufficient distress, to be imprisoned in the gaol at Bracebridge and there kept at hard labour for 14 days.

R. M. Browning, J.P.
James Boyer, J.P.

Paid and fine refunded.
Constable $1.25
Conviction returned.

Magistrate's Court — February 28th, 1896
Before James Boyer and Singleton Brown, J.P.s
Thomas Dodd, Sanitary Inspector v James Boyce

For having, on February 28th, 1896, at the Town of Bracebridge, offered for sale certain meat, to wit, beef, intended for but unfit for the use of man.

Defendant pleaded not guilty.

Thomas Dodd sworn

I am the sanitary inspector for the board of health of this town. I saw some meat in a sleigh in the yard at the Dominion Hotel in charge of defendant. I asked if he had the meat for sale and he said he had. I examined the meat and think it very unfit for human food. It was covered all over with blue mould on the outside. There were two or three quarters of beef that were bad, and some mutton which did not appear to be as bad. I didn't cut into it or smell it.

Jonathan Leeder sworn

I am a butcher in this town. I saw the meat in question and do not consider the beef fit for food but the mutton would be all right.

Defendant convicted and fined $3 and $4.50 costs, and in default, to be imprisoned in the common gaol at Bracebridge for 21 days. Meat to be confiscated and destroyed.

James Boyer, J.P.
Singleton Brown, J.P.

Paid constable $2.50
Conviction returned.
Paid.

Magistrate's Court — March 26th, 1896
Before James Boyer and Peter M. Shannon, J.P.s
Thomas Dodd, Sanitary Inspector
v Alfred Willoughby

For having, on or about the month of February, at the Town of Bracebridge, permitted the accumulation of dead animals and other filth on his premises, contrary to the bylaw relating to public health. Defendant pleaded not guilty.

Thomas Todd sworn

I am the sanitary inspector for the Town of Bracebridge. The defendant in February was living in a house belonging to Mr. Wm. Ross in the fourth ward of this town. I went with Mr. Alfred E. Hunt on March 23rd to the house where defendant resided. On the 24th I went again, took a spade and dug into a pit about two feet below the ground. I found the body of a horse, seemingly quartered. There were shoes on the feet of the animal. The carcass was covered only with a few lumps of earth and snow, and was within 200 feet of the dwelling house.

Alfred B. Hunt sworn

Defendant rented the house in question from me about October 20th last. He left about the 1st of the present month. Defendant had three horses die while he was living there. I went with Mr. Dodd on March 23rd and showed him where the horses were supposed to be buried. The house is now occupied by a man named Beatty. Defendant was home when one horse died.

Thomas Dodd recalled

When I dug down to the carcass I distinguished a bad smell. I believe it was dangerous to the public health. Defendant's wife admitted to me that one of the horses belonged to him and two to the man boarding with him.

Defendant convicted and fined $7 and costs $4.30, to be paid forthwith, and in default, to be levied by distress, and in default of sufficient distress, to be imprisoned in the common gaol at Bracebridge for 14 days with hard labour.

James Boyer, J.P.

Peter W. Shannon, J.P.

Fine paid to the town treasurer
Paid constable $1.50
Paid May 2nd, 50 cents
Conviction returned.

MAGISTRATE'S COURT — APRIL 18TH, 1896
BEFORE JAMES BOYER AND SINGLETON BROWN, J.P.s
THOMAS DODD, SANITARY INSPECTOR v JAMES RUTHERFORD

For having, on or about April 15th, 1896, at Bracebridge, unlawfully suffered the accumulation upon his premises of refuse and other filth dangerous to the public health.

The charge having been read to defendant, he pleaded not guilty.

Thomas Dodd sworn

I am sanitary inspector of the Town of Bracebridge. On the night of the 15th, in passing defendant's place I found a very offensive smell. The next morning I found kitchen refuse and decaying vegetable matter in the rear of the defendant's kitchen, about 20 feet from the window and about 30 feet from the kitchen of the adjoining house. I found it was stuff that couldn't be burned and that it was dangerous to the public health. On November 18th last, I notified defendant and his landlord not to put any rubbish on that place. The rubbish was nearer the street than the rear of the lot.

Complaint dismissed.

James Boyer, J.P.
Singleton Brown, J.P.

Magistrate's Court — July 15th, 1896
Before James Boyer and Singleton Brown, J.P.s
Thomas Dodd v William Hearns

For that defendant, on July 9th, 1896, at Bracebridge, did willfully empty the contents of a certain water closet,[1] without having first deodorized or disinfected the same, and did deposit the same upon a certain lot of land in said town.
Defendant pleaded guilty.

Fined $1 and $2 costs, to be paid forthwith, and in default, to be imprisoned in the common gaol at Bracebridge for 10 days.

James Boyer, J.P.
Singleton Brown, J.P.

Constable paid $0.50
Conviction returned.

Magistrate's Court — July 16th, 1896
Before James Boyer, J.P. and H.S. Bowyer, Reeve
Thomas Dodd v Joseph Ellis

For having, on or about July 11th, 1896, committed a nuisance by

---

[1] Toilet.

depositing the carcass of a dead horse upon certain land in the Township of Monck, having removed the same from the Town of Bracebridge leaving it unburied.

Defendant pleaded guilty and fined $1 and $5.25 costs, to be paid forthwith, and in default, to be imprisoned in the common gaol at Bracebridge for 10 days.

James Boyer, J.P.
H.S. Bowyer, Reeve

Paid.
Constable paid $3.75
Conviction returned.

Magistrate's Court — August 1st, 1896
Before James Boyer, J.P. and Singleton Brown, Mayor
Thomas Dodd v William S. Shaw

For permitting the deposit and accumulation upon premises belonging to him of fleshings and other refuse dangerous to the public health.
The charge having been read to defendant he pleaded not guilty.

Thomas Dodd sworn

I am the sanitary inspector of the Town of Bracebridge. Defendant has a tannery within the limits of this town. On the 28th of July last, I went down by his tannery to a pier on the river bank, a part of the tannery premises. I found a quantity of decayed matter composed of the fleshings of hides. This was covered by some ground tan bark. Part of it was entirely exposed. It appeared to have been recently deposited there. It covered a space of six or eight feet and slanted to the water's edge. There was so bad a smell that I could not stay there. I consider it was a nuisance dangerous to the public health. There are people living within two hundred feet of the place.

I was informed that Mr. Shaw was looking after the tannery. I think Mr. Shaw is the owner or manager of the tannery.[2] Last fall I found some objectionable matter on the tannery premises. I went and saw Mr. Shaw about it. He told me he didn't know there was anything objectionable but that he would stop it.

Mary Jane Lequier sworn
I am the wife of Bernard Lequier and live in the fourth ward in Bracebridge. I know where Shaw's tannery is. Last Saturday there was a disagreeable smell and I had to close my doors. It came from towards the river. The wind was blowing from that direction. The house is about two hundred feet from the place where the smell came from. It came from the direction of the tannery. I have found other bad smells before.

Cross-examined
I found a bad smell about six weeks ago.

Minnie Dodd sworn
I am the wife of Alfred Dodd of Bracebridge. I live near Mr. Shaw's tannery. I live next door to Mrs. Lequier, and about the same distance as her from the tannery. One day last week I had to close the doors and shut the windows on account of the bad smell. The smell came from where they are filling up on the tannery premises. I thought something was being deposited there. This is the only time I had to shut up the house.

Cross-examined
I have lived in the 4th ward four weeks and only noticed the smell once.

---

[2] William Sutherland Shaw was manager of the tannery, having arrived in Bracebridge during May 1891 to run the operation. He was a cousin of Charles Orlando Shaw, who owned the tannery in Huntsville.

James D. Shier sworn

I live in Bracebridge near Shaw's tannery. There was an offensive smell coming from the tannery last week. If smell continued I would have to change locality. The family had to close doors and windows on one or two different occasions. The smell seemed to come from the tannery. I told my bookkeeper to tell the Inspector to see about it.

Cross-examined

I have lived in the 4th ward as long as the tannery has been there, and have not noticed a smell very often. We had diphtheria in my house twice since I have come here.

Defendant convicted and fined $5 and $5.40 costs, to be paid forthwith, and in default, to be levied by distress, and in default of sufficient distress, to be imprisoned in the common gaol at Bracebridge for the space of 14days.

James Boyer, J.P.
Singleton Brown, J.P.

Court $2.90
Constable $2.50
Total $5.40
Paid.
Conviction returned.

Magistrate's Court — October 12th, 1896
Before James Boyer and Singleton Brown, J.P.s
Thomas Dodd v Jonathan Leeder

For having, on October 8th, 1896, at the Town of Bracebridge, fed offal or meat of dead animals to hogs without such offal or meat having been previously boiled or steamed, contrary to the Public Health Act.

Defendant pleaded not guilty.

Thomas Dodd sworn

I am Sanitary Inspector of the local Board of Health. On October 8th I was at defendant's slaughterhouse in Bracebridge. I found 3 hogs in one divide, 2 in another, and a sow and litter of pigs in another divide. There was a trough in the place where the 2 hogs were, and some blood and entrails of an animal in it. I went and examined the entrails and blood and found it had not been steamed or boiled.

I also saw a large paunch of an animal in the yard. Part of the paunch appeared to have been eaten. It was raw, had not been cooked. There are two buildings there. I didn't go in them. I have notified defendant several times as to cooking the food for the hogs. I met defendant as I was coming away. I went back with him. I showed him where I had been. He admitted it was wrong and said his man had done it contrary to orders.

Cross-examined

The end of the trough was near a spout where the blood runs from the building.

Defendant sworn

I own the slaughterhouse and pigs. I have fed them on shorts and offal cooked. I have not fed offal uncooked since being notified. I have given instructions to have the offal boiled. We drew the paunch out at the end door where the sow was. When I went with Dodd the small entrails were across the trough part in the mud.

Cross-examined by prosecutor

The offal found by you on the day in question was not cooked.

Jonathan E. Leeder sworn

I am son of defendant and in his employ. I generally fed pigs on shorts and offal boiled. I haven't fed any raw offal to pigs. I threw the small offal out and drew out the paunch. I went hunting and forgot all about boiling the offal.

Defendant convicted and fined $1 and $3.85 costs, to be paid forthwith, and in default, to be imprisoned in the common gaol at Bracebridge for 14 days.

James Boyer, J.P.
Singleton Brown, J.P.

Paid.
Paid constable $1.75
Conviction returned.

Magistrate's Court — April 17th, 1897
Before James Boyer and Singleton Brown, J.P.s
Thomas Dodd, Sanitary Inspector v Jesse Hunt and John George Hunt

For having, on or about April 12th, 1897, at Bracebridge, deposited the carcasses of two certain calves upon premises in their possession, the same being likely to endanger the public health.

The charge having been read to defendants, the defendant Jesse Hunt pleaded guilty, and defendant John George Hunt was dismissed.

Defendant Jesse Hunt fined $5 and $4.35 costs, to be paid forthwith, and in default, to be levied by distress, and in default of sufficient distress, to be imprisoned in the common gaol at Bracebridge for 14 days with hard labour.

James Boyer, J.P.
Singleton Brown, J.P.

Paid in full.
Paid constable.

Magistrate's Court — July 29th, 1897
Before Messrs. Boyer and Browning
Thomas Dodd v Augustine Russell[3]

For that defendant, on July 26th, 1897, at Bracebridge, by then and there exacting the trade or calling of a butcher, did have in his possession meat intended to be used as food, such meat being unsound and unfit for food and dangerous to the health of persons living on the premises and in the immediate vicinity of such premises.

Defendant pleaded not guilty.

Thomas Dodd sworn

I am Sanitary Inspector of the Board of Health. On July 19th I went to inspect the cellars of defendant and Mr. Harper. I found defendant's cellar covered with clay animal secretions, ashes. It was a brick floor. A barrel about half full of meat, which I believe was beef, had a very bad smell. I told defendant I wanted the place cleaned. He asked me how he was to do it. I told him to well clean it with water and use carbolic acid in the water. I said I would return the following Monday to see it was properly cleaned.

I went there on the 26th and found it had not been cleaned. I seized the barrel and the meat in it. It had a very bad smell and was full of maggots. I went to get a man to remove it. When I returned it had been taken away. The meat was not fit for food. Defendant is a butcher.

Cross-examined

A sign over the door of the shop reads TRY OUR CORNED BEEF. There is no

---

[3]Augustine Russell, like other Muskokans, including Magistrate Boyer who tried this case, started as a farmer to get free-grant land, but later moved into town for better work. A farmer in 1896, Russell was operating a Bracebridge butcher shop by 1897. At that time, he was charged for having contaminated meat on the premises. In an 1896 case, Augustine Russell and his brother Vincent were sued by Samuel Christiansen for unpaid wages, a case found in Chapter 17: Bartering for Work, Fighting for Wages.

communication inside with the cellar but there is outside. Defendant told me the cellar belonged to the premises, and he would clean it. Defendant told me he owned the meat but he intended to send it to the farm to feed the hogs. The meat was bad on July 19th. Defendant told me he didn't think the meat was so bad. In my opinion the smell was dangerous to public health.

Asa Harps sworn

I live in part of the house occupied by defendant butcher's shop. Defendant lives adjacent to me. On July 19th Dodd came and asked to see my cellar. I went with him to defendant's cellar. We found the cellar very filthy. Dodd told defendant to clean it and have the barrel of meat removed. Defendant promised to do so and asked Dodd what was best to use to do so. Defendant did not claim that the meat did not belong to him. On the 26th Dodd called me in. I saw Dodd coming up from the cellar. The cellar was still very filthy. The stench was terrible. The meat on top of the barrel was covered with maggots. The inspector seized the meat and said he would take care of it.

Cross-examined

I had told defendant before the 19th that there was a terrible bad smell. He said he couldn't see what it was. The cellar is under the apartments occupied by defendant on the 2nd flat, a shooting gallery is on the ground floor above the cellar.

George Dennis sworn

I am boarding at Mr. Harp's. I have been boarding there all this month. About the 15th instant, I noticed a very bad smell at the front of the house, and in the hall leading to and sometimes in the dining room. I spoke of it to other parties in the house. I noticed the smell along to the 26th. I didn't notice it after that.

Annie Bigelow sworn

About 3 weeks ago I was at Mr. Harp's. I noticed a very bad smell in the hall and in the sitting room. From what I said to Mrs. Harp, she took me to the sitting room and I found blood coming through the partition between the defendant and Mr. Harp's room. It was a wooden partition. The rooms of defendant and Mr. Harp's where the blood was coming through were both on the ground floor.

Elizabeth Smith

I am living at Mr. Harp's. For about 3 weeks there has been a very disagreeable smell in Mr. Harp's rooms and on the street in front of the house. I am a servant at Mr. Harp's. The smell was not caused by anything put on the premises by Mr. Harp's family. I saw offensive matter running under the partition from the defendant's shop. The smell has continued for about 3 weeks. I've not smelled it since Monday.

Defendant sworn

The cellar is not under the butcher's shop. There is no entrance into cellar from inside of shop. I didn't occupy the cellar. Mr. John Russell owns the cellar. I told Dodd the stuff in the cellar did not belong to me. The barrel of meat in question belonged to me and was put by me in the cellar. It was corned beef in pickle and it had partly dried off the top. It was all right when I put it in. It was not in good condition when I saw it last. It was not intended to be used as food. I didn't notice any offensive smell. I had enquiries for corn beef. I told them it was tainted. I arranged with Mr. Gibbs to take it away shortly after Inspector was there.

Cross-examined

I sell fresh beef and corned beef. The meat was good when I put it there. I intended to sell it to be used as food. Robert Whaley asked me for corn beef about July 19th. I refused to sell it to him or to Mr. Newton. I knew it was tainted at that time. The chips and ashes were cleaned out between the 19th and 26th, and I sprinkled chloride of lime in the cellar, about 4 inches out of the pickle.

Robert Whaley sworn

I applied to defendant's about a week ago for corn beef. I said, "How's the corned beef?" He said, "I have some but it's not good." He didn't let me have any.

W. Pfafenberg sworn

I know the cellar in question. I keep a shooting gallery over the cellar. I hadn't noticed any smell from the cellar. I didn't hear any complaints as to bad smell.

Cross-examined

I complained to Harp of a bad smell on the 18th and 19th.

Asa Harp recalled

Witness Pfafenberg said to me at one evening between 19th and 26th, "What a terrible smell arising from this grating. It smells like a dead cat or dog." The grating is in the cellar under the shooting gallery. On the 26th, the meat was decomposed and rotten.

Defendant convicted and fined $2 and costs $6.75, to be paid forthwith, and in default, to be levied by distress, and in default to be imprisoned in the common gaol at Bracebridge for 14 days.

James Boyer, J.P.
R.M. Browning, J.P.

Court $4.
Paid constable $2.75
Conviction returned.
Paid.

Magistrate's Court — January 28th, 1898
Before James Boyer, J.P. and Singleton Brown, J.P.
Thomas Dodd, Sanitary Inspector
v Samuel H. Armstrong

For that defendant, on January 21st, 1898, at Bracebridge, did unlawfully allow the intestines of animals to be fed to pigs without such intestines having been previously boiled, contrary to the Public Health Act. Defendant pleaded not guilty.

Robert Robinson sworn

I live in Bracebridge in Mr. Rose's house near the slaughterhouse of defendant. On January 21st I was coming along the railroad track and saw two pigs near defendant's slaughterhouse. It was about half-past 2 p.m. The pigs were standing by a trough and they then got to a paunch of an animal. I went on to Bracebridge, and afterwards, waiting till after 4 p.m., I saw Mr. Dodds, and I went with him to the slaughterhouse. When we got there we saw 3 pigs eating the raw insides of an animal. We took a sample of what the pigs were eating which I now produce. Neither one of the samples produced has been cooked. I didn't see any one around there or go into the building.

Cross-examined

I live about 200 yards from the slaughterhouse.

Thomas Dodd sworn

I am sanitary inspector for the local Board of Health. On the afternoon of the 21st instant, I saw the last witness in the Post Office. After hearing what he told me, at my request he went with me to the slaughterhouse. It was 20 minutes to 5 when we got there. I went into the yard and the last witness followed me. I saw a large paunch (apparently beef) partly under the slaughterhouse. I saw three hogs eating it at one end. Robinson took a knife and cut a piece off the outside of the paunch. There was another part of an animal lying in the yard and he cut a part off that. To the best of my belief the samples produced are the same Robinson cut off. In my opinion they were not cooked.

Cross-examined

I saw a stovepipe through the building and there was apparently a stove and fire in the building. A paunch of a cow couldn't be taken out of a pot after being cooked without breaking it. I am satisfied the part where the sample was cut off hadn't been cooked. The paunch had not been emptied.

For the Defence

William Jelly sworn

I was at the slaughterhouse on the day in question. We killed a pig in the yard and dressed it and a beef in the slaughterhouse. We boiled the offal. I was there from 2 to 5:30 p.m. I fed the offal to the pigs.

We killed one pig and one cow. I didn't see any other offal there. We boiled it about 20 or 30 minutes. There was no other offal in the yard. It was near 5 when we boiled it. I didn't see the men.

Edward Masters sworn

I was with last witness on the day in question from 2 to 5:30 p.m. We boiled the intestines. I don't know for how long. I didn't see any other intestines in the yard.

Jonathan Leeder sworn

I am a butcher in the Town of Bracebridge. I have examined the samples of offal now produced and in my opinion one of the samples has been in hot water and the other not.

Adjourned to 29th, instant, at 4 p.m.

29th January 1897

Fined $1 and $4.30 costs, to be paid forthwith, and in default, to be levied by distress, and in default of sufficient distress, to be imprisoned in the common gaol at Bracebridge for 14 days.

James Boyer, J.P.
Singleton Browning, J.P.

Fine paid.

Conviction returned.

Paid constable.

Magistrate's Court — July 6th, 1898
Before Messrs. Boyer and Spencer, J.P.s
Christopher T. Thrift v Samuel H. Armstrong

For that defendant, on July 4th, 1898, at Bracebridge, did unlawfully allow the offal of animals to be fed to pigs without such offal having been previously boiled or steamed, contrary to the Public Health Act. Defendant pleaded guilty.

Defendant fined $1 and $2.55 costs, to be paid forthwith, and in default, to be levied by distress, and in default of sufficient distress, to be imprisoned in the common gaol at Bracebridge for 10 days.

James Boyer, J.P.
Wm. H. Spencer, J.P.

Paid.

Paid constable.

Conviction returned.

Chapter Nine

LIVESTOCK AND DEADSTOCK

Whether worked as beasts of burden, raised to trade or sell at profit, kept as field and barn livestock, slaughtered for meat and hides, or treasured as pets, domesticated animals share a mutual dependence with humans.

An inordinate percentage of the thirteen animal cases from 1890s Bracebridge concern the problem of cows wandering loose on the streets. In addition to dairy cattle on township farms, many cows were kept in town to give households a daily supply of fresh milk. Often they "got away," when owners turned them out to graze and forage freely. Keeping cows off the streets and out of people's gardens was not just a problem in Muskoka's capital, of course. In the provincial capital, entrance to and from the spacious grounds of Ontario's most prestigious courthouse, Osgoode Hall on Queen Street, was restricted by narrow, wrought-iron gates designed to keep stray cows off the premises, an enduring feature to this day. Such counterpart barriers in Bracebridge were the humbler wooden picket fences around lawns, gardens, and the Land Registry Office.

Manitoba Street, the main thoroughfare of Bracebridge, sometimes abounded with crowds and excitement in the 1890s. Farmers' wagons coming into town would be drawn by any available means — horses, oxen, or even cows.

The problem of cows running at large was a recurring issue on Bracebridge council's agenda. As with most issues, there were at least two sides, and positions on the cow question in this highly political town were strongly held and vehemently expressed. The final council meeting for 1895, taking place just before the January 1, 1896 municipal election, became highly animated when town clerk James Boyer scheduled the hearing of a ratepayers' petition seeking repeal of the animal-control bylaw. Against this pressure, council upheld its existing policy, which stated that it was not acceptable for cows to be at large on the streets. Councillors believed the community's collective interests overrode the benefits of cheap foraging and convenient pasturing that free-range dairy farming offered for some cattle owners. They knew keeping cows off the streets would help reduce the manure problem on Bracebridge's already muddy and slippery thoroughfares. They welcomed to the town's treasury the fines Magistrate Boyer levied against cow owners under the existing animal-control bylaw. Finally, in an era when Canada's steam engines were built defensively with "cow catchers" in front, Bracebridge councillors also felt compelled to uphold and enforce the Railway Act, a statute of Canada's Parliament that

Muskoka dairy farmers, such as these three men pictured here with their herd of cows and dog, often found it easier to let their milk cows graze on the uneven slopes and in the woods of their property than growing crops in their stony fields. A cheese factory opened in Bracebridge once farmers pledged to provide a steady supply of milk.

prohibited cows running at large within a half-mile of a railway crossing.

Although the 1895 citizens' petition to repeal the cow-control measure was rejected by council, it was not, however, turned down for any of these rational policy grounds. That would have required council members to join issue with the petitioners on the eve of the elections and risk losing their votes. The petition was disqualified, instead, thanks to painstaking checking by town clerk Boyer, on the technical grounds that a large number of signatures should not have been on it. For whatever reasons, the petition, gathered in June, had not been presented to council until the end of December, and some signatories had moved away while others had died in the interim.

Even with the bylaw intact, Bracebridge's straying cow problem continued. Two and a half years later, a new council moved to tighten the restrictions with Bylaw Number 89, "To prevent certain animals running at large within the Municipality of the Town of Bracebridge." It was drafted by Clerk Boyer and passed by council June 6, 1898. Immediately that same month, Bracebridge pound keeper James Arnott began laying charges, getting the owners of stray cows into Magistrate's Court to appear before Boyer in his role as justice of the peace, at a court held in the Town Hall.

To any observer, Bracebridge would appear a tightly run municipality.

The result by the late 1890s was that stray cows began coming under more effective control. Yet this did not end the controversy over animals in Bracebridge. With cows dealt with, the animal issue on council's agenda for the next decades would be dogs running at large in the municipality.

Horses and oxen, sheep and pigs, also crop up in this catch of 1890s cases, rounding out the problematic relations between humans and animals. A further aspect of this relationship, cruelty to animals, seemed of little concern to the justice of the peace, or most others.

MAGISTRATE'S COURT — DECEMBER 29TH, 1893
BEFORE MESSRS. BROWNING AND BOYER, J.P.s
ALFRED HENRY LEE V ROBERT GRAHAM, JAMES GRAHAM

For having on, December 21st and 22nd, 1893, at the Township of Stephenson, unlawfully and wilfully abused and tortured a certain ox. The charge having been read to defendants, they severally pleaded not guilty.

W. Mahaffy for Defendants

John Smith sworn
I live in Macaulay. On December 22nd I was going from my place to Utterson. I saw broken sticks and blood on the road, and from where I saw the blood to defendant's yard, there was a stream of blood along the road.

Cross-examined
It was about 11 a.m. Saw blood about 35 or 40 rods along the road. Sticks were 8 to 9 inches long. Some shorter. One or two were nearly an inch in diameter. Others about half that size.

James Nickason sworn

I live on 1st Concession, Stephenson, Lot 25. I know defendants. On different days during the present month I saw defendants drawing logs. They went through my field with an ox team. I saw them strike the oxen. I don't know what it was with. I was too far away. That was the only time I saw them beat the oxen.

Roy Everitt sworn

I live in Macaulay. I know defendants. Defendants have been drawing logs, with oxen and horses. On the 22nd they were drawing logs. I saw one of them striking one of the oxen with a club about 2 feet long and 2 to 3 inches thick. He struck it 8 or 9 times. I was close to them when it happened.

Case dismissed with costs of $5.05 to be paid forthwith, and in default, to be levied by distress, and in default, to be imprisoned for 21 days.

James Boyer, J.P.
R.M. Browning, J.P.

MAGISTRATE'S COURT — APRIL 20TH, 1894
BEFORE BOYER AND BROWNING, J.P.s
JOHN MYERS V ROBERT TRIBE

For having, on April 12th, 1894, at the Township of Oakley, wantonly and cruelly beaten, ill-treated and abused two sheep, property of the informant.
Case withdrawn on payment of $5.30 costs.

James Boyer, J.P.
R.M. Browning, J.P.

Paid.

Magistrate's Court — August 12th, 1896
Before James Boyer and Singleton Brown, J.P.s
Thomas Dodd, Sanitary Inspector v John T. Marsland

For having, on August 8th, 1896, kept hogs in a pen within the Town of Bracebridge without such pen being regularly cleaned.

Defendant pleaded not guilty.

Thomas Dodd sworn

I am the sanitary inspector of local Board of Health. On August 8th I was on my way down to the river. I came to the hog pen belonging to defendant. I noticed the smell and examined pen. I found two hogs in a bad, uncleanly state. No bedding and a quantity of excreta from the pen around the floor of pen. Old excreta from the pen was around the pen on the rock. Part of the excreta was oozing out one side of the pen down the rock. In my opinion no disinfectant had been used and the pen had not been regularly cleansed. There had been no rain the day or so before.

Samuel Richardson sworn

I am the scavenger for the town. I went to the pigpen in question and saw two hogs in the pen, and in one corner was a lot of excreta. There seemed to have been some offal dumped onto the rock around the pen. I have no doubt that the smell came from the pen. There was no roof to the pen.

For the Defence

John T. Marsland sworn

The pen was regularly cleaned out. They were cleaned out about once a week.

Dalton Stephens sworn
I have been around Mr. Marsland's place quite a bit lately. I never noticed a bad smell there but once or twice.

Silas Booth
I have been boarding with Mr. Marsland for over three months. I never smelt a bad smell but once and then I was but a short distance away.

Case dismissed.

James Boyer, J.P.
Singleton Brown, J.P.

MAGISTRATE'S COURT — DECEMBER 28TH, 1896
BEFORE JAMES BOYER, J.P.
JOHN JOHNSON V THOMAS CAVE

Assault and battery at the Township of Oakley on October 5th, 1895.
The charge having been read to prisoner, he pleaded not guilty.

Complainant not being present, prisoner remanded to December 31st at 2 p.m. Prisoner to be summoned to appear.

John Johnson
I am a farmer and live in Oakley. On October 4th, 1895 I was bringing home 4 calves bought off William Denniss. One got away from us. I went back for it next day. My sons Thomas and Hugh went with me. I met defendant in a field of a man named Rice, through which people occasionally travel both with wagons and on foot.

I had two young colts, which followed us the day before and remained away all night. We met defendants in the field. I asked him where the colts were. He said they were on the old road. We went to find them. Defendant got ahead of us and drove them towards the barn on the farm. I said I would take care of them. He said he would put them in the pound. I said it was not his place. He said he would damned soon show me and threw the stone, now produced, at me, striking me on the left breast. He threw another stone at my head. I dodged it.

He then tried to run a pitchfork in me but I got behind a fence. He then said, "You damned son of a bitch. I'll shoot you," and ran into the house to get his gun. His wife said he had better leave that alone. I got the colts and went home. I was very sore for a few days after the blow.

Hugh Johnson sworn
I am a son of the last witness. I saw prisoner throw the stone, now produced, at my father striking him on the breast. He, prisoner, ran at my father with a pitchfork. He also threatened to shoot him.

Thomas Johnson sworn
I remember October 5th, 1895. Son of John Johnson. Saw prisoner throw two stones. The one now produced struck my father on the breast. Prisoner threatened to shoot my father.

For the Defence

Defendant sworn
The day before October 5th, complainant's colts were annoying me as I was ploughing. I took them home that day. The next morning they were in my field again. The field was fenced. I was going to take them to the pound. I met complainant and his sons. He asked me what I was going to do with the colts, and called me names. There were no stones used or pitchfork either. I did throw a stone at him but not the one now produced.

Defendant convicted and fined $10 and costs $13.84, to be paid forthwith, and in default, to be imprisoned in the common gaol at Bracebridge and there kept at hard labour for 2 months.

James Boyer, J.P.

Constable $12.09 paid
Court $ 1.75
Total $13.84
Committed to gaol, but afterwards paid.
Conviction returned.

MAGISTRATE'S COURT — JULY 5TH, 1897
BEFORE MESSRS. BOYER AND BROWNING, J.P.S
ALFRED STUNDEN V ROBERT IRWIN

For that defendant, on or about June 20th, 1897, at the Township of Ryde, did wantonly, cruelly and unnecessarily beat, ill-treat, abuse and overdrive a certain horse.
Defendant pleaded not guilty.

Robert Heffren sworn
I live in the Township of Ryde and know defendant. A week ago last Saturday I was at the corner near Barkway post office. I saw defendant's horse tied to a wagon. The horse was harnessed to a covered buggy. Defendant got into the buggy, ran the horse about 200 yards or more and came back again. He whipped him going and coming.

When he got back, the horse fell, got up and fell again and then the horse died. I didn't see him whip him when he was down. The horse was going as fast as he could. I drew the horse away and buried it.

Cyrus Long sworn
I live in Ryde and know the defendant. I saw defendant get into the rig and

drive the horse about 200 yards as far as I could see. Defendant was out of sight about 5 minutes. He then drove back and the horse fell. He was driving as fast as the horse could go and defendant was using the whip. He got out of the rig and helped the horse up. He fell again. Defendant then took the harness off and the horse died.

Richard Rush sworn
I live in Muskoka Township but was in Ryde on the day in question. I saw defendant get in the rig and drove the horse as far as I could see. Drove it fast. He used the whip. I saw him return driving at the same rate. The horse fell twice and died.

Cross-examined
Defendant said he would drive him a piece to see if he would stand better.

Case dismissed without costs.

James Boyer, J.P.
R.H. Browning, J.P.

During the month of June in 1898, Bracebridge constable James Arnott, in separate charges against John Brotherston, Charles Barnes, James Shelly, Anderson Boyd, and John Duval, produced five cases before Magistrate James Boyer. The accused were charged with unlawfully permitting their cows to run at large upon the public streets of Bracebridge, which was contrary to Bylaw Number 89. In four cases, they pleaded guilty and were fined a standard $1 penalty, plus costs ranging from $1.75 to $4.40.

But in the case of Shelly, below, whose plea was that of not guilty, the case was dismissed, and it is not unreasonable to suppose that James Boyer felt sympathy for the boy, an intended keeper of the cow, who was preoccupied reading a book.

MAGISTRATE'S COURT — JUNE 27TH, 1898
BEFORE JAMES BOYER, J.P.
JAMES ARNOTT V JAMES SHELLY

For permitting his cow to run at large upon one of the public streets at Bracebridge on June 19th, 1898.

Defendant pleaded not guilty.

Bylaw No. 89 produced, dated June 6th, 1898, signed by the mayor and clerk and under the seal of the corporation, and initialled, "To prevent certain animals running at large within the Municipality of the Town of Bracebridge."

Isaac H. Waltenbury sworn

I live in Bracebridge and am one of the pound keepers of the town. On Sunday evening, June 19th, my attention was called to a cow on Ontario Street, opposite my house. I waited for some time and saw a boy lying on the opposite side of the street. He appeared to be reading.

I went to the door, stayed there some time before I went out. I went and asked who owned the cow. I didn't understand what he said and he wrote down the name of Shelly on it. I told the boy if he didn't take the cow away I would take charge of her myself. He then went off with her. The cow was loose. I saw the cow on the street for 15 minutes.

Case dismissed.

James Boyer, J.P.

In August and September that same year, Constable Arnott was again laying charges against townsfolk over cows being in the streets in violation of Bylaw 89. Accused John Demara and James W. Bettes both pleaded guilty, getting the $1 fine and paying costs of $2.30 and $3 respectively. Once again, when a defendant pleaded not guilty, as in the earlier case of John Leishman, James Boyer, joined this time by two other JPs, found grounds to dismiss the case.

Magistrate's Court — September 15th, 1898
Before James Boyer, Singleton Brown, and William Sword, J.P.s
James Arnott v John Leishman

For permitting his cow to run at large upon one of the public streets of said town, contrary to bylaw, on September 13th, 1898.
The defendant pleaded not guilty.

John Gibbs sworn
On September 13th I saw two cows running at large upon one of the streets of this town and the cows belong to either John Leishman or Robert Leishman. They were near the planing mill. They were on the road for about an hour. I know the cows well.

Defendant sworn
The cows got out that morning, as the man who looks after them had probably left the bars down. The cows belong to my son Robert. This was the only time the cows have been out.

Robert Leishman sworn
The cows have never run at large before until this time, and I suppose they must have broken out of the field. The cows are my property.

Case dismissed.

James Boyer, J.P.
Singleton Brown, J.P.
William Sword, J.P.

Chapter Ten

A DOG'S LIFE

A dog is a man's best friend. However, there can be complications.

MAGISTRATE'S COURT — NOVEMBER 28TH, 1894
BEFORE JAMES BOYER, J.P. AND A.C. FLETCHER, J.P.
ROBERT IRWIN V ALLIS EDWARDS

For unlawfully killing a dog at the Township of Ryde on November 15th.
The charge having been read to defendant, he pleaded not guilty.

Robert Irwin sworn

I am a farmer living in Ryde. On November 15th I was out hunting. The dog was with me. It was a collie dog. I left the dog with Hugh Cox to put out after deer. The dog came back to me at the runway. I sent the dog to Mr. Benn's, about 500 yards from the runway. I saw him at Benn's about 1½ hours afterwards. He had been shot and died that night. I saw marks of blood on a hill near Benn's. The valuators valued the dog at $15. Defendant chose one man and me the other to value the dog.

Cross-examined

It was a valuable dog, both for farm work and for running deer. I never had the dog tied up. He was not vicious. I never heard of my dog killing sheep.

Allan McMillan

I live in Ryde between complainant and defendant. I went to see defendant at complainant's request to see if he would settle for the dog without having any trouble. I saw defendant. He admitted shooting the dog. About an hour afterwards he said the dog had worried[1] one of their sheep on the road quite a while ago and he was mad at him. Defendant came up to my house. He called on the way on Hugh Cox to act for him as to valuing the dog. I acted for complainant Cox, and myself valued the dog at $15. The dog would run deer.

Cross-examined

The dog was very obedient to his master. I have seen him run deer alone.

Robert Benn sworn

I live in Ryde near complainant and defendant. Have known the dog more than 2 years. He was a good farm dog, supposed to be a collie. He would fetch cattle up alone. If I wished to get a dog, I would have given $15 or $20

---

[1]Worry, in this context, means to harass or treat roughly with continual biting or tearing with the teeth. e.g., "The dog was worrying an old shoe."

for it. I never heard or knew of the dog going to other houses except mine. I am the father-in-law of complainant. I never heard of his worrying sheep.

Dennis Long sworn

I live in Ryde opposite complainant. I have kept sheep since complainant had the dog. He never interfered to my knowledge with my sheep. I never had any injured by dogs. Complainant kept sheep. Other people had sheep at defendant's to pasture.

Cross-examined

I don't know the value of the dog.

For the Defence

Sanford Edwards sworn

I am brother of defendant. On a Sunday, about the end of October or beginning of November, my brother and father had some sheep on the road in Ryde. One or two belonged to my brother, the defendant. The sheep got out by the gate being left open. I saw the dog go along the road with complainant. I did not see the dog touch the sheep. I saw one of the sheep the same day. It was torn back of the front leg and a cut on the side. I don't know what done it.

Cross-examined

The sheep were on a side road. It was a public road. The cut was about 3 inches long.

Joshua Matz sworn

I live in Ryde near complainant and defendant. On a Sunday in October or November I was on the road in question. I saw a sheep on the road that had some marks back of the front leg. It looked as if it had been torn. The sheep was walking on the road alone. It was walking and limped a little. I saw defendant and his brother some distance from the sheep. They were not driving it.

Cross-examined

I saw a place where the wool had been pulled out but don't know in what part. I don't know whether it had been bitten by a dog or not. I never have seen a sheep that had been injured by a dog.

Ira Davy sworn

I live in Ryde, about ¾ miles from complainant. I have seen the dog in question. Have seen him following deer. I have seen the dog in my place at night in my yard. I believe it to be the dog. That was during the fall. I had a sheep killed during harvest. Don't know what killed it. Defendant told me he found his dog eating the carcass of a sheep. Myself and Mr. Matz had a dog that would kill sheep. We both killed our dogs, and Mr. Fielding killed his dog as he had killed some sheep. Defendant lives 2½ miles from complainant.

Cross-examined

You might have been on the road when the dog came to my place at night. I live about 65 rods from Benn's.

Henry Edwards sworn

I am the father of defendant. On Sunday, October 14th, I saw my two boys take the horses to pasture. They left the gate open and the sheep went out on the road. I thought I would let them stay there awhile. I then went in to read. I went out shortly after and saw one running down the road. I then saw three more following it. I went to look after the others. I met some others trotting along with their mouths open as if tired — and then a ram lamb walking. I then met my son. Matz was sitting on a log on the side of the road. I then met defendant. We followed the sheep home. One appeared to be injured. We caught it and examined it and found a wound behind the front leg. For several days that sheep didn't eat much. It was a ram lamb. I saw complainant come down the road. I didn't see the dog. The dog is called a collie.

Cross-examined
I didn't make any complaint about the sheep for the sake of peace.

Allis Edwards sworn
Am defendant in this case. On the Sunday in question I saw the complainant go along the road. About 15 minutes after, I saw some of the sheep coming towards home. I saw the dog hanging on to the sheep. I went up and struck the dog with a stick. He let go of the sheep and ran away. I met Mr. Irwin, he caught the dog and gave him a beating.

Cross-examined by complainant
I passed you on the corner. We had been there about half an hour and you came back in about 15 minutes. I shot the dog about 3 or 4 weeks afterwards. He had hold of the sheep by the front leg and was chewing it.

Re-examined
I went twice to try and get the money to pay for the dog.

Defendant convicted and fined $1 and $5, the value of the dog, and $4.85 costs, to be paid forthwith, and in default, to be imprisoned in the gaol at Bracebridge for 21 days.

James Boyer, J.P.
A.C. Fletcher, J.P.

Constable $3.25
Court $1.60
Defendant Allis Edwards committed to gaol.

Magistrate's Court — March 14th, 1896
Before James Boyer and P.M. Shannon, J.P.s
James Barber v John Hall

For having, on or about December 29th, 1895, at the Township of Watt, stolen a dog.

Defendant pleaded not guilty.

James Barker sworn

I live in the Township of Watt. On December 29th I had a white and tan thoroughbred spaniel dog. I saw it there about half-past one. I heard the dog barking and saw defendant coming along the road in front of my place. I got the dog from a man named Wilson, living in Cardwell. I made a conditional trade with David Veitch to trade my dog for one of his. We exchanged dogs. The dog didn't suit me and I sent him back to Veitch and I got mine back. The dog was a good hunting dog and I have got as much as $2.00 a day for lending him out for hunting purposes. I think the dog was worth $20.00, and wouldn't want to take any less for it . Defendant didn't have a dog with him when he passed my place.

Cross-examined by Mr. Mahaffy

The dog was about three years old. The trade mentioned was made five or six months ago. Defendant is a brother-in-law of Mr. David Veitch.

Maud Bogart sworn

I know defendant. I saw a man who I thought was defendant on a Sunday shortly after Christmas. He was leading a black and white dog by a string or a rope.

John Bogart (evidence taken not under oath)

I have seen defendant once or twice before. I had seen the dog before at Mr. Barber's house. He was a black and white dog.

Hugh Tiffle sworn

I live near Raymond. I remember the Sunday after Christmas I met defendant on the road leading a dog by a small rope. I met him near Ullswater. Defendant was going towards Rosseau. It was a brown and white dog. I have seen the dog at Mr. Becker's and with members of his family. It was about a quarter to two.

George Tibble sworn

I live near Raymond. I remember December 29th. I was at Skeleton Lake River. I was not acquainted with defendant but saw a man like him leading a dog by a small rope. He was going towards Rosseau. It was just like Mr. Barber's dog.

Charles Kingshott sworn

I remember December 29th. I saw defendant near Ullswater. He was going towards Rosseau. He was leading a dog by a rope. It was a dark brown and white Spaniel. I said, "That is a nice little dog you have." He said he had two of them but didn't need them both.

William Barber

I saw complainant's son. On December 29th I was standing out in front of the house. I saw defendant coming along the road with a small bundle under his arm. The dog was barking when defendant was passing. I went in the house and haven't seen the dog since.

James Barber sworn

I saw defendant about the dog and told him I had heard that he had taken my dog. I told him he had better settle it. All I wanted was my expenses and a little for my time. He asked me what that would be. I said, "$5.00." He said that if I could find anyone who saw him with my dog he would give me the $5.00. He admitted he had no dog before he got to my place, and I told him that three of Mr. Bogart's family (next neighbour living near the road) saw him with the dog. He said he would give me the $5 but couldn't give me the dog. I said I wanted both the dog and the $5.00.

Cross-examined by Mr. Mahaffy
This was about a month after I lost the dog.

For the Defence

David Veitch sworn
I am the brother-in-law of the defendant and know complainant also. I know the dog in question. About the middle of June 1898 I made a trade with complainant. My brother, Mr. Barber and I were present. He wanted to trade dogs with me and to give me a dollar to boot. I charged him a dollar on my books and it was paid by Mrs. Barber. Miss Barber came and claimed the dog. She did not get the dog. I never gave the dog to the Barbers. According to the agreement the dog should belong to me. It was an absolute trade. I kept the dog there and fed him sometimes.

Cross-examined by Mr. Barber
I never asked you about the spaniel.

Addington Veitch sworn
I am the brother of the last witness. I was present at the trade at Windermere in June 1893. Complainant told my brother to put the dollar on his account.

Willmetta Veitch
I am the wife of David Veitch. I was standing in the door when the trade took

place between Mr. Barber and my husband. Mr. Barber offered a dollar to boot.

Sarah Longhurst sworn
I live in Rosseau and know defendant. I saw him on December 29th, 1895. He stayed with me all night. He had no dog with him.

Case dismissed with costs $14.60, to be levied by distress, and in default, to be imprisoned in the common gaol at Bracebridge for one month.

James Boyer, J.P.

Wit's fees Geo. Raymond $4.30
Sarah Longhurst $2.45
Constable $5.75
Court $ 2.10
Paid $14.60

Magistrate's Court — May 16th, 1896
Before James Boyer, J.P.
Margaret N. Browning v William Gleason

For stealing a dog at Bracebridge on May 11th.
The dog having been given up to the prosecutor, she withdrew the charge upon defendant paying the costs.

James Boyer, J.P.

Paid $3 costs
Paid constable $1.50

Magistrate's Court — April 17th, 1897
Before James Boyer and Singleton Brown, J.P.s
Thomas Dodd v Osceola Gladiator

For having, on or about April 2nd, 1897, at Bracebridge, unlawfully deposited the carcass of a certain dog upon or in a certain gully, which may endanger the public health.

The charge having been read to defendant, he pleaded not guilty.

Mr. Arnold for the defendant.

John Anderson sworn

I live in Bracebridge. I employed defendant to dispose of a dog belonging to me. The dog was alive. I paid him to dispose of the dog.

Thomas Dodd sworn

I am sanitary inspector for the Town of Bracebridge. About a week ago I heard some firing near the mouth of Fenn's gully. I went there. In about 2 days afterwards I went there again and found the carcass of a dog in a tree. It was smelling very bad.

I got a man named Richardson, who identified the dog. After I had seen Anderson I went to defendant and asked him how he came to hang that animal. He said Anderson paid him to dispose of the animal. He said he choked it and hung it up there but he didn't know it was in the limits of the corporation. I know it was within the corporation limits. I said I would have to prosecute him. He said he didn't know he was breaking the law.

After serving him with the papers, he said he had cut the dog down and buried it, but didn't tell me where. From where the animal was hanging water would run from there into the water course or creek. It was in a tree part of the way down the hill towards the gully.

Cross-examined
He said Anderson paid him to dispose of the dog and he had choked it and hung it there.

Re-direct
It was smelling very bad. I don't know who owns the lot.

John Anderson cross-examined by defendant
Defendant told me he had disposed of it on Samuel Armstrong's place.

Complaint dismissed.

James Boyer, J.P.
Singleton Brown, J.P.

MAGISTRATE'S COURT — DECEMBER 1ST, 1898
BEFORE JAMES BOYER, J.P.
JAMES E. TAVERNER v JOHN FOX

For that defendant, on November 24th, at Ryde, was the owner or harbourer of a certain dog which killed a sheep belonging to informant of the value of $6.
Defendant pleaded not guilty.

James E. Taverner sworn
I am a farmer living in Ryde. On November 24th I had 9 sheep. I had been in Bracebridge that day. On my return I found that one had been worried and torn. The sheep was dead when I got home. It was a thoroughbred Southdown Ewe, and was worth $6. Defendant had a dog

of a yellowish brown colour, some Collie breed.

Cross-examined

I left home about 1 p.m. for Bracebridge. I keep 2 dogs: one black, and one black and white — ordinary sized dogs. I left them at home that day. Defendant has had a dog since the hunting season. I saw him on defendant's premises and I saw him the next day near defendant's on the road. I passed the school house near Fox's, within a quarter of an hour of 1 p.m., on the way to Bracebridge. I saw nothing of the sheep then. If it had been near or on the road at that time I must have seen it. My dogs run loose but I never knew them to chase sheep. The sheep was 8 months old.

Stephen Brundage sworn

I live in Ryde and am a farmer. On November 24th I started from home and passed Fox's house on the way to the old school house. I noticed bunches of wool on the left-hand side of the road. I looked across the road and saw the dog and the sheep. I said to the dog, "Get out!" and he skulked into the bush.

The dog was middle size, reddish brown and darker on the outside. I had seen the dog in defendant's doorway. I saw the same dog the day before yesterday, chained up in defendant's stable. I went back to the post office and told defendant what I had seen. I could see the sheep was badly torn and, as I believed, could not live. It was somewhere near 1 o'clock. It is about three-quarters of a mile from my house to where I saw the sheep. I first saw the dog about 2 weeks since.

Cross-examined

I live on Lot 7, Concession 4. Defendant lives on Lot 6, Concession 5. It took 6 or 7 minutes to reach the place where I saw the dog and sheep from my house. I was driving rather fast. The dog was gnawing the sheep and pulling at it. The sheep was alive and bleeding freely. I do not remember Fox asking me if the dog had been at the sheep, or me saying in reply, "If he had been, I would have shot him." I won't swear I did not say so. I had my rifle loaded in my rig. I don't recollect any conversation about the rifle at that interview.

I saw the glimpse of another dog going into the bush but could not tell the colour. It was a dark colour. The dog I saw at the sheep had considerable blood round his jaws and head. I sold lambs to the butcher at $3 each, not thoroughbred. I have sheep I wouldn't sell at $8 each, and I want money.

John Loshaw sworn
I live in Ryde. On November 24th I saw some boys bringing the sheep in question on a hand-sled. It was alive but badly torn. I examined it and believed it would not live. I cut its throat to put it out of its misery.

The skin was torn from the gamb of the hind leg to the body. A large piece of the flesh had been torn from the thick part of the leg. It was badly bitten on the back and badly bitten or torn in the neck. The blood was dropping from the mouth. I know defendant's dog, saw it that day on the side of the road about 15 or 20 rods from the place where I was informed the sheep was found. It was between 10 and 11 a.m. when I saw the dog. I know Taverner had sheep but didn't see any when I saw the dog.

George Loshaw sworn
I live in Ryde. Fox's son and myself were in the field. I heard a dog barking. I saw Mr. Taverner's sheep in the field and drove them to the house. I drove the sheep, there were 8 of them. It was after dinner.[2] It was the same day the sheep was killed. I know defendant's dog, a shaggy dog with a shaggy tail, brown with dark hair.

Charles Fairies sworn
I am reeve of Draper and keep sheep. Taverner bought his sheep off me — all purebred Southdowns, except one. I think the sheep in question would be cheap at $6.00.

---

[2]Noon meal. The evening meal, today widely called *dinner*, was usually called *supper* back then.

Cross-examined

I saw the sheep in question about the first of the last month. Any of them would be cheap at $6.

Case adjourned to December 12th at 2 p.m.

For the Defence

Mr. Mahaffy objected that the action for damages cannot include an order to have the dog destroyed.

Norman Fox sworn

I live with my father, the defendant. I remember November 24th. I was at home. Father had a dog. Brother Fred was with me. The dog with was me. I let him out the middle of the forenoon. He was playing around me. I was cutting wood till 11 a.m. The dog didn't leave us. I went with George Loshaw to get a load of wood. The dog was barking near a tree. He came back. I went and worked at a stable. The dog went to Loshaw's stable and came back again. He told me to tie the dog up and I did so. It was about 12 o'clock at noon.

After Loshaw went past with the sheep, Taverner went by. He told his son to go after the sheep. I saw Brundage pass. He came back and said a sheep had been nearly killed, and to go and see to it. We went and found the sheep lying down. It appeared to have been worried.

Taverner's boy and me looked at the dog and found no blood or marks on him at all.

Cross-examined

The dog was tied up 2 hours before we found the sheep. The dog was running around loose while we were at the bush for wood, sometimes in sight and sometimes not. He wasn't out of my sight more than a minute or two. John Donaldson showed me some blood on the dog's leg after I had tied him up. I am not sure whether it was blood or not.

Frederick Fox (not sworn — 9 years of age)
On November 24th I was cutting wood near the house. Norman let the dog loose. He was with us. He didn't go away. I went with the other two to get the wood and came back with them. The dog was running around there. Father told Norman to tie the dog up.

Matilda Fox sworn
I was home November 24th when father came home at 20 minutes to 12 o'clock. The dog was round with the boys that morning. We had dinner shortly after 12. I saw the dog afterwards tied up in the stable. The dog was tied up in the stable when Brundage went past.

Ada Fox sworn
Was at home on November 24th all day. The dog was playing round that morning with the boys. My husband told the boys to tie him up. He got home at 20 minutes to 12 and the dog was tied up immediately after. Had dinner about half-past 12. Brundage went past after dinner. Taverner went past before we got our dinner.

John Fox sworn
Am postmaster at Lewisham. On November 24th I carried the mail to Barkway. Got back at 20 minutes to 12. The dog came running out of the shed to me. No marks of blood on him. I told the boys to tie him up. Had the dog about 10 days. I afterwards saw the dog tied up. I saw George Loshaw go past with the sheep.

In Rebuttal

James E. Taverner (not sworn)
On the November 24th Norman Fox had the dog out with a rope on and he took it off. We were at the stable. I saw him hauling wood. The dog was there.

James Fenton sworn
Norman Fox told me that morning his dog had chased the sheep out of Brook's field. Loshaw was bringing the dead sheep home.

Case dismissed with costs.

James Boyer, J.P.

Costs paid $2.30.

Magistrate's Court — February 16th, 1899
Before James Boyer, J.P.
James E. Miller v William Stiles

For that defendant, on February 5th, 1899, at Bracebridge, did shoot and wound a certain dog, the property of the informant.
Defendant pleaded not guilty.

James E. Miller sworn
I am a farmer living in Monck. On February 5th I had a collie dog, black body and legs of a lighter colour. I saw the dog about 9 a.m. on Sunday morning. He had been shot through the top of the shoulder. I kept the dog all day Sunday. He couldn't get up and he was shot on Monday morning to put him out of his misery. The dog was given to my son, who is under age and who lives with me. The dog was worth $10. I was offered $12 for him. He was a good cattle dog.

Fred Miller sworn

I am 19 years of age and live with my father. The dog in question was given to me by Samuel Morris in December last, and we had it from that time till it was shot.

Cross-examined

Joseph Hewitt killed the dog on the Monday. The dog was given to me. It is about a half a mile to defendant's from our place.

John Dunn sworn

One evening, some time since Morris came to the skating rink, the dog followed him in. Fred Miller was playing with the dog. Morris said, "Do you want a dog, Fred?" Miller said, "Yes!" and he got a strap and took the dog home that night.

Thomas Hewitt sworn

I live on the lot next to defendant. On Sunday morning February 5th the dog was at my place. It had been there all night. I heard the dog yell. It was at the door bleeding. I looked round the house to see if I could see any one. I went to defendant's. I asked him if he shot a dog at my place that morning. He said, "Yes, why?" I said it was a dirty mean trick to do. He said he didn't think I had anything to do with it. I said he might have to pay for it.

I took the dog to Millers. He was very lame. I told Miller what had happened to the dog. I think it was right to kill the dog, as I don't believe he would ever be any use after getting the bullet in his shoulder.

Cross-examined

I don't know whether the dog would have died from the first wound. The dog had been at my place a few times. Defendant told me the dog was on the road when he shot it. He shot it because it annoyed him.

For the Defence

William Stiles sworn

I am the defendant. I heard the evidence of Thomas Hewitt. The dog was shot on the road. It had annoyed me. I had driven it away repeatedly and my wife also. The dog had been howling round the house and scratching the door. I took the gun in the morning and shot at the dog to scare him. I happened to strike him. I didn't put the gun to my shoulder. I was about 4 rods from him. When I went out the dog was on my lot.

Re-direct

Fred Miller recalled

The dog slept in the stable at night. He hadn't been away except on 3 or 4 Saturday nights.

Joseph Hewitt sworn

I work for the complainant. The dog stays in the stable at night, put in every night. He followed me home 3 or 4 Saturday nights.

Defendant fined $2 with $3 damages and costs $3.70, to be paid forthwith, and in default, to be imprisoned in the common gaol at Bracebridge for 30 days with hard labour.

James Boyer, J.P.

Paid.

Conviction returned.

Chapter Eleven

WORSE FOR THE LIQUOR

Canada's temperance movement surged in the 1890s, fuelled by the moralistic urge of righteous people to "uplift" drinkers to a higher plateau of personal living and civil behaviour, and by secular realism that sought to confront rampant social and economic problems caused by alcohol. What started as "temperance," or balanced moderation in the use of alcohol, increasingly hardened into "prohibition." Prohibitionists sought to solve the problems of the drunken wretches and their victims who were drowning in alcohol by drying up the source, closing down distillery operations and the business places of those who sold booze and profited from the misery of others.

The move to restrict and ban alcohol was certainly driven by religiosity, but another motive was the social realism of those who were critical of the long row of beckoning bars and taverns interposed between the paymaster at a mill or factory and the workingman's waiting wife and hungry children at home. When the bars closed late on a weekly pay

The British Lion Hotel anchored the northwest corner of Ontario and Dominion streets, running steeply uphill from the wharf and Bracebridge Bay. Here the owner and employees pose during a quiet daytime moment. At night the dining room was busy, the bar crowded, and, after hours, sleeping accommodation often overflowed onto the lobby floor. Brawls inside and out kept the town constable busy, producing a steady flow of cases for Magistrate's Court.

night, many anxious and agitated women, huddling at home with crying youngsters, received not only an empty pay packet but also a slap across their face, or worse, from a lurching, hounded husband.

In 1893 the Liberal Party convention voted to hold a national plebiscite on prohibition, to address "the admittedly great evils of intemperance," showing how, by this date, Canada's political parties, in addition to churches, temperance organizations, and provincial parties, were coming to grips with the alcohol issue. The Liberals included this plank in their 1896 election platform, were victorious at the polls, and on September 29, 1898, gave Canadians our first national referendum: a ballot question about prohibiting alcohol.

Ontarians, including those in Bracebridge and across the rest of Muskoka, voted by a strong majority in favour of prohibiting the

In the 1890s a well-stocked pharmacy offered Bracebridge men an imposing choice of cigars: from cheap and hot to expensive and mellow, with prices ranging from five cents to one dollar. Pharmacies also sold beverage alcohol, when the "local option" law in Bracebridge permitted.

manufacture, sale, and consumption of alcohol. These results were not duplicated everywhere in the country, however. As a result of uneven support for the measure, the resolve of the Liberal government in Ottawa weakened. The counted ballots revealed strong differences of opinion about the desirability of allowing the continued sale of alcohol between French-speaking Catholics in Quebec and English-speaking Protestants elsewhere. With a deep cultural divide separating the two major Canadian communities, Prime Minister Laurier decided to leave it for each provincial government to regulate the "great evil" in a way most appropriate for its jurisdiction, rather than trying to impose a single national standard.

Bracebridge voters, in addition to casting their ballots in the 1898 national referendum, had already voted in Ontario's January 1, 1894 province-wide plebiscite on the prohibition of liquor, as they would again vote in Ontario's December 4, 1902 ballot on the same question. On October 20, 1919, they cast ballots on four questions respecting repeal of the Ontario Temperance Act and the sale of beer. Yet again, on April 18, 1921, Bracebridgites, along with all Ontarians, voted on whether to ban importation of liquor into the province. Under the "local option" provision of the Ontario Temperance Act, the contentious liquor question was also posed a couple of times to Bracebridge voters: first, in a 1908 ballot to approve a local-option bylaw, when the town voted to remain wet; then again in 1911, when the citizens, by more than the requisite two-thirds majority, voted themselves dry — a decision that resulted in the town's four hotel bars and one liquor store being shut down.

The liquor-related cases in this chapter came before Magistrate Boyer during that tumultuous 1890s decade. It was a time when public pressure over alcohol in Bracebridge was mounting, as "drys," advocating temperance or even outright prohibition, vied with "wets" in the long shadow cast by the town's hotels and taverns.

There were brawls in the bars. There were fights between fellows who had been close friends until one glass of liquor too many loosened a man's lips, causing him to let escape slurs about the character of another man's wife — the insults resulting in an argument that culminated in bare-knuckle blows. Drunkards in the street engaged a crowd of bypassing school children. Many residents of Bracebridge floated or jostled their way through a perfect alcoholic haze: some guided home by boys or friends; others fighting in the streets; still others causing late-night commotion and waking townsfolk; and not a few falling down dead drunk on the commons.

A majority of those charged with being drunk and disorderly admitted the charge or pleaded guilty. In return, JP James Boyer responded, according to the facts of each case, which regrettably are not disclosed on the record, with a variety of verdicts: fines; prisoner discharged; defendant discharged with a caution; fourteen days in jail when defendant admitted he could not pay his fine; dismissing the charge when a complainant declined to prosecute; dismissing a case for lack of strong evidence; accused not fined but discharged upon payment of costs; reducing the costs a convicted drunk had to pay by twenty cents, because after paying a $1.00 fine and $4.80 in court costs the man had no money left; dismissing with a caution and no fine a defendant who pleaded guilty, because the man had lost or had stolen $105 while he was drunk — punishment enough; discharging with a caution a defendant who pleaded guilty to being drunk, because he had to be in assizes court as a witness; deferring the sentence, which effectively meant no punishment; and deferring sentence for a patriot drunk while celebrating Dominion Day.

This Bracebridge bar had a brass rail along the top for patrons to steady themselves if they grew wobbly.

All these instances saw the sobering light of day in Magistrate's Court, where justice was meted out to those who, in the description of one witness, had been "the worse for the liquor."

MAGISTRATE'S COURT — MAY 5TH, 1893
BEFORE JAMES BOYER, J.P.
ROBERT E. ARMSTRONG v ALEXANDER TAYLOR

For being drunk and disorderly at Bracebridge on May 5th, contrary to Bylaw No. 8, passed September 4th, 1879.
The charge having been read to prisoner, he pleaded guilty.

Prisoner fined $1.00 and $4.00 costs, to be paid forthwith, and in default of immediate payment, to be levied by distress, and in default of sufficient distress, to be imprisoned in the lock-up at Bracebridge for 21 days.

James Boyer, J.P.

Paid June 17th, 1893.

Conviction returned.

Magistrate's Court — July 20th, 1893
Before James Boyer, J.P.
Gustavus A. Binyon v David A. Pringle

For being drunk and incapable at Bracebridge on July 20th.
Defendant pleaded guilty.

Defendant discharged with a caution.

James Boyer, J.P.

Magistrate's Court — September 7th, 1893
Before James Boyer, J.P.
Robert E. Armstrong v Alexander McGregor

For being drunk and incapable at Bracebridge on September 6th, 1893, contrary to Bylaw No. 8, passed September 4th, 1879.
The charge having been read to prisoner, he pleaded guilty.

Prisoner fined $1.00 and costs $4.00, to be paid forthwith, and in default, to be imprisoned in common gaol at Bracebridge for 14 days, defendant having admitted he had no goods and chattels whereon to levy the amount.

James Boyer, J.P.

Paid constable $2.50
Conviction returned.

Magistrate's Court — December 23rd, 1893
Before James Boyer, J.P.
Alexander Foster v William Dawe

For being drunk and disorderly at Bracebridge on December 22nd, 1893.
Defendant discharged, complainant declining to prosecute.

James Boyer, J.P.

Magistrate's Court — February 21st, 1894
Before James Boyer, J.P.
Robert E. Armstrong v Duncan McCallum

For being drunk and disorderly at Bracebridge on February 20th, contrary to Bylaw No. 8, passed September 4th, 1879.
Defendant pleaded guilty.

Defendant fined $1 and $4 costs, to be paid forthwith, and in default, to be imprisoned in the lock-up at Bracebridge for 14 days.

James Boyer, J.P.

Magistrate's Court — March 17th, 1894
Before James Boyer, J.P.
Robert Armstrong v August Vohlstrom

For being drunk and incapable at Bracebridge on March 17th, contrary to Bylaw No. 8, passed September 4th, 1879.

The charge having been read to the prisoner, he pleaded not guilty.

Robert Armstrong sworn

I am a constable of the District of Muskoka living in Bracebridge. About four o'clock this afternoon I was on Front Street near Dominion Hotel. I saw a horse and wheeled vehicle. He was backing up and broke the lines and got loose and fell. I took the horse to the Dominion Hotel stable and put him in there. Mr. Manley came and said that a man was lying drunk on the commons with his face cut. I went with Manley and found the prisoner. He was drunk and lying down on the commons asleep. I arrested him, and found that he owned the horse. He was not in a fit state to look after his horse.

Prisoner convicted and fined $2 and $4 costs, to be paid forthwith, and in default, to be imprisoned in the common gaol at Bracebridge for 21 days.

James Boyer, J.P.

Paid.

Magistrate's Court — December 28th, 1894
Before James Boyer, J.P.
Robert E. Armstrong v Frederick Bennett

For being drunk and incapable at Bracebridge on December 27th.
Constable withdrew charge and prisoner discharged.

James Boyer, J.P.

Magistrate's Court — May 15th, 1895
Before James Boyer, J.P.
Robert E. Armstrong v James Tarbox

For being drunk and disorderly at Bracebridge on May 14th.
Prisoner pleaded guilty.

Ordered to pay $1 fine and $4 costs, forthwith, and in default, to be imprisoned in gaol at Bracebridge for 21 days in default of sufficient distress.

James Boyer, J.P.

Paid.
Paid constable.
Conviction returned.

MAGISTRATE'S COURT — JULY 2ND, 1895
BEFORE JAMES BOYER, J.P.
ROBERT E. ARMSTRONG V THOMAS CROMBIE

For being drunk and disorderly at Bracebridge on July 1st, 1895.
Defendant pleaded guilty but sentence deferred.

James Boyer, J.P.

MAGISTRATE'S COURT — MAY 22ND, 1896
BEFORE JAMES BOYER, J.P.
THOMAS DODD V GUSTAVUS A. BINYON

For being drunk and disorderly at Bracebridge on May 21st, 1896.
The charge having been read to defendant, he pleaded not guilty.

Thomas Dodd sworn

I am a constable for the District of Muskoka. Yesterday afternoon between 2 and 3 o'clock I was at the British Lion. Moore, the bartender, asked me to stay there a minute or two as there was a "racket" at his house. He returned, and from what he told me, I went to his house. I found defendant lying on his back outside the house. He was using blasphemous language and threatening to be revenged on someone but I did not understand who. I arrested him.

Defendant convicted and fined $1 and costs $4.50, to be paid forthwith, and in default, to be imprisoned in the common gaol at Bracebridge for 14 days.

James Boyer, J.P.

Paid.

Paid constable.

Conviction returned.

MAGISTRATE'S COURT — JUNE 4TH, 1896
BEFORE JAMES BOYER, J.P.
ALFRED STUNDEN V DANIEL BROWN

For being drunk and disorderly at the Township of Medora on June 4th, 1896.

Prisoner admitted the charge.

Fined $1 and $4 costs, to be paid forthwith, and in default, to be imprisoned in the common gaol at Bracebridge for 21 days.

James Boyer, J.P.

Paid.

Paid constable $2.50

Conviction returned.

MAGISTRATE'S COURT — AUGUST 28TH, 1896
BEFORE JAMES BOYER, J.P.
THOMAS DODD V PETER MASTERS AND ERNEST EDWARDS

For being drunk and disorderly at Bracebridge on August 24th, 1896.

The charge having been read to defendants, they severally pleaded guilty.

Fined $1 each and $2.35 costs, to be paid forthwith, and in default, to be imprisoned in the common gaol at Bracebridge for 21 days with hard labour.

James Boyer, J.P.

Paid.
Paid constable $2.25.

Magistrate's Court — August 28th, 1896
Before James Boyer, J.P.
Thomas Dodd v Henry Waller

For being drunk and disorderly at Bracebridge on August 25th, 1896.
Defendant did not appear.

Thomas Dodd sworn
I am a constable for the Town of Bracebridge. On August 26th I personally served Henry Waller with a summons in the above case, requiring him to appear at the Town Hall, Bracebridge, at 2:00 p.m. today to answer the above charge. Defendant did not appear in obedience to the summons.

Warrant to be issued for his arrest.

James Boyer, J.P.

Just over two weeks later, Constable Dodd found and arrested Waller, resulting in his receiving, if not his day, at least his several minutes, in court:

Magistrate's Court — September 15th, 1896
Before James Boyer, J.P.
Thomas Dodd v Henry Waller

For being drunk and disorderly at Bracebridge on August 25th last.
The charge having been read to defendant, he pleaded guilty.

Defendant fined $1 and $3.90 costs, to be paid forthwith, and in default, to be imprisoned in the common gaol at Bracebridge for 21 days.

James Boyer, J.P.

Court $1.90.
Constable $2.00. Paid.
Total $3.90.

Magistrate's Court — October 17th, 1896
Before James Boyer, J.P.
Thomas Dodd v Alexander Taylor and John McIntyre

For being drunk and disorderly at Bracebridge on October 15th, 1896.
The charge having been read to defendants, they severally pleaded not guilty.

Susan McLean sworn
I live at the back of A.B. Bettes planing factory. On October 15th I saw defendants sitting on logs on the road near Mr. Copeland's house. They were there from 9:00 a.m. till between 1 and 2 p.m. Defendant McIntyre was drinking out of a bottle and swearing. I believe it was whiskey. I saw them both drinking more than once. Between 12 and 1, a number of school children, between 20 and 30 in number, were around them.

McIntyre used very bad language. Both were drunk. I did not hear Taylor use bad language. I went for Constable Dodd to arrest defendants.

Cross-examined
I heard McIntyre tell Tommy Loughery to go for whiskey. He had a flask in his hand.

Isaac Press
I live in Bracebridge. On October 15th I saw defendants sitting on timbers on the roadside. McIntyre was swearing at me and another boy. I saw both men drinking out of a flask.

William McDonald sworn
On October 15th I saw defendant sitting on logs near Copeland's. They were both drinking out of a flask. They were there when I left school at 12 and also when I went back about 1:30. McIntyre was swearing at the last witness. There were a crowd of children round them.

Defendant Taylor discharged. Defendant McIntyre convicted and fined $2 and $5 costs, to be paid forthwith, and in default, to be imprisoned in the common gaol at Bracebridge for 21 days.

James Boyer, J.P.

Conviction returned.
Defendant McIntyre committed to gaol.

MAGISTRATE'S COURT — JULY 16, 1897
BEFORE JAMES BOYER, J.P.
THOMAS DODD V DENNIS GUINEY

For being drunk and disorderly at Bracebridge on July 8th, 1897.

Prisoner pleaded guilty and was discharged on payment of costs, $4.50.

James Boyer, J.P.

Paid constable $2.50.

Court $2.00.

Paid.

MAGISTRATE'S COURT — JULY 17TH, 1897
BEFORE JAMES BOYER, J.P.
THOMAS DODD V GEORGE DAVIS

For being drunk and incapable, and impeding and incommoding peaceable passengers on one of the public highways of Bracebridge on July 10th, 1897.

[No plea entered, as accused failed to appear.][1]

Edward Dodd sworn

On Wednesday last I served George Davis with a summons to appear this day in this matter. I handed it to him personally. He said he didn't want it. I saw him reading it.

---

[1]George Davis did not appear in court despite the summons served on him by the town constable, a deviation from the fundamental principle that a person must be brought before the judge hearing the charges against him, rather than be tried in absentia. At some point, though, David must have become connected with this process because his fine was recorded as paid.

Thomas Dodd sworn

I am a constable for the Town of Bracebridge. On Saturday night July 10th, about 11 p.m., defendant was being led along by two boys on the east side of Manitoba Street. He was very much under the influence of liquor. The sidewalk was full of people and they were impeded and incommoded by defendant jostling and tumbling against them. I took him across the street. The boys said if I would let him go they would see he went home. I did so. At 20 minutes past 12 the next morning I again found the defendant among a lot of men making a disturbance in the yard at the British Lion Hotel.

Joshua Yeoman sworn

I was sitting near Mr. Merrill's store on Saturday night last and saw the defendant being led along by two boys as stated by Constable Dodd. He was very drunk and impeding people passing along the sidewalk.

Defendant convicted and fined $1.00 and $4.55 costs, to be paid forthwith, and in default, to be imprisoned and kept at hard labour in the common gaol at Bracebridge for 21 days.

James Boyer, J.P.

Court $2.30.
Paid constable $2.25.
Paid.
Conviction returned.

Magistrate's Court — August 30th, 1897
Before James Boyer, J.P.
Alfred Stunden v Arthur Tiffon and Charles Donahue

For that defendants, on August 21st, 1897, at Bracebridge, were drunk

and did unlawfully commit a breach of the peace in or near a certain street or public place in said town.

Defendants pleaded not guilty.

Frederick Gleason sworn

I live in Bracebridge. On August 21st, after 6 p.m., I saw a crowd in Higgins' yard. I went to the place and saw Tiffon tear the shirt off Donahue, who fell over a drain. Tifton struck him on the nose and made it bleed. I don't know if they were sober or not. They were angry with each other.

Frederick Gimson sworn

On August 21st I went to Higgins' yard to get a rig. The two defendants went from the street into the yard. Defendant Tiffon was going to strike the other defendant. They went to the gate leading to the street. Donahue said he would hit Tiffon if he was bigger. Tiffon took off his coat and went to strike at Donahue. They struck each other and Donahue fell over something and Tifton grabbed him and tore his shirt. It was not a friendly scrap. The men were the worse of liquor.

For the Defence

Charles Donahue sworn

I am a defendant. We work together. We came to Bracebridge together. We had a scuffle together. Tiffon said he would get me another shirt when he tore mine. I did not strike the other defendant.

James Boyer, J.P.

Case dismissed.

On Christmas Day, 1897, James Boyer heard the charges against James Leonard, whom Constable Thomas Dodd had found "drunk and disorderly" earlier that same day. Leonard pleaded guilty. Two days later, Dodd brought to

Magistrate's Court two others, George Filbert and William Lynn, who'd been, as they admitted, "drunk and disorderly" on Christmas Eve. They each paid $4.50 in fines and costs, and the constable, for his efforts, was paid $4.50.

The new year, 1898, began much as the old year ended. Frank Malone was charged by Constable Robert E. Armstrong "for being drunk and disorderly by fighting" at Bracebridge on New Year's Day. He paid his $1.00 fine and $4.50 costs, and Boyer paid over $3.00 of it to Constable Armstrong. Things then settled down, until spring.

MAGISTRATE'S COURT — MAY 13TH, 1898
BEFORE JAMES BOYER, J.P.
ALFRED STUNDEN V THOMAS MAHONY

For being drunk and disorderly at Bracebridge on May12th, 1898.
Defendant pleaded guilty, but as defendant had either lost or had stolen from him $105 the defendant was discharged with a caution.

James Boyer, J.P.

MAGISTRATE'S COURT — MAY 26TH, 1898
BEFORE JAMES BOYER, J.P.
JAMES ARNOTT V JOSEPH RIVARD

For being drunk and incapable at Bracebridge on May 26th, 1898.
Defendant pleaded guilty.

Defendant, being a witness in a case to be heard this day before the assizes, was discharged with a caution.

James Boyer, J.P.

Magistrate's Court — June 4th, 1898
Before James Boyer, J.P.
James Arnott v Mark Weston

For being drunk and disorderly at Bracebridge on June 4th, 1898.
The charge having been read to prisoner, he pleaded guilty.

Fined $2.00 and costs $4.75, to be paid forthwith, and in default, to be imprisoned in the common gaol at Bracebridge for 21 days.

James Boyer, J.P.

Fine paid.
Conviction returned.

Magistrate's Court — August 5th, 1898
Before James Boyer, J.P.
Alfred Stunden v Ira Broadway and David Laur

For that defendants, on July 31st at Bracebridge, were drunk and did use profane language on one of the public streets of said town, to the disturbance and annoyance of Her Majesty's peaceable subjects residing in the immediate neighbourhood.
Defendant Laur did not appear.
Defendant Broadway pleaded not guilty.

Alfred Stunden sworn
I am a constable of the District of Muskoka. I served a summons on David Laur on August 3rd, requiring him to appear at the Town Hall this day at 7 o'clock to answer the above charge.

Herbert B. Appleton sworn
I live in the 4th ward, Town of Bracebridge. On Sunday night, or early Monday morning, I was in bed. I heard a noise which woke me up. I heard someone say, "Put down the stone." Another said, "You can't hit me." The parties were making an unusual noise and swearing. The noise was sufficient to disturb the people in the neighbourhood. It was between 11 p.m. and 1 a.m. There were 3 when I first saw them, but one was not making any disturbance. One of the parties wanted the others to be quiet.

John Shier sworn
I board with the last witness. I was awakened out of my sleep on Sunday night last by a noise. I got up. I saw two men on the street making a noise. I don't know who they were. One said, "Put down that stone." It was about the middle of the night.

William C. Edwards sworn
I board with Mr. Appleton. On Sunday night I was awakened by the noise. I went to the window and I saw them pulling each other about. One was using bad language. A third man came up and tried to get them to be quiet and went away again.

Ira Broadway, one of the defendants, sworn
I live in Bracebridge and work in Shaw's tannery. On Sunday night I had been working at the tannery up to 12 a.m. As I left the premises I heard a noise. I recognized the voice. I went up and found defendants Laur and Samuel Robinson. I said to Laur, "You should be ashamed of yourself, getting drunk and hollering on the street."

I know Laur was drunk. He attempted to strike me. I had a pail and coffee pot in my hand; I swung my arm round to prevent him striking me, and hit him in the face. He attempted to strike me two or three times afterwards. I kept him off and he picked up a stone. I caught him by the two arms.

Robinson came up and took the stone and was very noisy and using very bad language. The noise was sufficient to disturb any people living in the neighbourhood. I was at work till 12 o'clock that night.

Case dismissed against defendant Broadway.

Defendant Laur convicted and fined $5.00 and costs $6.05, to be paid forthwith, and in default, to be committed to the common gaol with hard labour for 2 months.

James Boyer, J.P.

Defendant absconded.

Magistrate's Court — August 11th, 1898
Before James Boyer, J.P.
Gustavus A. Binyon v William French

For being drunk and incapable at Bracebridge on August 11th, 1898.
Charge withdrawn. Defendant came to town on an excursion from Orillia and was not disorderly.

Defendant discharged.

James Boyer, J.P.

Finally, two "drunk and disorderly" cases in 1898 highlight the dollar value placed on people's time in that era. Both Andrew Tribe and Thomas Jackson pleaded guilty, and each was fined one dollar. While the former was able to pay the dollar, the latter was not and, instead, as an equivalent, served twenty-one days in jail.

Chapter Twelve

Assault, Battery, and Plain Fighting

Because many defendants and accused persons pleaded guilty in assault and battery cases, no evidence was adduced, so all James Boyer recorded were the names of the parties, the date of the episode, the charge, and the sentence he imposed. Only a few, of several dozen, are included in this chapter as samples. The rest of the cases in the chapter were contested, with testimony about fighting and disturbing the peace that further rounds out a portrait scrappy Muskokans and late-night scenes in 1890s Bracebridge.

The hot feelings that provoked these fights of course went in both directions, not only in the moment but in the law suits later: fighting between the Ellsworths and Stevenses resulted in cross-suits between the two men, plus an additional suit by Ellsworth's wife, Lillian, against Alton Stevens. Other times, however, the parties actually settled between themselves in the presence of the JP once the charges had been read out.

This summertime view of the Queen's Hotel on the main street of Bracebridge, with Thomas Street running down at the right to the train station and river, shows the early evening busyness of Muskoka's central town by the late 1890s. The Queen's Hotel was another of the town's drinking establishments; several of the cases of fighting that landed before James Boyer originated inside the hotel or on the street outside.

These were not pre-trial settlements, but resolutions in court where the austere and intimidating presence of James Boyer, plus the fact that the combatants involved benefited from a day or two for their tempers to cool down, produced a relatively amicable compromise. Who knows? Perhaps even a few laughs were exchanged.

Anyone who's ever witnessed or participated in a bar-room brawl understands how, above all else, confusion reigns. This is reflected in several cases where it is not apparent, either from the bench book or the many names of those involved, just who was culprit and who was the victim. Magistrate Boyer found a way to resolve such confusion, in the cases involving combatants Gilbert McGinnis, Thomas Warlow, and others; he convicted all concerned. Reappearance of the same individuals in different cases of assault and battery, or causing public disturbance, shines the spotlight on the rowdies of Bracebridge's community stage, and their penchant for acting in gangs. Law enforcement (in the person of town constable Robert Armstrong) and speedy justice (from ever-on-the-job Justice of the Peace Boyer) hardly paused for

Christmas.

Magistrate's Court — December 26th, 1893
Before Messrs. Hunt and Boyer, J.P.s
Robert E. Armstrong v William Dawe

For having, on December 23rd, 1893, at the Town of Bracebridge, by riotous and disorderly conduct on Manitoba Street, wantonly disturbed the peace and quiet of the inmates of the dwellings near said street.
The charge having been read to prisoner, he pleaded guilty.

Prisoner fined $50 and costs $2.75, and in default of immediate payment, to be imprisoned in the common gaol at Bracebridge for the space of six months with hard labour.

Alfred Hunt, J.P.
James Boyer J.P.

Conviction returned.
William Dawe committed to gaol.

Magistrate's Court — December 26th, 1893
Before Messrs. Hunt and Boyer, J.P.s
Robert E. Armstrong v Thomas George Pull

For having, on December 23rd, 1893 at the Town of Bracebridge, by riotous and disorderly conduct on Manitoba Street, wantonly disturbed the peace and quiet of the inmates of the dwelling near said street.
The charge having been read to prisoner, he pleaded guilty.

Prisoner fined $50 and costs $2.75, and in default of immediate payment, to be imprisoned in the county gaol at Barrie for the space of six months with hard labour.

Alfred Hunt, J.P.
James Boyer, J.P.

Fine and costs paid.
Conviction returned.

MAGISTRATE'S COURT — DECEMBER 26TH, 1893
BEFORE JAMES BOYER, J.P.
THOMAS SMITH V BROOK WATSON

Assault and battery at Bracebridge on December 25th, 1893.
The charge having been read to prisoner, he pleaded guilty.

Defendant fined $1.00 and $2.75 costs, to be paid forthwith, and in default, to be imprisoned in the common gaol at Bracebridge for 14 days.

James Boyer, J.P.

Paid.
Conviction returned.

MAGISTRATE'S COURT — FEBRUARY 12TH, 1894
BEFORE JAMES BOYER, J.P.
WESLEY ELLSWORTH V ALTON STEVENS

For that defendant, on February 11th, 1894, did use the following threat: "By Jesus Christ, I'll put a knife into you. I'll rip you with the knife."
The charge having been read to defendant, he pleaded not guilty.

Wesley Ellsworth sworn

I live in Bracebridge. I know defendant. Last night I met defendant near Dr. Bridgland's store near ten o'clock. I was alone. Defendant's wife was with him. I took hold of his coat sleeve. I said, "I want to settle these lies." I walked along with them. I said, "If you are a man, give the youngster to the woman and settle it." He said, "You are no more than a pimp in the house." I walked towards him; he had a knife in his hand, and said, "By Jesus Christ, I'll rip you if you come towards me." I said, "I'll see about it tomorrow." I saw he had a knife in his hand. I did not strike defendant. I am afraid defendant will do me a bodily injury.

Cross-examined

I never offered to thrash defendant nor followed him up on Christmas night. I did not strike him. He threatened to put the knife into me.

For the Defence

Alton Stevens sworn

I am defendant in this case. I reside in Bracebridge. Last night I was coming along the street with my wife and child. I met complainant opposite Foster's hotel. He passed me, and then turned and struck me on the back with his fist, and said, "If you put down the kid, I'll punch your face into a jelly." I walked on. Complainant punched me in the back and shoved me.

When I got to my own house my wife tried to push him back. He reached over my wife's shoulder and struck me in the breast. All I said to him was to go on about his business and leave me alone. I did not have a knife with me. I do not carry a knife. I had both arms about the child. I did not use the language I am accused of. I never used any threats against complainant.

Cross-examined

I did not have a knife with me last night.

Annie Christina Stevens sworn

I am the wife of defendant. It was between 9 and 10 last night. I was coming home with my husband. Met complainant opposite Foster's hotel. He passed us and turned and struck defendant on the shoulder. My husband put the child down and asked him what he did that for. He said he would have revenge, if he sent defendant to the grave. He told defendant to put the kid down and he would smash his face.

I had to go between them several times. When we got to the house my husband opened the door; he struck over me at my husband. I did not see my husband with a knife. My husband did not say the expression used.

Cross-examined

Complainant and I did all the talking. My husband did not call him a pimp.

Complaint dismissed with costs $2.85, to be paid forthwith, and in default, to be levied by distress, and in default of distress, to be imprisoned in the gaol at Bracebridge for 30 days with hard labour.

James Boyer, J.P.

Paid.

Magistrate's Court — February 12th, 1894
Before James Boyer, J.P.
Alton Stevens v Wesley Ellsworth

Assault and battery at Bracebridge on February 11th, 1894.

The evidence in the last case is to stand as the evidence in this case by consent of the parties.

Complaint dismissed with costs $2.85, to be paid forthwith, and in default, to be levied by distress, and in default of distress, to be imprisoned in the gaol at Bracebridge for 30 days with hard labour.

James Boyer, J.P.

Paid.

MAGISTRATE'S COURT — FEBRUARY 14TH, 1894
BEFORE JAMES BOYER, J.P.
LILIAN ELLSWORTH V ALTON STEVENS

Assault and battery at Bracebridge on December 22nd, 1894.
Evidence taken down on paper.

Defendant convicted and fined $5 and costs $5.80, to be paid forthwith, and in default, to be imprisoned in the common gaol at Bracebridge for 6 weeks.

James Boyer, J.P.

Paid.

MAGISTRATE'S COURT — APRIL 9TH, 1894
BEFORE JAMES BOYER, J.P.
ANSON ROWLEY V DAVID NEWMAN

For having, on April 6th, 1894, at the Township of Macaulay, assaulted and threatened to shoot the informant.
Charge having been read, prisoner pleaded guilty.

Prisoner fined $1 and $2.50 costs, to be paid forthwith, and in default, to be imprisoned in the common gaol at Bracebridge for 10 days and also bound in the sum of $100 to keep the peace for 12 months.

James Boyer, J.P.

Paid.

MAGISTRATE'S COURT — DECEMBER 22ND, 1894
BEFORE JAMES BOYER, J.P.
ROBERT E. ARMSTRONG V JAMES DURNO, ALEXANDER FRASER, WILLIAM FRASER

For causing a disturbance in the public streets at Bracebridge on December 22nd, 1894.

Defendants Alexander Fraser and William Fraser pleaded guilty, and the other defendant, Durno, pleaded not guilty; case adjourned till 24th at 2 o'clock p.m.

Defendant Alexander Fraser and William Fraser each fined $1 and $4 costs, to be paid forthwith, and in default, to be imprisoned in the lock up at Bracebridge for 21 days with hard labour.

James Boyer, J.P.

December 24th, 1894
Case resumed against defendant Durno.

Robert E. Armstrong sworn

I am a constable of the District of Muskoka. On Saturday night, last, between 11 p.m. and 12 a.m., I saw prisoner and Alex Fraser lying down on the sidewalk in front of Burt's store. They had hold of each other. Prisoner's face was bloody. They were making a noise and there was a crowd round them.

For the Defence

James B. Brown sworn

I was in Burt's store on Saturday night between 11 p.m. and 12 a .m. When I came out, prisoner and Fraser were quarrelling. I heard some scuffling. I saw two men scuffling and saw them fall on the sidewalk but didn't see a blow struck. There were quite a number of people gathered there.

James Rutherford sworn

I was in front of Woods' store nearby, opposite, at the time it happened. I heard prisoner and Alex Fraser quarrelling and I went across. I went away for a few minutes. When I got back they were both down on the sidewalk. They were tussling. I saw William Fraser strike prisoner on the head. They were obstructing the sidewalk. It was 11 o'clock or past 11 at night.

Defendant convicted and fined $1 and $4 costs, to be paid forthwith, and in default, to be imprisoned in the lock-up at Bracebridge for 21 days with hard labour.

James Boyer, J.P.

Paid.

Conviction returned.

MAGISTRATE'S COURT — SEPTEMBER 12TH, 1895
BEFORE JAMES BOYER, J.P.
CHARLES DONOHUE V JOSEPH FISHER

Assault and battery at Bracebridge on the tenth day of September A.D. 1895

The charge having been read to defendant, he pleaded not guilty.

Charles Donohue sworn

On the night of the 10th instant, I was going home from Bracebridge. Defendant was going that way. When on the bridge, defendant got his arms round me and tried to take away a pipe I was smoking. I wouldn't let him have it. I got away from him. Defendant said I pushed him. He got me against the bridge and struck me in the eye, making it black and cutting the skin. He struck me 3 or 4 times afterwards. Oliver Marshall and William Booth and his father were present.

Cross-examined

I didn't try to crowd you over the bridge.

Hollie Marshall sworn

I was going home with complainant and defendant on the night in question. Complainant was smoking and defendant tried to take his pipe from him. I saw defendant strike complainant. They were together. I couldn't see if more than one blow was struck. I didn't see complainant strike defendant at all. I think Mr. Booth had gone up on the hill.

Prisoner convicted and fined $5 and $5.55 costs, to be paid forthwith, and in default, to be imprisoned in the common gaol at Bracebridge with hard labour for 6 weeks.

James Boyer, J.P.

Costs court $ 1.80
Paid constable $3.75
Total $ 5.55

Magistrate's Court — March 30th, 1896
Before James Boyer, J.P.
Robert E. Armstrong v Gilbert McGinnis

For that defendant, on the 28th day of March instant, at the Town of Bracebridge, did cause a disturbance in a certain public place near to a public highway by fighting and swearing.

Defendant pleaded not guilty.

Remanded until Tuesday 31st instant, at two o'clock in the afternoon.

George Harper sworn

I was in Bracebridge last Saturday night and saw the fight between the two men, defendant and Warlow, at the British Lion Hotel. They were wrestling in the backroom. I saw blood on defendant's face. I saw them on the floor.

James Lambert sworn

I saw defendant bleeding but saw no blows struck. They were wrestling around on the floor. The other man was Thomas Warlow. I did not hear any bad language.

Thomas Warlow sworn

On Saturday night last, two men, one was named Cochran, came and raised a disturbance. One man was wanting to fight, and the other, who was named Atkinson, didn't want to fight. Cochran tried to force him to fight. I tried to make peace between them with Mr. Sibbett, the landlord.

Defendant came up and struck me in the top of the head. He started to take off his coat to fight. This was in the back room of the British Lion. We clinched and rolled around the floor a little. I just tried to defend myself. I am quite positive that he struck me first. I struck him afterwards. There were several blows struck between us.

Cross-examined by Mr. Palmer

Defendant was trying to get Atkinson and Cochran to fight. I told defendant that Atkinson didn't want to fight. I stepped in front of him and he struck me. We clinched and had a scuffle.

Charles McTurk sworn

I saw two boys scuffling in the hall at the British Lion last Saturday night. Defendant interfered by inciting one of them on to fighting. I saw defendant and Warlow scuffling but couldn't say which one started it.

Cross-examined by Mr. Palmer

I did not see defendant attempt to leave. From what I saw he was not creating a disturbance.

George Williams Atkinson recalled

Cross-examined

Defendant and a man named Jimmy came up to me at the hotel. Jim Cochran wanted to fight me. I wouldn't fight. Cochran had my cap in his pocket. I asked him for my cap once or twice but he wouldn't give it to me. I didn't fight. There was no one backing me up.

For the Defence

Gilbert McGinnis sworn

I live at South Falls. Last Saturday, March 28th, I was at the British Lion Hotel. I heard a row start between Atkinson and a man called Jimmy. I went to go out and take Jimmy out too. Atkinson said we couldn't go out until Jimmy gave him his cap. I went out with Jimmy, and went around to the back and tried to come in again, when Warlow opened the door and struck me in the eye. He struck me again when I was trying to get my coat off. We clinched and rolled on the floor.

Taken as a common assault. See next case.

Magistrate's Court — March 31st, 1896
Before James Boyer, J.P., and Peter M. Shannon, J.P.
Gilbert McGinnis v Thomas Warlow

Assault and battery at the Town of Bracebridge on the 28th day of March, 1896.

Gilbert McGuinnis sworn
On Saturday, March 28th, I was at the British Lion Hotel. I went to go with a man named Jimmy. (Evidence in the other case of the present witness to be considered as evidence in this case.) This was part of the fight that was going on at the same time.

Defendant pleaded guilty to a common assault and the complainant pleaded guilty to a cross action of assault.

Defendant and complainant each fined $5.00 and $4.55 costs, to be paid forthwith, and in default, to be imprisoned in the common gaol at Bracebridge for the space of six weeks.

James Boyer, J.P.

Defendant Warlow paid.
Defendant McGinnis paid.
Paid constable.
Conviction returned.

Constable $7.35
Court $1.75
Total $9.10

Magistrate's Court — April 23rd, 1896
Before James Boyer, J.P.
William Nichols v Mark Weston

Assault and battery at Bracebridge on 22nd April instant.

The charge having been read to prisoner, he pleaded not guilty.

William Nichols sworn

Last night near 10 o'clock I was at the Queen's Hotel. Prisoner was with me in the bar room. We had a drink together. Prisoner was standing next to me. He struck me in the eye. He took me unawares as he had not threatened me. He cut me by the side of the eye. I had no quarrel with him.

Cross-examined

I had three drinks and a cigar.

John R. Higgins sworn

Prisoner and complainant were talking in front of the bar last night. They were not quarrelling. I saw prisoner strike complainant without giving him any notice or using any threats. He struck him once.

Defendant sworn

Mark Weston sworn

I was with complainant. We had several drinks together. We had been good friends up to that time. He said something about my wife and I struck him. He said she was nothing but a stinker, as she didn't use him well the last time he was up. I told him not to say that again. He repeated it and I struck him.

William Nichols recalled
I did not use the words or say anything to the effect that prisoner's wife was a stinker.

Defendant convicted and ordered to pay a fine of $20.00 and costs $2.00, to be paid forthwith, and in default, to be imprisoned and kept at hard labour in the common gaol at Bracebridge for two calendar months.

James Boyer, J.P.

Constable $5.00
Court $2.00
Total $7.00
Conviction returned.

MAGISTRATE'S COURT — FEBRUARY 3RD, 1897
BEFORE JAMES BOYER, SINGLETON BROWN AND JOHN INGLIS, J.P.s
EDWARD SWITZER V JOSEPH BOYD

Assault and battery at Bracebridge on February 2, 1897.
The charge having been read to defendant, he pleaded not guilty.

Mr. Mahaffy for defendant

Edward Switzer sworn
I was on the train last evening coming home from Gravenhurst to Bracebridge. I went into the smoking car. Defendant was sitting opposite me, and he with others shouted out to me "Tan bark," and said, "You are a son of a bitch of a tan bark man." I said, "Mr. Langford has been posting you on that and he is a damned liar." Defendant struck me twice on the head. He called me names afterwards.

Cross-examined by W. Mahaffy
I have asked the price of tan bark and what it could be purchased for. Defendant pleaded guilty to a common assault.

Defendant fined $5 and $4.50 costs, to be paid forthwith, and in default, to be imprisoned and kept at hard labour in the common gaol at Bracebridge for one month.

James Boyer, J.P.

Conviction returned.

More cases of civil suits by two combatants continued. For instance, John Coleman the Younger was brought by William R. Berry before James Boyer on April 13, 1897, for assault and battery at Macaulay, and fined $1.00 and $4.70 in costs. However, to round up a gang of fighters, it was more common for police officers, such as Bracebridge Constable Thomas Dodd, to be the prosecutor.

Magistrate's Court — July 15th, 1897
Before James Boyer, J.P.
Thomas Dodd v Alfred Hillman, James Hillman, Charles Bradshaw and Thomas Duncan

For having, on Sunday, the 11th day of July, 1897, at Bracebridge, unlawfully caused a disturbance in a certain public place in said town by fighting and swearing.
Defendant Bradshaw appeared and pleaded guilty for himself and the other defendants.

Each defendant fined $1 and $2.50 costs, to be paid forthwith, and in default, to be imprisoned and kept at hard labour in the common gaol at Bracebridge for 21 days.

Defendant Bradshaw paid fine and costs for each defendant.

James Boyer, J.P.

Fines $4.00
Court $5.50
Paid constable $4.50
Conviction returned.

Accused persons normally travelled to the court in Bracebridge from outlying communities, but on one occasion, in high summer of 1897, a pleasant trip to Port Carling may have been incentive enough for James Boyer to journey out of town and up the lakes.

Little more can be learned from this case, however, since the evidence taken was recorded "on paper" rather than in his bench book. Yet, the fine was stiff in comparison to those levied in other cases of assault and battery, while the higher than normal court costs no doubt included the extra expense of holding court in a different municipality. The Village of Port Carling received the fine.

Magistrate's Court held at Port Carling this 17th day of August 1897
Before James Boyer and John McDermott, J.P.s
Peter M. Shannon v William Pooler

Assault and battery at Port Carling on the 9th August instant.
Defendant pleaded not guilty.

Depositions taken on paper.

Defendant convicted and fined $5 and $8.33 costs, to be paid forthwith, and in default, to be imprisoned and kept at hard labour in the common gaol at Bracebridge for 6 weeks.

James Boyer, J.P.

Paid fine to Port Carling Village Treasurer, F.D. Stubbs.
Paid constable $4.53
Paid 2 witnesses $1.50
Conviction returned.

The following spring, Muskoka Magistrate's Court again travelled, this time to the Village of Utterson, with pretty much the same outcome.

MAGISTRATE'S COURT — MAY 20TH, 1898
HELD AT UTTERSON
BEFORE JAMES BOYER, J.P., DANIEL BAIN AND W.G. STIMPSON
NELSON BARRAGER V WILLIAM INGRAM

Charge of assault at the Township of Stephenson on 14th instant.
Depositions taken on paper.

Convicted and fined $2 and $6.48 costs, to be paid forthwith, and in default, to be imprisoned and kept at hard labour in the common gaol at Bracebridge for one month.

James Boyer, J.P.

Paid fine to Treasurer of Municipality.
Paid constable.

George Bunting sued James Durno twice in March 1898, on his own and, separately, on behalf of his wife, the two cases arising out of a single fight.

Magistrate's Court — March 30th, 1898
Before James Boyer, J.P. and W. George Stimpson, J.P.
George Bunting v James Durno

Assault and battery at Bracebridge on 26th instant.

Defendant pleaded guilty.

Fined $2 and $3.80 costs, to be paid forthwith, and in default, to be imprisoned in the common gaol at Bracebridge for one month with hard labour.

James Boyer, J.P.
W.G. Stimpson, J.P.

Fine paid.
Paid constable.
Conviction returned.

Magistrate's Court — March 30th, 1898
Before James Boyer, J.P. and W. George Stimpson, J.P.
George Bunting v James Durno

Assault and battery on Mary Elizabeth Bunting at Bracebridge on 26th instant.

Defendant pleaded not guilty.

George Bunting sworn

About 6:30 p.m. last Saturday night defendant met me and accused my child of stealing eggs. I told him I didn't think she had done so. I went home. Defendant struck me and said he would pound me to a jelly. My wife was present and told him to leave me alone. Defendant told her to get in the house you bloody bitch. He struck my wife and knocked her down and tore her dress. Mr. Baxter and his wife were near at the time.

Cross-examined
I didn't call you names.

Mary Elizabeth Bunting sworn
Am wife of George Bunting. I saw defendant strike my husband and knock him down. He then struck me and knocked me down. I got between my husband and defendant and he knocked me down. He called me a bloody bitch and told me to go in the house. He tore my dress. He told my husband if he met him up street he would pound him till he was all of jelly. I was not much bodily hurt.

Cross-examined
You struck me on the breast.

Sarah Jane Baxter sworn
I live next to Mr. Bunting. Last Saturday evening I was outside my house. Defendant accused my daughter of stealing eggs. I saw him meet Mr. Bunting and strike him and knock him down. Mrs. Bunting went to prevent him striking her husband. He (defendant) shoved her back and she fell. I was not near enough to hear what was said.

Cross-examined
You struck him at his own fence.

John Baxter sworn
Defendant came on Saturday night and accused my girl of throwing hay

out of the stable. He went on to Buntings. I heard they were talking. I didn't see defendant strike Buntings but I saw them both lying on the ground.

For the Defence

Defendant sworn

After I left Baxter's I was going to the Mill. Bunting came out, and called after me and said, "What damned lies have you been telling about my young ones?" He started to abuse me. His wife said something. I thought he was going too far and I struck him. His wife grabbed him and they both fell alongside the fence. She said, "That's all we want. George, go downtown and we will have him pulled." He blackguarded me and I went away.

Defendant convicted and fined $5 and $3 costs, to be paid forthwith, and in default, to be imprisoned in the common gaol at Bracebridge and there kept at hard labour for 6 weeks (not to run concurrently).

James Boyer, J.P.
W.G. Stimpson, J.P.

Paid.
Paid constable.
Conviction returned.

Magistrate's Court — August 13th, 1898
Before James Boyer, J.P.
William Eneas Toshack v Joseph Fisher

Assault and battery at the Township of Draper on the 16th day of April, A.D. 1897
Defendant pleaded not guilty.

William Eneas Toshack sworn

I live on the Town line in the Township of Draper. I know defendant. On the 16th of April 1897, when I was fishing at the mouth of Sharp's Creek I saw defendant, who was acting rather queerly. He grabbed my hat. My hat had some fish-hooks in the front of it. When he grabbed it I caught hold of it, and in jerking it away, one of the fish hooks ran into his finger. I was taking the hook out of his finger when he struck me on the nose and I found myself on the ground. My nose bled for quite a while. The bridge of my nose was bruised so that my face was black right across for some time.

I said, "Fisher, you fool, you'll suffer for that." He got mad, walked up and down for a while swearing, and then took me by the pants and the coat at the neck, and was going to throw me in, but Holly Marshall who was there told him to leave me alone. He then dropped me, kicked me a little and then left me alone. Holly Marshall, Norman Simmons, two Post boys, Melville Arnott, Tom Boyer and a lot of little boys whose names I do not know were there . I went home but came up the same day and laid proceedings against him.

Hollie Marshall sworn

I live on the Town line near Macaulay. I know last witness and defendant. I went with Toshack to the mouth of Sharp's Creek to fish on the 16th April 1897. Defendant was there. I saw defendant strike Toshack in the face and said something to him. The blow knocked him down, made his nose bleed and blackened his eye.

Thomas Boyer sworn

I live in Bracebridge. I know Toshack by sight. I also know defendant. I saw defendant and Toshack at Sharp's Creek sometime last in April 1897. Defendant grabbed Toshack's hat. Toshack grabbed at his hat to get it back and a fish hook in it went into defendant's hand or finger. Defendant struck Toshack in the nose or face and made his face bleed.

Defendant convicted and fined $5.00 and costs $18.20, and in default of immediate payment, to be imprisoned in the common gaol at Bracebridge with hard labour for the space of six weeks.

James Boyer, J.P.

Defendant Joseph Fisher committed to gaol.

Conviction returned.

The high costs in this case arose because, in addition to $2.05 paid to the constable for interviewing five witnesses, there was a charge of $1.50 for arresting Joseph Fisher, who then escaped from jail, a further $1.50 to the constable for re-arresting him, $2.75 for assistance in the arrest, $3.90 for mileage of thirty miles travelled in the exercise, a charge of $3.90 for conveying the prisoner, as well as fees for the remand, two witnesses, and the constable's attendance at court.

Chapter Thirteen

Early Road Rage

"Road rage" has been diagnosed as a product of human stresses, aggressive personality disorders, accelerating dependence on technology, imploding frustration, exploding frustrations, pressures of overpopulation, and overcrowding on roadways jammed with jostling SUVs, transport trucks, passenger cars, and motorcycles. This phenomenon presents a bleak contrast to the situation found on the roads long ago, in what was an earlier and gentler era, a golden age when slower people never became hostile, but instead perched peacefully on horse-drawn wagons along sleepy country roads. Or were "the good old days" so perfect?

Many of the cases James Boyer heard in the 1890s reveal that the Muskoka roadways of that era were also places where simmering resentments erupted into aggressive acts. The roads also produced an odd case or two involving not damage to other humans, but, rather, to the means of transport itself. Even the issue of the construction of the roads could land citizens before the magistrate, if they refused to comply with an order under Ontario's draconian "statute labour" laws, which required men, by statute, to stop their own work and provide unpaid labour to construct or repair local public roadways. This law may have been defensible public policy in the early days of settlement, but it was much criticized by James Boyer outside his courtroom; his view was that public roads should be built and maintained under government contracts, and the workers paid from public funds. Yet as a magistrate responsible for upholding the established law, James enforced statute labour laws in court by fining those who refused to provide their labour as required.

Magistrate's Court — December 26th, 1893
Before James Boyer, J.P.
Elias H. Traves v Alexander Fraser

For using blasphemous and indecent language upon public highway at the Township of Oakley on December 22nd, 1893.
The charge having been read to defendant, he pleaded not guilty.

Mr. Palmer appeared for the defence

Elias H. Traves sworn
I live in the township of Oakley. On December 22nd between 8 and 9 o'clock in the evening I was going home with my team and I met a team of horses and a pair of bobsleighs that were on the road without apparently anyone in charge of them. There was not sufficient room for me to pass. When I found I could not pass I shouted and a boy came out from Mr. McLellan's house. He tried to remove the horses and sleighs but could not on account of the snow crust.

Defendant came out of the house. I spoke to him. Defendant and the boy started to tramp a road. Defendant then drove off the road in order to let me pass. As the roads were bad, my harness struck his in passing.

Defendant then said to me, "Jesus Christ, you want the whole God-damned country," and furthermore called me a "son of a bitch" and "a bastard" and wanted to fight. I said I was sorry if I had done anything to him. I then drove on, defendant all the time using bad language. I told him I would summons him.

Cross-examined by Mr. Palmer
I did not turn out of the centre of the road.

For the Defence

Defendant sworn
I am the defendant and in this case. My team was in front of Mr. McLellan's house. I left Henry Anderson in charge of the horses. I was in the house ten minutes. We heard a shout and Anderson and I went out of the house. I turned off the horse as much as I could but my horse's forefeet were on the road. I called him a "damned hog." I said, "Some people when they get the world want a fence built around it."

He started off and the bunk of the sleigh caught the horse's hind leg. The horse jumped out of the way. He called me a "danged fool." I told him if he would come back off the sleigh I'd break his mouth and show him, if I was drunk or not. He said he wouldn't dirty his hands with a drunken man. I did not use such language as the complainant says I did.

Mary Ann McLellan sworn
I live on the town line in the township of McLean. I remember Friday night the 22nd. Defendant was at my house that night. I heard Mr. Traves call and opened the door. Anderson went to turn the horse out of the road. Defendant also went. I was in the doorway but left when Mr. Traves had passed defendant's team.

Adjourned till Wednesday, January 3rd, 1894 at 2 p.m.

For the Prosecution

Henry Anderson sworn

I live in Oakley. On December 22nd I was at W. McLellan's. Defendant came while I was there in the evening. Defendant had a team in front of the house. Traves had a team coming from direction of Bracebridge. He stopped to get defendant to move his team off the road. I went out and moved the team. The hind bunk of the sleigh was on the road. Defendant came out and we went to tramp a road.

Defendant said, "Jesus Christ, if you break the horse's leg you'll pay for it." Fraser called Traves "a son of" something. I didn't hear what it was. He said, "Go home, you bastard and fetch the whole gang." I was standing beside the sleigh. Defendant said, "If you come back I'll lick you."

For the Defence

Maud McLellan

Daughter of Mrs. McLellan. I was standing on the doorstep. Fraser went to the horses. Traves was speaking loud. Traves said as he was going up the road he wouldn't dirty his hand with a drunken man. I was about 120 feet away from them. Defendant said, "Jesus Christ, if you get off that sleigh I'll show you whether I am drunk or not."

Defendant fined $1.00 and $4.65 in costs, to be paid forthwith, and in default, to be levied by distress, and in default of sufficient distress, to be imprisoned in the common gaol at Bracebridge for 20 days.

James Boyer J.P.

Paid.
Witness $1.60 paid.
Constable $1.25 paid.
Conviction returned.

MAGISTRATE'S COURT — JANUARY 4TH, 1895
BEFORE JAMES BOYER, J.P.
MARY ANN PRENTISS V JOHN OUDERKIRK

For malicious injury to a certain sleigh, the property of James Prentiss.
Prisoner pleaded not guilty.

Edward Appleton sworn
I live in the township of Monck near Bracebridge. Yesterday afternoon I saw young Michaux with a dog hitched up to a sleigh. After going along a piece I saw him run away. Defendant came up, caught hold of the sleigh by the two front runners, and dashed it on the ground. One runner was broken off and split in two. I do not believe it was done accidentally.

Cross-examined by Mr. Palmer
Defendant said the dog was his. There would have to be a new runner made to fix the sleigh.

James Prentiss
I am seven years old.

Mary Ann Prentiss
I bought the sleigh a year ago Christmas. It cost $1.40. It was hardwood with iron runners. It was broken into three parts. I went over and asked defendant if he was going to pay for the sleigh. He said, "Not by a damn." He said he broke the sleigh.

For the Defence

Defendant sworn
I live in the township of Monck. I was keeping the dog. The dog came to my place on Sunday.

Caroline Ouderkirk sworn
I am defendant's mother. The dog came to us on Sunday afternoon. We kept the dog.

Blanche Ouderkirk sworn
There was nobody near the sleigh when the dog was untied.

R.E. Armstrong sworn
Defendant said he broke the sleigh.

Defendant fined 50 cents, and 50 cents damages and costs of $2.75, and in default of payment, imprisonment in the common gaol at Bracebridge for 21 days.

James Boyer, J.P.

Paid.
Paid 50 cents to prosecutor.

Magistrate's Court — January 14th, 1895
Before James Boyer, J.P.
George Henry Taylor v Jacob Winch

Assault and battery at Township of Macaulay on January 12th, 1895.
The charge having been read to prisoner, he pleaded not guilty.

George Henry Taylor sworn

I live in Draper. I know defendant. On Saturday last I was coming along the town line between Draper and Macaulay. I was going home driving a horse and sleigh. I saw defendant. He had passed the town line and was on a saw log road. He was riding on a load of saw logs. He was about 50 yards past the town line. He ran back to the town line. He stopped my horses. They were at the junction of the two roads.

Prisoner said Archie Yuill said I was going to knock the hell out of him. I said I didn't say that. He called me a liar and tried to pull me off the sleigh. I went to get down and fell. He struck me several times and bit me with his teeth several times. The marks on my face and eyes and neck are the result of his striking and biting me. He struck me with his fist. I got the wounds and I was on the ground.

I said let me up and don't be eating me like a dog. He said he'd be damned if he would till he had given me a good thrashing. He then got off me and ran to his load. It happened about noon on Saturday. No one else was present. He caught my horses by the lines and stopped them.

Cross-examined

I have not had any bad feeling towards defendant. I met defendant last Wednesday. We were both driving teams. Prisoner's sleigh was empty, mine was loaded. He turned out part of the way. I took off my coat after he put his whip in my face and said, "Throw me in the ditch if you can." He threatened to do so. I didn't offer to fight him. I did not use any threatening language to prisoner or strike him at all.

For the Defence

Defendant sworn

I was going along the road on Wednesday last. I met complainant driving a loaded team. I turned out into the ditch, as my sleigh was empty, and struck a rock. I had a pair of lumber bob sleighs with bunks on. I asked him if he could turn out. He said, "What the hell is the matter of your turning out?" I said, "I am in the ditch and can't get any farther." He said he couldn't turn off. I said if he didn't I would throw him in the ditch.

He took off his coat and told me to throw him in the ditch if I could. We both had a whip. He offered to strike me with the whip. I went on and left him there. He called me bad names. I didn't say anything about getting him in a corner.

I met him several times on the road between Wednesday and Saturday. On Saturday I had passed the town line. I saw him coming and stopped, and I said he had told Hale he was going to lick me. He took off his coat and took a piece of chain and said he would knock my brains out. I was not within 12 feet of his sleigh.

He said he would get something, would let my God-damn guts out, took a ring out of his pocket with 3 prongs on, put it on his finger and shook it under my nose. He told me to strike him and I told him to strike me. He struck at me. I warded off the blow and struck him and knocked him down and gave him a few blows with my fist. He hollowed murder. I struck him again and then let him up. He then called me a God-damned son of a bitch. He said he would knock my brains out if I didn't let him go. I didn't bite him.

Cross-examined
I struck him four or five times with my clenched fist when he was on the ground. I made the marks on his face. I had my hand on his throat and may have scratched his face. I went back to him on the road. It wouldn't have occurred if I hadn't went back. I went back to give him a beating. He was 12 feet from his sleigh. I had knocked him down.

In rebuttal

Archibald Yuill sworn
I live in Draper. I know the parties. I saw them last Wednesday on the town line between Draper and Macaulay. They each had a team. We met prisoner. Prisoner turned off a short piece and asked Taylor to turn out too. Taylor said he wouldn't. Prisoner said if he didn't he would put him in the

ditch. They had some words which I don't remember. Prisoner turned out and gave him the road. Prisoner's sleigh was empty and Taylor's was loaded.

Cross-examined
Taylor took off his coat and told prisoner if he wanted to fight he had a chance. It was an uphill grade and there was a good chance for an empty team to turn out.

Prisoner fined $10 and $4.25 costs, to be paid forthwith, and in default, to be imprisoned in the gaol at Bracebridge and there kept at hard labour for the space of 2 calendar months.

James Boyer, J.P.

Paid.
Paid constable $2.75.
Conviction returned.

MAGISTRATE'S COURT — FEBRUARY 10TH, 1896
BEFORE MR. WM. SPENCER, J.P.[1]
THOMAS DODD V JAMES FITZMAURICE

For furious driving upon a public highway.
Defendant pleaded not guilty.

William Galbraith sworn
On February 3rd I saw a team belonging to the best of my knowledge to

---

[1]Uncommonly, William Spencer took this case on his own. Magistrate James Boyer, serving in his other capacity as town clerk, was in Toronto on municipal business.

the defendant going up the street, furiously. I thought it was a runaway. Mr. Dodd was out on the street and tried to stop the team. I heard prisoner say "No you don't, Mr. Dodd." They slowed up at Kirk's and stopped at Webster's place. There was a boy on horseback alongside the team. He was driving at a faster rate than was safe for people passing on the street.

Thomas Dodd sworn

On February 3rd I saw a team coming up the street very rapidly. I, thinking that it was a runaway, ran out on the street to stop them. I saw defendant with either a whip or gad in his hand. He said, "No, you don't stop me, old man Dodd," when I asked him to stop. The sleighs were two heavy bobs and had a binding pole tied on with chains, projecting behind. There was a boy on horseback running along with the team.

James L. Fenn sworn

I was going up the street on the day in question when I heard a great noise and, looking around, saw a team coming very rapidly up the street. Mr. Dodd tried to stop the team but could not do so. There was a young man driving the team. They stopped in front of Lawrence's. I consider it was furious driving, unsafe for the public on the streets. The young man seemed to be trying to hold them back and the horses appeared to have got the better of him.

Augustine Russell sworn

I am a farmer and know the team in question. I have known them to run away. They would run some distance before they could be stopped.

Osborne Hewitt sworn

I was on the sleigh with defendant when this occurrence took place. Defendant pulled on the reins to stop them. He had no whip or gad. I think it was the horse coming alongside that cause them to run.

Case dismissed.

Wm. H. Spencer, Police Magistrate
Justice of the Peace

MAGISTRATE'S COURT — SEPTEMBER 9TH, 1896
BEFORE JAMES BOYER, J.P.
WILLIAM HANNON THE ELDER V WILLIAM ATKINSON

For having, on July 29th, at the township of Stephenson, being then and there in charge of a certain wagon drawn by two horses, wilfully obstructed the public highway and prevented complainant, who was then and there travelling along said highway with a horse and buggy, from passing along said highway.

The charge having been read to defendant, he pleaded not guilty.

Thomas Pickering sworn

I know defendant. About two months ago I was in a wagon with defendant coming from Utterson about six o'clock p.m. William Hannon came along driving a horse and buggy. We were in front in a wagon drawn by a team. Mr. Hannon caught up to us and tried to pass but defendant drew the horse over to the right hand side. Mr. Hannon asked to get by. Defendant drove on a piece further then turned out and let him by.

William Hannon Sr. sworn

I was coming from Utterson and was in a hurry to get home. Defendant, when I tried to pass, pulled his team right across the road in front of me two or three times. I asked him to let me pass as I was in a hurry. He drew on one side and said, "Whenever you want to pass, you will have to ask leave." He then let me pass.

Cross-examined by Mr. Palmer
I was at my house about five or ten minutes before he came up there. Atkinson was on the left hand side of the road.

Thomas Pickering recalled
Atkinson was about in the middle of the road. Mr. Hannon tried to pass on the right and defendant drove across on that side.

For the Defence

William Atkinson sworn
I was travelling from Utterson with team and wagon. I was about half way home. I kept nearly up to him after he passed. He went to pass on the right. I went off to the right and left him nearly all the road to pass on the left hand side. He tried it but once. I was home before he got the horses unhitched.

Cross-examined by Mr. Ashworth
As he did not pass when I turned out for him, I went back to the centre of the road.

Case dismissed with costs $6, to be paid forthwith, and in default, to be levied by distress, and in default of sufficient distress, complainant to be imprisoned in the common gaol at Bracebridge for 21 days.

James Boyer, J.P.

Court $1.30
Witness $2.15
Constable $2.55

Magistrate's Court — September 9th, 1896
Before James Boyer, J.P.
WILLIAM ATKINSON v PETER HANNON, WILLIAM HANNON JR. AND JOSEPH HANNON

For an assault and battery at the township of Stephenson on August 22nd, 1896.

The charge having been read to the defendants, they severally pleaded not guilty.

William Thomas Atkinson sworn

I live in Watt. I am complainant. I remember August 22nd I was driving a team from Utterson. Mr. and Mrs. Spencer, Mrs. Clearwater and Isaac Ouderkirk were with me. We met Peter Hannon. It was about 6 p.m. He was driving a team with a load of grain. He kept the middle of the road and wouldn't turn out. I asked him to turn out. He said he wouldn't. I said if he didn't I would put him off. There was room for 2 teams to pass if he had given me half the road.

We both got off our wagons. He struck at me and I threw him down. We were both on the ground. Hannon was undermost. He told Joseph Hannon to stick the pitchfork into me. Joseph got the pitchfork and ran at me with the fork. Barnard Spencer pulled me off Peter. I got in the wagon.

The women got the team past. Mrs. Spencer led the team past the other. Peter Hannon caught my horses by the head. William Hannon tried to pull me out of the wagon and tore my shirt.

Cross-examined by Mr. Ashworth

I was coming from Utterson. Defendants were going towards there. They were at the foot of the hill. I had turned out into the ditch, and told Peter Hannon, who was driving, to turn out. He said he wouldn't. I didn't say I could lick any one of the Hannons. He came towards me and struck at me. I clenched him and threw him down. Spencer jumped off the rig and prevented Joseph Hannon sticking the fork in me and threw it away. He took me off Peter. Mr. Hannon Sr. was not there then but came afterwards, and took hold of me.

Question by the court

When Joseph Hannon came at me with the fork he was near enough to have stuck it in me if he hadn't been prevented.

Barnard Spencer sworn

I live in Stephenson. I remember that on August 22nd about 6 o'clock I was driving with complainant, my wife and Mrs. Clearwater. We met a team loaded with grain driven by Peter Hannon. Joseph Hannon was there. We met them at the foot of a hill past Mr. Hannon's house. Atkinson drove out as far as he could and stopped close to the other team. There was room for both to pass. Atkinson said, "Come on." Peter Hannon said get out of the road. Atkinson said I have given you half of the road. Peter Hannon said, "If it is a fight you want, you will get it."

He got off the wagon and came to Atkinson. Atkinson got off the road. Hannon came and struck at him. They clenched and fell in the ditch hugging one another. I saw Joseph Hannon coming with a pitchfork. I caught hold of the fork. He was near enough Atkinson to strike him with the fork. Peter Hannon said, "Stick it in him." Joseph Hannon kicked Atkinson. I told him to step back and I would part them. I separated them by shoving them apart.

Atkinson attempted to get in the wagon. Joseph Hannon struck him on the head. Peter Hannon then struck him. Atkinson got in the wagon and caught the horses by the head. One of the other Hannons attempted to pull Atkinson out of the wagon and said, "You damned son of a bitch. I'll whip you." Isaac Ouderkirk was sitting in the wagon.

Cross-examined by Mr. Ashworth

Atkinson didn't say he could lick any of the Hannons. Joseph Hannon attempted to strike Atkinson with the fork but I prevented him. Atkinson didn't kick at anyone that I saw.

For the Defence

Peter Hannon sworn

I met Atkinson's rig on the day in question. I drove down and turned out within 6 inches of the ditch. Atkinson's team could have passed. There was no ditch on his side. Atkinson drove up and didn't pull out a bit but pulled in facing my horses. He told me to turn to hell into the ditch. I told him he had over half the road. He said he could lick me, and called me "a son of a bitch." He said he could lick the best man of the Hannons.

I jumped off the load. He jumped out of his wagon. He ran and struck at me. I struck him. We clenched and both went down. Spencer came and took hold of me and opened my fingers. I called to Joe and said if Atkinson struck me to hit him with the fork. Spencer kept us apart.

Father then came up. Atkinson told Spencer to stand back as he wanted to get a crack at that old dog. He struck at my father. Joe struck Atkinson. I knocked him against the wheel. Atkinson got into the wagon, and kicked at me. I didn't touch him again. My brother Will came along and told Atkinson if he wanted a fight Richard Patterson was there and he would show him fair play. Atkinson kicked at Will and Will ran up and caught hold of him. Mrs. Spencer led the horses up the hill.

Cross-examined by Mr. Palmer

I measured the distance the same evening. I didn't strike Atkinson when he was getting into the wagon.

Joseph Hannon sworn

I remember August 22nd. I was walking behind my brother on the road. I heard Atkinson say, "Turn into the ditch or I'll put you there." My brother said, "If you want to go by you have lots of room." He then called my brother a son of a bitch and said he didn't care for any of the damned family.

He jumped off the wagon and was pulling his coat off when my brother was getting off the load. They went towards each other and struck at each other. Atkinson got my brother down in the ditch. Spencer came along and jumped off the wagon. I told Spencer to take Atkinson off my brother.

My brother told me to strike Atkinson with the fork if Atkinson struck my brother when he got up. I picked up the fork to throw it back and Spencer caught it. Atkinson said to Spencer to let him get a whack at my father, who had come along. He raised his hand to hit my father, when I jumped in and struck him. As the team passed my brother, Atkinson kicked at him.

My brother then jumped forward and caught the horses' heads. My brother Will came up and asked Spencer what the row was about. As he passed, Atkinson kicked at him. My brother told Atkinson if he wanted to fight, Patterson was there and would see fair play. My brother turned out as far as he could.

Cross-examined by Mr. Palmer
I did not strike at anyone except when I struck Atkinson. I can't say I saw anyone struck by Atkinson.

William Hannon sworn
When I got to where the row occurred Atkinson was getting in the wagon. He kicked at my brother Peter. I went up and said that if it was fight he wanted Richard Patterson was there and would show him fair play. He kicked at me and I caught him by the shirt or vest near the neck to pull him out but my father came between us on the edge of the road and Atkinson's team was standing with their heads to them. He was close to the edge of the ditch.

William Hannon Sr. sworn
I saw my son's team stopped on the road. I ran down. I saw Atkinson, my son Peter, and Spencer as if they had hold of each other. Joseph was there. I said to Atkinson you had better get in your wagon and get out of here. He said to Spencer "Get out of the way and let me get a whack at that old bastard," and he struck him. Peter did not strike Atkinson after I got there. At the time there was no ditch between where the oats stood on Atkinson's side and the fence.

Defendants convicted and fined $2 each and $5.65 costs, to be paid forthwith, and in default, to be imprisoned in the common gaol at Bracebridge for 6 weeks with hard labour, and each to enter into his own recognizance in $200 to keep the peace for one year

James Boyer, J.P.

Paid and each party entered in recognizance as above.
Conviction returned

MAGISTRATE'S COURT — SEPTEMBER 9TH, 1896
BEFORE JAMES BOYER, J.P.
WILLIAM HANNON THE ELDER v WILLIAM ATKINSON

For having on August 22nd at the township of Stephenson obstructed a certain highway.

By consent of both parties, the evidence in the preceding to be considered as taken in this case.

Case dismissed with costs of $4.35 to be paid forthwith, and in default, to be levied by distress, and in default of sufficient distress, to be imprisoned in the common gaol at Bracebridge for 21 days.

James Boyer, J.P.

Conviction $1.80
Constable $2.55
Total $4.35 Paid

MAGISTRATE'S COURT — DECEMBER 28TH, 1897
BEFORE JAMES BOYER, J.P.
THOMAS DODD V PETER SWORD

For furious driving upon a certain public highway in the township of Macaulay on December 24th, 1897.
Defendant pleaded guilty.

Fined $2 and $4.67 in costs, to be paid forthwith, and in default, to be levied by distress, and in default of sufficient distress, to be imprisoned in the common gaol at Bracebridge for 14 days.

James Boyer, J.P.

Paid constable $2.67.
Conviction returned.

MAGISTRATE'S COURT — AUGUST 29TH, 1898
BEFORE JAMES BOYER, J.P.
WILLIAM MCNEIL V JOSEPH SEYNE

Refusing to do Statute Labour on Road Division No. 31, Draper, on August 27th, after being duly notified to do so.
Defendant pleaded guilty.

Fined $5 and costs of $2.14, to be paid forthwith, and in default, to be levied by distress, and in default of sufficient distress, to be imprisoned and kept at hard labour for 10 days.

James Boyer, J.P.

Paid.
Paid constable.

Magistrate's Court — August 29th, 1898
Before James Boyer, J.P.
William McNeil v Louis Bellafoy

Refusing to do Statute Labour on Road Div. No. 31, Draper, on August 27th, after being duly notified so to do.

Defendant pleaded guilty.

Fined $5 and costs of $1.75, to be paid forthwith, and in default, to be levied by distress, and in default of sufficient distress, to be imprisoned and kept at hard labour for 10 days.

James Boyer, J.P.

Paid constable.

Paid.

Chapter Fourteen

Ill-Gotten Game

Visitors to Muskoka in the 1890s hunted animals for sport, fished, and took pleasure being photographed with their trophies. Meanwhile, hungry locals hunted to avoid starvation, supplementing garden patch vegetables, wild berries, milled grain, and provisions from the general store with whatever fowl they could bag, fish they could catch, and deer, moose, or bear they could shoot. Because they harvested food on sight, most men walking the woods, rowing a boat, or driving a wagon carried a fully loaded rifle with them. No creature that could fly, walk, or swim was safe.

The dozen-and-a-half hunting cases decided by James Boyer in the 1890s surely represent just a small fraction of the incidents involving game harvested by Muskokans in violation of the rules. Even these scattered charges were laid only because someone witnessed illegal hunting and was prepared to prosecute a neighbour or relative.

It was illegal to shoot deer while they swam, but the "unsportsmanlike" hunting practice was so common in Muskoka that several artists produced renditions of the kill, routinely seeing it, as in this work by Seymour Penson of Port Carling, a "typical" Muskoka scene.

Provincial game laws governed catches and kills in several ways. The government designated seasons as either "open" or "closed" for harvesting specified species. It also stipulated the maximum quantity that could be taken, a quota known popularly to sportsmen as "the limit." Another rule made it unlawful to shoot swimming deer, even during deer season. Using nets or nightlines to catch fish was likewise prohibited, but, as with shooting swimming deer, it was an established practice in pioneer Muskoka. Hunting rules were routinely broken, as these cases show. As homesteader Thomas Osborne would later record about Muskoka hunting in the late 1870s, "There is no law here." Artists' engravings published in two separate books depicting Muskoka pioneer life of this era show men shooting frantically swimming deer from their canoes.

Other restrictions concerned human safety, more than sportsmanship. Hunting ducks with a shotgun was no problem, but doing so with a rifle was. Whereas buckshot scattered, a bullet risked the safety of anyone on the far shore as it could skip dangerously across the water's surface. In under-populated Muskoka, few considered that a serious risk, but most hunted with shotguns anyway because the scattering pellets improved their odds of hitting a flying bird.

The rules governing trapping did not concern themselves with cruelty to animals, or the manner of death for creatures of the waters or woods, only the numbers in which they died. Quotas for beaver and muskrat were specified. Trapping laws were enforced because the market for animal pelts constituted a lucrative commercial enterprise. The fur trade generated healthy profits, with little financial outlay, so the temptation to exceed quota or take animals out of season was real, as is shown by these cases of Muskoka muskrats taken out of season.

There was certainly no real concern that overhunting and overfishing might result in the eradication of the animals. Game management in 1890s Ontario was founded on the belief that the woods were deep and animals could reproduce endlessly. Absence of game wardens and failure by trappers to adhere to legal limits could, as a consequence, have seen Ontario's forests and streams stripped of fur-bearing animals, just as buffalo had been hunted to extinction on the Prairies by this date, and most species of whales and larger marine mammals harvested to depletion off Canada's Atlantic coast.

Had trapping been allowed to run unchecked, the woods might quickly have become a dangerous place, one where poachers and trap-line vigilantes battled in a state of frontier anarchy. Extending the rule of law into the bush was a challenge of wills. Law enforcers had to suppress the hunting instinct of men who owned firearms, lived in the teeming woods, liked the thrill of bringing down an animal, and above all needed to feed themselves and their families. A good way to control illegal hunting and fishing was through the vigilance of a roaming, busybody game warden, since people are generally more circumspect when they fear law enforcement officers are nearby. Consequently, the provincial government appointed many game wardens and deputy game wardens, whose effectiveness is seen by their presence as prosecutors in these cases.

Another way to ensure that those violating game laws faced prosecution was to offer a sort of "finder's fee." As has been noted, Canadian courts in this era paid prosecutors an incentive known as a moiety. The magic of moieties was its instant multiplication of law-enforcement personnel, beyond anything that could be achieved by naming more game wardens, bringing the rule of law to Muskoka's even most isolated townships. How else would Fritz Ross, with his catch of 192 muskrats trapped out of season, have been prosecuted, but for the vigilance of Charles E. Mawdsley, who earned half of Ross's five-dollar fine for his effort? Earning a share of the fine could prove stronger than even the bonds of family, as one of these cases demonstrates. In a few instances, it seemed the accused's neighbour was even more ardent hunting for moieties than his human quarry was in tracking down game.

Under the moieties system, even game wardens themselves could collect a portion of the fine, which greatly improved their hearing when it came to guns being fired in the woods. Judging from the number of cases he profitably prosecuted (including some not included here due to space), Warden Elias H. Traves seems to have been constantly hunting for money in the forests — an astute hunter bagging his own catch of unwary human prey, the one animal on which there was no statutory quota.

If some private citizens prosecuted illegal hunters who were their own relatives, proving that money can be thicker than blood, it is also true that, on occasion, official game wardens were not always as zealous as they could be in doing their duty. Thomas Osborne wrote in *Accidental Pioneer*, his memoir of 1870s bush life in north Muskoka, how as a youthful homesteader he served out-of-season venison to a game warden for dinner, put him up for the night at his cabin in remote Franklin township, then served him illegally caught fish for breakfast, receiving in return for all his free hospitality only a mild warning about "next time" as the well-satisfied officer departed.

This offhand relationship with game seemed natural in the Muskoka frontier setting, and developed into a well-established practice. In a hunting case heard by James Boyer on August 25, 1896, one of the defendants was A.C. Fletcher, the same man who had sat with him as a justice of the peace in a case two years before.

The well-known method of issuing hunting and fishing licences to keep anglers and hunters in check used by the government today would have to await the emergence of Ontario's regulatory state in the twentieth century, as licensing was not yet part of this 1890s scene. On the other hand, one heavily regulated aspect of life in the 1890s that would wither away as the twentieth century advanced was strict Sunday observance. The officially religious Victorians were zealous in keeping the Lord's Day, which meant that those hoping to arrest anyone for hunting or fishing illegally had a watertight case if the activity occurred on Sunday: a firearm discharged in the woods on the first day of the week, even without a deer or rabbit being stopped in its tracks, could be prosecuted as a violation of The Lord's Day Act. Even so, one of the cases involving a Sunday hunt that came before James Boyer did not proceed on those grounds, presumably because of all the other game law infractions it manifestly entailed. Many other cases of Sunday sport did, however, involve charges under The Lord's Day Act, as seen in cases of hunting or fishing on Sunday in Chapter 21: Saving the Sabbath.

Once Magistrate Boyer one time tempered the law's severity when, "in consequence of the defendant's age," he sentenced seventy-four-year-old John Marling to imprisonment "for a short term" of only one week for trapping muskrat out of season. A week later, however, the day Marling was being released from jail, a much younger muskrat trapper faced the same charge. Stuck with his own kindly precedent, James had no choice but to send George Ditchburn to take Marling's place, again only for seven days.

Although these cases involve the killing of moose, muskrat, ducks, deer, partridge, and a chipmunk (shot, a settler claimed, to feed his dog), not all "hunters" sought their quarry in the wild. Why traipse through the rough woods for uncertain prize, when a farmer's hen house was close at hand?

Magistrate's Court — November 11th, 1893
Before James Boyer, J.P.
John H. Willmott v Christopher A. Stong, Woodbridge

For having in his possession parts of a certain moose then recently killed during the time prohibited by law at the township of Monck on November 11th, 1893.

John H. Willmott sworn

I am one of the game wardens of the Province of Ontario. I heard about 8 or 10 days ago that a moose had been killed at Axe Lake in or near the township of Cardwell. I was informed that a charge had been laid before James Wilson, Reeve of Cardwell, for unlawfully killing a moose. He fined the party $20. On November 4th I interviewed Mr. Wilson and found it was correct.

I got possession of the head and hide from Mr. Wilson, which was afterwards stolen from me at Rosseau. I have since been on the lookout for any portions of the moose. I found that some of the hunting party had left, and left one man behind to bring the things away. I found prisoner on the boat coming from Rosseau today and partially searched his baggage and found the foot of a moose which had been recently killed. On a further search of his baggage I found a foot and shank and another foot of a moose. Also a fish spear. The articles found I now produce. I arrested the prisoner.

Prisoner convicted and fined $50 and $4.50 to be paid forthwith, and in default of immediate payment, prisoner to be imprisoned in the common gaol at Bracebridge for the period of 3 months. The feet of the moose confiscated. Committed to gaol, but afterwards paid.

James Boyer, J.P.

Conviction returned.

MAGISTRATE'S COURT HELD AT UFFINGTON
FEBRUARY 8TH, 1894
BEFORE JAMES BOYER, J.P.
ELI J. LONG V EDWARD CLEMENT

For having, between the 18th and 31st of December 1893, at the township of Ryde, unlawfully killed deer within the time prohibited by law.

The charge having been read to defendant, he pleaded not guilty.

Eli J. Long sworn

I live in Ryde. I know defendant. He resides about a half mile from my place. Last December I was in the bush cutting roads on Lot 19, Concession 11, Ryde. It is my lot. I heard a noise a little distance from me. I looked up and saw a deer coming. I watched it a short time. It ran among some bushes and stopped there.

I looked back at its track and saw defendant come in sight. He walked slowly in the direction the deer had gone. I saw him raise a gun, which he pointed in the direction the deer had stood. I saw the flash and heard the report of the gun and saw the deer fall. Defendant started to walk towards it. I looked at him till he got about half the distance to the deer and then went on with my work. I didn't speak to him.

Cross-examined by Mr. Fletcher

I was within about 125 yards. I am sure it was defendant. I didn't see any horns on the deer. I believe it was a doe.

For the Defence

Edward Clement sworn

I believe I was working for Matts. I was not in Long's bush following a deer between the times mentioned, nor did I shoot a deer or shoot at a deer during the month of December nor during last summer.

Eva Clement sworn

I am the wife of the defendant. My husband has not brought home any deer during this winter. He was home three days about Christmas. My husband has a rifle.

Adjourned for judgment to February 9th, 1894 at Bracebridge.

Defendant fined $20 and costs of $6.20, to be paid forthwith, and in default, to be imprisoned in the common gaol at Bracebridge for 2 calendar months.

James Boyer, J.P.

Fine $20.00
Court $2.30
Witness $1.20
Constable $2.70
Total $26.20
Conviction returned.

MAGISTRATE'S COURT — MARCH 7TH, 1894
BEFORE JAMES BOYER, J.P.
ELIAS H. TRAVES V WILLIAM TERRY

For having, on March 6th, 1894, unlawfully in his possession portions of seven deer within the time prohibited by law.
The charge having been read to the defendant, he pleaded guilty.

Defendant convicted and fined $10 for each deer found in his possession, with $8.40 costs, to be paid forthwith, and in default, to be imprisoned in the common gaol at Bracebridge for 3 months; and the rifle, ammunition, meat, and deer skin seized to be confiscated.

James Boyer, J.P.

March 8th, 1894.
Traves paid half fine of $35 to Crown Attorney Thomas Johnson.

Fine $70.00
Constable $6.40
Court $ 2.00

Total $78.40
Paid $35.00
Owing $43.50

Rifle $5.00
Deer Skin $0 .25
Total $ 5.25
Conviction returned.

A subsequent reconciliation of accounts in James Boyer's bench book indicates William Terry's confiscated rifle was sold April 2, 1894, to D. Hidd for five dollars. In this next case, however, nothing was confiscated.

Magistrate's Court — October 18th, 1894
Before James Boyer, J.P.
Charles E. Mawdsley v Fritz Ross

For having in his possession 192 muskrat skins at Bracebridge on October 17th, being within the time prohibited by law.

The charge having been read to defendant, he pleaded guilty.

Prisoner fined $5 and $3.50 costs, to be paid forthwith, and in default, to be imprisoned in the gaol at Bracebridge for 30 days.

James Boyer, J.P.

Paid.

Conviction returned.

Half the $5 fine paid over to the prosecutor, Charles Mawdsley.

MAGISTRATE'S COURT — JUNE 22ND, 1896
BEFORE JAMES BOYER, J.P.
ELIAS H. TRAVES V JOHN ANDREWS

For having in his possession 3 deer at Draper on June 22nd, during the closed season.

The charge having been read to defendant, he pleaded guilty.

Defendant fined $20 and costs of $5.10, to be paid forthwith, and in default, to be imprisoned in the common gaol at Bracebridge for 3 months; and the deer to be confiscated.

James Boyer, J.P.

Constable $3.10 Paid

Court $2.00 Paid

Total $5.10

Paid complainant $10.00, being half the penalty for this breach of the game law.

Conviction returned.

MAGISTRATE'S COURT — AUGUST 25TH, 1896
BEFORE JAMES BOYER AND SINGLETON BROWN, J.P.s
THOMAS M. BAIRD V ANTHONY C. FLETCHER, THOMAS FLETCHER, HENRY NICHOLS AND FREDERICK NICHOLS

For having, on August 19th, at the township of Morrison, hunted deer during the time prohibited by law.

The charge having been read to defendants, they severally pleaded not guilty.

Thomas M. Baird sworn

I live in Bracebridge. On Wednesday August 19th I was on Kah-she Lake in a boat between 10 and 11 a.m. Two other parties were with me. We were fishing. We went from that lake to Three Mile Lake, which is about 25 rods distant from Kah-she Lake. Before we landed from Kah-she Lake we heard some dogs giving tongue quite lively, a little west of Three Mile Lake. I heard two shots fired whilst the dogs were giving tongue. The dogs were silent after the shots were fired.

We landed and put the fish we had caught in some bushes. When we got in sight of the lake, a spaniel dog came towards us. We drove it away. We saw defendant A.C. Fletcher about 2 rods from the water of the lake. He was standing to one side of a path and a gun was near him on the ground. I said, "Good day, Mr. Fletcher, are you hunting?"

He didn't answer but asked me if I was fishing and said I had come to the wrong lake for fish. We passed on to the water. After getting into the boat and getting out into the water I saw one of the other defendants standing a few feet from where I saw Mr. Fletcher. I then heard a shot fired by one of the two men. It was fired in the air.

We ran our boat alongside an island in the lake. In about 10 or 15 minutes afterwards, defendant Henry Nichols and one of the young men came in a boat from the west corner along the east shore of the lake. After they passed us we followed, and when they landed they took 2 guns out of the boat, shouldered the boat and walked off. That was all I saw of them. I was only two or three rods from them when they shouldered the boat. I saw all the 4 together. The defendants are the same men. I saw 2 dogs. One was a hound or part hound.

Cross-examined

There were two dogs barking. I saw a marsh on the west side of the lake. The boat was coming from that direction. There were 4 men. One carried the 3 guns.

Richard Tyler sworn

I live with my grandfather, W.H. Brooks, near Housey's Rapids in the township of Ryde. I know all the defendants. I went with Mr. Baird last Wednesday. We fished in Kah-she Lake. I heard dogs barking and then heard 2 shots. We then took our boat over to Three Mile Lake. I saw Mr. Fletcher on the path, a gun was lying behind him. I also saw a dog with him. When we got on to the water I saw the defendant Fred Nichols standing close to Mr. A.C. Fletcher. Before Baird went into the boat he said, "Are you hunting, Mr. Fletcher?" He didn't answer.

We heard a shot as soon as we got off the boat. It appeared to be fired in the air. We went and fished near an island. Defendant Henry Nichols and Thomas Fletcher came in a punt along the side of the shore. We followed them. They pulled the boat up. The 2 in the boat came to where Mr. A.C. Fletcher and F. Nichols were standing. I am quite sure the defendants are the 4 men. I have known them some time.

Cross-examined by defendant A.C. Fletcher
I am sure the gun was lying behind you. It was a dog that had been clipped. Baird didn't say, "Are you out for a shoot?" I am quite sure I saw Fred Nichols. I didn't notice if it was a punt or skiff. I saw 2 dogs, one was a hound.

George Baird sworn
I live with my father in Bracebridge, and was with him last Wednesday. On Kah-she Lake we heard some hounds giving tongue, and then 2 shots were fired. We went in the direction of the shots, and saw a dog, and then we saw Mr. Fletcher. The dog was a spaniel. A gun was lying behind him. My father asked him was he hunting. He answered "Are you fishing?"

We went on to the lake. We then saw another young man with Mr. Fletcher. I was not acquainted with the parties. We heard a shot fired. We went to the island to fish, and saw defendant Henry Nichols and a young man come along in a boat. We followed them to where we had seen Mr. Fletcher. We got within a few rods of them. I am quite sure as to A.C. Fletcher and H. Nichols, and I believe the other defendants to be the other two men. When we first came to the landing I saw his two dogs. The other dog was a hound between brown and black in colour.

For the Defence

Frederick Nichols sworn
I was at home all day August 19th sawing wood. George Smith was helping me. I was not near Three Mile Lake all day.

Henry Nichols sworn and examined by A.C. Fletcher
I am a defendant. I was at Three Mile Lake fishing part of that day. I didn't see you up the lake. I didn't see A.C. Fletcher touch a boat that day. I saw him between 6 and 7 a.m. at his own house. I saw you at home when I came back from fishing. I didn't hear hounds running or dogs barking that day. I was fishing. Thomas Fletcher was with me.

Cross-examined
I generally take a gun with me when I go fishing. The other man had a gun. My gun was leaded with shot, not heavy shot. I got back from fishing about noon.

Thomas Fletcher sworn
I went with Henry Nichols fishing on Three Mile Lake. I left my father at home in the morning. I had a shotgun with me. I didn't see my father till I got back.

Anthony C. Fletcher sworn
Nichols came to my house Wednesday morning to ask my son to go fishing. He went. After being gone an hour, I started on foot to a marsh on Three Mile Lake. I had a spaniel dog with me. I crossed the marsh and shot a squirrel, and afterwards, another. I went to see if I could see the boat.

My dog barked and I had the gun in my hand. Baird and the two boys came up, and Baird said, "Out for a shoot?" I said you are going in the wrong lake, there are better fish in the big lake. I fired at a pine tree thinking my son would hear it. I then started for home. When I got home, H. Nichols had just got to my house. I didn't see Fred Nichols that day. I was not at the landing when Nichols and my son came to it. I didn't see another dog. I have two dogs.

Defendant F. Nichols discharged. Defendants A.C. Fletcher and H. Nichols fined $30 each and costs $4.61, or 3 months in Bracebridge gaol. Defendant Thomas Fletcher fined $20 and costs $4.61, or 2 months in Bracebridge gaol in default of immediate payment.

James Boyer, J.P.
Singleton Brown, J.P.

Conviction returned.

A week later, Thomas Baird initiated another prosecution in the same matter:

MAGISTRATE'S COURT — SEPTEMBER 2ND, 1896
BEFORE JAMES BOYER, J.P.
THOMAS M. BAIRD V IRA NICHOLS

For having on August 19th, at the township of Morrison, hunted deer within the time prohibited by law.
The charge having been read to defendant, he pleaded not guilty.

Thomas M. Baird sworn
I live in Bracebridge. On August 19th I was on Kah-she Lake fishing. I was in the bay near to Three Mile Lake. Between 10 and 11 a.m. I heard dogs giving tongue in a southwesterly direction from where I was. I then heard 2 shots fired in the same direction. I then passed over a portage of 300 or 400 yards to Three Mile Lake.

Just as we sighted the lake we met a spaniel dog and then saw Mr. A.C. Fletcher. He was standing on or near to the portage road. There was a gun lying behind him near a log. I said something to him and passed on into the lake a distance of 10 or 12 yards. I then saw another dog, part black with tan coloured legs and belly.

When I got away from the shore a shot was fired from the direction where Mr. Fletcher was standing when I passed. The smoke from the gun ascended straight up. Shortly afterwards Henry Nichols and Thomas Fletcher came along in a boat. When we left the shore I saw a young man standing on the shore with Mr. A.C. Fletcher. I don't know if it was the defendant. There were two guns taken out of the boat. Henry Nichols and one of the young men shouldered the boat. The other young man took up the guns and went to Kah-she Lake.

Ira Nichols sworn

I am a son of Henry Nichols of the Township of Ryde. I was at home all day on the 19th August last. I did not at any time during that day go near the Kah-she Lake or Three Mile Lake. I did not see either of the Fletchers that day before 6 p.m. I did not have any gun or other firearm in my hands on that day.

Case dismissed.

James Boyer, J.P.

MAGISTRATE'S COURT — FEBRUARY 25TH, 1897
BEFORE JAMES BOYER, J.P. AND SINGLETON BROWN, J.P.
JAMES CALVERT V HARRY WALLER, JAMES HILLMAN, ALFRED HILLMAN, BROOK WATSON AND CHAS. E. LOUNT

For having, on or about February 20th, at the Town of Bracebridge, unlawfully stolen five fowls of the value of about seven dollars.

Defendant Waller did not appear. The other defendants appeared and pleaded not guilty. Mr. Johnson, Crown Attorney, appeared on behalf of the Crown. Each of defendants present entered into $100 recognizance to appear on Wednesday, March 3rd, at two o'clock in the afternoon to answer above charge.

March 3rd, case resumed before same magistrates. Mr. Arnold appeared for defendants and put in plea of *autrefois acquit.*

The court held that, as the proceedings before Messrs. Browning and Boyer were subsequent to the information laid before Boyer, the case was *sub judice,* and the above plea held not to dispose of the case. Certificate of dismissal put in marked A.

The court decided to hear the case.

James Calvert sworn

I live in Bracebridge. I lost some fowls on the night between February 20th and 21st. Lost 5 hens and a rooster. One was left on the premises. I sent for Stunden between 8 and 9 o'clock. Stunden came. I went with him to defendant Watson. We traced the blood on the snow to Watson's and Waller's. The marks started from my barn where the chickens were left. We saw blood outside Watson's. I left Stunden at Waller's and came back to Watson's. Watson said he had nothing to do with taking the fowls. I went back to Watson's with Stunden. He was shovelling snow where the blood was.

Stunden asked defendant Watson if he had any fowls in his place. Watson said there was one bird there, and showed Stunden where it was. It was my rooster and was over a loft at Watson's place. The rooster and 3 hens now produced are my property. Stunden took the rooster and three hens to my place. Myself, Stunden, Waller and Watson went to Hillman's. This was between 9 and 10 a.m. on Sunday the 21st February.

Stunden went in and the two Hillmans came out. One of the parties said they had been on a spree and having some drink, and if they had done wrong they were willing to make it right. Watson said the boys had been on a drunk and some had killed the chickens, and they were willing to pay for the fowls.

We then went to Mr. Boyer. They wanted to pay me for the fowls. Mr. Boyer was sick in bed and got up. One of the Hillmans suggested that they be summoned instead of giving bail to which the Magistrate agreed. I laid an information against the defendants at that time before Mr. Boyer which was signed and sworn to. [Information produced] That is my signature to it.

The fowls were in the woodshed. The value of the fowls is about $8.00. I then went home. Defendants had left ahead of me.

Mr. Arnold for defendants
Produced subpoenas (Exhibits B and C).

Re-direct
Witness produced subpoena (Exhibit D) to appear before Messrs. Boyer and Browning. I was served with the last subpoena (D) on Monday, the 22nd February last between 8 and 9 a.m. I never authorized anyone else to lay an information, and did not know another had been laid till I got the subpoena (D). I appeared upon subpoena (D) and gave evidence. I just answered such questions as Mr. Arnold asked me. There were the 5 defendants, the two magistrates, Mr. Arnold and myself. They were the only parties present at that trial. I didn't tell them I had laid an information before.

Alfred Stunden sworn
I am a constable for the District of Muskoka. About 8:30 a.m. on the 21st February Mr. Calvert sent for me. I went there and, from what he told me, traced the blood from the Calvert barn to Watson's. Calvert went with me. Watson was not in. We then traced the blood to Waller's. I went in there and got the 3 hens, now produced, in a wood shed. I arrested Waller and took him with me to Watson's, and asked Watson if he had any fowls. He said he had Mr. Calvert's rooster overhead. Watson got it and handed it to me. I then arrested him.

Waller told me as we were going to the magistrate's that the two Hillman boys and Charles E. Lount were with them. Waller objected to go any further unless I got the Hillman boys. I went to Hillmans and arrested both of them. Both Hillman boys wanted to settle the matter with Mr. Calvert. I told them I couldn't settle it. I might have said I was in the hands of the law.

I took them to Mr. Boyer's. I told him the parties were under arrest. Mr. Calvert asked Mr. Boyer if he couldn't let them go and summon them. Mr. Boyer agreed to do so and the defendants (except Lount) left with the understanding they were to appear on the Thursday evening at his house. Mr. Boyer at first told them they would have to give bail.

Cross-examined

Defendants were arrested without warrant. Calvert never told me he didn't want to lay an information. Calvert asked me if he could settle it. I said I couldn't and he would have to go to Mr. Boyer in any event. I was appointed constable in the year Mr. Kinsey was mayor. [1891] I have had no appointment by the council since.

Mr. Arnold contended that if there was a conviction it must be a joint conviction and if an acquittal it must be a joint acquittal, and that there could be no separate acquittal or conviction. Overruled.

Case dismissed as against defendants Lount and the two Hillmans, and defendant Watson convicted and fined $5 penalty, $8 the value of the fowls and $6.65 costs, to be paid forthwith, and in default, to be imprisoned and left at hard labour in the common gaol at Bracebridge for 21 days.

James Boyer, J.P. for Muskoka

Singleton Brown, J.P.

Conviction returned.

Complainant gave up to defendant his claim for the $8 and Mr. Arnold paid the balance of $11.65 under protest. ~ J.B.

Magistrate's Court — March 26th, 1897
Before James Boyer, J.P.
Joseph Hey v Stewart W. Nicholls

For having, on or about the 18th March instant, at the Township of McLean, hunted deer during the time prohibited by law.
Defendant[1] pleaded not guilty.

Joseph Hey sworn
I am a Deputy Game Warden for Muskoka. I made a search of the house and premises where defendant resides yesterday afternoon. I saw defendant. Defendant's mother, in his presence, said that the defendant had been out hunting but didn't get anything. Defendant admitted having been out on snow shoes, and that he had a gun with him. I asked him if was it within a week of the 18th instant. He said it was about that time. I had seen tracks of snow shoes leading from defendant's place to the woods. Defendant said he had seen a deer track and followed it.

Charles Jackson sworn
I live in the Township of Macaulay. I know the defendant. A little over two weeks ago I went up to defendant's place to go with him to see a lot of land. We had one gun between us and it was loaded. We came across a deer track and followed it about a quarter of a mile. We fired once each. That is the only time I have been out with defendant.

Complaint dismissed.

James Boyer, J.P.

---

[1] The Nicholls family in McLean Township was unrelated to the Nichols family of Morrison Township. They lived in different parts of Muskoka, spelled their surname differently, but did share in common some time in Magistrate Boyer's court on hunting charges.

Magistrate's Court — August 7th, 1897
Before James Boyer, J.P.
Charles G. Grimes v Henry Ensom

For having, on Sunday the 25th July last, at the Township of Wood, unlawfully killed game, to wit, ducks.

Defendant pleaded not guilty.

Charles G. Grimes sworn

I live in the Township of Wood. I know the defendant. On Sunday the 25th last, between 9 and 10 a.m., I saw a flock of wild ducks in the bay between his house and mine. Defendant has a brush cover on the shore of the lake. I saw him shoot at the flock of ducks. He killed one. The others fluttered along the water. He got into a boat and went and picked up the duck he had killed. The ducks swam to a point. Defendant went round the point and fired several other shots at them. I was about 10 rods from him across the water when he shot the first one.

Cross-examined

I was on my own clearance near defendant's house at the line between the two lots when I saw you shoot. It was a young duck.

Alexander Walker sworn

On Sunday, the 25th July last, I went to Grimes's. I had been there a few minutes when I heard a shot from a small building on the shore. I saw defendant run out of the building. He got into a boat and rowed out after a dead duck lying on the water. He came to the shore with the duck in his hand. Took up his rifle and followed the flock of ducks along the shore and fired 2 or 3 shots afterwards.

Cross-examined by defendant

I am sure it was the 25th of July I heard the ducks quack when you shot into them.

For the Defence

Henrietta Ensom affirmed

I am the wife of defendant. Three Sundays ago my husband was down at the lake. He came in after the gun. I heard the gun fired shortly after. I saw some birds fluttering on the bay. I thought they were loons. I saw my husband in the boat. I could only see his head. He brought up a chipmunk. Last Sunday but one he was out near a lake in the same township.

William Ensom sworn (11 years old)

I was at home a week ago last Sunday. My father started away from home at 8 o'clock a.m. I saw him leave the house. Didn't get back till night. It would take me 2 hours to walk to Devil's Lake from our house. I didn't see him take anything away or bring anything back. I didn't see any one round or hear any shooting on that day.

Defendant affirmed

Three Sundays ago I went to the shore and sat on my logs. I heard a chipmunk, got the gun and shot him. I got into the boat picked him up and gave it to the dog. Two Sundays ago I was at Devil's Lake.

Defendant convicted and fined $5 and 21 cents in costs, to be paid forthwith, and in default of immediate payment, to be imprisoned in the common gaol at Bracebridge for the term of two calendar months.

James Boyer, J.P.

Court $1.75.

Constable $4.46.

Recvd. $6.50 on account.

1897 August 19th, paid complainant $2.50, half penalty.

Conviction returned.

MAGISTRATE'S COURT — AUGUST 28TH, 1897
BEFORE JAMES BOYER, J.P.
AND J.H. WILLMOTT, GAME WARDEN
ROBERT D. BROWN v MARK BAILEY, THOMAS BAILEY, RICHARD BAILEY, JOHN PATTERSON JUNIOR, THOMAS PATTERSON, RICHARD PATTERSON, WILLIAM PATTERSON AND AMOS BARRAGER

For that defendants, on the 13th and 14th days of August A.D. 1897, at Skeleton Lake in or near the Township of Cardwell, did unlawfully hunt and kill deer within the time prohibited by law.

The charge having been read to defendants, Mark Bailey and John Patterson Jr. pleaded guilty, and the rest of the defendants not guilty.

George Barrager sworn

I live in Stephenson about five miles from Skeleton Lake. On the 14th of August I was at Skeleton Lake with George Hughes. We went out in a boat. While out I heard a few shots fired and heard some dogs. Amos Barrager was in the boat with us. I saw Mark Bailey and John Patterson Jr. in a boat. They had a deer in their boat. There were some dogs there. I also saw Richard Patterson, Thomas Bailey, William Patterson, Richard Bailey. I didn't see Thomas Patterson. I don't know whether there were any guns there or not. I can't remember what was said. There are quite a few deer near where I live. I don't think the road where these men were is a concession or side line. I am related to some of these defendants.

George Hughes sworn

I remember the 14th of August last. I was on Skeleton Lake. While I was there I heard shots fired and dogs barking. We went to where the noise was. I saw two men in a boat. They were John Patterson Jr. and Mark Bailey. They were going to shore. I saw a deer in their boat. I saw Richard Patterson and Thomas Bailey and the rest of the defendants, except Thomas Patterson. They came out of the bush to where the deer was. I saw two dogs there at least. One was a brindle and the other black. There were some guns on the ground. I don't know how many there were. We left the other parties, the defendants, there.

I was talking to the defendants today. I think there was some talk about the evidence I was to give today. They asked me what I was going to say and I told them that I was going to tell the truth. Three or four of the defendants live near the lake shore.

Cross-examined by Mr. Arnold

This road or trail runs through the bush. The guns on the shore did not come out of Mark Bailey's boat.

Defendant William Patterson sworn

On the 14th August last, I was on Skeleton Lake about noon. I went to see my brother on the shore of the lake. We went over the farm. I had a gun. My brother got his gun from the house. His was a rifle and mine was a rifle and shot. I heard some shots near the lake and went down. I saw my brother on the shore.

We were hunting that day, in a way. There was a party of us. Thomas Bailey was also with us. He had no gun. All the defendants were in the party except Amos Barrager, who was in the boat. I heard a shot fired. My brother's name is Richard. There were two dogs there. I heard them giving tongue near the lake. I went back to my brother's.

We would have shot deer if we had seen them. Richard Bailey's house is ten or twelve minutes' walk from the place where the deer was. I had an idea that John Patterson Jr. was going out hunting. A wagon went from our place to Skeleton Lake that morning. There was a boat and a canoe in it.

Cross-examined by Mr. Arnold

The boat was to be left at my brother's. I always carry a gun when I go through the bush.

Robert D. Brown sworn

I had a conversation with William Patterson in Utterson, yesterday morning. I asked, what scrape was this he was getting into. He said it was a deuce of a note. He said he had taken a boat up to his brother to the lake. They had found this other party hunting, and they didn't think there would be much harm in it, and they went into it just for the fun of the thing.

Richard Bailey sworn

On the 14th August I left the house in the forenoon and went down to Skeleton Lake with a rifle and dog. He is a black and white dog. He started with me. I heard two or three shots. I also heard a dog barking. The shots were fired after the dogs tongued. I saw my brother and John Patterson Jr. in a boat with a deer. I saw them in the morning.

My brother was at my place the night before. I am not prepared to say whether we talked about hunting or not. Mark Bailey left my place in the morning with a gun. John Patterson took some of the meat home and Mark Bailey the rest. I expected I would shoot anything that came in my way, deer or anything else. I took my gun, and if I had seen a deer I would have shot it. My dog was at the shore when I got there. Richard Patterson and Thomas Bailey each had a dog. I have seen my dog after deer.

(Mr. Arnold claimed the defendant John Patterson Jr. could not be called as a witness till judgment had been given against him upon pleading guilty.)

Defendants Mark Bailey and John Patterson Jr., having pleaded guilty, be fined $20 and costs $3.95, to be paid forthwith, and in default, to be imprisoned in the common gaol at Bracebridge for two months.

Case against remaining defendants resumed. Mr. Arnold for defendants raised the objection that the conviction of the above two defendants disposed of the whole case. The objection was overruled.

John Patterson sworn

On the 13th of August I went to Skeleton Lake. Part of the way my brother was with me. We had one gun, my gun. On the 14th I went out to hunt deer with Mark Bailey. I told my brother I was going to kill deer, and I left them at the house. Mark Bailey shot the deer. We didn't arrange to go hunting. I took Thomas Patterson up to Briese's with me. He had a gun. I didn't see him at the lake. Mark Bailey and myself made the arrangements to go hunting, the night before at my brother's house. Martin Bailey fired two shots. Mark Bailey and I had the deer. I heard dogs in the bush.

Cross-examined by Mr. Arnold

The other defendants, other than Mark Bailey and myself, had nothing to do with killing the deer.

Case dismissed in connection with Amos Barrager and Thomas Patterson. Defendants Thomas Bailey, Richard Bailey, Richard Patterson and William Patterson each fined $20 and $3.73 costs, to be paid forthwith, and in default of immediate payment, each of said defendants to be imprisoned in the common gaol at Bracebridge for two months.

James Boyer, J.P.
John H. Willmott

Conviction returned.

Richard Patterson and John Patterson Jr. paid $23.98 each, including commission.

Paid constable $4.00.

Paid informant half the fine, $20 less $6 costs for 2 dismissed.

Paid Crown attorney half the fine, $20.00.

Magistrate's Court — September 13th, 1897
Before James Boyer, J.P.
Joseph Hey v William Brown

For having, on the 11th September instant, at the Township of Macaulay, hunted partridge within the time prohibited by law.

Defendants pleaded not guilty.

Joseph Hey sworn

I am a Deputy Game Warden for District of Muskoka. About 1:30 on Saturday last I heard that someone was shooting near Fletcher Phillips. I went up round there and saw defendant come out of the bush on to the road. Defendant had a rifle with him.

I asked him what he was shooting at in the bush. He said, "At a stump." I said, "What are you doing out with a gun?" He said he was hunting partridge. I said, "Did you know hunting season is not in?" He said it was on the first of September. I told him I should arrest him for hunting and did so. I heard two or three shots fired.

Cross-examined

I did not see any target. Defendant said he fired 4 shots. I did not see any partridges but it is a place where partridges congregate. I showed my badge and told him what the law was.

Defendant convicted and fined $5 and $5 costs, to be paid forthwith, and in default, to be imprisoned in the common gaol at Bracebridge for one calendar month.

James Boyer, J.P.

Constable paid $3.00
Fine and costs paid.
Conviction returned.

Complainant was paid half the penalty, $2.50.

The other $2.50 was paid to the Crown Attorney.

Most instances of taking game illegally combined men's enjoyment of the hunt and their need to provide food. Yet the 1894 conviction of Fritz Ross for trapping muskrat out of season, reproduced earlier in this chapter, as well as the following three cases, are reminders that Muskoka's economy extended beyond lumbering, farming, and tourism, to include the less visible though then highly lucrative fur trade.

Magistrate's Court — December 29th, 1897
Before James Boyer, J.P.
Elias H. Traves v John McMillan

For having furs, to wit, 4 muskrat skins, in his possession at Bracebridge during the time prohibited by law.

Defendant pleaded guilty and fined $5 and costs $7.32, to be paid forthwith, and in default, to be imprisoned in the common gaol at Bracebridge for one month, and the skins confiscated.

James Boyer, J.P.

Constable $4.82

Court $2.50

Total $7.32

Fine paid.

Paid constable costs $4.82 and half the fine $2.50

Total $7.32

Conviction returned.

MAGISTRATE'S COURT — DECEMBER 30TH, 1897
BEFORE JAMES BOYER, J.P.
ELIAS H. TRAVES V JOHN MARLING

For that he, the said John Marling, on or about the 23rd day of December A.D. 1897, at Bracebridge, did unlawfully have in his possession furs, to wit, muskrat skins, taken during the time prohibited by law.
Defendant pleaded guilty.

Fined $5 and costs $7.34, to be paid forthwith, and in default, to be imprisoned in the common gaol at Bracebridge for one week. (In consequence of defendant's age, 74 years, the imprisonment was made for a short term.)

James Boyer, J.P.

Constable arrest $1.50
Mileage (18 miles) $2.34
Attorney Court $1.50
Sub-total $5.34
Court costs 50 cents plus $1.50
Court total $2.00
Grand-total $7.34
Committed to gaol.
Conviction returned.

MAGISTRATE'S COURT — JANUARY 6TH, 1898
BEFORE JAMES BOYER, J.P.
JOSEPH HEY V GEORGE DITCHBURN

For that defendant, on or about the 20th day of December A.D. 1897, at the Township of Muskoka in said District, did unlawfully take fur, to wit, muskrat skins, within the time prohibited by law.

The charge having been read to defendant, he pleaded guilty.

Defendant fined $5 and $5 costs, to be paid forthwith, and in default, to be imprisoned in the common gaol at Bracebridge for 7 days.

James Boyer, J.P.

> Committed to gaol.
> Constable $3.00
> Court $2.00
> Total $5.00
> Conviction returned.

Shooting a deer while it swims in a river or lake is illegal. However, killing deer in the water was common practice in Muskoka in the 1890s. If people were routinely doing it, the reasoning ran, it must not be against the law.

The memoirs of several district pioneers treat shooting swimming deer as standard practice, and the 1872 Atlas of Parry Sound & Muskoka *includes the illustration reproduced earlier in this chapter by Port Carling artist Seymour Penson of two men in a canoe, one paddling while his companion in the bow takes aim at a deer they are pursuing, innocuously entitled "A scene on Lake Rosseau."*

Trapping laws seemed indifferent to cruelty to animals, but protecting deer in the water was one instance where animals were, at least in law, given a fair chance. Even so, it may not have been so much that this practice was cruel and unsportsmanlike but simply reflected concern for humans of ricocheting bullets if hunters fired across water.

MAGISTRATE'S COURT — DECEMBER 28TH, 1898
BEFORE JAMES BOYER, J.P.
JOSEPH HEY V GEORGE BROWN, ANSON BROWN, WILLIAM ARMSTRONG, GEORGE WILTON AND THOMAS GOHM

For hunting and wounding deer in the waters of Muskoka Lake, or immediately after the deer leaving such waters, during the open season

at the Township of Macaulay on the last day of November 1898.
Mr. Mahaffy for defendants claimed that each case should be taken separately as the summons did not disclose that it was a joint offence.

Case taken as against George Brown.

George E. Langford sworn
During the last day of the hunting season I met defendant on the bank of the river. He had a gun. Defendant Gohm was with him.

Samuel Taylor sworn
About the last of the open season I was along the river, heard shots fired.

Defendant sworn
I was not with Wilton and others when they fired at a deer. I did not shoot a deer in the water.

Case dismissed against defendant.

Case against William Armstrong.

Defendant sworn
I saw a deer on the bank of the river. It was dead.

Wilfred Hellett sworn
Case dismissed against defendants with costs and witness fees 75 cents.

James Boyer, J.P.

2nd case against Gohm withdrawn.

Magistrate's Court — December 30th, 1898
Before James Boyer, J.P.
Elias H. Traves v William Stonehouse and George Stonehouse

For that defendants, on the 9th day of December A.D. 1898, at the Township of Oakley, did unlawfully take and kill deer within the times prohibited by law.

Defendants pleaded not guilty.

Elias Traves sworn

I am a Deputy Game Warden. On the 10th December last, in Oakley, I saw where a deer had been killed. There was fresh blood. I found sleigh tracks to and from where the blood was. The blood and tracks were on the bank of the south branch. The ice was broken on the river as if some animal had passed.

I made inquiries, and defendant George Stonehouse admitted to me that they got the deer, and that it wasn't quite dead when they got there but it died shortly afterwards. He said that his brother and Henry Chamberlain were with him. He said they went back to his place for a canoe. That would be about 1½ miles. He said it was a buck and the head was at James Clarke's to be set up. I asked him if he had the skin and he said he could get it or part of it if required. There was a great quantity of blood and the snow was tramped down. I tracked the blood to the road and thence towards Oakley Bridge where defendants reside.

Cross-examined

I asked defendant George Stonehouse if they bled the deer. He said, "No, the blood came out of its nose."

Defendant George Stonehouse sworn

I am one of the defendants. I remember complainant speaking to me about the deer. I was informed on the 9th of December that a deer was in the river and couldn't get out. Henry Chamberlain told me. He asked me what we had best do, had we better take it out as he thought it might be dead if left there. My brother, Chamberlain and myself went down to take it out. The deer was still in the river and we couldn't see it move.

We got the canoe and took an axe to break the ice with and my brother went in the canoe to where the deer was. He brought the deer with him. We brought it up to where I live. We skinned it and divided it between the three of us, and I ate part of it. The deer bled after we got it out of the water. I didn't see if the deer bled before my brother went to it.

Cross-examined

It was bleeding from the nose and mouth but I didn't see any marks or wounds on it when we skinned it. We drew it to the road, put it on the sleigh and brought it home. There are no bullet marks or cuts on the skin. The ice was about 1¼ inches thick. I told Traves the deer was dead when we got him out of the water.

Henry Chamberlain sworn

On the 9th Dec I was going out to Oakley Ridge. I saw a deer in the river. It was 10 or 10:30 a.m. He was nearer the opposite bank to where I was. He was trying to reach the further bank. I went on to the bridge. I had about three-quarters of a cord. After throwing off the load I went to the store and saw defendants. I told them what I had seen. We agreed to do so and went back in the sleigh. We took a rope with us. We all three went back for a canoe and returned.

William Stonehouse broke the ice and put the canoe in the water. The ice was not safe. He went in the canoe to the deer. He put the rope on it and drew it to shore. We saw the deer move when we got there. I saw blood on the ice and on the shore, and there was some blood on the sleigh where its nose was. We didn't bleed the deer. It was dead when we got it.

Minnie Traves sworn

I saw a quantity of blood on the road this morning. It was near the track where something had been drawn out of the water. On Sunday the 11th instant, there was a track of a sleigh between the road and the river. There was quite a lot of blood on the road then going in the direction of defendants'. My husband called my attention to it. There would have been more than a tea cupful of blood on the road.

Complainant recalled

I have hunted a great deal. A deer will live in the water for a number of hours and swim a great many miles. I am quite certain a deer in the water would not drown in 3 hours. An inch and a quarter of ice would carry a deer so he wouldn't break through. The shore on the opposite side of the river is low. A deer, if in the water, could break through 1¼ inches of ice. The ice was broken to the opposite shore. A deer would not bleed after being drowned in the water. The blood I saw was very light colour which showed that the deer had been living a short time before.

Cross-examined

I can't say how long the deer in question would live in the water on the 9th December. I can't give an opinion on the point. I have seen at least 4 struggling in the water.

Case dismissed.

James Boyer, J.P.

Chapter Fifteen

BOYS' DOINGS

"Boys will be boys!" The affectionate reproval that is usually laced into this hackneyed phrase is mirrored by the other and equally valid side of the equation: constables will be trouble-sniffing busybodies.

Where would our rich supply of stories about bad boys come from if some Dudley Gumshoe had not been on the prowl? Who but the town constable would swat around a kid for stealing a girl's ticket to the circus, arrest a boy for throwing a stone at a sign on a bridge, or traipse before the local magistrate a troop of the town's young men for conducting an old-fashioned charivari outside the honeymoon habitation of a newly married couple?

Breaking windows is a bold excitement for boys, testing in a single throw one's nerve, aim, and strength, as well as providing a rush of excitement and the thrill of a vandal's accomplishment upon hearing the crash and sound of tinkling glass. But six weeks in jail for a single pane?

By the end of the 1890s, the forest of utility poles visible in downtown Bracebridge was a sign of the town's progress. Its dirt main street, however, remained in a primitive state, alternating between clouds of dust and puddles of mud for much of the year. A wooden boardwalk, on the other hand, provided convenience for pedestrians and some help for retailers. Despite a bylaw forbidding it and the town constable's patrolling eyes, lads on bicycles rode the roller-coaster sidewalks, both for the thrill of greater speed and, in rainy weather, as a way of ensuring that less mud would be thrown up by their bicycles' fenderless tires.

As a boy who grew up in Bracebridge myself, living warily next door to the police station and across a narrow laneway from the same stone lock-up referred to in these cases by my great-grandfather as the "gaol," I can only mutter, as perhaps even you, gentle reader, can also: "There, but for the presence of a constable, go I!"

Magistrate's Court — December 21st, 1893
Before James Boyer, J.P.
Elizabeth F. Piper v Alfred Coleman, Thomas Nicholson, Edward Murphy, Albert Read

For having, on the 16th and 17th December instant, at the Town of Bracebridge, unlawfully and maliciously damaged and injured a certain dwelling house belonging to Henry Piper.

Defendants pleaded not guilty.

Henry Piper sworn

I live in Bracebridge. I know the defendants. On Saturday the 16th instant, about eight o'clock at night, I heard Alfred Coleman speaking in front of the house while I was working in the rear. I went to the door and, as I opened it, two missiles struck the house, and I heard a crash behind me. The felt paper on the house was broken in places and a large square of glass in the window, 20 x 24 ½, was smashed. I saw Coleman and some other boys running away.

The damage done to the building was about one dollar. Defendants have damaged the house on several previous occasions.

Frances E. Piper sworn

I am the wife of the previous witness Henry Piper. It was soon after eight o'clock. I heard some boys hollering. I heard the crash of the missiles as they struck the house. I know that the defendants were there. I followed defendants right down to the town to Dill's old store and did not lose sight of them all the way down.

For the Defence

Edward Nicholson sworn

The defendant Thomas Nicholson is my son. Said defendant was with me all the time on the night in question from between 6 and 7 o'clock to late at night. I did not go home till after 10 o'clock.

John Coleman sworn

Defendant Alfred Coleman is my son. It was ten minutes past eight when we left home to come to town. Said defendant went on an errand for me as we were coming to town and was gone about 20 minutes.

Defendant Nicholson discharged.
   See next case.

MAGISTRATE'S COURT — DECEMBER 21ST, 1893
BEFORE JAMES BOYER, J.P.
ELIZABETH F. PIPER V ALFRED COLEMAN, ALBERT READ

For having, on the 17th December instant, at the Town of Bracebridge, unlawfully and maliciously damaged and injured a certain dwelling house belonging to Henry Piper.
Defendants pleaded not guilty.

Henry Piper sworn

On Sunday afternoon, the 17th of December, the defendants Coleman and Read, and two other boys, stopped and talked together at the end of my lot. Said defendant, Coleman, broke the ice-crust on the snow, and defendant Read and a smaller boy threw it at the house. Defendant Coleman told them they couldn't reach the house from there and to go further forward to do so.

They did so and threw ice again, some of which struck the window but did not break it, but some pieces broke the felt paper on the house. My wife went out to speak to them, when they began throwing at her. None of the pieces struck her as far as I know. She then came in the house and the boys began to throw at the house again.

Frances E. Piper sworn

On the 17th instant, the defendants came and began making a noise at the corner of our lot. Defendant Read and the younger Coleman picked up pieces of ice, and came and threw them at the house, breaking the felt paper in three or four places. When they began to throw at the window I went out and remonstrated with them. As soon as I went out they threw ice at me and used indecent language towards me. I then went in the house and they threw at the house again.

For the Defence

Thomas Good sworn
[No testimony recorded.]

Defendants Alfred Coleman and Albert Reed adjudged to pay damage 50 cents, fine $5 and costs $2.15 to be paid forthwith, and in default, to be imprisoned in the lock-up at Bracebridge for 30 days.

Defendant Edward Murphy adjudged to pay damage 50 cents, fine $2 and costs $2.15, to be paid forthwith, and in default, to be imprisoned in the lock-up at Bracebridge for 30 days.

James Boyer J.P.

Read paid $7.65.
Coleman paid $7.65.
Murphy paid $4.65.
Conviction returned.

Magistrate's Court — March 24th, 1894
Before James Boyer, J.P.
William Rutherford v George H.O. Thomas

Assault and battery at Bracebridge on the 21st day of March, 1894.
Charge having been read, the defendant pleaded not guilty.

Joseph Boyer sworn
I live in Bracebridge. On the 28th day of March I was going home when I saw Harry Rutherford and William Taylor standing near the entrance to the Orange Hall. There were some parties there. As Harry was standing there defendant came out, struck him two or three times in the face and choked him. There had been no noise to disturb anyone for twenty minutes. I did not hear defendant say anything.

Cross-examined
I saw a rattle in Harry Rutherford's hands, but he did not make a noise with it. Harry Rutherford and I went into the porch. He struck him two or three times on the cheeks with his open hands. I saw him take hold of his throat.

Harry Rutherford sworn
I live in Bracebridge with my father near the Orange Hall. Last Wednesday night some of the girls came to wait outside till they were ready for the taffy. Bert Post and William Taylor and Joe Boyer were in the porch with me. We did not make a noise. Mr. Thomas came out, jumped out at me, struck me on the cheek and head and then choked me.

Cross-examined
I had just come to the porch. I rattled it several times at the open door of the building in the porch. Robert Howard told me that Mr. Thomas had

chased them away before. They were not singing when I went there.

Bert Post sworn
Last Wednesday night I was in Rutherford's house, cutting taffy. When I went over to the hall, Harry Rutherford, Joe Boyer and Dodd were there. Harry Rutherford had a rattle in his hand. I was out on the sidewalk when defendant struck Rutherford. He only struck him on the face. Harry Rutherford and I were at the side window. We made no noise.

William Taylor sworn
There was a taffy pull at the Orange Lodge this week. I was coming up street and went to see what was coming. D. Dodd was there. I went away but came back again. I saw defendant strike Harry Rutherford.

George Jelly sworn
Several nights ago my brother, Bob Howard and Ed Post went to the Orange Lodge building, where a taffy pull was going on. I saw defendant grab Rutherford and then I ran away.

For the Defence

John Volumne sworn
I was at the taffy pull at the Orange Hall. Mr. Thomas was chairman of the meeting. At the first part of the meeting they were yelling at the windows. Mr. Thomas went out to the door and then the noise ceased. Before defendant went out the second time there was a rattling noise.

James Hillary sworn
I was at the taffy pull. There was a noise outside which sounded like two shingles being clapped together. They would often open the door. Bob Howard, Ed Post,

Frank and George Jelly were at Rutherford's house. I promised to give them some taffy if they would go home and keep quiet. Harry Rutherford was at the window near the stage and would disturb the actors by speaking in the window.

Trevor Boydell sworn
I was at the taffy pull the other night. There was a bag on the window in the north which was knocked down inside. I heard a rattling noise twice.

Claude Perry sworn
I was at the taffy pull the other night. I heard a noise two or three times. The entertainment was badly disturbed. The boys were yelling at the windows.

Ernest Perry sworn
I was at the taffy pull the other night taking part. There were some boys with a rattle at the door. The first time defendant went out, I heard the boys running away. We could hear the door open. The entertainment was stopped three times.

Fred Miller sworn
I was at the taffy pull the other night. There were several noises made by boys which badly disturbed the meeting.

Aubrey Henderson sworn
I was at the taffy pull. I heard several noises. There was so much noise we could not hear. The first time Mr. Thomas went out and spoke to the boys.

George Davidson sworn
I was at the taffy pull. The boys came in and made a noise by upsetting pails, etc. Mr. Thomas went out and I heard the boys run away. They came again and continued the noise. I saw Joe Boyer and Harry Rutherford there

before the meeting began.

George H.O. Thomas sworn

I am the principal of the public school at Bracebridge. I was chairman of an entertainment in the Orange Hall. It began about 8:15. There was so much noise in the lobby that I had to go to stop the noise, but did not see anyone. A rattle was sounded at the north window, near the stage. I heard Harry Rutherford's voice. A bag of books was pushed in. The noise was again continued at the front of the building. I went outside and waiting a moment caught Joe Boyer and Harry Rutherford. I did not choke Harry Rutherford. I took hold of him, gave him a slap on the left cheek with my open hand, and then put him out. I then asked Rutherford for the rattle and he gave it to me.

Case dismissed.

James Boyer, J.P.
R.M. Browning, J.P.

Magistrate's Court — April 7th, 1894
Before Justices Boyer and Hunt
George Bolton Ford v Stuart Rutherford and William Rutherford Jr.

For having, on the 5th and 6th days of April, 1894, unlawfully and wilfully broken windows in the house of the Informant.

Charge having been read defendants pleaded not guilty.

George Bolton Ford sworn

I live in Bracebridge, opposite defendant's house. On the 5th of April last, both defendants were throwing stones at my place and broke the windows.

Defendant William Rutherford Jr. admitted to me today he broke the windows. On the 6th of April defendant Stuart Rutherford threw a stone at me and struck me between the shoulders. On the 6th William Rutherford broke a window glass. Both defendants were there on both times.

Cross-examined
I threw stones at them into the drain. They did not have to get out of the drain. They were not in the drain. It was not a chip of wood that broke the windows.

George Boyer sworn
Yesterday morning I was in the yard at home and saw defendants working at a drain. I heard a smash of glass and heard complainant swearing at defendants. They answered him back. Defendant W. Rutherford said the party throwing had run along the street. There was no one on the street, running along Willis St. I did not see either throw stones.

Hannah Boyer sworn
Yesterday morning I saw William Rutherford Jr. throw a stone or something at complainant's house and immediately heard a crash of glass. Complainant was chopping wood. He had not been throwing stones at the Rutherfords'. William Rutherford Jr. was at the side of the drain. William Rutherford Jr. told Mr. Ford that the boy had run along Willis Street. Mr. Ford used bad and indecent language after this was thrown.

Harry Wallis sworn
Yesterday morning I saw William Rutherford throw something in the direction of Mr. Ford's house.

For the Defence

Hannah Boyer wrestles wind-dried laundry behind the family's Manitoba Street home. From this yard, on April 6, 1894, she witnessed a boy smash a window in neighbour George Ford's house. She testified in the resulting vandalism case her husband, Magistrate James Boyer, wearing a clean white shirt, heard the very next day.

Charlie Arnott sworn

I have been working on the front street in front of Mr. Rutherford's house. On Thursday morning I was in the drain and the two defendants were working filling in the drain. Neither of defendants threw stones at Mr. Ford, and Mr. Ford threw stones over at us. He said, "You God-damned son of a bitch, I'll kill you." I had to leave the drain on account of the stones. He kept us from work for about three minutes. Neither of us threw any stones.

Cross-examined

There was not bad language used until Ford found his window was broken.

William Rutherford sworn

I am one of the defendants in this case. On Thursday I was working filling in the drain. I first saw complainant throwing over sticks and stones. I told him to go in the house. I had to leave my work on account of the stones. I did not nor did any of the others throw anything at him. After we left he still kept throwing into our yard. On Friday morning I saw complainant standing in the yard. I picked up a piece of clay and threw it over. I happened to break the window.

Stuart Rutherford sworn

I was working in the ditch near our place. On Thursday morning, Ford began throwing stones at us. He used bad language to me. I left work when he began throwing. I threw stones back at him. We did not strike his house that day. On Friday morning my brother threw a piece of hard clay and broke the window of Ford's house.

Magistrates disagreed. Defendants to be re-summoned.

James Boyer, J.P.
Alfred Hunt, J.P.

The witness Hannah Boyer was wife of Magistrate James Boyer, who was hearing this matter, and witness George Boyer, his son. The episode of the broken window occurred at a neighbour's house, near the Boyer residence. Because of the possible conflict of interest, as well as due to the requirement that two justices of the peace hear cases involving wilful damage to property, the Mayor of Bracebridge Alfred Hunt, an ex officio J.P., also presided. This case appears to have ended inconclusively. The magistrates did not agree. There is no record that the defendants were ever re-summoned.

MAGISTRATE'S COURT — MAY 15TH, 1897
BEFORE JAMES BOYER, J.P.

THOMAS DODD V ARTHUR POST, WILLIAM LYNN, ALBERT MURPHY, JOHN O'DONNELL, MICHAEL LUNDY, LEMUEL SCOTT JR., MURTAUGH MCCOUBRAY, CHARLES KENNEDY, FREDERICK GLEASON, FERGUSON GIBSON, LESLIE MAHAN AND JOHN STEWART

Murphy and Stewart not served.

For having, on the 5th day of May instant, at the Town of Bracebridge, by riotous and disorderly conduct in a certain public street or highway in said town during the night time wantonly disturbed the peace and quiet of the inmates of several dwelling houses near such street or highway. Each defendant pleaded not guilty.

William A. Ryckman sworn

I live with my father on Richard Street, Bracebridge. I was home that night. The house is 13 or 14 feet from street. A number of persons gathered in front of the house between 10 and 11 p.m. They were beating on tin ware and on a saw. Something sounded like cow bells in front of the house. I was in bed.

The noise roused me and I got up. I looked out of the window. I should judge 18 or 20 or more were there. One said, "Stop the noise for a few minutes to see if we are going to get anything." One said, "We will take $5 and settle." They continued the noise.

They stopped for a while again, and one said, "Put up, or put up the bride." I had been married that day. Noise again. Just before they left, I spoke to defendant Lynn. Part of the crowd were then there. I recognized defendants Lundy, Lynn, Joseph Boyer, and Ferguson Gibson as being there. I knew them before and recognized them by their voices. Arthur Post brought a report that old Dodds was coming and told them to get the hell out of this. It was probably more than 15 minutes the noise was being made.

The next day I saw Joseph Boyer and Leslie Mahan. I saw Lundy the day following. He asked me to treat. I refused. He said, we will be over there again tonight.

Cross-examined

I spoke to Lynn from the window. I was not frightened.

Albert B. Ryckman sworn

I am father of last witness. He lived with me on 5th instant, and does so yet. On that night a crowd came to charivari my son — about 18 or 20 in one group and a number near them. It was about 11 p.m. We were in bed.

The noise of the bells and the pans caused us to get up. They were yelling and swearing. They demanded $5 to go away. I was in the front bedroom with window open. They then demanded $2 and 50 cents, and then something to eat, and said if we couldn't do anything else, to put up the bride. One said, "Here comes Dodd; we'll have to get to hell out of this." I knew Lundy was there by his voice.

I saw Mahan the next day. He said they had his name down, he had got into trouble. He said he was there outside the crowd. I considered it was a disgrace that people should be so disturbed.

Cross-examined

I was not frightened. I am not aware of any damage to property being done. I did not speak to them.

Joseph Boyer sworn
I was near Ryckman's on the night in question. I went up there with Lynn. I was near the Queen's Hotel, heard a noise, and went there. A number were beating tin pans and blowing horns, about 10 of them were beating the pans. I was there 20 minutes. I couldn't distinguish what was said for the noise. I went up to the crowd and then went back. Lynn went with me and remained there. Defendants O'Donnell, Lynn, Lundy, Gleason, Gibson and McCoubray were there.

James Bruce sworn
I live near Ryckman's. On the night of the 5th instant, I heard a great noise of cow bells, tin pans, hollering. As near as I could tell, it was at Ryckman's. The noise was so great as to attract my attention. I was not in bed. I didn't go to the place.

Cross-examined
I live on the next street about 100 yards away. I was not much annoyed.

George Brooks sworn
I live on same street as Ryckman. I heard the noise of cow bells and tin pans in front of Ryckman's. I was awakened by the noise. I live across 3 lots from Ryckman. I was not annoyed.

Philip Leeder sworn
I live 6 lots from Ryckman.

James Hey sworn
I live about a quarter mile from Ryckman. I heard the cow bells and tin pans and boys yelling. The noise was in the direction of Ryckman's. I was in bed and got up. I didn't go to where the noise was.

William Large sworn
I live 150 feet from Ryckman's. Heard noise about 10:30. I got up. The noise was from cow bells and tin pans and shouting.

Thomas Dodd sworn
I am constable of Bracebridge. On night of 5th instant, I went to Ryckman's. I was at the power house on the main street. I heard the noise. I saw defendant Post at the top of the hill. He asked if I was going to the charivari. I said, "None of your business." Post started to run to where the noise was, and said, "Get to hell out, here's old Dodd." This was said to the crowd.

I saw defendants O'Donnell, Lundy, and McCoubray there. I saw all 20 there. I saw defendant Mahan as he was coming away. He said, "I went there to notify the boys you were coming." He gave me the names of William Lynn, Joseph Boyer, and Arthur Post as being there.

I served a summons on each of the defendants. All except McCoubray and Lundy admitted being there, but they all denied taking any part in the charivari. I served a man named David Taylor with a summons to appear here as a witness. The summons was served at 12:30 today.

Cross-examined
I went there to get the names of the parties to bring them up. My duty is to keep the peace.

Medical evidence of Samuel Bridgeland that David Taylor, a witness in this case, is sick and unable to attend court, put in by Mr. Johnson, who applies for an adjournment on that ground.

Defendant Kennedy discharged.
Adjourned to 22nd at 2 p.m.

May 22nd, 1897, case resumed.
Case withdrawn against defendant Lemuel Scott Jr.

For the Defence

Richard Leeder sworn
I live near Ryckman, about 132 feet on same side. I remember the night in question. It occurred about 10:30 p.m. It continued about 15 minutes. I didn't think it unusual noise. I was watching the parties, and could hear what took place. I don't think it was such as to frighten people. There were tin pans or stove pipes beaten. Mrs. Ryckman spoke to them. I know it was not very loud noise.

Cross-examined
I was up late just going to bed. I heard noise of tin pans, loud enough to call me out. I didn't go near. I thought it better to stay away as I expected they would be broken up. I heard cow bells and hollering. I couldn't distinguish the voices, except those of the two Mrs. Ryckmans. One of the boys said, "Damn it, let's go up to the door, then they'll come out." It was said by one of the crowd. I was afraid if I went I would get into a row.

William Large re-sworn
I heard old Mrs. Ryckman say to the boys that they needn't go away.

Cross-examined
I don't know who she spoke to. The boys said they wanted $2.00.

Leeder recalled
What Mr. Large said is true.

George Mills sworn

I live about 200 yards from Ryckman's. Remember the night in question. I was at home in bed. I heard the noise. I thought it was a dozen cows got out with bells on. I was subpoenaed by prosecution last week.

Cross-examined

It sounded like a dozen cow bells. I heard it was going to take place. I heard the noise 200 yards away. I was not surprised, as I knew what was to take place. I am a constable for the District.

Alton Stevens sworn

I live 20 or 30 rods from Ryckman's. I got home that night at 10 p.m. No very bad noise. I was sitting outside, expecting it. I thought it didn't amount to much and went to bed.

Cross-examined

I heard there was to be a charivari. I didn't go over the Ryckman's. About 10:30 it began. Lasted 10 or 15 minutes.

Samuel Spencer sworn

I live about 50 rods from Ryckman. I am a constable. I heard there was to be a charivari. I didn't hear any noise, as I was not at home. I went home about 11 o'clock. I was at the Town Hall. There was a concert going on there.

Defendants Arthur Post, William Lynn, Michael Lundy, F. Gleason, Ferguson Gibson, Leslie Mahan, John O'Donnell and Murtaugh McCoubray each fined $1 and $2.50 costs, to be paid forthwith, and in default, to be imprisoned and kept at hard labour in the common gaol at Bracebridge for 21 days.

James Boyer, J.P.

Paid O'Donnell, Mahan, Gibson, Post, Lynn, Gleason, McCoubray.

All 8 defendants paid.

Conviction returned.

Magistrate's Court — September 2nd, 1897
Before James Boyer and Singleton Brown, J.P.s
Hubert Mills v Thomas Dodd

For having on the 31st day of August, 1897, at the Town of Bracebridge, unlawfully assaulted and beaten one Ernest Mills.

Defendant pleaded not guilty.

John Scott sworn

I live in the Town of Bracebridge. On the 31st of August two young girls were buying a ticket to go into some show. A boy took it from one of the girl's hand, and the girl ran out onto the road after him. The boy got away from the girl and ran away. Ernest Mills was standing alongside of me.

Defendant came out on the road and beckoned to Ernest Mills to come to him. When Mills went to him defendant caught him by the shoulder with one hand and struck him with his open hand on the head. I judge that the blow would have knocked Mills down had not defendant held him with one hand. Mills was walking into the tent with me.

Cross-examined by defendant

I was standing about 8 feet from defendant. There were marks on the boy's face the same night. I did not hear defendant speak to him at all.

Richard W. Ryan sworn

I was going up to the tent. I saw a girl chase a boy up the road. The boy fell down. I didn't know the boy. I took the girl to be Georgina O'Brien. When

I got to the corner I heard a noise as if someone had struck another a slap. I heard Mr. Dodd say to Mills that he wouldn't stand it any longer. Mills was crying. I asked afterwards who it was he slapped. He said he didn't know. At the time I took it to be defendant's own boy.

Joseph Gleason sworn
I saw defendant strike Ernest Mills one blow in the side of the head. I guess the side of the boy's jaw wouldn't get cold that night. Mills was not scuffling with Georgina O'Brien.

Ernest Mills sworn
I was up near the tent, and the show people promised me a ticket with some other boys. William Scott was fooling with Georgina O'Brien, and Frances Martin, and ran off with Frances Martin's ticket. Georgina O'Brien took after him and cuffed and kicked him. I went to see what she was doing to him. Mr. Dodd called me to him, and caught me by the arm and struck me with the other hand on the face. I heard him say something but couldn't tell what it was as I was crying.

For the Defence

Thomas Dodd, defendant, sworn
I was told by the reeve that there was trouble the night before at the show, and was advised to come down that night in question. I saw a boy snatch a ticket from Frances Martin. Georgina O'Brien chased him. Frances Martin came up and told me a boy had taken her ticket. I saw Georgina O'Brien scuffling with the boy on the road. I came back then.

A few minutes afterwards Mills came running into me. I caught hold of him and questioned him. He said he didn't have to answer, it was none of my business and stuck out his tongue at me. I struck him a light blow with the tips of my fingers on the ear. I hadn't hold of him when I struck him.

Gustavus A. Binyon sworn
William Scott and Georgina O'Brien were scuffling about a ticket. Defendant walked over to Mills and said to him, catching him by the arm, "I have put up with your fooling long enough. Now get you home," at the same time giving him a slap on the side of the head.

Henry S. Bowyer[1] sworn
Defendant came to me and said he heard of the row at the show, and asked me as to whether he should go. I said, "Yes." The language used around the tent was bad. I told defendant to go there to keep order.

John McQuade sworn
On the night in question there was very bad behaviour in front of the tent by boys and grown up people. I heard defendant telling the boys to keep quiet and heard them answering back. Defendant did not use language that would indicate he was in a temper.

William Sibbett[2] sworn
On the previous night, boys threw stones into the tent, and the proprietor came out and made a disturbance. On account of this, defendant was requested to attend to keep order.

Patrick Sullivan sworn
I was there Monday and Tuesday. Boys and young men cut up shamefully up there. Young Mills was there. He has used bad language to me.

The assault being of too trivial a nature, and having been provoked, the case is hereby dismissed with costs $5.25 to be paid by complainant and

---

[1]H.S. Bowyer was a Bracebridge town councillor at this time.
[2]William Sibbett was also a town councillor.

in default, to be levied by distress, and in default of suffering distress to be imprisoned in the common gaol at Bracebridge for 21 days with hard labour.

James Boyer, J.P.
Singleton Brown, J.P.

Magistrate's Court — September 2nd, 1897
Before James Boyer, J.P. and Singleton Brown, J.P.
Thomas Dodd v William Scott, Lemuel Scott Jr.

For having, on the 27th day of August A.D. 1897, at the Town of Bracebridge in said District, unlawfully damaged and injured a certain Notice posted upon a certain bridge the property of the Corporation of the said Town.

Defendants pleaded not guilty.

Thomas Dodd sworn

On the night of 27th of August I came down street about 10 o'clock. I saw three boys carrying on rather unruly on the street. I went down and saw who they were. Lemuel Scott had a banana stalk in his hand, and was swinging it round his head. They started down towards their home. I followed them down as far as the railroad crossing. Lemuel Scott Jr., William Scott and Arthur Pelkey were the three boys.

Just as they got to the bridge William Scott picked up a stone and threw it right at the notice on the bridge. I saw and heard the stone strike, and saw it fall after it struck. I followed up. Lemuel Scott Jr. swung the banana stalk at the sign but missed it. The stone now produced is the one thrown at the sign. The sign is a metal one of some kind painted and lettered.

Cross-examined by Mr. Mahaffy

I saw the sign move also.

Arthur Pelkey sworn

I was with the defendants that night. I went down towards home with them. I didn't see the boys pick up a stone. I didn't see them throw a stone. I heard something strike on the bridge at the far end of the bridge. Lemmel Scott had the banana stalk. I was near the far end of the bridge when I heard the blow strike.

Cross-examined by Mr. Mahaffy

I would have heard the noise if William Scott had thrown the stone.

Case dismissed.

James Boyer, J.P.

MAGISTRATE'S COURT — FEBRUARY 16TH, 1898
BEFORE JAMES BOYER, J.P. AND SINGLETON BROWN, J.P.
REG EX REL *JOHN A. ROSS V CHARLES ROACH*

For having, on the 8th day of February, 1898 A.D., at the Town of Bracebridge, stolen a string of sleigh bells of the value of $5.00, the property of the said John A. Ross.

Case taken under the Juvenile Offenders Act, defendant being only 15 years of age.

Depositions taken on paper.

Defendant pleaded guilty.

Defendant ordered to pay a fine of $3 and $5 costs, to be paid forthwith, and in default, to be imprisoned in the common gaol at Bracebridge for 6 weeks with hard labour and the property to be restored.

James Boyer, J.P. for Muskoka

Conviction returned.

Received $5 on account, balance to be paid on 26th.

February 26th, received $1 on account.

Magistrate's Court — February 22nd, 1898
Before James Boyer, J.P.
George Spence v George L. Sinclair

Assault and battery at the Township of Draper, on the 17th instant, on George Frederick Spence, an infant under the age of 13 years.

Mr. Arnold for Prosecution.

Mr. Ashworth for Defendant.

Defendant admitted that the punishment may have been too severe under the circumstances and the case was withdrawn on payment of costs.

James Boyer, J.P.

Magistrate's Court — May 17th, 1898
Before James Boyer, J.P.
J. Henry Wilson v James Samuel McCord

Assault and battery at the Township of Muskoka upon one Harvey Wilson.

Defendant pleaded not guilty.

Harvey Wilson sworn

I am 10 years of age. On the 13th May instant, as I was coming from South Falls School I had to pass defendant's house to get home. Defendant came and took hold of me by the back of my neck, jerked me, and tore the button off my shirt collar and kicked me on the hip. He asked me if I had taken the dog away. I said, "No, it followed me." I went and told my father. There was no bruise where he kicked me.

Cross-examined

I didn't coax the dog away.

Norman Scott (not sworn)

I am 11 years of age. I was with the last witness at the time in question. I saw defendant take hold of Wilson and jerk him. I did not see defendant kick Wilson. I could see all that took place. Defendant lifted his foot as if he was going to kick him but I am not sure if he did kick him.

Percy Magee (not sworn)

I am 8 years of age. I was with the other children coming from school. Defendant took hold of Wilson and shook him. I saw him raise his foot but didn't see him kick him.

Rosa Meeks sworn

I am 13 years of age. I was coming home with the other children on the day in question. When passing defendant's house he came and took hold of Wilson and gave him a push. Defendant lifted his foot as if he was going to kick him but I don't think he did. I didn't notice if the boy's shirt was torn.

For the Defence

Eliza Vincent sworn

I saw defendant take Wilson by the shoulder, give him a jerk and push him off.

Defendant convicted and judgment suspended, and to be brought up for judgment when called upon.

James Boyer, J.P.

MAGISTRATE'S COURT — AUGUST 29TH, 1898
BEFORE JAMES BOYER, J.P.
WILLIAM DAWE V JAMES NELSON

For having, on the 24th August instant, at Bracebridge, unlawfully and wilfully committed damage and injury to a certain window, the property of complainant.

Defendant pleaded not guilty.

Richard Harper sworn

I live in Bracebridge. I know defendant. Last week, I think on Wednesday, I saw defendant coming up the hill on Ontario Street opposite Dawe's house. He picked up a stone and threw it, and I heard the glass break. I should estimate the damages at 25 cents. The other boy didn't pick up any stone.

William Griffith sworn

Last week, on Wednesday or Thursday, about 4 p.m., I was coming up the hill on Ontario Street with defendant. I was 5 or 6 yards ahead of him. I heard the crash of the glass and saw the window was broken. There was no one else around there except the last witness. Mrs. Dawe came out and asked defendant his name. There was a small dog near the gate. The dog didn't interfere with either of us.

Defendant convicted and fined $10 and 25 cents damages and costs $4.95, to be paid forthwith, and in default, to be imprisoned and kept at hard labour in the common gaol at Bracebridge for 6 weeks.

James Boyer, J.P.

Committed to gaol.

MAGISTRATE'S COURT — SEPTEMBER 13TH, 1898
BEFORE JAMES BOYER, J.P.
FLOYD DODD V JOHN BEERS

For having, on the 29th day of August instant, at the Township of Wood in said District, unlawfully assaulted and beaten the said Floyd Dodd. Defendant pleaded not guilty.

Floyd Dodd sworn

On Monday about 3 weeks ago I saw defendant Beers. I was picking berries with my aunt, Mrs. Dodd, and my cousins Raymond and Frank. Defendant's dog and Mrs. Dodd's dog fought, and I separated them. Lizzie Beers hit me with a stick on the head and I hit her back. When going home we met defendant, who caught hold of me and hit me and shook me. I was holding on to my Auntie and he told me to let go. My aunt and cousins Raymond, Francis and Della were there. John Beers Jr. was also there.

Cross-examined

I had a fight with Willie Beers. I ran to hide behind my Auntie. He came and hit me, and I tried to hit him back. I can't remember whether it was while I was trying to hit Willie Beers that defendant caught hold of me. He held me by the ear with one hand and hit me with the other. Defendant told Willie Beers to fight me.

Isabella Dodd

I am plaintiff's aunt. I remember Monday, 29th August instant. That day I saw defendant. Francis, Floyd and Raymond Dodd were with me. Mrs. Beers, Lizzie, Johnny and Willie Beers were there. Defendant came out and told Johnny and Willie Beers to fight Floyd. Raymond Dodd said if they did, he would fight too, so only Willie came to fight Floyd. I told Floyd to run home and not fight. Mr. Beers caught Floyd by the ear and shook and hit him. Floyd had hold of me when defendant caught hold of him. Willie hit Floyd two or three times.

Cross-examined

I did not catch hold of Willie Beers. Floyd had nothing in his hand.

Raymond Dodd sworn

Defendant set Willie and Johnny on Floyd. Willie went. Mrs. Dodd told Floyd to go home. Defendant caught hold of his ear, pulled it, hit him and shook him.

Francis Dodd sworn

Defendant asked Floyd why he hit Lizzie Beers. Floyd said she hit him first. Defendant set Willie and Johnny on Floyd. Defendant hit Floyd and shook him.

For the Defence

Defendant sworn

I was coming from the bush. Willie was with me. Mrs. Dodd caught hold of my boy. Willie and Floyd were fighting. I caught hold of Floyd to keep him from hitting Willie. I caught hold of his ear but I didn't hit him. Mrs. Dodd had hold of Willie when Floyd was going to strike him.

Mary Jane Beers sworn
Mrs. Dodd had hold of Willie, and Floyd was trying to strike him. My husband caught hold of Floyd and pulled him back. My husband did not strike him.

Cross-examined
Willie asked Floyd why he hit Lizzie, and Floyd said he hit her and could lick him too. Willie hit him several times. Willie struck Floyd before Mrs. Dodd caught hold of him.

Lizzie Beers sworn
Willie came down from the bush with my father. Johnny told Willie that Floyd had hit me and told Willie to hit Floyd. Willie went to hit Floyd, and Mrs. Dodd caught hold of Willie. Floyd then had a stone in his hand and went to strike Willie. My father caught Floyd by the ear. My father did not strike Floyd. When my father caught Floyd by the ear he dropped the stone.

William Beers (not sworn — 10 years old)
Johnny told me Floyd hit Lizzie and for me to hit Floyd. I went to hit Floyd. Mrs. Dodd caught hold of me. Floyd went to hit me and my father caught him by the ear and kept him from hitting me.

Cross-examined
He struck me a couple of times on the breast.

John Beers (not sworn — 8 years old)
Corroborated last witness.

Defendant convicted and fined $2 and costs $8.05, to be paid forthwith, and in default, to be imprisoned in the common gaol at Bracebridge for one month.

James Boyer, J.P. for Muskoka

Fine and costs paid.

Magistrate's Court — November 4th, 1898
Before James Boyer, J.P. and John Thomson J.P.
Arthur Patrick v Lawrence Murphy, Joseph L. Jacques and Patrick Carleton the Younger

Juvenile Offenders — for having, on or about the 17th day of October A.D. 1898, at the Township of Monck, stolen a certain boat of the value of $4 the property of the informant.
Defendants by their parents wished the case disposed of by the magistrates. Defendants severally pleaded not guilty.

Arthur Patrick sworn
I live in Bracebridge. On or about the 20th September last, my boat was taken from the wharf at the old tannery. I didn't see the boat again until it was brought to the wharf at Thomas Robinson's, after the boys had been summoned. One of the defendants said they had brought the boat back after they were summoned. The boat was worth $4.00.

Cross-examined
It was lost from the tannery wharf. The defendants said Mrs. Robinson had lent them a paddle and allowed them to take the boat. I never loaned the boat to any or either of the defendants.

Alice Robinson sworn

I am the wife of Thomas Robinson and live in the Township of Monck. I know the defendants. On the 17th October last, the boat in question was at our wharf. I saw the defendants taking the boat in question. They had not asked my permission to take the boat. I told them if they took that boat to bring it back. They never brought it back. I had not any authority to let the boys have the boat, but said if they did take it they were to bring it back. I didn't know the owner of the boat. The defendants never returned the boat till Wednesday last. The defendants brought the boat back to the wharf on Wednesday last.

For the Defence

Lawrence Murphy, defendant, sworn

I am 13 years of age. We got the boat from Robinson's wharf. I asked her if we could have the boat and asked for the loan of the paddle. She said if we took the boat to bring it back. The other defendants were present. We left it at Beaver Creek and went to Ripke's. We got half way between Beaver Creek and Robinson's house, we pulled it up on shore and left it. We left the paddle at Robinson's wharf.

On questioning by the court

There were 2 boats and a scow at the wharf. I had seen the other boat often at the wharf. Mrs. Robinson had the paddle, which I asked her to lend me. I didn't return the boat till after I got the summons.

Patrick Carleton the Younger, defendant, sworn

I am 13 years of age. I was present when Murphy asked for the boat. She said we could have it if we fetched it back. She lent him the paddle. I knew the boat belonged to Patrick.

William Murphy sworn
It is about 50 rods from the wharf at Robinson's to Beaver Creek. I never measured it.

The Magistrates disagreed.

Defendants were bound (by their parents) in $100 each to appear on Friday 11th November at 2 p.m. to answer the charge in consequence of magistrate's disagreeing.

Patrick Carleton paid in $100.

William Murphy paid in $100.

Samuel St. Jacques paid in $100.

On November 11th, 1898
Case again resumed before Messrs. Boyer and Browning. Defendants objected to the case being tried under Juvenile Offenders Act, and they were committed for trial.

James Boyer, J.P.

Chapter Sixteen

Pressures on the Sex Trade

Prostitutes, whether working in Bracebridge or at a remove in the convenient brothels of adjacent townships where fewer public complaints might arise, faced the same double standard in the1890s that sex trade workers have experienced before and since.

They and those who kept or organized the "common bawdy house" or "house of ill-repute" where these women plied their trade to eager townsmen and visitors to the community were intermittently rounded up by the local constable. His charges against them were often based on his own scouting around, other times in response to complaints from neighbours.

While the fifty-dollar fines for prostitution were dramatically higher than those levied for fighting or killing animals out of season, Magistrate Boyer seems to have been less than even-handed, with men getting lower fines than women for keeping a common bawdy house or for being found-ins.

In a number of cases, the convicted women passively paid their fine, if they had money enough, in order to get quietly back to business with the least delay so that they could recoup their loss. Yet some women served long sentences because the high fifty-dollar fine, plus costs, was more than they possessed. Sometimes there was no option to even pay a fine because the only sentence handed down to a prostitute was jail time with hard labour. On other occasions, Magistrate Boyer offered indigent prostitutes an alternative to serving time in jail: "Get out of town!"

Magistrate's Court — April 30th, 1894
Before Alfred Hunt and James Boyer, J.P.s
Robert E. Armstrong v John Took, John Smith

For having, on the 3rd May, 1894, at Bracebridge, been frequenters of a certain house of ill fame kept by one Queenie Dufresne.
Both parties pleaded guilty.

Each prisoner fined $10 and costs $3.50, to be paid forthwith, and in default, to be imprisoned in the common gaol at Bracebridge and there kept at hard labour for 2 calendar months.

Alfred Hunt, J.P.
James Boyer, J.P.

Constable $3.00
Court $4.00
Total $7.00
Fines paid.

MAGISTRATE'S COURT — MAY 4TH, 1894
BEFORE MESSRS. HUNT AND BOYER, J.P.s
ROBERT E. ARMSTRONG V QUEENIE DUFRESNE

For having, on the 3rd day of May A.D. 1894, at the Town of Bracebridge, been the keeper of a certain house of ill fame.

Prisoner pleaded not guilty.

John Gibbs sworn

I live in Bracebridge, the second house from prisoner. Prisoner has resided there about two weeks. I know that for some time past a number of men have been in the habit of frequenting that house at night, and myself and family have been disturbed by men coming to enquire for the residents of that house. I have seen a number of men go in and out there at night. The house has borne a bad reputation for some months.

Cross-examined

I have seen three men go there either last Monday or Tuesday.

Prisoner admitted that she knew the reputation of the house before she came to live there, and that she came to look after the interests of Mrs. Rogers, a former resident.

Joseph Lacombe sworn

I live just across the street from the prisoner. The house has borne a bad name since last fall. A number of men going in and out there every night. Have seen men going in and coming out of there at half past 10 o'clock at night. Have seen a number going in and out there during the last two weeks.

David Hidd sworn

I live in the house next to the one in question. Have lived there nearly a year. My house is about 3 feet from the one in question. Since about August last, the house has borne a reputation on account of men going there as late as midnight or beyond that time. Since prisoner has lived there I have seen men going in there late at night. Myself and family have been disturbed by noise in the place at night, and by parties coming to my house to inquire for that place. I saw a man go there between 12 and 1 o'clock this morning.

John Anderson sworn

I have been living near the house in question up to the day before yesterday. I have seen men going in and out there both day and evening.

Robert E. Armstrong sworn

I am a constable for the District of Muskoka. About one o'clock this morning I made a raid upon the house in question under a warrant. I found prisoner and another woman and two men in the house. They were in a sitting room. The residents of the house have borne a bad reputation for some time. I have warned them they would get into trouble.

For the Defence

Elizabeth Dempsey sworn

Prisoner has been in Bracebridge for 2 weeks. I have seen nothing wrong going on in that house. Men have not come there during the day and all hours at night since I have been there. The two men last night came to ask for Mrs. Rogers.

Cross-examined

I was with Mrs. Rogers, went away and came back two weeks ago. I don't know whether there were numbers of men staying there late at night as I slept upstairs. We were having supper when the men came last night.

Prisoner convicted and fined $50 and costs $5.55, to be paid forthwith, and in default of immediate payment, to be imprisoned in the common gaol at Bracebridge and there kept at hard labour for 6 calendar months.

James Boyer, J.P.
Alfred Hunt, J.P.

Court $2.80
Constable $2.75
Total $5.55
Fine paid.
Conviction returned.

MAGISTRATE'S COURT — MAY 4TH, 1894
BEFORE MESSRS. HUNT AND BOYER, J.P.s
ROBERT E. ARMSTRONG V ELIZABETH DEMPSEY

For having, on the 3rd May 1894, at Bracebridge, been an inmate of a certain house of ill fame.

Plea of not guilty.

Robert E. Armstrong sworn
I am a constable for the District of Muskoka. About one o'clock this morning I went to the house kept by Dufresne in Bracebridge and I found the prisoner and the woman, Dufresne, and two men in the house at that time, and arrested the whole of them.

Prisoner convicted and fined $50 and costs $5.55, to be paid forthwith, and in default, to be imprisoned in the common gaol at Bracebridge and there kept at hard labour for the space of six calendar months.

Alfred Hunt, J.P.
James Boyer, J.P.

Committed to gaol.

Conviction returned.

Magistrate's Court — March 11th, 1895
Before James Boyer, J.P.
Robert E. Armstrong v Elizabeth Weston

For keeping a bawdy house at the Township of Monck on the 9th March instant.

Case adjourned to 13th instant, at 2 p.m., to procure evidence.

* * *

March 13th case dismissed for want of evidence.

James Boyer, J.P.

Magistrate's Court — December 6th, 1895
Before James Boyer, J.P.
James Armstrong v James Winters

For having, on the 4th day of December A.D. 1895, at the Township of Draper, been the keeper of a house of ill fame.

Prisoner pleaded guilty.

Prisoner ordered to pay a fine of $20 and $4.95 costs, to be paid forthwith, and in default, to be imprisoned in the common gaol at Bracebridge and there kept at hard labour for 3 calendar months.

James Boyer, J.P.

Committed to gaol.
Conviction returned.

MAGISTRATE'S COURT — AUGUST 28TH, 1896
BEFORE JAMES BOYER, J.P.
THOMAS DODD V HENRY WILSON

For that defendant, on 26th August instant, at Bracebridge, was the keeper of a house of ill fame, and that a number of women were kept in said house for the purpose of prostitution.
The charge having been read to prisoner, he pleaded guilty.

Defendant Wilson fined $2 and $18.40 to be paid forthwith, and in default, defendant to be imprisoned in the common gaol at Bracebridge with hard labour for 6 months.

James Boyer, J.P.

Paid constable $10.00
Court $6.90
Paid 2 Witnesses $1.50
Total $18.40
Conviction returned.

Magistrate's Court — August 28th, 1896
Before James Boyer, J.P
Thomas Dodd v Lily Hay, Maud Sutherland and May Murray

For that defendants were, on the 26th day of August instant, at Bracebridge, inmates of a certain house of ill fame kept by one Henry Wilson.
The charge having been read to prisoners, they severally pleaded guilty.

Each prisoner committed to the county gaol at Bracebridge, with hard labour for 3 months. Sentence not to be enforced if prisoners leave Bracebridge and its vicinity and remain away for above period.

James Boyer, J.P.

Magistrate's Court — July 23rd, 1897
Before James Boyer, J.P.
Matthew Small v Mark Weston

For having, on the 21st day of July A.D. 1897, at the Township of Macaulay, kept a bawdy house or house of ill fame.
Prisoner pleaded not guilty.

Matthew Small sworn
I am, at present, residing at the British Lion Hotel, Bracebridge. Wednesday afternoon Dennis Guiney took me to a house to have some fun. I went up the railway track to a house 1¼ miles from the town. He introduced me to two women who are now present. I didn't see prisoner in the afternoon. I had connexion with one of the women. I paid $2 for the fun. I bought some liquor, treated the girls. Dennis Guiney took the liquor up.

I went to the concert with Guiney in the evening. After it was over I went with Guiney to the same house. In consequence of what Guiney said, I gave him $2 and a bottle of whiskey to see me through the night. After I got there I was going to bed with the girl. I told her Denny was to settle with her. The girl went and saw Denny. She wouldn't accept it, as $2 was not enough for two of us for the night. Prisoner was sitting in the room with Guiney drinking. I had my coat and vest off. I asked Guiney for my money. He said he wouldn't give it me, as he couldn't travel with me for nothing. I then left.

Thomas Dodd sworn

I am a constable residing in Bracebridge. I know the prisoner. Last Monday, about 4 o'clock a.m., I saw two rigs with 2 wheels each driving into Leishman's yard. The first rig contained James McCord and a woman. The 2nd rig contained a man and woman and canvas (like a tent) tied to each. They drove through the brick yard. I went up to the English Church, and then saw it was prisoner driving the second rig. The party had 3 dogs, a black, a Collie and a white one.

Defendant afterwards pleaded guilty and fined $2 and $5.25 costs, to be paid forthwith, and in default, to be imprisoned in the common gaol at Bracebridge with hard labour for one month.

James Boyer, J.P.

Fine paid $2.00
Costs collected $2.25
Paid constable $3.00
Total $7.25
Conviction returned.

Magistrate's Court — July 23rd, 1897
Before James Boyer, J.P.
Matthew Small v Elizabeth Weston, May Sykes

For being inmates of a house of ill fame at the Township of Macaulay on the 21st day of July, 1897.

Defendants pleaded guilty and fined $2 and $3.25 costs each, and in default, to be imprisoned and kept at hard labour in the common gaol at Bracebridge for one month, but not to be enforced if defendants pay the costs and leave the neighbourhood within 48 hours.

James Boyer, J.P.

> Costs: Constable paid $3.50
> Court $3.00
> Total $6.50

Magistrate's Court — July 11th, 1898
Before James Boyer, J.P.
James Arnott v Lucy Rickard

For that defendant, on 11th July instant, at Bracebridge, being a person not having any visible means of maintaining herself and living without employment.
Defendant pleaded not guilty.

James Arnott sworn
I am a constable for the District of Muskoka. On the 26th of June last, I was informed that the prisoner was a loose character. I saw her that night on the street between 10:30 and eleven o'clock. She went into the British

Lion Hotel to get a place to stay but they wouldn't keep her. I met her going from there towards the Dominion Hotel.

I asked her what she meant by being on the streets at that time of night. She said she had lots of money and could get a place to stay. She then went to Foster's Hotel but the proprietor would not keep her. She came up the street with a young man and tried to get shelter at Mr. Adair's and Harp's boarding houses. She at last got shelter at Harp's boarding house.

Next morning she was around trying to get a place to work. She got a place at Johnson's boarding house and was there two nights. On the 29th, prisoner and a man left town. The same night the prisoner and the man with her applied for lodgings about a mile and a half out in the country. On the fourth of July she returned to town. She engaged to work at Bradshaw's and stayed there two nights. On Saturday night, the 9th of July, prisoner and another man applied for lodgings at a reputed house of ill fame in the Township of Draper, applying thereto as man and wife, but were refused.

On Sunday the 10th of July, at 7:30, prisoner was seen going in the direction of South Falls. On Monday the 11th she was at Mr. P. Sherwood's.

About 9 o'clock that night I arrested prisoner. Prisoner goes by the nickname of "Spot" around town.

Prisoner committed to the gaol at Bracebridge for the term of six months with hard labour.

James Boyer, J.P.

Conviction returned.

Chapter Seventeen

BARTERING FOR WORK, FIGHTING FOR WAGES

A justice of the peace is not commonly understood to be a collection agency for workers or an arbitrator between employers and employees. But fifty-six times during the 1890s, James Boyer spent a lot of effort adjudicating their claims and counterclaims in cases that shed rare light on that era's working conditions and economic relationships.

With many Muskoka farms so marginal, farmers often sought income by providing wage labour, logging in the big lumber companies' winter bush camps when their snow-covered fields meant that only the milk cows, chickens, and other livestock needed tending anyway, which their wives and children did. By the 1890s Muskoka's main towns had become more industrialized, and men increasingly abandoned their farms to join the "working class" recruits employers were bringing into the district for their mills, shops, factories, and tanneries. These workers typically put in days of ten hours or more, six days a week.

Everyone in this 1890s work camp near Bracebridge looks across slash and stumps into the camera, including the woman who was the cook, giving us a sense of their time and place. Often workers' wages were not agreed to in advance, time records were haphazardly kept, and payment was subject to offsets, delays, and excuses — as James Boyer heard in Magistrate's Court.

Magistrates had primary jurisdiction over cases involving employer-employee obligations, including specific disputes related to employment. The Master and Servant Act of Ontario, dating from 1847, clarified the jurisdiction and authority of magistrates for employment contracts. Despite such statute law, however, as these cases before James Boyer show, only the most basic provisions of contract law were usually applied. And there were instances when higher courts did become involved, as in one case when an employer ordered by Magistrate Boyer to pay a disputed amount to an employee appealed his decision, and in another, when he himself sought a warrant of distress from a higher court to enforce his judgment against a recalcitrant employer.

Legal historians Jeremy Webber and Randall Echlin have observed that the work performed by magistrates "was not undertaken in as orderly and formal an environment as might have been expected of judicial officers." Magistrates inhabited "a different legal universe" from superior court judges,

The two bargemen unloading this shipment of tanbark alongside a Bracebridge tannery in the 1890s are harder to discern in their dark clothes than the four visiting ladies in fine dresses who stand out in such an industrial scene. Leather tanning contributed thousands of jobs and dollars to Muskoka, bringing prosperity, production, and pollution.

often relying, for example, on "their own good sense" to supplement statute law and the magistrates' manuals. "Moreover, proceedings before magistrates were often informal and based on oral arguments and magistrates often took it upon themselves to intervene and encourage a solution. The role of magistrates in 19th century Ontario was much more than just a judicial one." Magistrates "were expected to play an important social role at a time during which the agrarian-based economy underwent a shift towards industrialism."[1]

A worker in Muskoka was his own negotiator because all these wage issue cases arose outside of any context of union representation. A worker also had to litigate his own claim for on-the-job injury, a costly inconvenience for

---

[1] Jeremy Webber, "Labour and the Law" in *Labouring Lives: Work and Workers in Nineteenth-Century Ontario*, ed. Paul Craven (Toronto: University of Toronto Press, 1995), 105–201; Randall Scott Echlin, "From Master and Servant to *Bardal* and Beyond: 200 Years of Employment Law in Ontario, 1807 to 2007," in *Special Lectures 2007: Employment Law*, eds. Randall Scott Echlin and Chris. G. Paliare (Toronto: Irwin Law, 2007), 4–9.

both worker and employer alike because cases for compensation continued to go to a higher court until Ontario's legislature enacted the Workmen's Compensation Act in 1914, which came into force in 1915 and provided an administrative trade-off in which workers relinquished their right to sue in exchange for compensation benefits.

Reproducing so many cases in this chapter may seem like overkill, because the core issues were often the same. One reason for doing so, as Edward Greenspan notes in his preface, is that these disputes "clearly had the potential to have a major impact on the lives of those involved," and "the justice of the peace may have been the linchpin who kept the developing community from anarchy." That conclusion stands up when one is able to see the nature and extent of these claims as a whole. Secondly, they provide raw evidence, otherwise not available, about the development of Ontario labour relations and contract law. For instance, when Justice Randall Scott Echlin of Ontario's Superior Court of Justice prepared his review of two hundred years of employment law in Ontario from 1807 to 2007, for a special lectures series of the Law Society of Upper Canada, he reviewed all fifty-six of these cases. A sociologist, or a novelist writing historical fiction, could equally mine them for evidence and insights about the human condition in Muskoka in the closing decade of the nineteenth century.

The claims for unpaid wages coming before James Boyer show just how loose the employment arrangements often were. In a surprising number of cases, the boss and hired man had not even discussed a rate of pay. Or, where they had agreed at least on that, the amount earned was often unduly diminished in the eyes of the worker, according to a number of these cases, by set-off deductions his employer deemed appropriate. What would surprise many people today is how workers were expected to provide or pay for supplies needed to keep their equipment running, such as a train engineer paying for oil in his locomotive. Thus a Muskoka man hired to keep an engine running was charged by his employer for the oil and grease to lubricate the machinery, but he also suffered deductions from his pay for downtime when the engine was not working. In some instances, a worker would go without any payment for time actually worked, even several weeks, if he left before the end of the month. To make matters worse, the system for keeping track of days worked, or reporting in, was often haphazard.

Men, horses, and boys logged the Muskoka woods until end of winter, felling trees by axe. They would soon return to their families and farms, often disputing in Magistrate's Court before James Boyer the amount claimed by their employer from their wages as set-offs for food, accommodation, tobacco, woollen socks, or a lost axe.

Logs cut and massed by riverbanks and streams all winter were rolled into spring waters as soon as ice melted so the annual log drive could begin. Available watercourses helped move logs to sawmills, but there was urgency to complete the drive while spring freshets still kept rivers high enough to float logs over rocky shallows.

Whatever modest remuneration these Muskoka drovers earned during the annual log drives, there was no extra "danger pay." Clearing log jams at waterfalls was part of their hazardous work, where death often found opportunity to present itself.

Wage "offsets" were common in the barter economy of 1890s Muskoka. An employer reduced a worker's earnings for the value of items consumed, such as an amount for room and board, the price of a pair of work pants, wool socks, or for tobacco "bought" from the company's stores deep in the bush. He would be charged for a lost axe. Spring's arrival culminated in months of earnings and deductions being tallied; there was frequently such confusion about offsets, and so many disputes over wages, that the parties were forced to rely on a justice of the peace to decide what amount, if any, should be paid. As magistrate, Boyer reviewed allowable deductions, heard evidence from witnesses about their calculation of accounts cross-owed, then settled exactly how much money remained to be paid or stood to be recouped.

*Workers complete a major wood-and-iron trestle over the Muskoka River into
Bracebridge. When the labourers had gone unpaid for weeks, they rioted in town, and
James Boyer, municipal clerk and magistrate, faced them down reading the Riot Act.*

There were further wrinkles too. In this barter economy, payment of
money or money's worth was sometimes made through a third party. A
logging company might give a local merchant authorization to bill the
logging company's account for up to, say, twelve dollars' worth of groceries
purchased at his general store for the wife of a man absent from home
because he was working in the bush, or it might arrange for a third party
to deliver a cord of hardwood to the man's home while he was away during
the winter and unable to supply firewood himself, with the wood's value
then deducted from the worker's pay. Such a triangle worked perfectly, so
long as everybody did what was expected, agreed on the values or prices
involved, and kept accurate records with which the others concurred. But
the accounting could become a mixture of real misunderstandings and
ambiguous set-offs which, once again, the reliable and handy justice of the
peace had to sort out.

Men and boys, horses and machinery, worked this Port Sydney shingle mill between Bracebridge and Huntsville to produce a constant stream of roof and wall coverings for the regional market. The three water barrels on the roof ridge were early fire extinguishers.

Still another wrinkle was illiteracy. In one document pasted into James Boyer's bench book, a receipt was signed by a worker using his mark, an *X*. No doubt, record keeping was hard for those unable to write, which contributed to haphazard records and reliance by workers on the fairness of their bosses.

A different complicating factor was the use of Magistrate's Court to collect unpaid wages when better direct communication between worker and employer might have resolved the matter. It appears some workers were not especially ardent in direct dealing, and one paid the price when James Boyer assessed court costs against him even as he ordered his back wages to be paid.

James's role as labour arbitrator did not stop even there. Parallel to Muskoka's barter exchange of goods and services, a cash economy was simultaneously operating, which generated quite a different variety of wage cases for Magistrate's Court. These cases arose when a workingman failed to get his money due and payable at the end of a week of laying

Ten men and a dog pose at this Muskoka lumber yard for an 1890s photograph. Progress is evident with buildings constructed of boards rather than logs, but less visible were advances for workers. In this era before Ontario's workers' compensation law, injuries on the job still required suing one's employer, while wage disputes, the result of such things as set-offs for food and gear, often led to actions in Magistrate's Court.

bricks, or upon completing a particular job such as digging a field of potatoes. The dispute was no longer over setoffs but the value of the work done, the competence of the labourer, and the time it took compared to what it ought to have taken. Sometimes, third party witnesses testified about how much they would have charged, a quest for objective standards in a highly subjective work setting.

Finally, a different variety of wage cases landing before Magistrate Boyer were more straightforward, involving as they did a hard-pressed employer unable, or a hardnosed employer unwilling, to pay a workingman his earned wages. Such contractors as Isaac Waltenbury, Andrew Boyd, John Ruttan, and Thomas and William Holliday were often in court. Several pleaded not guilty to a charge of failing to pay wages due, as if it was part of their overall tough-minded approach to running their construction businesses, and perhaps even their way to signal to workingmen that they would not easily be pushed around. Sometimes the court costs that Boyer levied against these employers, after also ordering them to pay a worker his wages, makes one wonder how long it took these contractors to get the message that, in terms of their money and time, it would be simpler to pay up in the first instance. Other contractors, however, such as the Hollidays, often admitted they owed the money, so were ordered to pay the wages, as well as court costs. From the record, it would seem they were not hard-boiled or recalcitrant employers, just men short of money, struggling to do their best and make ends meet in the poor economy of the late 1890s.

MAGISTRATE'S COURT — JULY 13TH, 1893
BEFORE JAMES BOYER, J.P.
JAMES PTOLEMY v SAMUEL H. ARMSTRONG

For wages of $6.50, which became due within one month past.
Defendant pleads not indebted.

James Ptolemy sworn
I went to work for defendant on June 26th, hoeing potatoes. I went to the work without any agreement as to wages. I worked 5 days and 2 hours and finished the job. I charged at the rate of $1.25 per day. That is the rate of wages I have been getting all summer. Defendant has paid me at that rate for work done before this. I had asked defendant for the money. He refused to pay.

For the Defence

Samuel Armstrong sworn
I am the defendant. I asked complainant to do the work. I didn't make any bargain. I sent him to hoe the potatoes. There is not a quarter of an acre in

the patch of potatoes. I told him to put the Paris Green[2] on the potatoes, dry mixed with flour. I claimed $6.50 was too much and offered him the potatoes as they stood in payment for his work. They were thinly planted. I think they could be hoed in a day.

Cross-examined
I didn't know how long you had been working when I saw you on Wednesday. I offered complainant $3.50 for the work.

William J. Mayes sworn
I planted the potatoes in question, about a quarter of an acre. I have been used to cultivating potatoes. I planted them in 13 hours, including cutting them and hoeing the weeds. Defendant asked me to hoe the potatoes but I had other work. I should have thought myself well paid at $3 if I had done the work.

Richard Ryan sworn
I planted the same land with potatoes last year and hoed them partly up. I paid a man $1.25 for hoeing them and helped him one afternoon. About 1/4 of an acre in the patch.

Judgment for plaintiff for $3.50 without costs.

James Boyer, J.P.

Costs paid.

---

[2]Paris Green, a pleasingly named but highly toxic chemical killer of potato bugs and other critters, made from combining copper acetate and arsenic trioxide, was often mixed into soil with the plantings.

Magistrate's Court — November 15th, 1893
Before James Boyer, J.P.
Matilda Wolfrem v Joseph Boyd, Gravenhurst

Claim for $27 in wages, due within one month from November 4th.
Defendant didn't appear

Matilda Wolfrem sworn
I am the complainant in this case. On Monday November 13th I served a summons on defendant to appear at Bracebridge on November 15th in this case. I handed it to him personally. After serving the summons, defendant gave me $2 on account of the debt. I have been working for him in a lumber camp in Medora. I left there last October 5th. At the time I left defendant owed me $27 for wages. I was working there as cook.

Judgment for complainant for $25 and costs of $1.75 to be paid forthwith, and in default, warrant of distress to issues within the time allowed by law.
James Boyer, J.P.

Magistrate's Court — March 3rd, 1894
Before James Boyer, J.P.
George Fennell v James I. Clark

For the sum of $9, for wages which became due within one month prior to February 22nd, and which defendant neglected to pay.
Defendant appeared and admitted being indebted to complainant in the sum of $9.52, for which judgment was given, together with $2.75 costs, making together $12.27 to be paid in 8 days or warrant of distress to issue.
James Boyer, J.P.

Wages and court costs paid in full.

Received above amount of $9.52 — [signed] "George Fennell."

Magistrate's Court — March 20th, 1894
Before James Boyer, J.P.
Richard James Leeder v Andrew Boyd

Claim for $22.20, for wages which became due and payable within one month from February 15th last.

Plea: "Not indebted."

Richard James Leeder sworn

On the 18th of October last, I first went to work for Mr. Boyd. I was hired in Bracebridge. I worked up till noon on February 20th. He still owes me a balance of $22.20. It was $22 for skidding and $20 after the skidding was finished. I worked three months all but one day skidding.

> Amount claimed $85.54
> Allowed as offset $82.39
> Total $ 3.15

Judgment for complainant for $3.15 and costs $3.35, to be paid forthwith, and in default, warrant of distress to issue at the end of 8 days.

James Boyer, J.P.

> Constable $1.75
> Court $1.60
> Total $3.35
> To complainant $3.15
> $6.50 Paid. ‑ *J.B.*

Bracebridge March 31st, 1894. Received from James Boyer three dollars on the account of Richard James Leeder. ~ *A.B. Ryckman*

This entry suggests a fifteen-cent administrative fee may have been levied. No evidence was recorded in the bench book about the full claim by Leeder for $85.54 and Boyd's $82.39 in offsets.

MAGISTRATE'S COURT — JUNE 25TH, 1894
BEFORE JAMES BOYER, J.P.
ISAAC H. WALTENBURY V FREDERICK EDWARDS

Assault and battery at Bracebridge on June 25th.

The charge having been read to defendant, he pleaded not guilty.

Isaac H. Waltenbury sworn

I live in Bracebridge. Defendant had been in my employ up to about 2 o'clock today. Defendant had brought a chum of his to work. I promised to give him a week's work or longer if I could. Defendant's chum came up.

I couldn't promise more than one or two weeks' work. Defendant used abusive language to me because I wouldn't promise to give him work longer than that. He struck me on the eye and gave me a black eye. I held him to try and prevent his striking me but I didn't strike him. He struck me three times.

Cross-examined

I did not strike you.

Defendant admitted he struck complainant twice.

For the Defence

Lawrence Gazeley sworn
I had been working for Mr. Waltenbury. This afternoon Waltenbury came to the work. Defendant asked when he was going to start another job. He said, "In the morning." He asked him if he was going to put his chum on. Waltenbury said, "No." Defendant asked why he told him to send him for his chum. Waltenbury said he didn't. Defendant said he did. Waltenbury called him a liar. They had a few words. Waltenbury struck defendant on the arm. They clinched and fell. I didn't see defendant strike Waltenbury. They were behind some old lumber and I couldn't see what happened. They both fell together. Defendant on top. Waltenbury struck him with his fist on the arm.

Cross-examined
It only lasted two minutes.

Defendant convicted and fined $1 and $3 costs, to be paid forthwith, and in default, to be imprisoned in the lock-up at Bracebridge for 7 days.

James Boyer, J.P.

Fine and costs paid.

Magistrate's Court — June 30th, 1894
Before James Boyer, J.P.
Isidore Labrie v Alonzo Boyd

For $10.50 in wages, due to complainant within one month now last past.
Defendant admitted the indebtedness.

Judgment for plaintiff $10.50 and $2.00 costs, to be paid forthwith, and if not, execution to issue at the time limited by law.

James Boyer, J.P.

Paid.

Magistrate's Court — July 16th, 1894
Before James Boyer, J.P.
John Hunter v John Greenwell

Claim for $7.78 in wages due to complainant within one month previous to July 11th.

Defendant pleaded not indebted.

John Hunter sworn

I live in Bracebridge. About 5 weeks ago I went to work for defendant. I was to get $18 per month and get my pay every two weeks. I worked 3 weeks and two days. I have received $5 and $0.50 at another time, and a half-pound of tobacco worth 30 cents. I left his employ about 3 weeks ago. I left of my own accord. I left because I could get higher wages. No time was stated as to how long I was to stay with him.

Cross-examined by W. Mahaffy

Complainant owes me about $7.78. The $5 was paid at the end of two weeks without me asking for it. I asked for the $0.50 and the tobacco. I told defendant I didn't think I would want any more money till July 12th.

Complaint dismissed, with costs of $2.50

James Boyer, J.P.

Magistrate's Court — August 29th, 1894
Before James Boyer, J.P.
James Hobson v Joseph Layne

For the sum of $37 for wages which became due within one month from August 25th, 1894 (the day information was laid), which defendant refused to pay.

Defendant admitted the indebtedness.

Judgment for complainant for $37.00 and costs $2.85, to be paid forthwith, and in default, distress to issue at the time limited by law.

James Boyer, J.P.

Constable $1.25
Court $1.60
Paid constable.

James Boyer's bench book records that James Hobson received $10.00 on account of the debt on the day this matter was heard, and three weeks later, a further installment of $8.40, but there is no record the balance of $18.60 of unpaid wages was ever tendered.

Magistrate's Court — September 22nd, 1894
Before James Boyer, J.P.
Albert R. Waltenbury v William Grinson

For $4.30 in wages, due to complainant within 30 days from September 20th, which defendant neglected to pay.

The defendant admitted the indebtedness.

Judgment was for $4.30 claim and $2.75 costs, to be paid forthwith, and in default, distress to issue within the time allowed by law.

James Boyer, J.P.

Paid $5.80

Defendant paid constable

October 8th, 1894, paid $4.30 to complainant

Magistrate's Court — September 25th, 1894
Before James Boyer, J.P.
Florence Dalwood v James L. Fenn

Claim of $2.50 for wages, which became due within one month now last past.

Defendant pleaded not indebted.

Florence Dalwood sworn

I went to work for defendant on August 21st at $5 per month. I remained there 2 weeks. I left there because Mrs. Fenn objected to my sister coming to see me. I asked Mrs. Fenn to pay me. She said Mr. Fenn objected to it.

Cross-examined

I understand I was hired for a month. I also understood that if I left before my month was up I was not to get any pay but was to get it if I stayed the month.

Case dismissed with costs $2.75.

James Boyer, J.P.

Magistrate's Court — October 3rd, 1894
Before James Boyer, J.P.
Frederick Dubois v Charles Smith

For $12 in wages, which became due within one month at township of McLean.

Defendant pleaded not indebted.

Frederick Dubois sworn

I live in Macaulay. I have been working for defendant. It is about a month now since I left. It was within a month before September 26th. I was working for him by the day at 50 cents per day and board. Defendant is owing me $12 for 24 days work.

Cross-examined

I have done other work for him. I worked 45½ days. In addition to the articles alleged, I got a coat and vest worth $3.00 two years ago on July 12th. I paid him in work. I got a bushel of potatoes. I worked and paid for them in addition to the work. Defendant charged me for other things: $1 charged for washing, 10 cents for beef, 30 cents for butter ($3 claimed as board for complainant and dog per week for 2 weeks). I was only there 3 or 4 days before I began work. I marked the day's work every time I was at home.

Charles Parker sworn

I know both parties. I saw defendant one day last week at the hotel in Macaulay (the halfway house). I heard defendant tell the hotel keeper he owed complainant $12 and he was going to bring a cow down on Monday to leave with John Richards till he could pay the money. Complainant was there at the time. I didn't hear him, defendant, say anything about Dubois' account.

For the Defence

Defendant Charles Smith sworn

I should judge complainant was boarding 9 or 10 days before he commenced work. Complainant told me he worked 40 days. Defendant was boarding after he left work, by the day, but he worked for his board.

Serena Smith sworn

I am the wife of defendant. Complainant had 11 loaves of bread. I marked the number on a piece of paper. Complainant was with us I think 9 or 10 days before he commenced work. Complainant said he worked 40 days.

Judgment for complainant for $6.00 and costs $4.50, to be paid forthwith, and in default, warrant of distress to issue at the time allowed by law.

James Boyer, J.P.

Paid constable and constable paid complainant.

MAGISTRATE'S COURT — JANUARY 21ST, 1895
BEFORE JAMES BOYER, J.P.
ALEXANDER McGINNIS V GEORGE KEILTY

For the sum of $8.81, for wages due within one month now last past.
Defendant pleaded not indebted.

Alexander McGinnis sworn

I have been working for defendant for 3 or 4 years. We settled up in the full about Xmas last. I commenced work again on New Year's Day. I hired with him at $22 per month to roll logs on skids. I worked for him up to last Tuesday morning. I worked 12¼ days, amounting to $10.35. I received

$1, also 50 cents and 50 cents, making $2, leaving $8.35 due. No time mentioned as to how long I was to work.

Defendant discharged me because I wouldn't shovel snow. While working in the fall I told defendant I wouldn't shovel snow. I don't know if he said anything in reply. On Tuesday defendant brought out a shovel and said if anyone objects to shovelling snow now is the time to say. A man named Malcolm McKinnon and myself objected. Defendant told us to go to the camp and he would settle up with us. We went to the camp. Defendant came in at noon and said he had no money and had no time to give me a settlement.

Cross-examined

I was engaged by the month. No distinct bargain made in January. I went on the old terms. No particulars as to my work. I was rolling logs all fall. Defendant said on Saturday we would have to shovel snow. I objected to doing so. I told him on Tuesday morning that I wouldn't shovel snow and he knew it. I am renting a place from Keilty. I was to pay 25 cents a month. I went in the place May 15th, 1890. I have only paid 50 cents on account of the rent. It was kept from my wages by defendant. I have paid no taxes or done any statute labour for the place. I put on 2 loads for the ¼ day.

For the Defence

Defendant sworn

I am the defendant. Complainant was to work for me till spring. He started January 1st, 1895 at $22 per month. There was 1 day's board at 50 cents. I had to pay at his boarding house after he ceased work. I have to be responsible for the board. I was paying him $2 a month more than the other rollers. Nothing said about shovelling snow till Saturday night. I didn't discharge him. McKinnon is back working for me.

They left me in the woods with five teams to do the best I could. I lost one of my horses through complainant's conduct. I have sustained loss through complainant leaving to the extent of $8.00. The rent was 25 cents a month. I have stopped 50 cents out of his wages. I was to keep the 25 cents out of his wages every month but as he claimed he needed the money I didn't deduct it. He is owing me $13 on account of this rent.

The rent being part of the contract and the amount being more than the amount claimed, the complaint was dismissed. Costs to follow the event. Defendant allowed 1 day, 75 cents, and mileage $2.50.

James Boyer, J.P.

MAGISTRATE'S COURT — JANUARY 25TH, 1895
BEFORE JAMES BOYER, J.P.
JOHN DEBNEY V WILLIAM J. FYKE

For the sum of $3.50, for wages due within one month now last past.
Defendant did not appear.

R.E. Armstrong sworn
I am a constable for the District of Muskoka. Yesterday afternoon I served a summons upon the defendant, requiring him to appear in this case at two o'clock this afternoon at the town hall, Bracebridge. When I served summons defendant stated he would not appear. Defendant afterwards appeared.

John Debney sworn
I went to work for defendant on January 14th. Defendant is owing me $3.50 for wages and gave me an order on Andrew Boyd. Boyd said he did not owe defendant anything. Twenty cents is to be deducted from amount for breakfast yesterday morning. The order now produced is the one I received.

Judgment for the complainant for $3.30 with costs $2.75, with warrant of distress to issue if not paid within time limited by law.

James Boyer, J.P.

Magistrate's Court — January 25th, 1895
Before James Boyer, J.P.
Thomas Cattell v William J. Fyke

For the sum of $3.50, for wages which were due within one month now past.
Defendant admitted owing $3.30.

Judgment for complainant for $3.30 and costs $2.75, with warrant of distress to issue if not paid within the time limited by law.

James Boyer, J.P.

Magistrate's Court — April 8th, 1895
Before Messrs. Browning and Boyer, J.P.s
James Crosbie v Andrew Boyd

For the sum of $27.04, for wages which became due and payable within one month now last past.
Adjourned by consent of the parties until April 9th at 2 o'clock in the afternoon.
Adjourned further until April 10th at 10:30 in the forenoon.
Defendant pleaded not indebted.

James Crosbie sworn

I went to work for Mr. Boyd on September 14th, 1894, and worked up to March 13th, 1895. Wages were to be $20 a month and board. The bargain was made in Bracebridge. There is now owing me $27.04. I saw defendant on September 3rd, and defendant and Mr. McConnell talked to me about this matter but no engagement was made.

About 2 days after I saw defendant on the street in Bracebridge. I told him that I was willing to go for $20 a month. Defendant agreed to give me that much. Defendant was to give me my fare one way to Wahapitae. About February 9th I saw him again and he asked what rate I was figuring my wages at. I said $20. Defendant said he wouldn't pay at that rate. I told him that was the agreement. I said I wouldn't work for less. I still continued to work there. There was never anything said about $15 a month until after I left. I worked until my services were no longer required.

Cross-examined

I swear positively that nothing was said about paying less than $20 a month until February 9th.

Andrew Boyd sworn

I saw Mr. Crosbie in the street here at Bracebridge. I saw him a few days after and complainant wanted to know what I would pay him. I said, "It would depend on what you can do." I told him I would want him to do the bookkeeping and as that wouldn't take much time, I said if he could do other work to fill up the time I could afford to give him $20 a month.

Judgment given for $27.04, the amount claimed, to be paid forthwith, and warrant of distress to issue if not paid.

James Boyer, J.P.

Court $1.50
Constable $1.25
Witness $1.50
Total $4.25

Paid.

Conviction returned.

Magistrate's Court — April 20th, 1895
Before James Boyer, J.P.
Henry White v Jacob Bogart

For the sum of $4.93, for wages due to complainant within one month now last past, which defendant neglected to pay.

Defendant pleaded not indebted.

Henry White sworn

I went to work for defendant on March 18th last. I worked 22 days at $18 per month, making $15.18. I have received $10 cash. Tobacco, 25 cents. I left on Monday last. I was sick with piles and had to leave. Defendant was willing I leave. Defendant gave me a $5 bill to get changed and to take $4.95 out of it. As I could not get it changed, I handed him the $5 back. Defendant promised to send it out to Witherson with my clothes the next day. He sent out the clothes but not the money.

Jacob Bogart, defendant, sworn

I hired defendant at Utterson for $16 per month. He worked 2 weeks, and then said I had better get another man. I said I would get another man if he couldn't stand the work. He agreed to finish the month. He worked the 22 days. Last Monday he said he would have to give up work. I gave him $15. He was to give me 34 cents out of it. He couldn't get the bill changed (the $5 bill) and returned it. I charged him for 5 days' board at 40 cents per day, $2.00 and $1.60 for washing a quantity of clothes. I told him I would send the balance of the money as soon as I got the bill changed.

Cross-examined

I gave you $10 in cash. I don't remember if I asked you to come on the Saturday. I asked him the first Monday he was there if he had any clothes to be washed. I did not say anything about clothes or working when he was leaving.

Complainant allowed 22 days at $16 per month, or $13.53
Less $10 cash and 25 cents tobacco, $10.25
Balance $ 3.28

Judgment for $3.28 and $1.50 costs. Warrant of distress to issue if not paid within the period allowed by law.

James Boyer, J.P.

Paid.
Conviction returned.

MAGISTRATE'S COURT — MAY 8TH, 1895
BEFORE JAMES BOYER, J.P.
JOSEPH THOMSON V ROBERT FORD AND ANDREW GILLESPIE

Claim of $13.53, for wages which became due within one month, which now has past.
Defendants pleaded not indebted in the amount claimed.

Joseph Thomson sworn

I commenced work for defendants on September 19th last. I was to get $25 per month, a free house and firewood. I worked for them up to Saturday April 20th. They owe me $7.28 balance of wages, and $6.25 which they have charged me for firewood. I asked them for the money. They refused to pay and said that was not the agreement.

Cross-examined

I agreed to pay 50 cents a month for the house. You said you would not buy hard wood but I could have wood as long as any was round the mill. There was wood round the mill all the time. When I ran out of wood I was to have the use of their team of horses and to have time to get it in my working hours. I was sent into the bush for 4 weeks with the team. I was away from home and my family required the wood. I had to get 5 cords of wood, costing $6.25. There was a settlement up to January 1st but nothing was said about wood. I got about one cord of the hard wood before January 1st and the other afterwards. I occupied the house up to May 8th (today). Defendants deducted 5 days' pay whilst I was sick. I was hired by the month.

For the Defence

Robert Ford sworn

We agreed to give defendant $25 per month, a house for 50 cents per month, to give him firewood for his house so long as there was any round the mill, but if none, then we were not to buy him any. In December complainant wanted wood. There was none at the mill that could be got. Complainant ordered the first load. We ordered 2 loads of wood. Mrs. Thomson requested me to order one and complainant the other. Complainant has not allowed us for 22 pounds syrup, which cost 75 cents.

Judgment for complainant for $6.05 claim and $3 costs, to be paid forthwith, and in default, warrant of distress to issue and at the time allowed by law.

James Boyer, J.P.

Paid.

Conviction returned.

MAGISTRATE'S COURT — MAY 23RD, 1895
BEFORE JAMES BOYER, J.P.
CHARLES J. WOOD v THOMAS M. BAIRD

Claim for $7.20, for wages which became due within one month now last past.

Defendant pleaded not indebted.

Charles J. Wood sworn

I went to work for defendant during the present month at the rate of 60 cents per day and board. I worked 12 days. Defendant has not paid me anything on account. I have asked for the money three or four times. No one was present when the bargain made.

Cross-examined

I worked all the time. I agreed to pay 30 cents for washing.

Defendant sworn

Complainant had 14 meals at my house to my own knowledge after he quitted my employ. I charge 12½ cents per meal, or $1.75.

Judgment for complainant for $5.15 and $2.75 costs, to be paid forthwith, and in default, warrant of distress to issue at the time allowed by law.

James Boyer, J.P.

June 6th, 1895, received $5 on account
Paid in full.

Magistrate's Court — July 23rd, 1895
Before James Boyer, J.P.
Frederick J. Coley v Isaac H. Waltenbury

Claim for $2.56, for wages due within one month now past .
Plea not indebted.

Frederick J. Coley sworn
I went to work for defendant on July 15th. Nothing was said about wages. I worked 4½ days. Defendant pays his other labourers $1.25 per day, and I claim wages at that rate. I was sick on Friday morning and said I couldn't work in the afternoon. I was working by the day. Defendant never found any fault with my work. The wages came to $5.62½. I have had $3.06, leaving balance due me of $2.56½.

For the Defence

Isaac Waltenbury, defendant, sworn
Complainant came to me on the Monday. I started him to work. I took him on for charity's sake. He refused to carry the hod when I asked him. I set him mixing mortar. I got Charlie Arnott to show him how to mix mortar. I accepted the order for $3.00. I expected him to do any labouring work I had to do. I tendered complainant the $1.50 which I thought was all he was worth.

Judgment in complainant's favour for $1.50, with costs.

James Boyer, J.P.

Paid.
Fifty cents costs paid.

MAGISTRATE'S COURT — AUGUST 22ND, 1895
BEFORE JAMES BOYER, J.P.
WILLIAM JAMES DUNN V ISAAC WALTENBURY

Information laid August 20th, 1895.
For the sum of $18.75, for wages which became due within one month last past, and which defendant neglected to pay.
Defendant pleaded not indebted in amount claimed.

William James Dunn sworn

I commenced work for defendant on May 8th at $2.50 per day. I left working for him on July 27th, at which time he was owing me $18.75, and still owes me that amount. I was working at stone work and brick laying. $1 for trowel and 10 cents for tobacco to be deducted.

Cross-examined

The book I now produce is the original entries.

Judgment for plaintiff for $17.65 and costs $2.85, to be paid forthwith, and in default, warrant of distress to issue at the time allowed by law.

James Boyer, J.P.

On September 3 a warrant of distress was issued to Constable Armstrong for $20.50. With the cost of the warrant being twenty-five cents, $20.75 was the full amount the office was to seize from the defaulting defendant. A week later, Constable Armstrong turned over to Justice of the Peace Boyer $20.75, procured through a garnishee summons issued September 10 in a Divisional Court application. That same day, the JP paid the $17.65, for plaintiff Dunn, to the clerk of the Divisional Court, and obtained a receipt. This process illustrates how rulings by a justice of the peace were upheld and enforced by a higher court.

Magistrate's Court — October 4th, 1895
Before James Boyer, J.P.
Noah Bennett v Isaac H. Waltenbury

Claim for $11.75, for wages due within one month from defendant to complainant.

Defendant pleaded not indebted in amount claimed.

Noah Bennett sworn

I went to work for defendant on August 19th in the afternoon. I worked for 3 weeks and three days at $1.25 per day. I have received $7 on account, leaving $11.75 due to me.

On cross-examination complainant admitted that he had worked only 13 days, 1 hour, leaving balance due him $9.37½.

Judgment given for $9.37½ and costs $2.75, to be paid forthwith, and in default, warrant of distress to issue at the time allowed by law.

James Boyer, J.P.

Paid in full.

Paid complainant.

Magistrate's Court — October 16th, 1895
Before James Boyer, J.P.
George Barnsdale v Andrew Boyd

Claim for $18.02, for wages which became due within one month now last past.

Defendant admitted the claim and judgment given for $18.02 and costs $1.75, to be paid forthwith. Warrant of distress to issue in 8 days in default.

James Boyer, J.P.

Paid.

Paid complainant $1.00, and $17 to be paid in order given by complainant to defendant. ~ *J. Boyer.*

Magistrate's Court — January 18th, 1896
Before James Boyer, J.P.
Duncan McLean v John L. Ruttan

Claim for $6.68, for wages which became due and payable within one month now last past, and which defendant neglected to pay.
Defendant pleaded not indebted.

Duncan McLean sworn
Defendant admitted owing $6.68 at the time plaintiff left his employ.

Cross-examined
I left on January 4th. I asked for an order on J.B. Johnston's store for goods. I asked for a little more than was due me as I did not intend coming out for a month or two. Before I left there he said he would give me my time and I needn't come back. I got an order from defendant on Mr. Johnston for $6.68. I presented the order and Johnston refused to pay it or give me goods on it.

John L. Ruttan sworn
I am the defendant in this case. Complainant asked me for the order and I gave it to him, for $6.68. I saw Johnston after giving him the order. Johnston told me the order would be all right. I thought complainant had

the money until I was served with the summons. I had paid him by orders on Johnston before. Complainant knew Bracebridge was my post office and knew I got my mail nearly every day.

Judgment for plaintiff for $6.68 without costs. Costs $3.55 to be paid by complainant.

James Boyer, J.P.

Paid.
Paid constable $2.05

The money owed was paid by Ruttan to McLean, as ordered. Evidently the JP felt the complainant could have obtained his unpaid wages directly from employer, Ruttan, rather than by using the court's time and resources. So, JP Boyer ordered McLean to pay the court costs, an amount more than half the wages he got by suing. Boyer in this instance seemed to send a message to the community that his court should not be used unnecessarily as a collection agency and arbitration centre.

MAGISTRATE'S COURT — FEBRUARY 8TH, 1896
BEFORE JAMES BOYER, J.P.
JOSEPH H. BOYER V ANDREW BOYD

For wages which became due and payable within one month now last past, and which the said Andrew Boyd has neglected to pay.
Defendant admitted the claim. Judgment for $7.00 for wages and $2.75 costs.

James Boyer, J.P.

Paid.
Paid constable $1.25

Joseph Henry Boyer, a nephew of James Boyer who heard this case, was the son of James's brother-in-law Harry Boyer and his wife, Florence. Andrew Boyd, whose family came to Muskoka in 1861 to first settle in Morrison Township, was one of Muskoka's prominent lumbermen. Paying wages was often an issue for the entrepreneurial Andrew Boyd, as several more cases attest, but he lived in grand style, and when he and his wife moved to Bracebridge, he built a large and stately riverside residence below town, on the Monck Township side of the Muskoka River, a place later called "Brofoco" when owned by Harold Brobst of the Brobst Forestry Company.

MAGISTRATE'S COURT — FEBRUARY 22ND, 1896
BEFORE JAMES BOYER, J.P. AND SINGLETON BROWN, J.P.
ALEXANDER MOOREHEAD v ANDREW BOYD

For $38.92, for wages which became due within one month now last past, and which the said Andrew Boyd has neglected to pay.
Defendant pleaded not guilty.

Alexander Moorehead sworn
I have been working for Andrew Boyd since November 9th, 1895. I was employed as cook at $1 a day. I worked for ten days at that. After November 19th I went to work as cook on the boat at the same salary for 12 days. After December 2nd I did chores around the camp as I was not able to work. On December 23rd I was taking care of the camp for eight days. I had to feed and look after the horses, and did the cooking. On January 1st, 1896 I started cooking again and did this work up to the 11th of that month. After that, up to January 31st, I took care of the camp again. From then up to February 15th I did the chores of the camp. I asked defendant for a settlement of a dollar a day. That was when I came off the boat. I asked for a settlement again on February 15th.

Cross-examined by Mr. Mahaffy
I have a claim for $34.02 due from defendant. I expected to get paid for that work. From December 2nd to December 23rd I worked for my board. I admit the offset of $27.65, except the overcharge of $1 on a pair of pants. I made an offer to settle for the board when I went to work in the mill but I haven't done so as the mill has not started running yet. Board would be worth $10 or $12 a month. I kept record of the board and it was between three and four weeks.

For the Defence

Andrew Boyd sworn
I am the defendant in this case and had dealings with Moorehead. I allowed complainant a dollar a day for ten days after he came off the *Lake Joseph*. Nothing was said as to his charges for work on the boat.

Cross-examined by Mr. Palmer
I told complainant to stay at the camp till his leg was better.

William Findlay sworn
I was captain of the *Lake Joseph* last November at the time complainant was there. He did part of the cooking while he was there. He did most of the cooking.

George Lloyd sworn
I was the clerk in Mr. Boyd's camp at the time Mr. Moorehead was there. The price of the pants in question was $4.

William McConnell sworn
I was the foreman in Mr. Boyd's camp when Moorehead was there. I allowed complainant $15 per month.

Statement of claim allowed
10 days cooking $10.00
On boat cooking $9.24
8 days at 77 cents per day cooking $6.16
Cooking $11.00
Chores in camp 12½ days at 58 cents $ 7.25
Total $43.65
Offset admitted $27.65
Board $6.00

Judgment for $6 and $2.75 costs, to be paid forthwith, and in default, warrant of distress to issue at proper time.

James Boyer, J.P.

MAGISTRATE'S COURT — MARCH 17TH, 1896
BEFORE JAMES BOYER AND PETER M. SHANNON, J.P.s
CHRISTY RUTTAN v JOHN L. RUTTAN

For the sum of $14.50, for wages due within one month now last past.
Defendant pleaded not indebted.

Christy Ruttan sworn
Defendant admitted the correctness of the complainant's claim but claims a set-off.

Cross-examined by Mr. Mahaffy
Set-off being for a claim for a horse sold two or three years ago. Court refused to allow it to be put in.

Judgment for the plaintiff for $14.50 and costs $2.75 to be paid forthwith, and in default, warrant of distress to issue at the proper time.

James Boyer, J.P.

Paid.

Paid constable on cost of distress $3.15.

April 7th, 1896. Served with garnishee summons in above case.

April 8th, 1896. Amount of judgment paid into court.

Magistrate's Court — April 11th, 1896
Before James Boyer, J.P.
John Bailey the Younger v Andrew Nichol

For the sum of $30, for wages which became due within one month now last past.

Defendant pleaded not indebted.

John Bailey the Younger sworn

I went to work for defendant on October 28th, 1895 at $13 a month. I worked for him four months and six and a half days. I lost a day and a half time. He has paid me $25 on account. I left him on March 10th. The wages were to be paid monthly and I left because he didn't keep the agreement. I asked him for the money.

Cross-examined by Mr. Palmer

I asked defendant for the money when I left him. Mrs. Nichol was present when I left to see the doctor. Defendant told me he would give me $13 a month. I didn't agree to cut a cord and a half a day. I was coming down on February 15th with defendant, and was left in charge of a sleigh with a buffalo robe, a chain, and a horse blanket. I returned all the articles mentioned and didn't lose anything. On October 31st I started to go to the camp.

Andrew Nichol, defendant, sworn

No one was present but complainant and myself. He wanted $13.50 a month but he wasn't ready to come for a month and a half. It was about September when I spoke to him about the work. I said I thought that was rather big wages but would see him when he came to work. There was nothing said about wages when he came to work. I never made any bargain as to the rate of wages. I didn't agree to give him $13 and had no further conversation with him re wages.

I consider he was worth about $10 a month. I paid Mr. Fraser of Port Cockburn a hotel bill of 75 cents for complainant. On November 18th in the camp I paid him $1.25. On February 19th I gave him an order on Judge Mahaffy for $25. I found that a horse blanket, buffalo robe and a chain were missing when I examined the sleigh complainant brought in. Complainant left an axe worth $1 on the dump and couldn't find it when he went to look for it next morning. There was only 28 cords of wood cut.

Charles Manley sworn

I heard defendant ask complainant to cut a cord and a half a day. Complainant said he thought he could do it.

David Scott sworn

Defendant came into the camp and told Bailey he wanted a cord and a half of wood out a day. Complainant said he thought he could do it.

Euphemia Jane Nichol sworn

I am the wife of defendant. I keep my husband's books. Complainant worked 28 days cutting wood.

Complainant recalled

The robes and chain were on the sleigh when I stopped. I was sent on to Mr. Bunn's because the farmer didn't like to turn his cattle out to make room for me. I had to drive all night because I could get no shelter at Bunn's. The team got stuck near Smith's and I left it and went to Smith's all night.

Complainant entitled to 108½ days at 50 cents. Deductions, $27 cash. Robes, $8. Order Mahaffy, $25. Wood not cut, $7.

Judgment for plaintiff for $12.25 and costs $2.85, to be paid forthwith.

April 25th, 1896, paid complainant the above amount, $12.25

James Boyer, J.P.

Paid.

Magistrate's Court — June 20th, 1896
Before James Boyer, J.P.
William Griffith v Thomas Shannon

For the sum of $8.75 in wages.

The case was settled between the parties.

James Boyer, J.P.

Paid.

Costs of court $0.50.

Constable $0.25.

Magistrate's Court — August 5th, 1896
Before James Boyer, J.P.
John McLean v Albert B. Bettes

Claim for $18.01, for wages which became due within one month now last past.

Defendant pleaded not indebted.

John McLean sworn

I went to work for defendant on March 13th at $5 per week. I worked

1¾ days on July 28–29. The 29th was the full day. I was working firing the engine. May 30th I worked overtime ¼ day fixing the engine after 6 p.m. July 1st and 3rd, I worked ½ day each day overtime. No particular engagement as to time. I was to get $5 per week. I worked for defendant every day. He has charged me for when engine not working. The engine was only stopped 3¼ days. I only got 2 bags of potatoes at 40 cents each. I also got tallow and oil necessary for the engine, 25 cents.

Cross-examined

I didn't lead defendant to suppose I was a certified engineer. I told him I fired boilers. I told him I had no papers. I left July 30th without giving any notice.

James Boyer, J.P.

Judgment for plaintiff for $9.90, and costs $3.25, to be paid half by each party.
Paid.
Paid complainant $8.25
Paid constable $1.75

Magistrate's Court — August 14th, 1896
Before James Boyer, J.P.
Samuel Christiansen v Augustine Russell and Vincent Russell

For the sum of $14.25, for wages which had become due and payable within one month now past, and which sum they have neglected to pay. Defendant admitted the claim and each party paid half costs, $1.98.

James Boyer, J.P.

Paid complainant.

Magistrate's Court — August 19th, 1896

Before James Boyer, J.P.
William Charles Liddard v Isaac H. Waltenbury

Claim for $12.17, for wages which became due within one month.
Defendant pleaded not indebted.

William Charles Liddard sworn
I went to work for defendant on June 15th at $1.25 per day, engaged by the day. Defendant owes me $12.17. I left on August 1st.

Cross-examined
I didn't work continuously as sometimes you have not had work for me all the time.

Judgment for plaintiff for $12.17 and $3.25 costs, to be paid forthwith, and in default, warrant of distress to issue at the time allowed by law.

James Boyer, J.P.

Paid complainant $12.17
Paid constable $1.75

Magistrate's Court — August 28th, 1896
Before James Boyer, J.P.
James Gazley v John Beaumont

Claim for $7, for wages which became due within one month last past.

Alfred Stunden sworn

I am a constable for the District of Muskoka. On August 26th I personally served defendant with a summons requiring him to appear at the town hall in Bracebridge at 2 o'clock p.m. to answer a claim by complainant of $7 for wages.

Defendant by his son admitted owing complainant $6.62, which complainant agreed to take.

Judgment for complainant for $6.62 and costs $3.90, to be paid forthwith, and in default, warrant of distress to issue at proper time.

James Boyer, J.P.

Constable $2.40
Paid.

MAGISTRATE'S COURT — AUGUST 29TH, 1896
BEFORE JAMES BOYER, J.P.
ARTHUR J. POST V ISAAC H. WALTENBURY

Claim for $39.30, for wages which became due within one month now last past.

Adjourned at request of defendant to September 2nd at 2 p.m. Jesse Hunt to be allowed witness fees. Defendant pleaded not indebted. Complainant reduced claim to $38.50.

Arthur J. Post sworn

I am the complainant. I worked for defendant. I started to work on March 27th last. Defendant told me I was to get $10 per month and board when I was working at the trade. When doing labourer's work I was to get labourer's pay. I worked one full month March 27th to April 27th at labour, $19.50. Worked right along to August 13th, 3 months 15 days at 75 cents and board, $35. I was sick one day but worked overtime to make it up. He was to learn me the trade.

I have recently been working at Whitten's new building with a number of others for defendant. Defendant put me to work on a chimney, between his son and his uncle. He told me to do some work which I didn't know how to do. He didn't show me how to do it. I did the work the best way I could. I was working on a scaffold 20 feet high and 40 inches wide. Defendant came and asked who did that work and told me to take it down again. I said, "What can you expect when you put me between 2 and 3, and they are rushing me?" He cursed and swore at me, told me to take it down and he would charge me the time it took.

He went off swearing, and said he would give me a slap in the mouth. I answered him back, and he said he would kick my arse off the scaffold and came towards me and attempted to strike me in the face. Palmer, a workman, caught hold of me. He said no fighting here. George Waltenbury, defendant's son, attempted to strike me. I got away from Palmer and took hold of George. He swore at me and said, "Hold on." I hung on to the wall. Robert Arnold the labourer came up and interfered to prevent any accident.

I packed up my tools and came home. I asked defendant to pay me, and he said he wouldn't give me a cent till I had worked the balance of this season and all next season. There were 5 people on the scaffold at the time.

Cross-examined by Mr. Ashworth
I was to get $10 per month and board. That was all the arrangement between us this year. I have received $10 on account of my claim

Jesse Hunt sworn
I am a bricklayer. I was working for defendant on August 13th. Complainant was working there. I worked 6 or 7 days on that job. Chimney building is more difficult than plain work. An apprentice in his 2nd year would not be able to build a chimney without showing. Complainant generally done his work well. I could have pulled down the part of the chimney that was badly built and re-built it in an hour at an expense of $1.00.

Defendant looked at chimney, cursed some and told him to take it down. Both used bad language. Waltenbury commenced it. Defendant put up his hands in a fighting attitude. I didn't see a trowel in complainant's hands. Defendant's son went and they clenched. Palmer said throw him down. Defendant said he would kick complainant's arse off the scaffold.

Cross-examined
Defendant tried to strike the complainant first.

Thomas Baird Jr. sworn
I was working for defendant on August 13th, carrying the loads. When I took a load of brick up, defendant was finding fault with a chimney being built. Complainant said it could have been done right if the men had not been rushing it. Defendant told complainant to take it down again, and said he would kick him off the scaffold. He started towards him. Palmer said shove him down.

Judgment for plaintiff for $27.50 and costs $4.95, to be paid in 8 days or warrant of distress to issue.

James Boyer, J.P.

Court $2.20
Constable $2.00
Witness $0.75
Total $4.95
3 months, $10.85 per month.
September 30th, recvd $10.85 on account.
November 2nd, recvd $10.00 on account.
Oct 1, paid complainant $5.90.

March 1897 — James Boyer issued a warrant of distress for the balance of $11.60 to Constable Stunden, who made the amount and paid it over to complainant, Arthur Post.

Magistrate's Court — September 3rd, 1896
Before James Boyer, J.P.
John McFadden v John Beaumont

Claim for $13.60, for wages which became due and payable within one month now last past, and which sum defendant neglected to pay.
Defendant did not appear.

Thomas Dodd sworn
I am a constable for the town of Bracebridge. On September 1st in the forenoon I served defendant personally with a summons in this case requiring him to appear this day at 2 p.m. at the town hall, Bracebridge.

John McFadden sworn
I went to work for defendant in June, at $20 per month and board. I worked 42 days, making $32.31. I have received $18.71, leaving a balance due to me of $13.60, which I have demanded but which defendant has neglected to pay. I received the paper produced, containing the account as above set forth, from defendant.

Judgment for complainant for $13.60 and costs $3.90, to be paid forthwith, and in default, warrant of distress to issue at the proper time.

James Boyer, J.P.

Paid in full April 8th, 1897.
Paid constable in full.

Magistrate's Court — November 7, 1896
Before James Boyer, J.P.
John Yeoman v John Baird

Claim for $8, for wages due and payable within one month last past.
Defendant pleaded not indebted.

John Yeoman sworn
I went to work for the defendant on October 20th at $2 per day and board. I worked 12 days and 8 hours, making $25.60. I have received $16.25 in cash and order, leaving a balance of $9.35 now due.

John Baird sworn
I admit $8 due. One order of $2 complainant has allowed me. There was another order of $2 but complainant didn't give me any order in writing. Hutchinson Brothers[3] sent me a bill of $2 in addition. Complainant never gave me any authority in writing to pay any but the first order of $2.

Judgment for complainant for $8 and $3.25 costs, to be paid forthwith, and in default, warrant of distress to issue at the time allowed by law.

James Boyer, J.P.

    Paid in full.
    Paid constable.

In early November 1896, just two weeks before John Yeoman sued his employer for unpaid wages, his wife, Mary Jane Yeoman, had brought him up before Magistrate James Boyer on a charge of assault and battery. He had been away three and a half weeks, working on the lakes. People in Bracebridge who owed

---

[3] A Bracebridge grocery store.

453

him money had promised to pay her while he was away. When he returned home, weary and hungry, John Yeoman found little to eat in the house. When he berated his wife, Mary Jane complained in turn that she'd not received any money lately, and thirteen dollars for rent was owing. Their fight then erupted. That case is reported in Chapter 6: Women's Fears and Women's Fates.

Magistrate's Court — December 1st, 1896
Before James Boyer, J.P.
Albert Rowley v Albert B. Bettes

For the sum of $10.85, for wages which became due and payable within one month now last past, and which defendant refused to pay.
Defendant pleaded not indebted, having tendered the money prior to this action.

Albert Rowley sworn
I've worked for defendant off and on over the past 3½ years. Recently I worked to about the last day of October. I worked for him again from November 13th to 27th. I worked for $1 per day. I worked 118½ hours, amounting to $11.85. I received $1 in cash, leaving a balance due of $10.85. I have asked for the money. Defendant disputed the account.

Cross-examined
The account is correct. Appleby was foreman. I don't remember him asking me to report to him each day so as to keep the time. I worked on November 19th. I spoke to Appleby that day. Don't know what I said. He set me at work that day. When I went to settle I was not offered any money or shown any. Wallis said there was $8.80 due me. He didn't offer me any money at all. I gave an order on defendant to John Gibbs for $2.50. The order was dated November 24th.

William H. Doidge sworn

I was working for the defendant at the tannery the same time as Rowley. I worked every day from November 16th up to 25th. Rowley worked every day that I worked. I generally went to work with him. I don't know if he worked all that day but he was there working.

For the Defence

Harry Wallis sworn

I am bookkeeper for defendant. Complainant came in the morning last Saturday and asked for his money. Defendant was present. He came again in the afternoon. I made up his time. I said it is $8.90. I had the money in my hand. Complainant said, "That's not right. It's a day short." I offered him the money. I said, "Here's your money. If there is anything wrong, go to Mr. Appleby and if he says it is a day short I'll give it to you tonight." He said he wasn't going down there again. I showed him the exact amount of money and offered it to him.

Henry Appleby sworn

I am foreman for defendant. On November 14th when the men were getting their pay I said to complainant I wanted him to report to me every day so that I could keep his time right. He agreed to do so. He didn't report on the 19th and I have not his name as being at work on that day. The entries were made each day. He worked 98½ hours altogether.

Defendant sworn

I admit owing defendant $9.85, subject to the $2.50 order. Defendant disputed the claim. I told him if he went to the tannery and it wasn't right I would make it right.

Judgment for the plaintiff for $7.35 (plus defendant to pay plaintiff's $2.50 order on John Gibbs), without costs.

James Boyer, J.P.

Amount paid.
Paid constable.

Magistrate's Court — March 3rd, 1897
Before James Boyer, J.P.
John O'Hare v Albert B. Bettes

Claim for $19.37, for wages which became due within one month last past.

Alfred Stunden sworn
I personally served defendant with a summons in this case, requiring him to appear on March 3rd, 1897 at the town hall to answer the above. I have not seen him here.

John O'Hare sworn
I have been working for defendant. I left working for him 2 weeks last Friday. He is owing me $19.37 for wages. Defendant's bookkeeper agreed that was the amount due me. I asked him to give me an account of my time. He said Mr. Bettes wouldn't allow him to do so. The bookkeeper told me that was the amount owing to me.

Judgment for complainant for $19.37 and costs $3.35, to be paid forthwith, and in default, warrant of distress to issue at the time allowed by law.

James Boyer, J.P.

Not all wages owed were easily collected, even with a court order, as several cases reveal. Some were never collected at all. In the above case, for the $19.37 Bettes was ordered to pay O'Hare, James Boyer made these two subsequent notations in his bench book:

March 19th, 1897 — Warrant of distress issued to Constable Stunden.

November 6th, 1897 — Received costs from sheriff.

MAGISTRATE'S COURT — MARCH 26TH, 1897
BEFORE JAMES BOYER, J.P.
WILLIAM ROUSHORN v JOHN L. RUTTAN

Claim for $40, for wages which became due within one month now last past, and which sum defendant has neglected to pay.

Defendant admitted the indebtedness.

Judgment for complainant for $40 and $4.29 costs, to be paid forthwith, and in default, warrant of distress to issue at the time allowed by law.

James Boyer, J.P.

Paid constable $6.72

Warrant of Distress issued.

Received $30 on account May 6, 1897 paid in full.

Costs –
Constable $2.79
Court $1.50
Warrant $0.50

Further Costs –
Warrant of Distress $1.50

(to constable) $0.91
$0.52
$1.00
Total $3.93

Magistrate's Court — May 7th, 1897
Before James Boyer, J.P.
Alexander McKay v J.J. Beaumont

Claim for $10.10, for wages which became due within one month now last past.

Defendant admitted claim and paid the sum of $10.10. The question of costs was adjourned till May 8th at 2 p.m.

May 8th. Judgment for plaintiff for $10.10 and costs $3.90, to be paid forthwith, and in default, warrant of distress to issue at the time allowed by law.

James Boyer, J.P.

> May 8th paid complainant in full.
> Also constable.
> Paid in full.

Magistrate's Court — May 17th, 1895
Before James Boyer, J.P. and Alfred Hunt, J.P.
Henry Slater v Samuel H. Armstrong

Claim for $11.50, for wages which became due within one month now last past.

Defendant pleaded not indebted.

Henry Slater sworn

I began to work for Mr. Armstrong on April 5th. No rate of wages mentioned. I have charged $1.75 which is a reasonable charge and less than I generally work for. My bill came to $20.12. I have received $7 in cash and $1.53 in meat, leaving a balance of $11.59. I demanded the amount from Mr. Armstrong and he refused to pay.

Cross-examined by Mr. Palmer

I worked 115 hours. I did not keep the bricklayers from working. I could not have done it in less time. No one could have done it in less time. I was in Mr. Armstrong's store on Wednesday. He objected to the amount and asked me to settle for $10 on condition that I put in a pane of glass. I offered to settle for $10 and take the $1.50 off.

Samuel Armstrong, defendant, sworn

Mr. Slater came and asked me for the work. I told him to do the work. He said he would do it cheaper. He asked me what I would give him. I told him $10 and when I offered it to him he refused to take it.

Herbert J. Denniss

I am a carpenter by trade. I have been over to Mr. Armstrong's house. I inspected the carpenter's work. I think the work could have been done for $15.25. Mr. Armstrong did not show me anything that was done inside nor a platform of a shed that was fixed. $1.75 is a reasonable amount to charge.

George Dillway sworn

I am working for defendant. On Wednesday at noon I heard a conversation between the two parties. Complainant asked defendant for some money. Defendant said he would settle for $10 if complainant would put some glass in a door. Complainant agreed to do so. I understood the $10 to be for the whole amount.

Judgment for plaintiff for $10 and costs $2.75, to be paid forthwith, and in default, warrant of distress to be issued at the time allowed by law.

Alfred Hunt, J.P.
James Boyer, J.P.

Paid.
Paid complainant $10 and paid constable.
Returned.

Magistrate's Court — July 14th, 1897
Before James Boyer, J.P.
Robert Arnold v Isaac Waltenbury

Claim for $8.69, for wages which became due within one month prior to July 10th.
Defendant pleaded not indebted.

Robert Arnold sworn
I went to work for the defendant May 3rd and worked for him up to and including June 14th at $1.25. There is now a balance due me of $8.69. Defendant told me to go to work at Mr. Palmer's on May 31st. On June 1st he took me away from Palmer's to work at Mr. Ford's. I worked there the first half day in June and went back to Palmer's June 2nd and worked a half day. Both Palmer and defendant told me what I had to do. Defendant was working there with me, except the first day. Mr. Palmer paid me for what I did there. Defendant told me to go to work at Ford's.

Cross-examined
I had worked for Palmer before. It was not contract work. Defendant saw Palmer pay me.

George Tyrrell sworn

I went to work for Palmer in May. I heard Palmer tell Waltenbury that he had paid complainant $1.30 per day. Defendant said, "I wouldn't if he was working for me. I would only give him $1.25." Complainant was not present at the time.

Adjourned to July16th at 7:30 p.m.
Resumed.

Peter Palmer sworn

I asked defendant whenever he could let complainant come to do so, to run off the mortar. Defendant said he would. He came and did the work. I was working at Ford's. I had told Arnold I wanted him to attend on the job for me. He did so and I paid him $1.25 per day. He said defendant agreed to give him more. On the Monday he agreed to take $1.25 per day. Defendant was working for me by the job. I did not tell complainant to go to work at Ford's. I said to defendant that whenever he could spare complainant, to let him come and run off the mortar at my place.

George Waltenbury sworn

I heard my father say Arnold was going to work for Palmer. Both my father and myself worked for Palmer. Arnold said, "Alright." Palmer said he wanted Arnold to run off the mortar and we let him go for half a day.

Defendant sworn

I told complainant it was a day's work at Palmer's. I took complainant away to work at Ford's.

Judgment for plaintiff for $8.69 and $3.25 costs, to be paid forthwith, and in default, warrant of distress at the time allowed by law.

James Boyer, J.P.

Paid.

Paid constable $1.75.

Paid complainant $8.69 July 31st, 1897.

MAGISTRATE'S COURT — NOVEMBER 13TH, 1897
BEFORE JAMES BOYER, J.P.
NEIL MCGILLVRAY V THOMAS HOLLIDAY AND WILLIAM HOLLIDAY

For the sum of $26.60, for wages which became due and payable within one month now last past.

Defendant Thomas Holliday appeared and admitted indebtedness.

Judgment for the plaintiff for $26.60 and costs $3.70, to be paid forthwith, and in default, warrant of distress to issue at the time allowed by law.

James Boyer, J.P.

Paid Stunden amount of claim and constable costs.

Complainant gave defendants 2 weeks additional time ~ *J.B.*

December 14th, 1897 — Issued warrant of distress to Constable Stunden.

Paid in full.

Document attached to the bench book with this case:

Bracebridge, November 20, 1897

I, Neil McGillvray, of the Town of Bracebridge in the District of Muskoka, assign any claim against William Holliday and Thomas Holliday of the Township of Macaulay in the said District of Muskoka for wages for the sum of twenty-six dollars and sixty cents or the full amount of claim to Alfred Stunden of the same Town of Bracebridge.

"X" Neil McGillvray — his mark Witness: C. Mawdsley

MAGISTRATE'S COURT — NOVEMBER 27TH, 1897
BEFORE JAMES BOYER, J.P.
ALBERT ROWLEY V THOMAS HOLLIDAY AND WILLIAM HOLLIDAY

For the sum of $19.20, for wages which became due and payable within one month now last past, and which defendants neglected to pay.
Defendant Thomas Holliday appeared and admitted the claim.

Judgement for complainant for $19.20 and $4.48 costs, to be paid forthwith, and in default, warrant of distress to issue at the time allowed by law.

James Boyer, J.P.

Constable $2.78, paid constable
Court $1.70
Total $4.48
Dec. 14th, 1897, issued warrant of distress to Constable Stunden.
Dec. 18th, 1897, paid complainant in full. ~ *J.B.*
Paid in full.

MAGISTRATE'S COURT — DECEMBER 16TH, 1897
BEFORE JAMES BOYER, J.P.
SAMUEL BAKER V THOMAS HOLLIDAY AND WILLIAM HOLLIDAY

Information laid December 11th, 1897.
For the sum of $17.97, for wages which became due and payable within one month then last past, and which defendants neglected to pay.
Defendant Thomas Holliday appeared and admitted indebtedness to the amount of $17.72.

Judgment for complainant for $17.72 and costs $2.90, to be paid forthwith, and in default, warrant of distress to issue at proper time.

James Boyer, J.P.

Court $1.70
Constable $1.20 — (½) paid
Total $2.90
Paid in full.
Dec. 18th, 1897, paid complainant in full.

Magistrate's Court — December 16th, 1897
Before James Boyer, J.P.
Joseph Hey v Thomas Holliday and William Holliday

Information laid December 11th, 1897.

For the sum of $14.91, for wages which became due within one month then last past, and which defendants neglected to pay.

Defendant Thomas Holliday appeared and admitted $7.27 as the balance due after deducting offset.

Judgment for complainant for $7.27 and costs $2.90, to be paid forthwith, and in default, warrant of distress to issue at the time allowed by law.

James Boyer, J.P.

Court $1.70
Constable $1.20 — (½) paid
Total $2.90
Paid in full.
Dec. 18th, 1897, paid complainant in full. ~ *J.B.*

Magistrate's Court — January 10th, 1898
Before James Boyer, J.P.
Martha Devitt v Joseph Morton

For that defendant is indebted to complainant in the sum of $4.50, for wages which became due and payable within one month now last past, and which sum the defendant neglected to pay.
Defendant pleaded not indebted.

Martha Devitt sworn
I worked for defendant one month and three weeks. I was to get $5 per month, till Mrs. Morton was sick, then I was to get $5 per week, nurse's pay. I was there one week at $5. I was paid $5 the first month and $3 afterwards, leaving a balance due me of $4.50. I told Mrs. Morton I would stay till the week before Christmas. I told her the Monday before I left I was going away. She said she would have to get another girl, and if I didn't like the place I need not stay.

Cross-examined by defendant
I was to get $5 for the time I acted as nurse. You were not in the house when your wife made the bargain with me.

Judgment for complainant for $4.50 claim and $3.25 costs, to be paid forthwith, and in default, warrant of distress to issue at the time allowed by law.

James Boyer, J.P.

January 27th, 1898, warrant of distress issued to Constable Armstrong.

Magistrate's Court — February 23rd, 1898
Before James Boyer, J.P.
William Medley v Thomas Holliday and William Holliday

Claim for $30.21, for wages which became due within one month and which sum defendants neglected to pay.
Defendant claimed a set-off of $2.50 for board, and admitted indebtedness to the amount of $27.71, for which judgment was given with $3.40 costs.

James Boyer, J.P.

Magistrate's Court — February 23rd, 1898
Before James Boyer, J.P.
Frank Malone v Thomas Holliday and William Holliday

Claim for $25, for wages which became due within one month now last past, and which defendants neglected to pay.
Defendants admitted claim of $25, for which judgment was given with $3.40 costs.

James Boyer, J.P.

In the last two cases, notations in James Boyer's bench book show the total amount to be recovered from the Hollidays, for both unpaid wages and court costs, came to $59.51. Evidently, it was not paid, as subsequent entries show payments of 50 cents for issuing a warrant of distress, and payment of $7.04 to a constable for "execution of same and mileage." This brought to $67.05 the total recoverable from the Hollidays. The constable got $50.00, by distress leaving $17.05 as the "balance not paid," with no record it ever was.

On March 23, William Medley was paid out $18.00, and Frank Malone $17.66. In both cases, it was less than what they had been awarded. By October 1 that year, Frank Malone was back in Magistrate's Court, this time as a defendant on a charge of creating a disturbance on one of the public streets of Bracebridge by fighting. Justice of the Peace James Boyer, upon receiving a plea of guilty, fined Malone and his co-fighter Robert Arnold $1.00 each plus $4.80 costs. Malone absconded. By December 17 a constable had apprehended him, and the $5.80 was paid.

Magistrate's Court — March 5th, 1898
Before James Boyer, J.P.
Charles Zehnder v Thomas Woods and James Brown

For that defendants are justly and truly indebted to informant in the sum of $31.98 for wages which became due and payable within one month then last past, and which defendants have refused to pay.
Defendants pleaded not indebted.

Charles Zehnder sworn
I know defendant Brown. I made an agreement to work for him at $18 a month, and a raise if wages went up. This was a little more than five months ago. I went to work for him in the bush for five months all but one day. I finished work a week ago today. The defendants still owe me the sum of $31.38. They paid me $58.02 in goods. As far as I know defendant Woods is a partner of defendant Brown.

Defendant Brown sworn
I never hired complainant for $18 per month. I had an interview with him at the Queen's Hotel. I asked him if he was going to the camp, and he asked me what wages I was paying and I said $14 and $18 for good men. That was all was said. I am in partnership with defendant Woods.

Thomas Woods sworn

We have not paid any men working the bush more than $14 per month except some teamsters. I saw him up at the camp and he never asked for more.

Complainant recalled

I told defendant that I would not work for $16 per month. I was the handyman in the bush and did whatever I was called upon to do.

Adjourned till next Saturday at 2 p.m. for judgment.

March 12th, 1898

Judgment for complainant for $31.38 and costs $3.70, to be paid within the time limited by law and in default, warrant of distress to issue.

James Boyer, J.P.

Defendants appealed.

No indication is made why sixty cents were deducted from the amount claimed, unless James made an error in recording the amount. No record has been found as to the results of this appeal.

Magistrate's Court — March 5th, 1898
Before James Boyer, J.P.
Harry Law v Thomas Holliday and William Holliday

For that defendants are justly and truly indebted to the informant in the sum of $37.43 for wages which became due and payable within one month then last past, and which defendants neglected to pay.

Alfred Stunden sworn

On Thursday March 3rd I personally served William Holliday with a summons to appear in the this case on Saturday March 5th at 2 o'clock p.m., and at the same time handed him a similar summons for Thomas Holliday. Defendant Thomas Holliday afterwards appeared.

Defendant admitted the amount claimed to be correct, namely $37.43 with $3.60 costs, and judgment given in favour of complainant for that amount payable in the time fixed by law and in default, warrant of distress to issue.

James Boyer, J.P.

Constable $2.00
Court $1.60
Total $3.60

MAGISTRATE'S COURT — JULY 21ST, 1898
BEFORE JAMES BOYER, J.P.
JOSEPH IRWIN V AARON WEIR

For that defendant, on July 18th, at the township of Ryde, was justly and truly indebted to complainant in the sum of $8.30 for wages which became due and payable within one month then last past, and which defendant has refused to pay.

Defendant pleaded not indebted.

Joseph Irwin sworn

I am the complainant. Defendant owes me for 8½ days work at $1 per day. I got a pair of socks from defendant on account, leaving $8.30 due to me. I went to work on July 6th at noon and worked up to and including July 16th. I did not work on the 12th. I worked by the day. I have been paid $1 per day before this by defendant for the haying season.

Cross-examined by Mr. Ashworth
I got the pair of socks on July 11th. He has not paid me any money.

Judgment for complainant for $8.30 and costs $4.84, in default of payment to be levied by distress at the time fixed by law.

James Boyer, J.P.

Court $1.50
Constable $3.34 Paid
Total $4.84
Paid.
Paid complainant balance of claim, $2.75, August 2nd, 1898.

Magistrate's Court — July 21st, 1898
Before James Boyer, J.P. and S. Brown, J.P.
Joseph Irwin v Aaron Weir

For that defendant, on July 18th, at Ryde, did unlawfully point a gun at and threaten to shoot the said Joseph Irwin.
Defendant pleaded not guilty.

Joseph Irwin sworn
I have recently been working for defendant. On July 18th I met defendant and asked if he was going to settle with me and give me my clothes. He called me a thief and threatened to shoot me. He had a gun with him. He pointed it at me and said he would put it into me.

Cross-examined
It was about 6 a.m., near Leehafer's Lane. Two of his boys were there. I was going west. I waited for defendant and the two boys to come. I asked for

my clothes and wages. He called me a thief. I didn't threaten him. I was walking away. He was about three rods from me at the time. He faced me. The boys were not on the road when he threatened to shoot me. We were talking loud. I went down to Henry Merkley's.

Defendant had both hands on the gun when it was pointed at me. I don't know if it was loaded.

For the Defence

George Seehafer sworn
I was with defendant last Monday morning. We met Irwin at the 10th Concession. Irwin said he wanted his clothes and wages. Defendant said they were hanging on the end of the house he couldn't give him his wages because he had robbed him. Irwin said he didn't rob him. They were about the length of the room apart. Defendant didn't threaten to shoot. He didn't point the gun. I went to defendant's with him. He wanted me to watch the house whilst he milked.

Cross-examined
Irwin spoke first. I didn't see Irwin as I was behind the fence. They were calling each other names. The gun was loaded. It had a cap on.

Albert Seehafer (not sworn, age 8 years)
I saw Irwin. He said to defendant he wanted his clothes. He didn't point the gun at Irwin or threaten to shoot.

Cross-examined
They left me in the lane. I saw Weir all the time.

Henry Merkley sworn
I was about 40 rods from the parties. They were yelling at each other.

Complaint dismissed with costs $5.55, to be paid forthwith, and in default, to be levied by distress and defendant to be imprisoned for 21 days.

James Boyer, J.P.
Singleton Brown, J.P.

Paid.
Court $1.80
Constable $3.75 paid
Total $5.55

Magistrate's Court — September 15th, 1898
Before James Boyer, Singleton Brown, William Sword, J.P.s
Moses Robinson v Andrew Boyd and H.R. McLeod

For the sum of $9.25, for wages which became due and payable within one month now last past, which sum Andrew Boyd and H.R. McLeod have refused to pay.
Defendants pleaded not indebted.

Moses Robinson sworn
I went to work for the defendants last August a year ago and quit four weeks ago last Monday. I missed five days. There was $9.25 due to me when I left, which is still due. I demanded the amount from Mr. Huckson and Andrew Boyd. I was to get $26 a month. I got my time from Mr. McIntyre, the foreman.

Cross-examined
I claim 37 and a half days. There were four days in June not paid for. The total amount due was $37.75 and I have been paid $27 in cash and $1.25 in tobacco.

John McIntyre sworn

I am foreman for Boyd and McLeod. I made the agreement with Robinson the first time. Then he was away and came back again. He was to get $1 a day the first time. The second time Robinson came back, he asked me about returning to work and I said, "Mose, you can take your place." Nothing was said about a reduction or change in wages.

Melissa Robinson sworn

I was present when my husband was hired by Mr. McIntyre for $26 a month. There was nothing mentioned about board. Boyd said he could work until somebody else was got to take his place, at $26 a month.

For the Defence

Defendant sworn

Robinson lost two axes. They were charged up to him. One was found and the other was not. His wages were to be $22 a month the last time. I didn't say anything to Robinson about the difference in wages but I did to his wife. The price of the axe lost is $8.00.

The judgment of the court is that defendant is indebted in the sum of $8.25 for wages and also liable for costs in this case of $5.05, to be paid within the time limited by law and in default, a warrant of distress to issue.

James Boyer, J.P.
Singleton Brown, J.P.
William Sword, J.P.

Paid in full.
September 15, 1898, paid complainant in full.
Paid constable.

Chapter Eighteen

The High Price of Stolen Goods

Muskoka Magistrate's Court considered a wide range of cases involving that timeless character: the thief. These were neither cases of grand larceny, nor the kind of embezzlement that got Bracebridge's treasurer fired in an 1890s town scandal. They were rather the work-a-day business of a justice system coming to terms with such commonplace realities as snatched chickens and stolen silk scarves.

Still, it would be wrong to think of theft as a trivial matter in Bracebridge. Stealing a pair of skids got one man two weeks in jail with hard labour. Someone who stole two pairs of socks, an undershirt, and a pair of drawers got a month's worth of the same punishment. At this rate, can you imagine how much time a woman might serve, with hard labour, for stealing a single silk handkerchief from the man she worked for, and for whom she perhaps felt an undisclosed romantic impulse? Read on.

Bracebridge dry goods stores like Fenn, Anderson & Co. offered a wide variety of footwear and clothing. Their goods also served as temptation to those who might "lift" a new scarf or pair of gloves without paying. Theft in town seemed well curbed, however, with Bracebridge's many churches inculcating right living and Magistrate's Court imposing harsh sentences.

There is, unfortunately, no evidence on the record for most of these cases, since depositions were "taken on paper"; these documents were not included in James Boyer's bench book, which does have the benefit of leaving plenty of scope for one's imagination.

Only one of these 1890s cases of theft was dismissed. This fact, taken together with the severity of punishments for this crime, no doubt sent a strong cautionary warning to everyone in the community and perhaps helps explain the relatively few cases involving stealing to be found in Magistrate Boyer's bench book.

Magistrate's Court — February 1st, 1896
Before James Boyer and Singleton Brown, J.P.s
Frederick Hill v William McNabb

For stealing one whip and two surcingles at the Town of Bracebridge on the 28th of January last.

Prisoner convicted and ordered to be imprisoned in the common gaol at Bracebridge for two days.

James Boyer, J.P.
R.M. Browning, J.P.

Conviction returned.

Magistrate's Court — February 24th, 1896
Before James Boyer and Singleton Brown, J.P.s
John G. Bruce v John Keeler

For stealing one pair of skids on or about the 20th of February instant, at the Township of Macaulay.

Prisoner convicted and sentenced to be imprisoned in the common gaol at Bracebridge for fourteen days with hard labour.

James Boyer, J.P.

Conviction returned.

Magistrate's Court — June 20th, 1896
Before James Boyer, J.P. and Singleton Brown, Mayor
James Newberry v John Walkinshaw

For having, in or about the month of March last, at Bracebridge, stolen two pairs of woollen socks, one undershirt, and one pair of drawers of the value of $2, the property of the informant.

Depositions were taken on paper.

Defendant convicted and sentenced to be imprisoned in the common gaol at Bracebridge for one month with hard labour.

Conviction and deposit returned.

James Boyer, J.P.

Magistrate's Court — November 20th, 1896
Before James Boyer and S. Brown, J.P.s
Frank Prosser v Peter Insley the Younger

For having, in or about the month of June past last, at the Township of Watt, stolen one pair of pants and one jack knife of the value of $3, the goods and chattels of complainant.

Prisoner consented that the charge should be tried summarily, and pleaded guilty to the charge and was sentenced to imprisonment in Bracebridge gaol for one week.

James Boyer, J.P.

Conviction returned.

Magistrate's Court — January 13th, 1897
Before James Boyer, J.P. and Singleton Brown, Mayor
Mary Ann Bigelow v William Fuller

For that defendant, on the 10th January 1897, at Bracebridge, stole 10 cents in money and one handkerchief and one piece of ribbon of the value of 10 cents, the property of Washington Bigelow.

Depositions taken on paper.

Defendant convicted and sentenced to be imprisoned and kept at hard labour for one month.

James Boyer, J.P.

Conviction returned.

Magistrate's Court — June 14th, 1897
Before Messrs. Boyer and Browning, J.P.s
The Queen v Charlotte Holmes

For having, on or about the 5th April last, at Bracebridge, being then and there servant to one Patrick Sherwood, did unlawfully steal one silk handkerchief of the value of $1.00, the property of the said Patrick Sherwood.

Depositions taken on paper.

Prisoner convicted and sentenced to be imprisoned in the common gaol at Bracebridge with hard labour for 2 calendar months.

James Boyer, J.P.

Conviction returned.

MAGISTRATE'S COURT — SEPTEMBER 20TH, 1897
BEFORE JAMES BOYER AND R.M. BROWNING, J.P.s
JOSEPH WILLOUGHBY V FREDERICK COLEMAN

For that defendant, being an infant under the age of 16 years, did on the 16th September instant, at the Town of Bracebridge steal a quantity of fire wood, the property of the said Joseph Willoughby.

Defendant elected to be tried before the magistrate.

Defendant pleaded not guilty.

Depositions taken on paper.

Defendant convicted and fined $1.00 and $4.50 costs, to be paid forthwith, and in default, to be imprisoned in the common gaol at Bracebridge for 21 days.

James Boyer, J.P.
R.M. Browning, J.P.

Fine paid.

Constable $3.00

MAGISTRATE'S COURT — SEPTEMBER 27TH, 1897
BEFORE JAMES BOYER, J.P. AND SINGLETON BROWN, J.P.
SAMUEL M. CORD V JOHN HENRY HALE

For that defendant, on or about the 16th day of September A.D. 1897, at the Township of Muskoka, did unlawfully steal one axle of a horse rake of the value of about $5, the property of the said Samuel McCord.

Defendant consented that the charge shall be tried by the magistrates.

Defendant pleaded not guilty.

Depositions taken on paper.

Case dismissed.

James Boyer, J.P.
Singleton Brown, J.P.

Magistrate's Court — January 6th, 1898
Before James Boyer, J.P. and R.M. Browning, J.P.
The Queen ex rel William A. Brown v Ronald D. Johnston

For that prisoner, on the 1st November 1897, at Bracebridge, did unlawfully steal one halter of the value of $1.25, the property of W.A. Brown.

Prisoner consented that the case be disposed of summarily.

Depositions taken on paper.

Prisoner convicted and sentenced to be imprisoned at the common gaol at Bracebridge and there kept at hard labour for the sum of six weeks.

James Boyer, J.P.
R.M. Browning, J.P.

Conviction returned.

Magistrate's Court — April 30th, 1898
Before James Boyer and S. Brown, J.P.s
The Queen ex rel Priscilla Edwards v Frederick Nichols

For that defendant, on the 5th day of August 1897, at the Township of Ryde, did steal 15 cents in silver, the property of Priscilla Edwards.

Defendant pleaded not guilty and consented to a summary trial.

Depositions taken on paper.

Defendant convicted and sentenced to the common gaol at Bracebridge for 10 days with hard labour.

James Boyer, J.P.

Deposition and conviction returned.

MAGISTRATE'S COURT — AUGUST 1ST, 1898
BEFORE JAMES BOYER, J.P.
RICHARD MILLS V CHARLES MACKINTOSH

For that defendant, on the 1st day of August instant, at the Township of Macaulay in said District, did steal a quantity of apples (then and there growing in a garden) of the value of 25 cents, the property of the informant.

The charge having been read to defendant he pleaded not guilty.

Richard Mills sworn

I live in the Town of Bracebridge. I own a house and lot in the Township of Macaulay, near Bracebridge, and have some apple trees on the lot, which are growing in an enclosed garden. I went there this morning and found defendant pulling apples off the tree and putting them in a basket. The apples and basket produced are the ones he had. They would be worth about 25 cents. Defendant offered to pay for the apples. I have trespass notices on the fences.

For the Defence

Defendant sworn

My impression was that the place where I got the apples belonged to Mr. Orr. Mr. Orr had told me we could go to his place, camp there and take anything we wished. There was a locked gate there.

Defendant convicted and fined $5.00 and 25 cents damages and costs $4.50, to be paid forthwith, and in default, to be imprisoned in the common lockup at Huntsville and there kept at hard labour for one month.

James Boyer, J.P.

Paid constable $3.00
Fine $5.00
Costs $4.50
Damages $0.25
Total $9.75
Conviction returned.

Chapter Nineteen

RELIGIOUS FERVOUR AT GROUND LEVEL

Religious life, associated with elevating the human spirit and right living, could also be manifested in ways more down to earth.

MAGISTRATE'S COURT — MAY 29TH, 1893
BEFORE JAMES BOYER, J.P.
ANNIE BIGELOW, WIFE OF WASHINGTON BIGELOW v CHARLES W. WATSON

Assault and battery at Bracebridge on 24th May instant.
The charge having been read to defendant, he pleaded not guilty.

Annie Bigelow sworn

I am the wife of Washington Bigelow and live in Bracebridge. About 8 p.m. on the evening of 24th May instant, I was with the Salvation Army on the march near the Post Office and was marching with them. Defendant came up to me and caught me by the shoulder and turned me round. He didn't say anything to me. He turned me round purposely. It was not accidental. My shoulder pained me from the force used by defendant in taking hold of me.

Gustavus A. Binyon sworn

I was present on the occasion above mentioned. I saw defendant take hold of prosecutrix, and said to one of the officers of the Army, "That was a mockery of God." Prosecutrix had been kneeling down testifying. Defendant said prosecutrix owed him a dollar or a $1.25. He took hold of her intentionally.

Thomas M. Baird sworn

I was present with the Salvation Army on this occasion. I saw defendant speak to the captain. He said this hussy (meaning prosecutrix) is kneeling there and has been owing me these 3 months. I didn't see him touch her.

Defendant convicted and fined $1.00 and costs of $3.10, to be paid forthwith, and in default, to be imprisoned in the lock-up at Bracebridge for 21 days.

James Boyer, J.P.

Paid constable $1.50
Conviction returned.

MAGISTRATE'S COURT — JUNE 28TH, 1893
BEFORE JAMES BOYER, J.P.
ARTHUR BROWN V IRA BROOKS

For assault and battery at Bracebridge on 24th June 1893.

The charge having been read to defendant he pleaded not guilty.

W. Palmer for complainant

Arthur Brown sworn

I live in Bracebridge. On Saturday evening 24th instant, I went to Salvation Army barracks with Napoleon Duval about 8:30 p.m. I had not been drinking anything. Meeting had opened. I took a seat on left hand side, about 3 or 4 seats from door. A man came and sat beside me. I think his name is Fisher. He was a stranger to me.

Fisher started to throw candies. I hadn't any with me. I told Fisher to keep quiet. He appeared to be under the influence of liquor. Defendant came and said, "I want you 3 fellows to go out (Duval, Fisher, and myself)." Fisher went out. Defendant then told me to go out. I asked him his reason for pulling me out. He again told me to go out. I said I wasn't doing anything to go out for.

Defendant then caught me by the two shoulders, threw me out of the seat on the floor, and ripped the sleeve of my coat. I got up and went out quietly. I couldn't see the defendant from where I sat. I spoke to defendant on Sunday evening about it. He said I was with the crowd and was as bad as the rest.

Rose Arlie sworn

I live in Bracebridge. Was at Salvation Army meeting last Wednesday evening. I know complainant. Was sitting two seats ahead of him. A man named "Fish" was throwing candies.

Complainant was quiet and didn't have anything to do with throwing candies. I saw defendant go and speak to Fish — who went out. He then spoke to complainant who was sitting quietly in his seat. I looked round again. Complainant was on his back and defendant had hold of him. When complainant got up, he went out. I did not see or hear him make any disturbance.

Cross-examined by defendant
I saw Fish throw the candies.

Napoleon Duval sworn
I live in Bracebridge and know complainant. I went with him to Salvation Army barracks on 24th June about 8:30 p.m. We went alone. We were both sober. We both sat in the same seat. I had no candies with me. Fish came in and sat on the same seat. Complainant was perfectly quiet. Fisher threw some candies at the girls. The doorkeeper came to Fish and spoke to him. He kept on throwing them. Defendant came and told the three of us to go out. Fish went out. Complainant asked defendant reason for putting him out. Defendant took hold of complainant, threw him on the floor and tore his coat. There was no loud talking or noise to disturb the meeting. Complainant then went out. Complainant did not do anything to disturb the meeting.

William Lynn sworn
I live in Bracebridge. Last Saturday night I was at Salvation Army barracks. I saw complainant. I was sitting across the aisle from him and could see him all the time if I looked that way. Doorkeeper spoke to Fish, who kept on making a noise and throwing candies. Defendant was sitting quietly in his seat. Defendant came, and I told them to go out. Fish went out. Defendant spoke to complainant. I couldn't hear what he said. He then went in the seat, took complainant by the shoulders, pulled him out of the seat and threw him on the floor. Complainant got up and went out quietly. So far as I saw complainant behaved himself during the whole of the time.

George Jessop sworn
Was at Army night in question. Heard Joe Fish laugh. Saw defendant and someone scuffling on floor.

For the Defence

Defendant sworn
I am the defendant. I heard a noise in the barracks. I looked round and saw the three men "cutting up" behind 2 girls. During prayer I watched them. Either complainant or the man next to him was throwing candies. I could not tell which one it was. When prayer was over I went and told the 3 men I wanted them to go out. One man, sitting on the outside of the seat nearest me, went out. I told complainant to go, as I didn't want any trouble with him. He wouldn't go so I put him out. When I took hold of him, he caught the seat. I jerked him round and he fell on the floor.

Cross-examined by Mr. Palmer
Am Lieutenant in the Salvation Army at Bracebridge. I saw one of the 3 men throw candies. I can't say which one it was.

Lilian Rowbottom sworn
I was on the platform, looked down at the audience and I saw 3 young men misbehaving. I saw complainant with his hand up as if he was throwing. They were whispering and laughing, it was just before prayer. The Ensign was speaking. I can't say who threw the first candy. The girl, Arlise, looked round and laughed. I heard the defendant tell them to go out. I saw defendant take hold of complainant. Both were down on the floor.

Cross-examined by Mr. Palmer
Defendant took hold of complainant after prayer was over.

William Stiles sworn

I saw complainant. I saw his hand go but I couldn't swear he was throwing anything. I saw the 3 men talking and laughing during prayer and singing. It is customary during service for parties to throw their arms around. I saw defendant sitting next to the aisle. Defendant took him by the shoulders, jerked him out of the seat and got him down on the ground.

Robert Elvin sworn

I am doorkeeper at the Salvation Army. I was there last Saturday evening. I saw a man sitting on each side of complainant throwing candies at some girls. They were talking. I went and spoke to Fish, who was sitting on the outside nearest the aisle. I saw him throwing candies but didn't see complainant throw any. Complainant and Duval came in before Fish who sat in the same seat with them.

Cross-examined

I can't say that complainant did anything to interrupt the proceedings by loud talk or anything during prayer. He laughed but not out loud. It was a public meeting.

Defendant fined $5 and costs of $4.60, to be paid forthwith, and in default, to be imprisoned in the common gaol at Bracebridge for one calendar month.

James Boyer, J.P.

Constable $2.50
Constable $2.10
Total $4.60
Paid.
Conviction returned.

MAGISTRATE'S COURT — NOVEMBER 9TH, 1893
BEFORE JAMES BOYER, J.P.
PATRICK SULLIVAN V DAVID TAYLOR

Assault and battery at Bracebridge on 8th instant.
The charge having been read to defendant, he pleaded not guilty.

Patrick Sullivan sworn
I live in Bracebridge. Last night, between 8 and 9 o'clock, I was near the
Salvation Army. Prisoner was behind me. I was talking with Alfred Wilson.
Prisoner said, "You mustn't say anything against Gus Russell." He said you
have been talking about me and attempted to strike me twice. I then struck at
him. Prisoner took hold of me and tried to throw me off the sidewalk. I went
to the Salvation Army barracks. He called Frank Russell out. Prisoner walked
down the steps. I followed him and had my hands in my pockets. Prisoner
turned round and struck me on my face. I did not give him any provocation.

Cross-examined
I did not follow you up.

Alfred Wilson sworn
Last night a little past 8 o'clock I was going down Ontario Street. I saw
the complainant and defendant walking along together. Sullivan asked me
if I had seen James McMahan. I said I saw him about 5 o'clock when he
drove into the hotel yard with Gus Russell. Sullivan said that damned shit.
Defendant resented that speech. I was in front of them. They got fighting.
I don't know who struck first. I advised him to quit.

For the Defence

Defendant sworn

I met Sullivan and Wilson. Some talk about Gus Russell. Sullivan spoke disparaging of Russell. I resented it. He pushed me off the sidewalk. We clinched. I went to the barracks to see Russell. Sullivan used abusive language to me. I walked away. He followed me. He hadn't his hands in his pockets. We had a scuffle when the constable came up.

Joseph Jarbeau sworn
Sullivan called defendant "a God-damned liar." I saw Sullivan on the ground.

Judgment that defendant pay a fine of $1.00 and $3.50 costs, to be paid forthwith, and in default, to be imprisoned in lock-up at Bracebridge for 14 days.

James Boyer, J.P.

Magistrate's Court June 26th, 1895
Before James Boyer, J.P.
Albert Sims v Napoleon Duval

For having on the 24th June 1895, at Bracebridge, unlawfully and willfully damaged and injured the guy ropes of a certain tent the property of the informant.
Defendant pleaded "not guilty."

Oliver McNeil sworn
On Monday last I was at the Free Methodist Camp meeting. The meeting was conducted in a large tent. There were two poles supporting the tent attached to ropes. The prisoner had an open knife in his hand and was fooling with the ropes. There were three short ropes cut. He was alone at the time. He was passing the knife across the rope.

Cross-examined
This happened about nine o'clock. The ropes were not cut while I was there. I don't know that I went away first or not.

Montford Manaril sworn
I was at the meeting Monday last. I saw prisoner up there. He was standing at the rope alone with an open knife. He was drawing the knife across the rope. The rope was alright when he was at it.

Albert Sims sworn
I had charge of the meeting on Monday night. The guy rope would I think cost one dollar to repair.

For the Defence

Edward Archer sworn
I was at the camp meeting last Monday. Prisoner was there when I got there. We were both in the tabernacle.

Charles Bailey sworn
Prisoner was in the tent with me from 9:15 p.m. till about 9:30 p.m.

Archie Duval sworn
I am a brother of the prisoner. We went up to the camp last Monday. My brother was with me. We went in the tent before the meeting began. We came out of the tent together and went home together. He did not cut any ropes. He was in the tent all the time I was there.

Napoleon Duval sworn

I did not cut the rope. I was with the boys. I was standing beside the rope. I passed the back of my knife across the rope, but did not cut it. I did not cut the small ropes.

Prisoner convicted and fined $1.00 and $1.00 damages and $4.50 costs, to be paid forthwith, and in default, to be imprisoned in the common gaol at Bracebridge for one month with hard labour.

James Boyer, J.P.

Paid.
Conviction returned.
Paid complainant $1.00
Paid constable $3.00

Chapter Twenty

POWERS OF THE SPOKEN WORD

The use of words is always an art. Art, of course, is intended to provoke reaction.

MAGISTRATE'S COURT — JULY 11TH, 1893
BEFORE JAMES BOYER, J.P.
WILLIAM GIMSON v JULIUS BEYER

For unlawfully using blasphemous and grossly insulting language to informant on 12th July last.
The charge having been read to defendant he pleaded not guilty.

William Gimson sworn

I live in Bracebridge. On the 12th July last, in the afternoon, I was in my house. Prisoner came in under the influence of liquor. I told him to go out and go about his business. He went out of the house and said I know your place is only a whore house. I told him to go. He turned round and called me a God-damned son of a bitch. I then made a complaint to the magistrate.

Prisoner convicted and fined $1.00 and $4.00 costs, to be paid forthwith, and in default, to be imprisoned in the common gaol at Bracebridge for 20 days in default of goods and chattels whereon to levy the amount.

James Boyer, J.P.

Paid costs and fine remitted.

Magistrate's Court — December 6th, 1893
Before James Boyer, J.P.
Robert E. Armstrong v Patrick Sullivan

Charge: using blasphemous language on public street at Bracebridge on 5th instant.

Defendant pleaded guilty.

Defendant fined $1.00 and $4 costs, to be paid forthwith, and in default, 14 days in the lock-up at Bracebridge.

James Boyer, J.P.

Defendant paid costs and fine remitted.

Magistrate's Court — July 29th, 1895
Before James Boyer, J.P.
Robert E. Armstrong v Herbert Andrews

For using blasphemous language upon the public streets in Bracebridge on 27th July 1895.

Defendant pleaded guilty.

Fined $1.00 and $4.00 costs, to be paid forthwith, and in default, to be imprisoned in the common gaol at Bracebridge for 20 days.

James Boyer, J.P.

Paid.

Conviction returned.

Magistrate's Court — October 8th, 1895
Before James Boyer, J.P.
Charles Everitt the Elder v Robert Bond

For having, on the 22nd of September last, at the Township of Macaulay, used threatening language toward the complainant.

Case settled between the parties.

James Boyer, J.P.

Constable $4.50
Court $1.50
Total $6.00
Paid.

Magistrate's Court — May 7th, 1896
Before James Boyer, J.P.
Joseph Hey v. Frances E. Piper

For having, on the 4th day of May A.D. 1896, at the Town of Bracebridge, used indecent and grossly insulting language to the informant upon one of the public highways in said town.

Defendants failed to appear at the times and place mentioned in the summons.

Thomas Dodd sworn

I am a constable for the Town of Bracebridge. I served a summons on defendant on the 5th of May instant, requiring her to appear this day at 2 p.m. at the Town Hall, Bracebridge, to answer the above charge. Defendant has failed to appear in obedience to the summons which was served personally on her.

Warrant to issue for her arrest. Issued warrant to Constable Dodd.

James Boyer, J.P.

The defendant in this case is the same Frances Piper who, just twelve months before, in May 1895, had been jailed for a year because of her threats and coarse comments to neighbours.

Magistrate's Court — January 24th, 1898
Before James Boyer, J.P.
George Richardson v John Johnson

Assault at Township of Oakley on 27th December last.

Defendants pleaded not guilty.

George Richardson sworn

I live in the Township of Oakley. I know the defendant. I saw defendant on the 27th December last, at the nomination of councillors for Oakley at the municipal election. I was a candidate for reeve, and on addressing the electors said if I was elected I would spend no money on the Petersen Road.[1]

Defendant said I would have to do it as it was a government road. I said it was not a government road. Defendant said I was a liar, called me a liar several times. He came close to me, shook his fist in my face, and repeated it that I was a liar. He shook his fist in my face several times and said I was a damned contrary old bugger. He was close to me and his fist was within 6 inches of my face. I warned him to be careful.

Cross-examined

The nomination was held at Wood Lake. James Johnston and Albert Myers were candidates for reeve. There was a great deal of talk, feeling was running high. I did not say anything to annoy defendant.

James Cox sworn

I live in Oakley. I was at the nomination on 27th Dec. last. Saw complainant and defendant there. After the parties were nominated the chairman called upon the candidates to make a speech. Complainant said if he was elected he wouldn't spend any money on the west end of the Petersen Road. After Richardson got through speaking, defendant approached him and said, "If elected you won't spend any money on Petersen Road." Complainant said he wouldn't. Defendant went close to complainant, raised his hand to complainant's face and made some threatening remarks.

Thomas Weaver came and laid his hand on defendant and drew him away. The feet of the parties nearly touched, they were standing so close

---

[1]The Petersen Road was an east-west colonization road running from Peterborough, west, into the District of Muskoka through Oakley. Its construction proved costly, its survey line problematic, and its economic utility as a road for new development and settlement increasingly dubious — and thus controversial — at this time.

together. They were loud words that were used by defendant. I don't remember the words. It lasted 3 or 4 minutes. Defendant was about 15 feet from defendant and went up to him.

Elias H. Traves sworn
I live in Oakley and was at the nomination meeting on December 27th last. I saw both parties present. Complainant was speaking on township affairs standing near the table. Defendant was four or five paces off. He got up and went to Richardson, put his fist in his face and called him a liar. He was standing close to him. Richardson told him to be careful.

For the Defence

Albert Meyers sworn
I was at nomination meeting. I saw both parties present. I was a candidate for reeve.

Defendant convicted and to appear for judgment when called upon.

James Boyer, J.P.

MAGISTRATE'S COURT — JUNE 27TH, 1898
BEFORE JAMES BOYER, J.P.
JAMES ARNOTT V GEORGE BLACKWELL

For using blasphemous and profane language and being disorderly upon one of the public streets of Bracebridge on the 25th instant.
Defendant pleaded guilty.

Fined $1 and $4.50 costs, to be paid forthwith, and in default, to be imprisoned in the common gaol at Bracebridge for 14 days, defendant having admitted that he had no goods or chattels whereon to levy the amount.

James Boyer, J.P.

Paid constable $3.00

Conviction returned.

Chapter Twenty-One

SAVING THE SABBATH

The injunction to "Remember the Lord's Day and keep it holy" was not only accepted as gospel by Canadian lawmakers in the nineteenth century, but inspired them to enumerate the requisite ways for "saving the Sabbath" in The Lord's Day Act.

Hunting, shooting, and fishing on Sunday were unlawful. So was bathing in any public place, or in sight of a place of worship or a private residence. All public meetings, except in churches, were prohibited. The business of amusement or entertainment was off-limits, including all games, races, or other sports for money or prizes, or which were noisy, or at which a fee was charged. There could be no excursions for hire, by train, steamer or other conveyance, if the object was pleasure. Ontario's Sunday laws extended the effective reach of this ban by also prohibiting advertising of anything unlawful to take place on Sunday.

In the realm of business, it was unlawful to make contracts on Sunday, just as it was to buy, sell, or deliver anything, including liquors, cigars, and newspapers. Generally speaking, the only exceptions from this Sunday ban on deliveries were for passengers' baggage, milk for domestic use, or supplying meals and medicines.

One could not work on Sunday. The Lord's Day Act adumbrated all the ways workers had to remain idle. With certain exceptions, this prohibition included the work of labourers, mechanics, and manufacturers. No farm work, such as seeding, harvesting, fencing, or ditching, could be done. Building and construction work on railways, including repair work "except in emergencies," was banned. So was railway traffic, except for the forwarding of passenger trains and certain freight trains. The list went on. All building was prohibited. Teaming, and driving for business purposes, was prohibited. Bakers and barbers could not open their shops. The work of musicians and "paid performers of any kind" was likewise against the law. Only exceptional relief from these strictures against toiling on the Lord's Day was contemplated for "works of necessity and mercy."

Statutory prohibitions on Sunday activities, known commonly as "blue laws," were so extensive that it may seem surprising that only four alleged violations came before Justice of the Peace Boyer during the entire decade. Partly this was because many devout families imposed *even stricter* codes of Sabbath observance upon themselves. Another reason was that, because closed-down Sundays really did mean that nothing commercial or entertaining was going on, there was little scope for a person to violate the Lord's Day, even if he or she wanted.

Furthermore, people in these times were circumspect. If they did slip in for a Sunday swim, it was likely an inconspicuous dip in some secluded opening to Muskoka's abundantly scattered waters. In the same clandestine way, Muskokans became savvy in finding out-of-the-way places to drop a fishing line into a stream (the best fishing holes anyway), or to bring a deer into their rifle's sights.

There were doubtless many episodes that did not result in charges being laid. Where it not for deputy game warden Elias Traves out searching for moieties, his share of the fines levied against those he successfully prosecuted for hunting on Sunday, even three of these four cases would never have materialized. The fourth was easier to detect, as it involved a town barbershop open on the Lord's Day.

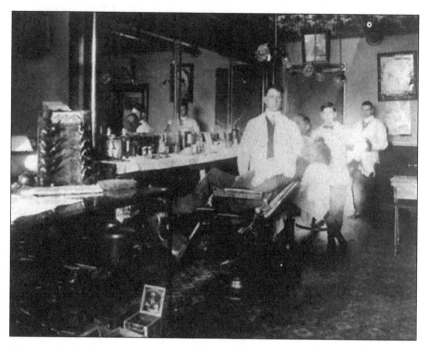

This Bracebridge barber shop extended the gentlemen's comforts on offer beyond a mere haircut and shave to include such things as briar pipes and cigars. Opening on Sunday was, however, strictly forbidden.

A certain gentility seems to have attended these prosecutions. Traves took the men he'd arrested home for dinner. Magistrate Boyer, in one case, "asked" rather than ordered the convicted men to pay their fine. Traves and Boyer seemed inclined to display Christian charity when doing the Lord's work.

MAGISTRATE'S COURT — MAY 20TH, 1895
BEFORE JAMES BOYER, J.P.
ELIAS H. TRAVES V JOHN O'HARE AND JOHN LEEDER

For fishing on Sunday the 19th May in Sharpe's Creek in Draper under Lord's Day Act (Chapter 203 R.S.O.)

Both defendants pleaded guilty.

Defendants asked each to pay fine $2.00 and $3.45 costs, forthwith and in default, to be imprisoned in the common gaol at Bracebridge for one calendar month in default of sufficient distress whereon to levy the amount.

James Boyer, J.P.

Paid.

Conviction returned.

Paid instalment $2 half fine and $3.90 costs.

MAGISTRATE'S COURT — NOVEMBER 4TH, 1895
BEFORE JAMES BOYER, J.P.
ELIAS H. TRAVES V HENRY PALMER, FRANK HAIGHT AND RICHARD M. APPLEBY

For hunting in the township of Macaulay on Sunday, the 3rd of November instant.

The charge having been read to defendants, they severally pleaded not guilty.

Elias H. Traves sworn

I am one of the deputy game wardens for Muskoka. Yesterday afternoon I heard shooting in a northwesterly direction from Oakley Bridge. That would be in Macaulay. I went in the direction of the firing to where defendants and others had a camp beside a lake in the woods. I found two men in the camp but neither of defendants there. Whilst I was at the camp Palmer and Haight came out of the woods to the camp. Each had a loaded firearm. I arrested them.

As I was going from the camp I found defendant Appleby on the edge of the woods. He had a rifle with six cartridges in it. I arrested him. I took all 3 to my house, gave them dinner and brought them to Bracebridge. One of them said they were out after a dog but if they had seen anything they would have shot it. They said they knew it was against the law carrying guns on Sunday.

Defendants convicted and fined $5 and $4.75 costs each, to be paid forthwith, and in default, to be imprisoned in the common gaol at Bracebridge for one month and firearms seized to be forfeited to the crown.

James Boyer, J.P.

Paid complainant half the fine, $7.50, and $10.60 costs.
Conviction returned.
Paid.

Magistrate's Court — April 27th, 1896
Before James Boyer, J.P.
Elias H. Traves v Anson Rowley and Albert Rowley

For fishing on Sunday the 26th April instant, at the Township of Macaulay.
The charge having been read to defendants, they severally pleaded guilty.

Each fined $1 and $3.50 costs each, to be paid forthwith, and in default, to be imprisoned in the common gaol at Bracebridge for 21 days.

James Boyer, J.P.

Conviction returned.

Magistrate's Court — June 15th, 1896
Before James Boyer, J.P.
Thomas Dodd v Napoleon Duval

For having, on the 14th instant, at Bracebridge, unlawfully exercised his ordinary calling as a barber on the Lord's Day.
Defendant pleaded guilty.

Fined $1.00 and $3.25 costs, to be paid forthwith, and in default, to be imprisoned in the lock-up at Bracebridge for 14 days.

James Boyer, J.P.

Fine $1.00
Court $1.50
Constable $1.75
Total $4.25
Conviction returned.

Chapter Twenty-Two

Unlicensed and Illicit Conduct

The idea that, on one hand, social order can be regulated and that, on the other hand, public revenues can be raised through the licensing of activities has, for a very long time, been a marriage of convenience in the governing process.

Governments do this by identifying discreet areas of human endeavour, and then setting out rules to be followed by those they authorize or licence to carry out those activities. Anyone can engage in the identified conduct — operating a hotel, running a pharmacy, shipping freight, transporting passengers — according to the stipulated rules, provided they first apply for the licence, qualify for it according to some objective criteria, and pay the licence fee. Under this regime, revocation of the licence, or even the threat that someone's licence may not be renewed, are further means by which government extends control and ensures compliance.

For just as long a time, this system of commercial orderliness and maintenance of public standards has had to contend with individuals and businesses intent on testing the reach of such regulation. A libertarian spirit drives some people to avoid this meddlesome arm of the state. A few, despite good intentions, just never get around to the required administrative formalities. Still others engage in illicit activity they prudently seek to keep away from the eyes of government inspectors, knowing they could never get a licence for what they are doing, such as distilling liquor in disregard for the system of quality control and payment of excise duties, even if they did apply.

Whatever statutory or other guidelines assisted James Boyer in setting the amount of a fine, or how much the amount reflected a JP's own sense of the seriousness of operating without a licence, these cases show a dramatic gradation in the fines and sentences imposed for the various activities, from hauling goods or selling cloth through to possessing a revolver, operating billiards tables, or distilling liquor, for which the defendants were convicted.

Such challenges to the state and its licensing process in the 1890s kicked up the cases grouped in this chapter; all of them collectively serve to demonstrate how greatly we have changed and how much we remain the same. In all but the case of operating an illegal distillery, the accused pleaded guilty, with the result that no evidence was recorded, yet even the stark reports, through the nature of the charges themselves, give an outline sketch of the community and its effort to establish the rule of law.

Magistrate's Court — September 1st, 1893
Before James Boyer, J.P.
Robert E. Armstrong v James Campbell

For having on the 1st September instant, at Bracebridge, teamed goods or chattels for hire or reward without having first taken out a carter's licence, contrary to By-law No. 7 of the Town of Bracebridge passed 6th May 1889.

Defendant pleaded guilty.

Defendants fined $1.00 and $2.75 costs, to be paid forthwith, and in default, to be levied by distress, and in default of distress, to be imprisoned in lock-up at Bracebridge for 14 days.

James Boyer, J.P.

Paid constable $1.25
Conviction returned

Magistrate's Court — April 30th, 1894
Before Alfred Hunt and James Boyer, J.P.s
George Bunting v Patrick Sherwood

For having, on or about the 23rd day of April, A.D. 1894, at the Town of Bracebridge, unlawfully conveyed merchandise for hire or reward without having first taken out a licence so to do.
Defendant pleaded guilty.

Defendant fined $1 and $3.25 costs, to be paid forthwith, and in default, to be levied by distress, and in default of distress, to be imprisoned in the lock-up at Bracebridge for 10 days.

James Boyer, J.P.

Paid
Conviction returned

Magistrate's Court — May 14th, 1895
Before James Boyer, J.P.
James Wallace v John Williams and John Wilson

For peddling and offering for sale certain goods, to wit, cloth not being

manufactured in the province of Ontario, without having a licence so to do, contrary to a bylaw of the township of Monck.

Defendants each pleaded guilty.

Each defendant fined five dollars and seven dollars costs, to be paid forthwith, and in default, to be levied by distress, and in default of distress, to be imprisoned in the common gaol at Bracebridge for the term of 21 days.

James Boyer, J.P.

Paid
Paid constable $10.00
Conviction returned

A receipt was attached to the record of this case:

Issued by William H. Spencer, Treasurer of Monck Township, to James Boyer, Esq., J.P. for the sum of ten dollars being amount of fine in the case of *Regina v Williams and Wilson* for selling goods without licence in the township of Monck.

MAGISTRATE'S COURT — JANUARY 31ST, 1896
BEFORE JAMES BOYER, J.P.
ALFRED STUNDEN V DAVID DERCKMAN

For that defendant, on 29th January instant, at the Town of Bracebridge, did unlawfully have in his possession upon his person a certain pistol or revolver, he the said defendant not being one of those persons allowed to carry such pistol or revolver by section 105 of the Criminal Code, 1892.

Defendant pleaded guilty.

Defendant ordered to pay a fine of $5.00 and costs $6.05, to be paid forthwith, and in default, to be imprisoned in the common gaol at Bracebridge for one month and revolver forfeited for the use of the corporation.[1]

James Boyer, J.P.

Paid in full
Conviction returned
Paid constable $4.05

Magistrate's Court — March 18th, 1896
Before James Boyer, J.P.
Thomas Dodd v Vincent Russell

For that defendant on or about the 11th March instant, at Bracebridge, and on other days and times within one month now last past did unlawfully have and use for hire or gain billiard tables, without having first taken out a licence so to do, contrary to bylaw 83 of the Town of Bracebridge.

The charge having been read to defendant he pleaded guilty.

Defendant fined $15 and costs $3.75 to be paid forthwith, and in default, to be levied by distress, and in default of sufficient distress, to be imprisoned in the common gaol at Bracebridge for 21 days.

James Boyer, J.P.

Paid
Court $2.50
Constable $1.25
Total $3.75
Conviction returned

---

[1] The "corporation" is a reference to the incorporated Municipality of Bracebridge.

Magistrate's Court — September 21st, 1898
Before James Boyer and John Thomson, J.P.s
Edward Floody v George Bilbrough

For having had in his possession, on or about the 10th day of September last, at the Township of Oakley in the District of Muskoka, a still and other apparatus for rectifying and distilling spirits on the premises owned by him or under his control, being Lot 29 in the 11th Concession of the Township of Oakley aforesaid, without having given notice thereof as provided by the Inland Revenue Act.

Prisoner pleaded not guilty.

Edward Floody sworn

I live in Toronto and am a Preventive Officer in the Inland Revenue Service and have been since 1895. I made a search on the 10th at Lot 29 in the 11th Concession of the Township of Oakley. I found a still, now produced in evidence, which is used for the distillation of spirits. I found it in prisoner's house upstairs. I also found about 6 or 7 gallons of black molasses in a barrel in a room downstairs. The kind of molasses found there is used in the manufacture of spirits. We also found a barrel that could be used as a mash barrel. The still was covered over with a bag evidently with the intention of hiding it. There were a large number of empty bottles around the place. From the smell of it, the still had evidently been used. Defendant was not there when we got the still.

Elias H. Traves sworn

I was with last witnesses when the still was found. What he says concerning it is true. I had been at prisoner's house on Monday the 5th instant. I was also there on the 6th and saw the still there. It was covered with a kind of sack made to fit it. The still was found in prisoner's house on what is known as his farm. I don't know of anyone but prisoner and wife living there.

William E. Stratton sworn

I am the Collector of Inland Revenue for the Toronto division, which division includes Muskoka. I believe the article produced to be a still such as is ordinarily used by those engaged in illicit manufacture of spirits. The tap at the bottom is for the purpose of drawing off the charge as if they did not have this they would have to lift the whole apparatus off the stove to cool every time. Prisoner has no licence from the Inland Revenue department to distil and I have received no notice from him at any time in regard to same.

Prisoner convicted and sentenced to be imprisoned with hard labour for six months and also to pay a fine of $200 and costs $7.20, and in default, to be imprisoned with hard labour for a further period of six months.

James Boyer, J.P.
John Thompson, J.P.

Received $6.70 in full for costs. ~ *J.B.*
Conviction returned.

Chapter Twenty-Three

LIFE AROUND THE LAKES

Opening into the southern edge of the Canadian Shield, Muskoka District is synonymous with lakes. Because its rock, pines, and waters evoke the "northern" image so compelling for people to the south, the district conveniently satisfies the yearnings of many who seek a closer connection to Nature and what they consider the essence of being Canadian. Yet whether one is a permanent resident, summer cottager, or guest at a majestic lodge or small resort, the Muskoka experience is seldom a passive encounter. Life can become intermingled with harrowing adventures up the rivers and mishaps around the lakes.

Some of these 1890s cases dealing with experiences around Muskoka's lakes might just as readily appear in chapters on unpaid wages, assault and battery, or unlicensed conduct, because they include those elements. For example, the case of Alexander Moorehead, cook aboard the steamboat *Lake Joseph*, who sued employer Andrew Boyd in February 1896 for $38.92

The steamboat Islander, *sailing upriver from Lake Muskoka, trying to reach Bracebridge, is blocked because logging companies choked navigation, sending their woodland harvest downstream toward sawmills in Gravenhurst. Conflicting watercourse uses, a constant problem, led to heated debate and court cases.*

A homesteader's hard work clearing land for a farm invariably left stumps and often exposed bedrock under thin soil, leaving the would-be farmer bereft — unless, as in this case, his land backed onto a lake. The two men in a boat, as hard to see here (one-third from right, behind island point) as the four people on shore, offer a foretaste of what was in store for Muskokans who made their homes into simple lodges for sportsmen, then later, grand resorts for summer vacationers.

of unpaid wages, is in Chapter 17: Bartering for Work, Fighting for Wages. Yet most are gathered here, together with other vignettes and controversies that could *only* have occurred on the boats and along the shorelines, embellishing those postcard views of picturesque Muskoka with behind-the-scenes realism about life on the district's waterways.

MAGISTRATE'S COURT — MAY 16TH, 1893
BEFORE JAMES BOYER, J.P.
DAVID E. BASTEDO v THOMAS H. STEELE

For having, on or about the 11th day of May A.D. 1893, at the Township of Stephenson, unlawfully thrown or permitted sawdust to drift into Mary's Lake in said Township, contrary to the provisions of The Fisheries Act.

Defendant pleaded guilty.

Defendant fined $10.00 and costs $5.70, to be paid forthwith, and in default, to be imprisoned in the lock-up at Bracebridge for 30 days.

James Boyer, J.P.

Constable $3.50
Court $2.20
Paid $5.70

Paid complainant $10.00
Paid constable $3.50
Conviction returned.

Magistrate's Court — November 29th, 1893
Before Messrs. Boyer and Browning, J.P.s

Thomas Harbottle, Inspector of Hulls, Etc. v Alfred Denton (owner), and Lorenzo McHenry (Master of Steamboat "Erastus Wiman")

For having, on the 25th day of August 1893, at the Village of Huntsville, unlawfully towed a certain scow in certain waters in District of Muskoka, without a certificate of inspection of said scow authorizing the same to be done.

The charge having been read to the defendants, they severally pleaded guilty.

Defendants fined $20 each and $8.20 costs, to be paid forthwith, and in default of immediate payment, to be imprisoned in the common gaol at Bracebridge for 2 months.

James Boyer, J.P.
R.M. Browning, J.P.

Paid $56.40.

Witnesses — $6.00 paid to A.A. Mahaffy.

Constable paid $3.35

Refunded defendants $5 on account of costs ~ *JB.*

Conviction returned.

Magistrate's Court — November 29th, 1893
Before Messrs. Boyer and Browning, J.P.s
Thomas Harbottle v Alfred Denton

For that defendant, being owner of steamboat "Erastus Wiman," did wilfully carry a greater number of passengers than that allowed by her certificate.

Defendant pleaded guilty.

Defendant fined $50 and $8.20 costs, to be paid forthwith, and in default, to be imprisoned in the common gaol at Bracebridge for 2 months.

James Boyer J.P.

R.M. Browning J.P.

Witness $3.00 paid A.A. Mahaffy.

Constable paid $3.10

Court $2.10.

Dec 11, 1893 — Issued commission to W.J. Hill

Dec 11 — Received from defendant, $40 per mail

Dec 12 — Received balance from constable.

Dec 13 — Obtained drafts for $90 (less 13 cents for draft) payable to Receiver General and handed same to A.A. Mahaffy to remit.

Conviction returned.

MAGISTRATE'S COURT — JUNE 30TH, 1894
BEFORE MESSRS. BOYER AND BROWNING, J.P.s
THOMAS HARBOTTLE, STEAMBOAT INSPECTOR v GEORGE FREDERICK MARSH

For having, on or about the 5th day of May last past, at the Township of Franklin, being then and there the owner of a certain steamboat called "The Lady of the Lakes" and also of a certain scow towed by said steamboat, did unlawfully carry passengers on such steamboat without it having been inspected as required by law.

The charge having been read to defendant he pleaded guilty.

Defendant fined $50 and $6.05 costs, to be paid forthwith, and in default of immediate payment, to be imprisoned in the common gaol at Bracebridge for 2 calendar months.

James Boyer, J.P.
R.M. Browning, J.P.

Fine $50.00
Costs $ 6.05
Costs on commission $3.05
Total $59.90

July 13, 1894. Commission issued to W.J. Hill, Constable.
July 14, 1894. Received $59.90 in full for fine and costs in above case.

The fifty dollar fine received by James Boyer as justice of the peace was turned over to A.A. Mahaffy, a Bracebridge lawyer who often acted for the Crown, and who in 1912 would become district judge, to transmit to the Receiver General at Ottawa. This was done because navigable waters and navigation are a national jurisdiction, thus requiring the fines be paid to the Government of Canada. This was also the procedure in the earlier case of Bastedo v Steele *involving The Fisheries Act, likewise a federal statute. This practice did not apply to fines for offences against the Criminal Code of Canada, however, which, though also a federal statute, went to cover the local costs for the administration of justice, as can be seen from many cases.*

MAGISTRATE'S COURT — JULY 21ST, 1894
BEFORE JAMES BOYER, J.P.
WILLIAM H. DODDS V STEWART RUTHERFORD

Assault and battery at Township of Monck on 19th July 1894.
The charge having been read to defendant, he pleaded not guilty.

William H. Dodds sworn
I live in Bracebridge. On the evening of the 19th instant, I went on an

excursion to Beaumaris. Defendant was also on the excursion. Whilst the boat was lying at Beaumaris, defendant said, "Here's a sneak." I said, "I don't know." He walked up behind me and struck me on the cheek with his fist. Lounden got up and stopped him.

Cross-examined
I don't know if I shoved you.

Mr. Lounden to be called after defence put in.

For the Defence

Minnie Kirk sworn
I went on the excursion. I was talking to defendant. Defendant said, "There's a sneak." I don't know who he referred to, as there were several people there. Complainant pushed defendant. I don't think it was accidental, as there was plenty of room to pass. Defendant said "Hold on there, partner." Complainant said you are a shade too late. Rutherford went towards complainant. I didn't see whether he struck him or not.

Ida Schaefer sworn
I was on the excursion. I was with complainant at the time it happened. I was about 3 feet ahead of complainant. I heard defendant say "Hold on there, partner." Dodd said, "You are a shade too late." I went away to another part of the boat. I didn't see any blow struck. There was plenty of room for complainant to pass without crowding against defendant.

Cross-examined
I did not see defendant strike complainant.

Adjourned to 7 o'clock p.m.

Alfred Lounden sworn
I live in Bracebridge. I was on the excursion in question. Complainant and defendant were on the boat at Beaumaris. I saw the parties scuffling. They had hold of each other. I could scarcely see what they were doing as it was dark. I went up to them and parted them. They were on one side of the boat and I was on the other. I caught hold of defendant and told him it was no place for that. We didn't want any fighting on the boat. I did not see any blow struck at all. I did not see complainant push defendant.

Cross-examined
I think both parties were in the wrong.

Complainant recalled
I pushed against defendant accidentally.

Complaint dismissed with costs $3 to be paid forthwith, and in default, to be levied by distress, and in default of distress, to be imprisoned in the common gaol at Bracebridge for 14 days.

James Boyer, J.P.

> Fine paid.
> Court $1.50
> Constable paid $1.50

MAGISTRATE'S COURT — MAY 6TH, 1896
BEFORE JAMES BOYER, J.P.
THOMAS DODD v THOMAS THRIFT AND EDMUND ARBIC

For having, on the 2nd day of May instant, at the Town of Bracebridge in said District, unlawfully thrown stump roots and other waste wood in the waters of the Muskoka River.
The charge having been read to defendants, they severally pleaded not guilty.

Thomas Dodd sworn
I am constable of the Town of Bracebridge. On the 2nd May instant, I was standing near the British Lion Hotel. I heard something plunge in the river. I went down and stood on the end of the Iron Bridge. I saw Thrift dump a barrow load of roots, stumps and brush in the river. Arbic was digging up the roots nearby. I asked if they knew they were breaking the law. They said they didn't. The river abounds with pickerel, trout, and other fish.

Cross-examined by Mr. Bird
I saw some of the roots sink as soon as they were put in, some of the stuff floated across the river towards the rack at the powerhouse.

Defendants convicted and fined $1 each and $2.10 costs each, to be paid forthwith, and in default, to be levied by distress, and in default, to be imprisoned in the common gaol at Bracebridge for 30 days.

James Boyer, J.P.

Paid.
Conviction returned.

Constable Dodd, in this case being paid $2.00 costs, plus 66 cents, received a moitie that was not half, but one-third, of the fines.

Magistrate's Court — July 29th, 1897
Before James Boyer, J.P.
Burton B. Wendover v Jacob Bogart

For having, on and previous to 24th July 1897, deposited sawdust in the waters of Three Mile Lake and in the waters of a certain creek running into said lake, to the injury and destruction of the fish in said lake. Defendant pleaded guilty.

Fined $5 and $4.78 costs, to be paid forthwith, and in default, to be imprisoned in the common gaol at Bracebridge for 21 days.

James Boyer, J.P.

Fine $5.00
Constable $2.58
Court $2.20

Paid complainant $2.58
Paid constable's fees and $2.50 (½ fine).

Magistrate's Court — August 20th, 1897
Before James Boyer, J.P.
The Township of Medora and Wood v John J. Beaumont

For having, on or about the month of July last, at the Township of Medora and Wood, being then and there a hawker or petty chapman, unlawfully peddled or sold goods, wares and merchandise in said township, without having first obtained a licence from the said Township for that purpose.

Defendant pleaded not guilty.

Mr. Johnson for the complainant
A.A. Mahaffy for the defendant

Henry C. Guy sworn
I am the clerk of the Municipality of the Township of Medora and Wood. I produce Bylaw No. 15 (Book No. 2, page 138) of the United Townships of Medora and Wood, signed by the reeve and clerk and duly sealed with the corporate seal, relating to hawkers and peddlers. I also produce Bylaw No.16 of the said municipality (Book No. 3, page 10). Bylaw is duly signed by the reeve and clerk and the seal of the municipality attached thereto. This bylaw amends Bylaw No. 115 and was passed on the 29th day of May 1897. I also produce Bylaw No. 135 (Book No. 2, page 204) amending Bylaw No. 115, duly signed and sealed, passed on the 4th day of June 1894. Those are the only bylaws in force in the municipality relating to the matter in question.

I have seen Mr. Beaumont's boat at Bala and passing my own house. Defendant does not live in the municipality of Medora and Wood and is not assessed there.

Cross-examined by Mr. Mahaffy
Bylaw No. 161 was signed by the reeve about an hour ago today. I signed it a few days after the meeting on the 29th day of May 1897 and the corporate seal was affixed thereto at the same time. The printed form now produced is the one printed and intended to show people the bylaw as it is to be now enforced. This form was issued by the corporation soon after the meeting. (Witness added that it was issued by him as Clerk of the Municipality.)

Re-direct
Defendant has no licence to sell goods in the Township of Medora and Wood from that municipality.

John J. Beaumont sworn
I live at Alport in the Township of Muskoka and am a farmer. I run a supply boat in connection with the farm on Lake Muskoka only. Farm produce and groceries are sold on the boat. I sell them to the tourists. I was engaged in that business in the month of July last. Tea, sugar, soap, fruit, etc. are sold. I do not go on the boat. My two sons, George and Frank, run the boat. I have no licence from the Township of Medora and Wood to sell goods in their municipality. The boat is a small steam yacht, with a deck and two cabins.

Cross-examined by Mr. Mahaffy
I do not go on the boat myself so have no personal knowledge of actual sales. It is chiefly farm produce my boat carries and is grown by myself. My farm is in Township of Muskoka.

The Nymoca, *one of several steamboats bringing provisions to cottagers and remote lakeside settlers in the 1890s, calls in at Walker's Point, Lake Muskoka. Charged for conducting this commerce without a licence, the boat's owners were brought before Muskoka Magistrate Boyer.*

Re-direct
Groceries and fruit are bought to sell again.

George Beaumont sworn
I run the engine on the *Nymoca*. The boat is engaged in carrying supplies around Lake Muskoka for sale. We sell farm produce, flour, tea, fruit, hams and bacon, sugar, apples and canned fruit and bananas and watermelons. We go to Beaumaris, Gibraltar, Port Keywaydin, St. Elmo, Mortimer's Point, Sandy Point, Torrance, and Bala. We have been selling these supplies at these places. We did so during July last. Mr. Young, Hamilton at Beaumaris, Mr. Fearman at Gibraltar, Mr. Gibson at Keewaydin, Mrs. Beddo of Sandy Point, Miss Dark of Torrance, and Mrs. Board of Bala have bought supplies from my boat. I believe that Bala, Mortimer's Point and Torrance are in the Township of Medora and Wood. My boat does not carry passengers.

Defendant submitted that there is no case.
Case dismissed with costs against the municipality.

James Boyer, J.P.

Sept. 23, 1897 — received from clerk of Medora and Wood $25.22
Paid constable's fees, $20.92
Paid magistrate's fee, $4.30

The payment by James Boyer of a $4.30 "magistrate's fee" to himself was not, as can be seen in most cases in this book, very common. At intervals, the Town of Bracebridge paid an amount toward the costs of the magistrate doing his work, but at other times council suspended the item from its budget and lobbied the provincial government to pick up the costs for paying its appointee. Boyer did not like the practice of JPs paying themselves, but had to be practical about remuneration for his efforts.

He was nonplussed about the foregoing case, and its counterpart, which follows, because of the interference it represented by a municipality in the work of farmers and boat operators to meet the needs of people whose summer residences at the lakes were important to the Muskoka economy and character. He had no reluctance levying a magistrate's fee against a municipality, in contrast to his hesitation taking it from costs paid by an individual, another part of James Boyer's struggle to shape "the rule of law."

MAGISTRATE'S COURT — AUGUST 20TH, 1897
BEFORE JAMES BOYER AND ISAAC WHITE, J.P.s
MEDORA AND WOOD v ROBERT WADE AND GEORGE HOMER

For having, in or about the months of July last past, in the Township of Medora and Wood, being then and there hawkers or petty chapmen, unlawfully peddled and sold goods, wares and merchandise, without having first obtained a licence from the corporation of said township for that purpose.

Defendant pleaded not guilty.

Mr. Johnson for complainant
Mr. Monroe Grier for defendant

Henry C. Guy sworn

I am the clerk of the Municipality of Township of Medora and Wood. I produced Bylaw No. 115 (Book 2, page 138) of the United Township of Medora and Wood, signed by the reeve and clerk and duly sealed with the corporate seal relating to hawkers and peddlers. I also produce Bylaw No. 161 of the said municipality (Bylaw Book No. 3, page 10). Bylaw is duly signed by the reeve and clerk, with the seal of the municipality attached. This bylaw amends Bylaw No. 115 and was passed on the 29th day of May 1897. I also produce Bylaw 135 (Book No. 2, page 204) amending Bylaw No. 115, duly signed and sealed passed on the 9th day of June 1894.

Those are the only bylaws in force in the municipality relating to the matter in question. Defendants do not reside in Medora and Wood and are not assessed there.

Cross-examined by Monroe Grier
Bylaw No. 161 was signed by the reeve about an hour ago today. I signed it a few days after the meeting (29th of May 1897) and the seal was affixed thereto by me at that time when I wrote to Mr. Homer. The letter produced is in my writing and is my letter to Mr. Homer. The document[1] put in before was therein enclosed.

George Stephens sworn
I am a lake captain. I am employed by the defendant George Homer. I have been in his employ since the 29th day of June 1897. The boat is called the *Edith May*. We carry supplies around the lake. We go around Lake Rosseau and Joseph. I run the boat to different islands and points around the lakes under direction of the salesman, and tie up at the wharves. We have tied up at Mr. Love's near Port Sandfield, Mackenzies on Lake Joseph, Wilson's, Orgles on Lake Joseph, Mr. Nixon's at Redwood post office, Judge Ardagh's,[2] and Chamber's near Redwood, Lee near Redwood, Hammill's Point on the mainland. I believe the places mentioned are in the Township of Medora.

There is a salesman on the boat named Rutherford who sells goods. He sells flour, pork, sugar, tea, bananas, apples, potatoes and other vegetables, and general groceries and fruit. We were carrying on that trade during the month of July last, at the different places mentioned. The people above mentioned came to the boat to get goods. I believe the salesman received the money for the goods sold. The *Edith May* is a small-decked steamboat.

---

[1] The printed form explaining the township's rules on hawkers and peddlers, produced in evidence in the preceding case.
[2] County Court Judge John A. Ardagh of Barrie, whose family's enjoyable experiences at this Lake Muskoka summer home influenced his lawyer son B.H. Ardagh to become a member of the Muskoka bar around this time.

Cross-examined by Monroe Grier

I am only the captain. The selling is done by the salesman, Mr. Rutherford. The Navigation Company's boats sell meals, candies, etc. on board. They have a regular passenger licence and we have also a like licence from the Dominion Government Inspector. Mr. Evans, the hull inspector, was on the boat about two weeks ago. Our last year's licence is not run out.

George Homer sworn

I am a member of the firm of Homer and Company. Robert Wade is the other member. We do business at Gravenhurst and Rosseau. We run a boat also for the purpose of carrying supplies. We have been running on Lake Rosseau and Joseph. We carry supplies for summer tourists and visitors and sell to them. We have been running this supply boat six seasons.

We carry everything in the way of feed, vegetables, groceries, and provisions. We were engaged in that business in July last. I am not on the boat myself, the business on the boat being conducted by my employees. I do not live in Township of Medora and Wood nor am I assessed there. I have no licence from the Township of Medora and Wood to sell goods. We have a steamboat licence which authorizes us to run the boat and carry passengers and freight. The account of the sales is made to Mr. Hooper, our manager at Rosseau. The boat is supplied from Rosseau.

Cross-examined by Monroe Grier

I pay taxes at both Gravenhurst and Rosseau.

Henry C. Guy recalled

The printed form now produced is the one printed and intended to show people that the bylaw is to be now enforced. This form was issued by the Corporation soon after the meeting.

Defendant submitted that there was no case.

Case dismissed with costs against the municipality.

James Boyer, J.P.

September 23rd, received from clerk of Medora and Wood $25.22

Paid constable's fees, $20.92

Paid magistrate's fee, $4.30

Late in the fall of 1897, a couple of prosecutors, William Evans and James Johnston, drew a bead on two Muskoka steamboat operators, George Marsh and Albert Mortimer, bringing them before Magistrate's Court on five separate charges pertaining to their boats.

Defendant Marsh pleaded guilty in only one of the three cases brought against him, and the other two charges were withdrawn. Defendant Mortimer pleaded guilty to both charges, although he protested the inaccuracy of one. As a result of these pleas and the summary disposition of their cases there is really no evidence in these reports to relish, yet again something can be gleaned about who was operating steamboats, and the licensing requirements they faced.

There is also an interesting twist to the outcome in Albert Mortimer's cases, proving once again that "It's not over 'til it's over!"

MAGISTRATE'S COURT — OCTOBER 28TH, 1897
BEFORE JAMES BOYER, J.P. AND SINGLETON BROWN, J.P.
WILLIAM EVANS V GEORGE F. MARSH

For that defendant, on the 12th day of July 1897, being then and there the owner of the steamboat *Mary Louise* on the Lake of Bays in the District of Muskoka, did unlawfully carry on said steamboat a greater number of passengers than allowed by her certificate, contrary to the provisions of the Steamboat Inspection Act.

Mr. Johnson for prosecutor

A.A. Mahaffy for defendant

The charge having been read to defendant, he pleaded guilty.

Defendant fined $50 and costs $33.96, to be paid forthwith, and in default, to be imprisoned in the common gaol at Bracebridge for 2 calendar months.

James Boyer, J.P.
Singleton Brown, J.P.

Conviction returned.

Magistrate's Court — October 28th, 1897
Before James Boyer, J.P. and Singleton Brown, J.P.
Williams Evans v George F. Marsh

For that defendant, being owner of Steamboat *Florence*, on the 12th July 1897 on Lake of Bays in District of Muskoka did unlawfully carry passengers on said steamboat, without said steamboat having a certificate.

Defendant pleaded not guilty.

Case withdrawn on payment of costs by defendant

James Boyer, J.P.
Singleton Brown, J.P.

Magistrate's Court — October 28th, 1897
Before James Boyer and Singleton Brown, J.P.s
William Evans v George F. Marsh

For that defendant, being owner of Steamboat *Florence*, did on 12th July 1897 on Lake of Bays unlawfully tow a scow, by means of said

steamboat, having passengers on board, without the certificate required therefor by the Steamboat Inspection Act.

Defendant pleaded not guilty.

Case withdrawn on payment of costs by defendant.

James Boyer, J.P.
Singleton Brown, J.P.

MAGISTRATE'S COURT — NOVEMBER 10TH, 1897
BEFORE JAMES BOYER AND H.L. BOWYER, REEVE
JAMES JOHNSTON V ALBERT MORTIMER

For that defendant, being then and there the owner of the steamboat *Ethel May*, did, on the 29th day of July A.D. 1897, unlawfully carry passengers on said steamboat, without a certificate authorizing said steamboat to carry passengers, contrary to the provisions of the Steamboat Inspection Act.

Defendant pleaded guilty but stated he did not carry passengers for hire. Defendant fined $50 and costs $12.30, to be paid forthwith, and in default, to be imprisoned in the common gaol at Bracebridge for two months.

James Boyer, J.P.
H.L. Bowyer

MAGISTRATE'S COURT — NOVEMBER 10TH, 1897
BEFORE JAMES BOYER AND H.L. BOWYER, REEVE
JAMES JOHNSTON V ALBERT MORTIMER

For that defendant, being then and there the owner of the Steamboat *Ethel May*, did unlawfully run said steamboat on Lake Muskoka on the 29th day of July 1897, without having the certificate required by the Steamboat Inspection Act.

Defendant pleaded guilty and fined $50 and costs $11.80, to be paid forthwith, and in default, to be imprisoned in the common gaol at Bracebridge for 2 months (not to run concurrently).

James Boyer, J.P.

H.L. Bowyer

1897 Dec. 14, costs paid, and fine remitted by Dominion Government. 1897 Dec. 14, sent post office order to Archdeacon & Sloan, Gravenhurst, to pay his costs, and witness fees to Jackson & Steele in this and preceding case (P.O. order $9.80).

Conviction returned.

It turned out, as can be extrapolated from James Boyer's bench book notations following this case, that the one hundred dollar fine Albert Mortimer paid on November 10 was refunded to him five weeks later on December 14, because the Laurier government in Ottawa, which had jurisdiction over navigation, authorized its remission. Such forgiveness, only extended in exceptional cases, would not have happened without representation having first been made to the federal government on behalf of the boat's owner, Mortimer. Such representation was likely made through the good offices and intercessions of Liberal Member of Parliament for the district, Duncan Graham, who had been newly elected for the district earlier that same year — by a margin of only seventeen votes — and who was eager to build his support among electors, including the influential Mortimer clan at Mortimer's Point settlement.

Chapter Twenty-Four

DOWN BY THE STATION

Once the Grand Trunk Railway reached Bracebridge in 1885, the train station became a second hub of community activity, its passenger and freight traffic a counterpoint to the bustling town wharf below the falls, where steamboat navigation was at its height. Like a magnet, the station drew transcontinental passengers and local drunks alike.

That year citizens celebrated the first passenger train to run through town on Monday afternoon, June 28, with the Bracebridge Firemen's Band playing jaunty airs and people waving Union Jack flags and crowding the station platform. By 1898 the growth of railway freight shipments from Bracebridge industries called for additional marshalling capacity, so the station building was moved a short distance, a switch installed, and additional track laid behind the building as sidings.

The railway accelerated the pace of life in Bracebridge, introducing a rougher, more exciting element. It was not just the transcontinental reach

By the 1890s, the train station in Bracebridge was a new hub of activity for passengers, freight, and mail. The railway brought progress but also opened the community to more uncertainty about individuals coming and going.

of the thundering trains steaming along its tracks, but also the exciting aura of modern times and uncertainty about the railway's human traffic catered to by hotels near the station that gave Bracebridge a rawer edge and a wider sense of adventure.

Symbolic of these bigger stakes, even before the trains began rolling through the community, was a riot that took place in Bracebridge. Unpaid construction workers, who had toiled long at hard labour building up the roadbed and laying down the tracks through unforgiving stretches of Canadian Shield rock and swamp, began a rampage in the central streets of town to protest the fact they had not been paid their wages for weeks. Most of these angry workers spoke little or no English. That did not prevent town clerk James Boyer confronting the tumult with a reading, in English, of the Riot Act. His open proclamation of this section of the Criminal Code was what it took to invoke the Riot Act's extraordinary powers of arrest, should the immigrant labourers not disperse forthwith and return peaceably to their construction camp along the railway line. The rule of law, now tested in a new way to Bracebridge, was upheld.[1]

James Boyer's street drama with rioting workers was emblematic of the deeper 1890s contest between the raw conditions of a Canadian town and efforts to impose some civil peace upon its disorderly elements. With the railway, just as with the two vast local tanneries operating in Bracebridge, only the smallest parts of that larger play can be glimpsed in Magistrate's Court. Serious criminal offences, major contract disputes, and liability for injury in cases arising from railway operations did not come before a justice of the peace. The misdemeanours represented by the following five cases at least offer a sampling of what life was like in that era, down by the station, early in the morning.

MAGISTRATE'S COURT — JULY 3RD, 1893
BEFORE JAMES BOYER, J.P.
J.D. McMINN v JOHN McINTOSH

For being drunk and disorderly at the Railway Station at Bracebridge on Sunday morning, the 2nd instant, contrary to Bylaw No. 8 passed 4th September 1879.
The charge having been read to defendant, he pleaded guilty.

---

[1] The next time the Riot Act was read in town, so far as I am aware, was when James's son George Boyer, by then a former mayor and local newspaper publisher, read the same text over the public address system at a 1950s Bracebridge Bears–Sundridge Beavers Saturday night hockey game that had descended into a bench-clearing, rink-wide brawl, involving all players and most fans. Although this audience understood English, it was also necessary to turn out the arena lights and play the national anthem in the dark to quell the flow of battle.

Prisoner convicted and fined $1.00 and $4.00 costs, to be paid forthwith, and in default, to be imprisoned in lock-up at Bracebridge for 21 days. Defendant admitted that he had no goods whereon to levy the amount.

James Boyer, J.P.

Paid constable $2.50
Conviction returned.

Magistrate's Court — October 24th, 1895
Before Messrs. Browning and Boyer, J.Ps.
Thomas Dodd, Sanitary Inspector, Local Board of Health v Alexander Foster

For having on the 10th day of October instant, at the Town of Bracebridge, deposited refuse and other filth dangerous to the public health upon the lands of the Grand Trunk Railway in said town.

The charge having been read to the defendant, he pleaded not guilty. Adjourned to 26th instant, at 3 p.m.

Defendant, by his council (W. Mahaffy), admitted the existence of the material.

J.W. Bettes sworn

I am chairman of the Local Board of Health. I saw defendant a week ago last Monday. I went and examined the drain. On that day the wash water was in barrels. I saw that it required the co-operation of the Grand Trunk Railway to put a drain under the track. I had some conversation with Mr. Gregg of the Grand Trunk Railway, and as I was going away I asked Mr. Dickie to see defendant. There were no slops being put in the drain at that time.

Defendant discharged from conviction under Section 861 of Code upon payment of $4 costs, in consequence of representations made by chairman of Board of Health.

James Boyer, J.P.
R.M. Browning, J.P.

Paid.

MAGISTRATE'S COURT — DECEMBER 13TH, 1895
BEFORE JAMES BOYER, J.P.
JOSEPH WILLOUGHBY V WILLIAM MURPHY

Fighting in the waiting room of the Grand Trunk Railway at Bracebridge on 13th December instant.
The charge having been read to prisoner, he pleaded guilty.

Prisoner fined $1 and $4.50 costs, to be paid on or before 21st instant and in default, to be imprisoned in the common gaol at Bracebridge for 21 days.

James Boyer, J.P.

Paid.
Paid constable $2.50
Paid Constable Stunden $4.00

MAGISTRATE'S COURT — SEPTEMBER 28TH, 1896
BEFORE JAMES BOYER, J.P.
THOMAS DODD V GEORGE BILBROUGH

Assault and battery upon complainant at Bracebridge on the 26th instant, whilst in the execution of his duty as a constable.

The charge having been read to prisoner, he pleaded not guilty.
Taken as a common assault.

Thomas Dodd sworn

I am a constable for the District of Muskoka. On Saturday morning last, near 1:00 a.m., shortly after the train left for the north, prisoner was at the railway station. I told him to leave. There had been a number of drunken men at the station but they went off on the train. Prisoner wouldn't leave, told me it was none of my business.

I took hold of him and put him off the platform. He fell. I picked him up, took him across the street to the sidewalk and told him not to come back. He followed me back to the station, used very insulting language, called me a shit. I took hold of him to put him off, he struck me in the eye. I then knocked him down three times. I again took him across the road. He sat down on the sidewalk and threatened me with the law.

Cross-examined

I struck you three times but didn't kick you. I was requested by the agent to ask you if you were going on the train. The train had gone.

Joseph Willoughby sworn

I am night agent of the Grand Trunk Railway at Bracebridge. On the Saturday morning, last, between 12:30 and 1 o'clock, I asked Constable Dodd to take prisoner from the station. The train had then gone north. The conductor had put a drunken man off the train.

Dodd spoke to prisoner. I didn't hear what was said. Dodd took him across to the sidewalk. Prisoner followed Dodd back. Dodd took him away a second time. He followed him back again. He went to put him away a third time. Prisoner Bilbrough struck Dodd. Dodd shoved him off the platform. He fell. He then got up and refused to go.

Dodd then struck him. He asked prisoner if he would go then, if that was enough for him. He said, "No it isn't." Prisoner called him an old shit and an old son of a bitch. Dodd came into the station. Prisoner went away threatening the constable. The constable was quite sober.

Prisoner has been in the habit of coming around the station late and trying to stay around there in the waiting room. I have put prisoner out of the waiting room on other occasions and had to use force to do so.

Cross-examined
I told Dodd to take you away. I didn't see him strike you.

Prisoner convicted and fined $5 and $4.70 costs, to be paid forthwith, and in default, to be imprisoned in the common gaol at Bracebridge for 6 weeks with hard labour.

James Boyer, J.P.

Paid.
Paid constable $3.00
Conviction returned.

Magistrate's Court — February 5th, 1897
Before James Boyer, J.P.
William W. White v Thomas Dodd

Assault and battery at Bracebridge on 27th January last.
The charge having now been read to defendant, he pleaded not guilty.

Mr. Mahaffy for complainant
Mr. Arnold for defendant

William W. White sworn
On the 27th January last, I was Assistant Baggage and Freight Agent of the

Grand Trunk Railway at Bracebridge. At about 7:00 p.m. that evening, I went with Roy Whitten to the station to practice on the telegraph key. I was there about half an hour. The agent had seen me practicing there at night.

I was leaving the office and locking it up. Willoughby the night operator was standing outside. Willoughby told defendant to arrest me. I went to go back in the office.

Dodd caught me by both shoulders, pushed me into the office against the counter, and said, "I have orders from the night agent to arrest you."

I said, "Did you see Mr. Cochrane about it?" and I said, "Show me the warrant for my arrest."

He said he had his authority from the agent (pointing to Willoughby). He said, "Come out."

I said I wouldn't till he showed his warrant.

He shook me round, pulled out the handcuffs and put one partly on my right hand. I said I would walk up with him and he put them back in his pocket.

He said, "Come on."

I walked out behind him. He said I couldn't stay on the premises, I had to get off. He caught me by the arm and twisted me round. He was cursing and swearing and said he would show me the law.

He left me by Higgins' Corner. Willoughby had told Whitten to leave the operating key of the telegraph alone, and he told me the boss (Mr. Cochrane) said I was to leave the operating key alone. Cochrane is the agent. I carry a key of the office door. I had been practicing on the instrument before. Cochrane had seen both Whitten and myself practicing on the telegraph key.

Cross-examined

I was not on duty at the time. I knew defendant was a constable. I refused to leave the telegraph key alone when Willoughby requested me.

General rules and regulations of the Grand Trunk Railway No. 107 put in.

DOWN BY THE STATION

Defendant admitted seeing such a rule in the regulations.

I had no permission from the superintendent to practice on the key. Cochrane said I could practice. I did not use any profane or bad language. I had my coat off to fight Willoughby.

Rule 201 admitted, and that Willoughby was in charge that night.

Rule 117 admitted, and that complainant went down to the station and took another person there that night, and that Whitten turned off the switch and that was when Willoughby first interfered.

Case dismissed with costs $4.10 to be paid forthwith, and in default, to be levied and distress and in default of sufficient distress, to be imprisoned in the common gaol at Bracebridge for 21 days.

James Boyer, J.P.

Paid.

Paid constable.

Magistrate's Court — January 18th, 1898
Before James Boyer, J.P.
Joseph Willoughby v Hugh Blair

For trespassing upon the property of the Grand Trunk Railway during the night time on the 18th instant.

Defendant pleaded guilty and sentence suspended.

James Boyer, J.P.

Chapter Twenty-Five

FENCE WARS

The adage "good fences make good neighbours" is only as valid as certain assumptions from which it arises: that one indeed knows where one's own property line runs; or that neighbours agree on where the line of division separates their land; or that a fence is a helpful containment rather than a hazardous hindrance; or that the bylaws have been complied with in the fence's erection; or even that one actually owns the land in question. Sometimes all such considerations evaporate entirely when, as occurred in at least one astonishing situation, a fence is simply stolen, or it is damaged in the darkness of night by someone committing an act of voyeurism.

Each of these circumstances arose in central Muskoka during the 1890s, not only testing that old bromide about happy neighbourly relations being based upon good fences, but resulting in cases that seemed to reveal the existence of its corollary: bad fences make for bad blood between neighbours.

If "mending one's fences" means making peace with a person, these nine cases reveal how such peace could be as elusive as a property line in a dense Muskoka forest.

Magistrate's Court — August 4th, 1894
Before James Boyer, J.P.
Isaac Bridgment v George Keilty

For having, on or about 31st July last past, at the Township of Draper, wilfully destroyed a certain fence and also a certain building, the property of informant.

The charge having been read to defendant, he pleaded not guilty.

Isaac Bridgment sworn

I live at Muskoka Falls and Lots 21 and 22 on Joseph Street and Lots 20 and 21 on the west side of William Street, and I have a house on the lots which are fenced. I bought the lots from Frank Prunty, and have lived there since last fall. Defendant's shingle mill is on the adjoining lot. Defendant has a burner attached to the mill. It is open to my line fence which is a board one, and the refuse falls right against my fence.

It has burnt my fence several times. The first time about 20 feet were burnt. I put up the fence. It was again burnt down for about the same distance. It was burnt a third time, and I went to defendant and asked him what he would do about it as the cattle got in. I have a meadow and garden inside the fence.

Defendant said he would go half the expense of building a wire fence if I run it on my own property around the burner. I agreed. He said his team was coming to Bracebridge and he would get the wire while here. He did not bring the wire and went away. I asked him about it and he said he was not going to do anything towards it.

While my fence was down through being burnt, cattle got in and spoilt my cabbage and trampled my meadow. The fence was burnt a fourth time.

I built it with blocks, running it around the burner on my own place. This was also burnt on Monday last.

There was a blacksmith shop on my lots when I bought them from Mr. Prunty, and it was included in the sale from him to me. On Tuesday last, Mr. Keilty and his men entered my lots after I had forbidden them to do so, and removed the building from off my lots by tearing it down and removing the materials. The value of the building was at least $10.

The value of the fences destroyed was about $4.00. The damage to my crops and hay was about $10.00.

Cross-examined by the defendant
I did not pile any crops or hay between the fence and the burner.

Frank Prunty sworn
I sold the property in question to complainant. The blacksmith shop on property was included in the sale. I owned the building at the time. Defendant's burner is so placed that the blocks come up against the complainant's fence. Complainant's valuation of the fence is reasonable. The blacksmith shop is worth $10. Blacksmith shop was on the land when he bought it.

Alexander Cameroon sworn
I value the damage to the property at $10 for the building and $7 for the fence to put it in place the last time. I saw the fence burning last Monday. Defendant told the fire started from the burner.

Henry Hall sworn
I was working for Mr. Prunty across the river and saw the fire start from the burner and burnt complainant's fence. Defendant's burner is right up close to the complainant's front fence.

Louis Belfuille
I saw fence burning about a month ago. I saw cattle in complainant's field and drove them out. I drove them out where the fence was down, near the burner.

Cross-examined by the defendant
I saw fence burning. I sent the cattle out between the burner and riverbank.

For the Defence

James Sinclair sworn
Blacksmith shop was put up in 1892 and was not of much value. It had no window or door to it. About 2 or 3 hundred feet of lumber in it.

John McVeigh sworn
I saw some ends of logs built up inside the fence, between the burner and his fence. The pile of logs ends was a very good fire trap. I heard complainant tell defendant to move the blacksmith shop out of that. I think it was the night before I moved the building. Complainant came to stop me when I went to take building down. Defendant told me to go on and move it.

Cross-examined by Mr. Mahaffy
It was Thursday morning when I heard the conversation between complainant and defendant. Complainant said to defendant, "I do not want this going up and down. It would be better to take the building out of that."

Alexander McGinnis sworn
The lumber in the blacksmith's shop was not worth anything.

Defendant sworn
Complainant's fence is almost about eight feet from the burner. I offered complainant to purchase enough wire if he would deviate his fence about 20 feet to Lot 22. He at first agreed to do that, but afterwards refused on account of its shutting him off from the river. The blacksmith shop was 8x10 and was of no value.

Cross-examined by Mr. Mahaffy
The fence was in danger of having burnt at any time. Fence would be worth about 14 cents a rod. If complainant will build a rail fence, it is liable to be burnt every time.

Defendant convicted and fined $5. Damages $10. Costs $4.70 to be paid forthwith, and in default, defendant to be imprisoned in the common gaol at Bracebridge for 6 weeks with hard labour.

James Boyer, J.P.

Fine $5.00
Damages $10.00
Costs $4.70
Total $19.70
Paid constable $ 2.00

MAGISTRATE'S COURT — JULY 13TH, 1895
BEFORE JAMES BOYER, J.P.
NORMAN WALLACE V JOHN PATTERSON THE YOUNGER, HUGH PATTERSON, JAMES PATTERSON, THOMAS PATTERSON AND WILLIAM McKENZIE

For having, on the 3rd July 1895, at the Township of Stephenson, willfully damaged and injured a certain fence, the property of complainant.

Plea of not guilty.

Norman Wallace sworn

I live on Lot 7, Concession 6, Stephenson, on the south half of the lot. The defendant, John Patterson, lives south half of Lot 6, Concession 6, Stephenson. On the 3rd July last, defendant pulled down the fence between my lot and Patterson's. The fence was put up the day previous. There had been no fence there since April last. Defendant's cattle had been running over the land previous. I had the line between my lot and defendant surveyed on the 8th May 1894. The defendant John Patterson was present on the occasion.

Defendant Patterson said to the surveyor that the line was not right. I notified defendant after the survey that the line was not right. I caused a notice to be served on the defendant and saw it handed to him. No copy of notice kept. It notified defendant to remove his portion of the fence onto the proper line. His portion of the fence was not removed to the proper line.

The surveyor went up on the 2nd July to stake out the proper line, and I put up the fence where he staked it out. Defendant came whilst I was building the fence and said we needn't build the fence, he would throw it down.

Mr. Pope P.L.S. had run a line there about 15 years since. He was employed by me and a Mr. Bailey to run a line but no fence was built on that survey. All defendants were present when the fence was pulled down. It took 7 men about 3½ hours to build the fence. They were Norman Wallace, Arthur Hughes, Gordon Barrager, James Hughes, George Hughes, Solomon Wallace, and Nelson Barrager. The fence was 35 rods of rail fence. It would cost $5 to build it. Defendant's land is cleared where the fence was built.

Cross-examined

I got Lot 7, Concession 6, as located, from the Crown. Have been located about 26 or 27 years. Had the patent 15 or 16 years. Lived on southerly end of lot ever since. Nelson Bailey, the man who located Patterson's lot, was located after me. He lived on Lot 5 and didn't improve Lot 6. John Patterson done the improvements on Lot 6 and went to live on it. I think about 15 or 16 years ago.

The piece adjacent to disputed fence was cleared 14 or 15 years as near as I can tell. My niece on the other side of disputed fence cleared her land about 12 years since. The fence between me and Patterson was put up 3 or 4 years, after he did the clearing. There was no fence put up for some years where Patterson had cleared. He put in hay. My side was partially cleared. The original fence was put on the line Pope ran. It stood over on my lot, facing to Galbraith's survey 45 to 35 feet. Pope, the land surveyor, was employed by Bailey and myself. No fence there before. Built the fence some years after surveyed by Pope. Half each was built by me and John Patterson Jr., who was then living on the lot. He has occupied and cropped the part in dispute ever since, up to the original fence.

We had a dispute about where the fence was built and we referred it to Joseph Weir about 9 years ago last spring as near as I can recollect, about 9 years last May. Weir set some pickets on the old line run by Pope. No fence had ever been built before in that part. We built the fence according to stakes planted by Weir. We built the 35 rods at that time. It stood there ever since till I removed it in April last, after Galbraith's survey, to the line surveyed by him. I built it at my own expense, the 35 rods. He put a crop in on the land in dispute this season, peas and oats. The new fence was put on his crop. I don't think the crop was damaged. The land was cropped by Patterson 4 or 5 years before the fence was built. I am referring now to the land in dispute marked or coloured pink on plan produced.

Re-examined

Mr. Pope started at the corner between Lots 6 and 7 on the concession at the original stake. The stake had figures on it. He didn't take any bearings. He ran it with a theodolite, the same kind of instrument Mr. Galbraith used.

Mr. Mahaffy for defendant raised objection to the jurisdiction of the court on the ground that adverse possession had been proved.

Case dismissed on the ground that defendant, John Patterson Jr., had adverse possession for over 10 years. Complainant to pay his own costs and witnesses, $7.25.

James Boyer, J.P.

Court $2.50
Constable $4.75
$7.25 paid

MAGISTRATE'S COURT — JULY 29TH, 1895
BEFORE JAMES BOYER, J.P.
EDWARD HENRY LIGHTHEART V JOHN A. HILL AND CHARLES MEDLAY

For that defendants on the 29th July 1895, at Bracebridge, did wilfully damage and injure a certain fence, the property of complainant.
Defendants pleaded not guilty.

Hannah Sophia Lightheart sworn
I live across the road from Mrs. Griffith near the stable on the fair ground. Am the wife of Edward Henry Lightheart. Was living there on 20th instant. Myself and little child were there alone on that night. My husband was away and had been for a week. I had been up to town. Got to bed at 11:30. May Wolfrem was with me. I fastened doors and windows after 12 a .m.

I heard someone pushing at the front door. They left and went to woodshed door. They went to the front door again and tried to get in. I woke the girl up. I looked out of the window, didn't see anyone. I hollered for Mrs. Griffith and then for Mrs. Davis. May called her mother. She came. Mrs. Griffith came and asked what was the matter.

The persons had gone round the house. A man came and stood within 12 or 15 feet from where I could see him. He was on my premises. The defendant Hill answers the description by his size and clothing. I saw another man on the place, near the corner of the fence. It was a man in dark clothes. The first one nearest the house walked to where the other was. They stood there for some time and went out where some pickets are broken off, which were not broken after dark that night. I could hear them at the fence. I saw the next day the fence had been broken near where the men stood.

I have seen defendant Hill several times during the last month or two, frequently. He had horses there. It was the first thought came into my mind that it was the defendant. I am reasonably certain defendant Hill was one of the men that came there that night. Have seen defendant Medlay several times. Didn't have as good a chance of seeing him. It was a quarter past 12 a.m.

Cross-examined
It was not moonlight. I could see from my light and a light in Griffiths'. I couldn't swear to Hill's features but I can to his clothes.

May Wolfrem sworn
I live on the hill going down to the hollow in Bracebridge with my mother. I stayed with Mrs. Lightheart on Saturday night, went there at 11 p.m. I went to bed. I was roused up about a quarter past 12 by Mrs. Lightheart. I looked out of the window and saw a man standing outside on the lot near the window. He looked like defendant Hill, he had on a light coat, a light coloured shirt, a soft felt hat, a black one. I yelled for my mother. The man went into the corner of the fence as my mother was coming down. Another man was in the corner of the fence. It was a light (thin) coat.

Caroline Wolfrem sworn
I live in Bracebridge. I know Lightheart. On the 20th instant, I was home at night. My daughter left home at 11 p.m. to go to sleep with Mrs. Lightheart. At a quarter past 12 I heard my girl shout my name. I answered the call and went down there. I didn't see any one there. I saw the fence had been broken.

Elizabeth Davis sworn
I live opposite Lighthearts. On Saturday the 25th instant, at night I heard May Wolfrem shouting. She was at Mrs. Lightheart's.

Case dismissed.

James Boyer, J.P.

MAGISTRATE'S COURT — MAY 26TH, 1896
BEFORE JAMES BOYER, J.P.
STANLEY ASHWORTH V ARTHUR TURLEY AND THOMAS TURLEY

For having, on the 12th of May 1896, at the Township of Stisted, willfully damaged and removed a certain fence then set up and used as part of a boundary line fence.
Defendants pleaded not guilty.

Stanley Ashworth sworn
I live in the Township of Stisted and am the owner of Lots 18 and 19 in the eighth Concession and 19 in the 9th Concession of the Township of Stisted. Arthur Turley is the occupant of Lot 18 in the 9th Concession. There is no road allowance between Concessions 8 and 9, as the road was closed up and the property sold to me by the council in 1886.

There was a fence on the boundary line between my property and the property of the defendant Arthur Turley. I repaired the fence in question last fall. The fence was erected by the former occupant of defendant Turley's lot. Defendant Turley did not contribute anything towards the fence. It was a pine worm fence.

I was away from home on the 12th of May. On the 14th May instant, I noticed that the fence had been moved. The rails were moved onto

Turley's lot, towards the creek. Some were piled up, and some not piled, on defendant's lot.

Taking away the fence left my field and my three lots exposed. There is a hay crop on Lots 18 and 19 in the 8th Concession. Nothing had been said by or to me about moving the fence. I would not undertake to rebuild the fence for less than $15.00. There is no other boundary line fence between us.

Cross-examined by Mr. Ashworth
There was a fence between my property and the concession 66 feet from Turley's. The fence was built before I got possession of the road allowance.

Jesse Thompson sworn
I live in the Township of Stisted and am a merchant there. I was home on the 12th of May and saw Thomas Turley taking the rails off the fence between Lots 18 in the ninth and 19 in the ninth, and I saw Arthur Turley drawing rails away. The fence is now quite removed. The fence on the road allowance was also taken away. I had noticed the fence there about a week before. There were about 20 rods of fence removed as near as I can tell. The fence before removal was a very good fence capable of keeping anything in reason out. The removal of the fence left the lots all open. I should judge it would cost at least $12.00 to replace the fence as good as it was before.

Cross-examined by Mr. Ashworth
I am quite sure that it was Thomas Turley who was moving the fence.

Eva Garside
I live in the Township of Stisted. I know complainant and defendants. I live with Mr. Thompson. On the 12th of May I was out with Mrs. Thompson and saw Arthur Turley drawing the rails away. I saw him drawing two or three loads away and put them down near the creek. I saw the fence before this time. The fence is now taken right away.

For the Defence

Defendant Arthur Turley sworn

The fence surrounded my property. I am removing the fence to put it around a potato patch. I thought I had a right to move the fence as those are my rails. It wouldn't cost five dollars to build a fence there as good as was there before.

Cross-examined by Mr. Mahaffy

I have not built the fence yet. I have got about eight rods built now. I knew that the fence was a line fence between Mr. Ashworth's land and mine. Cattle can come across my place to Mr. Ashworth's fields. I do not know that Mr. Ashworth had put any rails there and did not trouble to ask him. I do not know what pine rails are worth.

Defendants convicted and each fined $2.00 with $6.00 damages and $6.45 costs, and in default, to be imprisoned in the common gaol at Bracebridge for the term of two months.

James Boyer, J.P.

Conviction returned.

Magistrate's Court — June 6th, 1896
Before James Boyer, J.P.
Thomas Dodd v Silas Willoughby

For stealing part of a certain fence at Bracebridge on 4th instant, the property of Alfred Hunt.

The charge having been read to defendant, he pleaded guilty.

Fined $2.00 and $1.00 damages and $4.50 costs, to be paid forthwith, and in default, to be imprisoned in the common gaol at Bracebridge for 21 days.

James Boyer, J.P.

Paid.

Paid constable $3.00

Paid Mr. Hunt $1.00 damages

Conviction returned.

MAGISTRATE'S COURT — JUNE 11TH, 1896
BEFORE JAMES BOYER, J.P.
JAMES E. MILLER v THOMAS SHANNON

For having, on or about the 3rd day of June A.D. 1896, erected and built a certain wire fence contrary to the bylaws of the Township of Monck, thereby doing damage and injury to a certain cow the property of the informant.

The charge having been read to defendant, he pleaded not guilty.

Mr. Palmer for complainant

Mr. Johnson for defendant

Wm. H. Spencer sworn

I am the clerk of the Township of Monck. I produce original Bylaws 149 and 154 relating to building wire fences in the Township of Monck. I also produce Bylaw 199 of that Township imposing penalties for breach of bylaws. Each bylaw is signed by the reeve and clerk and is under the seal of the corporation.

Bylaw 149 regulates the height and width between the wires of wire fences, height to be 4½ feet, posts not more than 16 feet apart, space between wires not more than 6 inches for a height of 2½ feet from the ground. It was passed 30th June 1883. Bylaw 199, passed 15th December 1888, imposes penalty of not less than $1 nor more than $20 to be levied by distress, and in default, imprisoned, not more than 21 days. Each of said bylaws is in force.

James E. Miller sworn
I am a farmer living in Monck on Lot 1 Concession 2. Defendant is living on Lot 1 Concession 1, the adjoining lot. My share of the division line fence is a rail fence, except about 20 rods which is a plain wire fence. Defendant has recently attempted to put up a fence on his share, posts about 8 feet apart, with 3 strands of barbed wire. Most of it is 3½ feet high, some not over 2 feet. There is no scantling or pole on top of it. It has been up a week or 10 days. There are no poles or scantling on the ground. It is mostly built through hazel bushes. Cattle could not see it. I was pasturing a cow in that field. The cow, with some others, was there. She jumped a log fence and ran against the wire fence. It was about 30 feet from the log fence.

Cross-examined
I should say the fence was finished, as defendant had not worked at it for 8 or 10 days. There was no dog there when the cow jumped the fence.

Frederick Miller sworn
I am the son of the last witness. We were piling wood. The cow got in the field. I tried to head her off. She jumped the log fence and ran against the wire fence, breaking the top wire and forcing the staples out. Wire fence is about 3½ feet high, no top rail on it.

Cross-examined
Didn't see any one working there last Saturday. I didn't frighten the cow. I had no dog there.

William James Andrews sworn
The cow in question is my cow. She was torn. I saw the fence on Sunday. It

was a barbed wire fence of 3 strands varying from 4 feet to 2 feet in height. The fence could not easily be seen in some places on account of bushes.

Wm. Ball sworn
The barbed wire fence is a division line between my land and the land occupied by defendant. I first saw it on the 7th instant. I didn't know there was a fence there till that time.

For the Defence

Thomas Shannon sworn
I am the defendant and am the occupant of parts of Lot 1, 2, 3, Concession 1, Monck. I was looking after the building of the fence in question for Mr. Lount. It was started a week ago last Tuesday. I sent men to work at it last Saturday. They had been working at it up to that time. They haven't worked on it this week. Monday and Tuesday were wet days. Was served with summons on Tuesday evening. There was no top protecting. I had arranged with the men to put on the poles last Friday or Saturday.

Cross-examined.
The posts were put up a week ago last Monday. I didn't know how many strands of wire were required. Run the fence nearly along the 3 lots.

Bert Hughley sworn
I know Fred Miller. I saw him last Saturday night. I had conversation with him. He said the cow got into the hay field. He went after her. She jumped over a log fence and ran against the wire fence.

Robert Robinson sworn
I helped build the fence. I worked at it last part of last Saturday afternoon.

Defendant told me whilst I was working there he was getting some boards to put on the fence. I agreed with him on Saturday last to put a top on it. That was in the afternoon.

Cross-examined.
I helped put up the wire, 3 strands of them. We didn't have the boards to put up. We began on Tuesday, finished putting up the wires on Thursday.

Defendant convicted and fined $1 and $3.60 costs, to be paid forthwith, and in default, to be levied by distress, and in default of sufficient distress, to be imprisoned in the lock up at Bracebridge for 14 days.

James Boyer, J.P.

Conviction returned.
Conviction appealed from.

In this case, for which both complainant and defendant were represented by counsel, the appeal would have gone to Muskoka District Court. No record of the appeal has been located.

MAGISTRATE'S COURT — JUNE 11TH, 1896
BEFORE JAMES BOYER, J.P.
WILLIAM BALL v THOMAS SHANNON

For that defendant, on or about the 5th of June A.D. 1896, at Monck, did erect and build a certain wire fence contrary to the bylaws of the Township of Monck.
Defendant pleaded not guilty.
The counsel for defendant consented that the evidence in the last case shall be considered as taken in this case.

Defendant convicted and fined $1 and $3.60 costs, to be paid forthwith, and in default, to be levied by distress, and in default of sufficient distress, to be imprisoned in the lock-up at Bracebridge for 14 days (not to run concurrent).

James Boyer, J.P.

> Constable $2.75
> Court $3.30
> Witness $1.15
> Total $7.20
> Half in each case $3.60
> Conviction returned.

This conviction was also appealed.

Magistrate's Court — May 7th, 1898
Before James Boyer, J.P.
John M. Patterson v Caroline Hughes and James Hughes

For that defendants, on the 3rd day of May 1898, at Stephenson, did assault and beat complainant.

Defendants pleaded not guilty.

Mr. O.M. Arnold for prosecutor
Mr. Ashworth for defendants

John M. Patterson sworn
I am a farmer and live in Stephenson Township on Lot 6, Concession 6. On May 3rd instant, I went across my land to the road. I took down a fence on the land I recently bought from Arthur Hughes by the north

half of Lot 6, Concession 6, 50 acres except a small portion conveyed to Township of Stephenson for a road.

Defendant James Hughes came and told me he wanted me to leave the fence alone as it belonged to his mother. I said I had bought and paid for it and had the deed. He threw off his coat and swore he would make me. Defendant Caroline Hughes came running up and said, "Jim strike him, knock his brains out, kill him, do just as Mahaffy told you. And if you can't I can." She picked up a club, got over the fence and struck at me. I had a fence rail in my hand. I raised it to protect my head and to ward off the blow and I understand it struck her on the hand. Jim Hughes got another club and they both struck me.

I said to Jim, "Confound you, I'll knock your head off." I went for him and he ran. Nelson Barrager and Mrs. Wallace came for to assist the others. I thought they would mob me and I backed away. Mrs. Hughes struck at me as I passed her. I caught the club and held it whilst I walked back to the bridge.

Nelson Barrager came running up. Mrs. Wallace came up, ran at me and said, "By Jesus Christ. I can lick you myself," and slapped me in the face. I took hold of her hand and asked her to be civil.

Cross-examined
I didn't strike at Mrs. Hughes with the rail. It was about 12 feet long.

Jane Ann Patterson sworn
I remember 3rd May. My husband went and took down the rails. Jim Hughes forbid him doing so. My husband said he hadn't bought the property. Mrs. Hughes came out with a club and said, "Knock him down, smash his brains out. And if you can't do it I can." She said, "Kill him. If you can't do it I can." When she was getting over the fence she struck at my husband with the club. I screamed for help.

A young man named Bennett was passing. A younger son of Mrs. Hughes came up with a club. Jim Hughes struck at my husband's head with a club. He put up his arm to save his head and was struck on the arm. Mrs. Hughes struck my husband. He only used the fence rail to ward off the blow. I saw Barrager shake his fist and swear at my husband.

Cross-examined

I was about 6 rods away when it commenced. Mrs. Hughes struck at my husband before she got over the fence.

Richard Bennett sworn

I was passing on the 3rd May last. I saw James Hughes strike at Patterson. He struck him on the head or shoulder. I passed on along the road.

Cross-examined

I saw Patterson running after James Hughes after Hughes struck him.

Emma Patterson sworn

It was a fight between father and defendants. Defendants had club. They struck Pa.

For the Defence

Caroline Hughes sworn

I am one of the defendants. On the 3rd May, Patterson was removing the fence. I sent James down to stop him. I afterwards went down to them, came to the fence and tripped over it, had nothing in my hand. As I was getting up he struck me on the wrist with a stick. Defendant James Hughes got over the fence and struck at Patterson.

Defendants then ran after Jim and chased him with his club. He then came back and backed up to the fence at the bridge. I followed him. I struck at him after he struck me, but missed him. Jim only struck him once. Barrager and Mrs. Wallace then came up. It's not true that I struck him. He had a rail in his hand. He dropped it and picked up a stick.

Cross-examined
My son struck Patterson. I struck at him with my hand. I had no stick.

James Hughes sworn
I told Patterson to quit taking down the fence. He wouldn't. I took off my coat and said, "If you are a better man than me, you won't quit taking it down." Mother came down. She had no stick in her hand. She told me to lick him. She stumbled in getting over the fence. Patterson struck her with a stick. I jumped over the fence and struck him with a stick. He ran after me. He went back to the bridge. Mother followed him.

Margaret Trusetter sworn
I saw Patterson and Mrs. Hughes about 4 on the afternoon of 3rd May. I saw him taking the rails off. The son came and forbid him doing so. Mrs. Hughes then came down. She picked up a stick as she went. She fell as she was getting over the fence. He, Patterson, dropped the rail, picked up a stick and hit her on the hand. Jim ran and picked up a stick. Mrs. Hughes picked up a stick and struck Patterson. I don't know if the blow reached him. He backed up to the bridge. There was a number of sticks there.

Nelson Barrager sworn
I remember the 3rd of May last. On that day I saw Patterson taking rails down off the fence. Jim Hughes came and ordered him to stop. He said he wouldn't. Mrs. Hughes came down and went to get over the fence and fell. As she was rising he struck her with a club. Thereupon Jim Hughes struck Patterson. Then Patterson chased Jim with the club. Hughes backed up until he got over the fence. The club was about three or four feet long and about 6 inches around. Patterson did not strike her until she came over the fence.

Cross-examined by Mr. Arnold
Mrs. Hughes had a club too. She struck at Patterson but I am not sure if she struck him or not.

Fined $1 and costs $4.00, to be paid forthwith, and in default, to be imprisoned in the common gaol at Bracebridge for 21 days and to enter into their own recognizance to keep the peace for 12 months.

James Boyer, J.P.

Paid and recognizance entered into.
Paid constable.
Conviction returned.

Magistrate's Court — May 7th, 1898
Before James Boyer, J.P.
John M. Patterson v Lucy Wallace

For having, on the 3rd day of May, at the Township of Stephenson in District of Muskoka, unlawfully assaulted and beaten said John M. Patterson.

Defendant pleaded not guilty.

The evidence of John M. Patterson in the case of *John M. Patterson v. Caroline Hughes and James Hughes* to be taken as evidence in this case by consent.

Jane Ann Patterson sworn

I saw Mrs. Wallace on the 3rd of May instant. She slapped my husband in the face. My husband put up his hand and said, "Oh no, Mrs. Wallace, I won't touch you." She followed us down to our bridge.

Cross-examined by Mr. Ashworth

My husband had a club in his hand at the time.

Emma Patterson sworn

Corroborated evidence of previous witness. I did not see Mrs. Trusetter at all.

For the Defence

Nelson Barrager sworn
I am sure that Mrs. Wallace did not strike Mr. Patterson. She went up to him and said, "Johnny Patterson I could lick you myself." She shook her hand at him but did not touch him. I then went away.

Caroline Hughes sworn
Mrs. Wallace did not strike Patterson. She told him he was getting his pay for taking our land, and said, "You're no man for striking my daughter." Mrs. Patterson said, "John, has she hit you? Yes, she's hit you. I am witness to it."

James Hughes sworn
I was about 20 feet from Patterson. Mrs. Wallace did not strike him.

Margaret Trusetter sworn
Mrs. Wallace did not strike Patterson. She shook her hand at him and said, "I can lick you in two minutes." I was about 15 or 20 rods away. I was at Mrs. Wallace's kitchen.

Defendant sworn
I shook my hand at Mr. Patterson and said, "I can lick you in two minutes because you hit my daughter and took my land." I did not hit him.

James Boyer, J.P.

Case dismissed with costs $2.60.

Magistrate's Court — May 7th, 1898
Before James Boyer, J.P.
Caroline Hughes v John M. Patterson

For having, on the 3rd day of May, at the Township of Stephenson in the District of Muskoka, unlawfully assaulted and beat the said Caroline Hughes and James Hughes.

Defendant pleaded not guilty.

By consent the evidence taken in the case of *Patterson v Caroline Hughes and James Hughes* be considered as evidence in this case.

Case dismissed with costs.

James Boyer, J.P.

Costs $2.60.

Magistrate's Court — July 11th, 1898
Before James Boyer, J.P.
Alfred Stunden v James Nelson

For that defendant, on 6th July 1898, at Bracebridge, did unlawfully and wilfully commit damage and injury to a certain fence, the property of John Ewart Lount.

Defendant pleaded not guilty.

Alfred Stunden sworn

I am a constable for the District of Muskoka. On the 6th of July instant, between 7 and 8 p.m., I saw defendant rip off a picket from the fence of Mr. J. Ewart Lount. A large number of pickets have been taken and destroyed from the fence. The damage to get a new picket would be 25 cents.

Fined $1.00 and 25 cents damages and $3.25 costs, to be paid forthwith, and in default, defendant to be imprisoned in the common gaol at Bracebridge for 21 days.

James Boyer, J.P.

Committed to gaol, and afterwards paid.

Conviction returned.

Chapter Twenty-Six

CONTESTED LOGS

Once Muskoka was opened to logging in the 1850s and human settlement in the 1860s, the district witnessed a surge of economic activity. With it came hazards and conflicts.

The hard and dangerous work included clear-cutting the deep stands of white pines with hand-powered crosscut saws. Teamsters with sweating horses pulled record-setting loads of logs out of the bush along hilly winter logging roads. Rivers clogged spring and summer by log drives obstructed early steamboat navigation. River drovers drowned or were crushed to death falling between logs, and died dynamiting log jams at waterfalls.

Homesteaders and loggers competed over ownership of logs, even as they supported and depended on each other. Impoverished settlers rebelled at the Catch-22 of paying the provincial government its stumpage fees on trees they felled, because they were legally required to clear the land for farming in order to qualify for the provincial government's "free" grant of land ownership.

By the 1890s Muskoka's forests had already been heavily logged, but forestry remained an important industry and the area's waterways remained integral to the lumbering economy. Here, drovers pose with their pike poles while assembling a boom to be tugged to Gravenhurst's sawmills. When loggers, drovers, and rough shantymen visited Bracebridge's taverns and women, they sometimes ended up in Magistrate's Court.

Land use policies of the provincial government promoted heavy cutting in the forests because wood was needed by North American and British markets, and because timber concession fees and stumpage royalties filled Ontario's coffers. Clear-cut logging was also fostered by the policy that, because Muskoka was deemed suitable for agricultural development, lumbermen removing trees would facilitate farming.

In the first decades of "opening up" Muskoka, most timbering conflicts were between homesteaders and loggers, neither of them much helped by incompatible rules emanating from different departments of the same provincial government. With the logging boom ended by the 1890s, conflicts about logs and lumber, as these two cases show, then arose between settlers themselves.

Magistrate's Court — April 22nd, 1895
Before James Boyer, J.P.
James Thomas Colson v Harry D. Jackson and Thomas Jackson

Assault and battery at township of Draper on or about March 30th last.
The charge having been read to defendants, they severally pleaded not guilty.

Mr. A.A. Mahaffy for the prosecution

James T. Colson sworn

I live in Draper. Defendants are my nephews. On or about March 30th, last Saturday, I was working on the side line between 9 and 10 a.m., digging saw logs out of the snow. My son was with me. I had been there some time. Defendant Thomas Jackson came there and asked what I was doing. I said he could see. The other defendant then came and asked the same question and said I had better get out of that. I refused to go. Defendants said they were their logs.

Defendant Tom Jackson came and took hold of me by the shoulders and tried to push me away. The other defendant then caught me by the throat and got me down and held me down, and threatened to murder me. Tom Jackson then caught hold of my boy. They kept me down about 10 minutes, and was on top of me trying to choke me. I didn't strike either of them. I then got up and went on with my work. About 10 minutes after, Tom Jackson took hold of me again and pushed me around.

I said, "I can't stand this" and went away. I went to the house. I saw Adam Crozier and called him. I met defendant on the road near the clearing. I asked them what they had to say. They said they had said all they had to say. I had a sore throat for about 2 weeks from the assaults. Defendant Harry D. Jackson raised his axe, swung it over my head and threatened to murder me.

Cross-examined by defendant Harry Jackson
I did not push Tom first. You touched me before I touched either of you. I did not raise any weapon at all. I had a shovel in my hand when you took hold of me. I did not have a pistol that day.

Thomas Colson sworn
I was with my father at the time. He was digging out the log. Tom Jackson came first. Harry was behind. Tom asked father what he was doing. Father said, "You can see." Both told him to go and leave the logs, which they claimed. Tom jumped in the hole behind my father. I caught him by the shoulders. He tried to push father out.

I stepped in to make him let go and Harry jumped in. Tom had me down, and Harry had father down on his back and held him by the throat. I didn't see any one strike a blow. We were down about 10 minutes. Harry got hold of the axe. Tom got hold of father and Harry raised the axe within 6 inches of father's head. Father didn't attempt or threaten to strike either of defendants with the axe. Harry threatened to strike father with the axe. When father got to the house some of his whiskers were pulled out. His throat was bruised.

Cross-examined by Harry Jackson
You said you would murder Father when you had him down.

Adam Crozier sworn
Mr. Colson called to me. I went with him to where defendants were. I didn't see anything of the assault.

For the Defence

Thomas Jackson, defendant, sworn
I saw Mr. Colson and his son going with an axe and 2 shovels where I saw him at work at the edge of the road. I heard some chopping and thought it

was in our bush. My brother and myself went to see what it was.

I went first and saw what they were doing. I said they had no business to take them. I said, "I'll wait a while and see if you will go, and you'll have to go." I put my hand on his shoulder and said, "You had better go."

He raised the shovel and said, "You get out of here." He then put down the shovel and took up the axe. He was coming at me, and my brother took the axe from him and put him down. Complainant's son jumped on my back. I dropped down on top of him. I held him down after struggling some time.

Complainant got up on his feet. He came to me and clawed at me. I had to ward off his blows. He went away and I let his son get up. I waited to see if they would go. He said something about my sister. I went up and took him by the throat and set him down in the snow.

Cross-examined

The logs are not ours, nor complainant's. I am not in any township office, but complainant is pathmaster for the township. The logs are on the side road and belong to the township.

Harry D. Jackson sworn

There is a small deviation from the side road. It sounded as if someone was chopping in our bush. I went round by the travelled road. My brother went by the original road and got there first. The deviation is made on our lots and complainant's.

When I got there I saw Tom Colson and my brother wrestling. I threw my axe on the edge of the side road. I saw complainant reach over the log for his axe. He said, "I'll soon settle this business." I took hold of him. I may have caught him by the throat. In the skirmish I got my face badly scratched up. I don't know how it happened. Neither my brother or myself hold any township office.

Cross-examined

It was complainant that scratched my face in the scuffle.

Adam Crozier recalled
I saw Harry D. Jackson soon after it took place. He had one scratch on his face below the eye. That was all I saw.

Defendants convicted and fined $1 and costs $2.50 each, to be paid forthwith, and in default, to be imprisoned in the lock-up at Bracebridge for one month, and to enter into recognizance in $100 to keep the peace towards complainant for 12 months.

James Boyer, J.P.

Paid.
Recognizance entered into.

MAGISTRATE'S COURT — APRIL 22ND, 1895
BEFORE JAMES BOYER, J.P.
HENRY D. JACKSON V JAMES T. COLSON

Cross summons in above case.
Dismissed with costs $1.35.

James Boyer, J.P.

Conviction returned.

MAGISTRATE'S COURT — OCTOBER 4TH, 1897
BEFORE JAMES BOYER, W.H. SPENCER, S. BROWN, J.P.s
JOHN GIBBS V ROBERT LEISHMAN

Assault and battery at Bracebridge on September 30th last.
Defendant pleaded not guilty.

John Gibbs sworn

On September 30th about 7 p.m. I went to Mr. Leishman's and asked for him. Defendant said he wasn't home. I then told defendant I wished to speak to him. He said, "What you have to say, say it here." I said I wanted a re-measurement of my lumber, and that I had a man to look after it.

Defendant said the lumber had been measured and added, "Get out of here or I'll put you out." Defendant rushed at me and knocked me down. A number of persons rushed in. I was knocked senseless. When I came to myself, defendant was dragging me along the passage and beating me. I said, "What are you doing it for. For God's sake don't kill me."

Defendant used an oath and said, "I'll beat your brains out for the abuse you gave the old man last night." He dragged me outside and dashed me against the sidewalk. The contusions on my face were caused by the defendant.

Cross-examined by Mr. Mahaffy for defendant.

I was at Leishman's the evening before and Mr. Leishman and myself had some hot words. I said he had stolen my lumber. I had charged him with cutting the ends off the lumber before.[1] I didn't put up my hands to fight or attempt to take my coat off. I had no marks on my face before he struck me.

Joseph Ball sworn

I was at Leishman's when Gibbs came that night. I saw Gibbs go in and heard loud talking in the small room adjoining the bar. Gibbs and defendant were talking about logs. Gibbs said they had cut the ends off. Defendant denied it and told Gibbs to go, and said if he didn't go out he would put him out.

Gibbs said defendant couldn't put him out. I heard some scuffling and saw Gibbs on the floor in the hall with his face downwards. Defendant told him several times to go out and then caught him by one of his heels

---

[1] Ownership of logs was indicated by hammering a metal brand against the end to score it with a distinctive mark. Like cattle without a brand, logs in a river or a sawmill yard can be commingled and lost track of in the absence of such marking.

and dragged him out and left him on the platform outside the front door. Gibbs came in shortly after and went into the washroom. I didn't notice any marks on Gibbs' face when he came in. I saw defendant give Gibbs one or two slaps. There was blood in the passage way.

Cross-examined

I heard defendant ask Gibbs to leave the house several times, and he refused to go, and used abusive language.

For the Defence

Defendant sworn

On the night in question I was in charge of the hotel. Gibbs came in between 8 and 9 p.m. I was in the bar. Defendant told me he had brought a man to measure the lumber. I said it had been measured and he had the bill of it, and I told him that I wouldn't measure it again, but he could have who he liked to measure it. I asked him to leave, and told him to leave, and asked him a third time. He said none of the Leishmans could put him out. He said, "You dirty little scamp. You cut the marks off my logs and I stood and looked at you."

I said, "I didn't cut the mark off." He said I was a God-damn liar and I couldn't put him out. He put his hands up and tried to strike me. I struck him in self-defence, and shoved him out. He fell on his hands and I gave him a slap or two and drew him out by the heels. He again came and asked for his hat. He came in to wash himself as his nose was bleeding. No one else struck him. He wanted to shake hands. He has made a disturbance three times this summer.

John McDonald sworn

I was at the Albion Hotel on September 30th as a guest. Gibbs came in about 8 o'clock. I was talking to defendant. Gibbs asked defendant to come to him. He refused and told his brother not to give him a drink.

Gibbs accused defendant of sawing the ends off timber. Defendant denied it and told Gibbs to leave the house and not make a disturbance. He refused to go out and called defendant a liar and put up his fists to strike defendant, who again ordered him to leave.

Defendant walked to him and struck him but Gibbs struck at Leishman first. I then saw Gibbs on the floor. He said to Leishman "I'll make you suffer for this." The defendant again asked him to leave and said, "I don't want a disturbance. You raised a disturbance last night." Defendant caught him by the foot and drew him to the veranda. Gibbs was able to leave if he had wished. He was using bad language.

Case dismissed with costs $3.35 to be paid forthwith, and in default, to be levied by distress, and in default of sufficient distress, 14 days in Bracebridge gaol.

James Boyer, J.P.

Paid.

PART III: CURTAIN DOWN, CURTAIN UP AGAIN

Magistrates Court. Nov 27th 1895 Dec 3d 1895

Before James Boyer JP.

Thomas Dodd } For that Deft on the 2d Dec 1895 at the Town
       v } of Bracebridge is a loose idle or disorderly
William Fraser } person not havg any visible means of
maintaining himself did live without employment.

The charge having been read to Prisoner he pleaded
not guilty

Thomas Dodd sworn.

      I am Constable & Nightwatchman
of Bracebridge. On Sunday morning at 10 minutes past
12 a M. I saw Prisoner pushed out of Binyons. Binyon
asked me to take him away. I was going to meet the
train and couldnt do so. As I returned from the station
I saw a man on the sidewalk opposite Thomas St.
He fell down. I watched him awhile. He went as far
as Hidds hotel and tried to get in and then went
towards the British Lion. He fell two or three times
and fell off the platform at British Lion and crawled
towards the Sheriffs office. I took hold of him. I took
him to the Lock up but as the Gaoler wouldnt take
him without a warrant I put him in the fire Hall to
keep him from freezing. The night before last I again
found Prisoner in the fire Hall about ¼ past 10 very
much under the influence of liquor. He fell against
a ladder. I let him remain there that night. Last night
shortly after 10 o'clock I again found him in the Fire
Hall sleeping. The Reeve told me to have him arrested
Prisoner told me he had no money, nor no home.

Chapter One

NEW PLAYERS, SAME OLD SCRIPTS?

The 1890s was a time in Muskoka when abandoned women raised their children alone, people found it hard to make ends meet, laws to protect human health were circumvented, drivers menacingly enraged one another on the roadways, men drank alcohol and got into fights, employers dragged their feet about paying workers, prostitutes served the community, items disappeared through thievery, and laws to prevent water contamination were ignored.

Our present-day scene, adjusted for clothing styles, equipment, and perhaps the attitude of the actors, suggests human nature may not change much, that we just re-enact age-worn scripts, our contemporary performances propelled by timeless permutations of pride, envy, fear, anger, avarice, lust, vengeance, poverty, madness, love, idealism, and injustice.

Yet, since the 1890s, much *has* changed. Our population has multiplied many times over, bringing new social organization and different structures for governance, adding new demands on resources, and shifting expectations.

With the imaginative application of inventions from the twentieth- and twenty-first centuries, yesterday's science fiction is now reality. Transportation, communications, economic activity, commercial enterprise, health care, and environmental awareness, not to mention financial relationships, educational systems, forms of entertainment, sports, the nature of news reporting, and the wraparound role of government in all its forms, has each been transformed, several times over, since the end of the nineteenth century. Despite the familiarity of these human vignettes, life in 1890s Canada is a foreign country to our eyes. In fundamental ways, the framework itself has been revamped.

A Reconfigured Framework

The Muskoka venue itself has changed, in tandem with the rest of the modern world.

Huntsville playwright Stina Nyquist set her play about pioneer days, *The Raspberries Came in Haying Time*, among Muskoka's waters and the timberlands "in an era when joys were simple and the reality harsh; when people, animals and plants were closely bonded; when faith, humility and perseverance were necessary for contentment and survival." Her saga of families "who dream and struggle, rejoice and suffer, while constantly being challenged by a difficult climate and a poor soil" could not be set in today's Muskoka, with its good year-round roads and reliable vehicles, electric appliances, sports complexes, imported food, improved clothing, government support services, consolidated schools, modern hospitals, and its connections to a global communications network.

Bracebridge writer Andrew Wagner-Chazalon describes in *Muskoka Traditions* how the district has been "growing and changing, making long-time residents sometimes wonder where it is heading. The cottages and boats grow bigger and more numerous every year, and many of the traditional ways of life seem to be fading into memory."

Secondly, the framework today is also different because a positive role for government emerged during the twentieth century. The 1890s marked a high point of the "laissez-faire" philosophy: a let-it-be approach to economic activity and a hands-off attitude to social conditions. Government's response to the challenges of the day was mostly confined to erecting institutions to house society's problem people — jails, prisons, orphanages, and asylums. Hospitals were few, mostly privately owned or church operated. Schools were small, simple, scattered, and locally funded. Colleges, where the few existed, were often operated by religious denominations. Today's regulatory state has supplanted that minimalist approach, inspired by an interventionist ideology that witnessed the introduction of legal protection for consumers, investors, patients, workers, the environment, and most other realms of commerce and human enterprise.

Companion to that earlier laissez-faire approach was a tough-love outlook that was nothing like today's empathizing humanism. From the problem of a working man struggling to recover unpaid wages in the context of a barter economy's set-offs and uncertain rates of pay, to the harder question of finding fault between fighting spouses, or of requiring an indigent man to give financial support for his children, James Boyer rendered judgments reflective of a time when people were allowed to be educated without sentiment in "the school of hard knocks." In that decade, support to the indigent was provided, if at all, by families, churches, and the fraternal societies a person belonged to; today, support under many government assistance programs provides help to individuals who are in poverty, living with disability, or in need of medical services. Workers then had to take their employers to court for unpaid wages, and to recover financial compensation for injuries sustained while on the job; today, a Labour Relations Board and the Workers' Compensation program are the workplace reality. In the 1890s women abandoned penniless with their children had no choice but to sue in Magistrate's Court for redress; today, a legal regime for support payments is part of the system, and community and social services flow from government agencies to support mothers and children in need.

Hand in hand with the more interventionist role for government has come changing attitudes about what protections the law should provide and what freedoms it ought to guarantee. These are not minor adjustments but tidal changes in social, cultural, political, scientific, and economic life that have caused community attitudes to ebb and flow during the decades since the 1890s. As these newer attitudes have become codified into laws, they have continued to cause society's transformation, as well as being its effect. Thanks to attentive ongoing law reform in Canada, the enacted rules that courts now enforce mostly tend to be in phase with the society they govern, having largely emanated from it. Therefore, while some of these timeless human dramas, as captured from 1890s Muskoka, would play out much the same way in today's courtroom venues, many others simply could not, because of the altered values within which the justice system operates.

Sociologists look at the aggregate patterns of society to discern its "norms," those patterns of human conduct that are repeated often enough to seem normal rather than deviant, behaviours that become established over time as the accepted, and acceptable, way of doing things. Social scientists also identify "mores" (customs or conventions regarded as essential to a community, or characteristic of it) that are the higher-level values that influence normative behaviour. Society's norms and mores sooner or later become codified into laws, as shown by the transformation from the 1800s to present-day Canada. Being expressed in laws elevates norms and behaviours to a new status, where they are no longer just social patterns of behaviour but rules to be enforced on the "abnormal," the rule breakers. In this fashion, imposing such rules and determining the fates of offenders becomes part of Canada's civilized way of keeping society functioning "normally" according to the rule of law. What had once been social pressure for conformity now entails legal requirement for compliance. The instrument is law enforcement. Judges are pivotal to this process, for it is they who must, case by case, every step of the way, calibrate the community's tolerances, and either toss a case out or impose sanctions.

This process of making new laws moved into high gear as the twentieth century advanced and Canadian society's issues became more complex and our mores evolved. In the dynamic North American setting where "change" is worshipped upon a high altar, many of the beliefs, values, and behaviours that suited one era became incompatible, useless, and even counterproductive in following ones. Laws that had codified norms of behaviour and social standards for a horse-and-wagon age increasingly fell out of phase with the new realities of a world centred on motor vehicles, television, jet aircraft, space stations, and the internet.

While some of this revision of law took place in the hands of law reform commissions and legislatures implementing their recommendations, ongoing adjustment between law and society also occurred in the daily contentions of individuals struggling to make sense, first, of what they must do, and second, of which rules they thought bound them. Magistrate's Court was one venue among many where this evolution of Canadian society took place. It happened through continuous interaction between those pushing against laws and those deciding where the limits of law really lay, not abstractly but in real peoples' lives in specific Canadian communities. Everyone had, and has, a share in this project, because only when a law is pushed to its limits, and others push back, does it become clear whether it is still fair, or functional, or, above all, just.

In 1890s Bracebridge, as elsewhere across Canada, the testing of law's limits contributed incrementally to those changes that the twentieth century would usher in. Harsh experiences brought to light in Magistrate's Court more than a century ago contributed both to society's understanding of social and economic problems and to evolution in Canadian law and legislated responses. Cases in this book were the tips of larger icebergs, and those who experienced or witnessed the deeper conditions giving rise to them included activists and reformers creating "movements" for greater justice, pushing for improvements that seemed like lost causes at the time but which, over the decades, became victories.

The transformative effect of these general developments was felt at ground level. By government taking a more active role in social and economic realities, the specific legal context for these human dramas expanded widely through statutes, regulations, and the Charter of Rights and Freedoms. Enactment of new regimes in the Highway Traffic Act, the Environmental Protection Act, and the Young Offenders Act, and many dozens more, put in place rules that were absent in the 1800s. This revamped framework results not only in different outcomes, but in different processes to get there. The single largest contributor to James Boyer's workload as JP, labour relations cases, saw his 1890s docket mostly involve disputes over unpaid wages. Such issues, though still with us today, occur within a statutory framework that provides a minimum wage level, safety and hygiene rules, limits on hours of work, rules about the age of workers, the right to vacation pay, entitlement to maternity leave and further protections and benefits, as well as government officers to uphold and enforce these laws.

Still, the cases in this book do have a caché of the familiar to them, because comparing the 1890s cases from Magistrate Boyer's court with today's experiences reveals similarities (and differences) that extend beyond the legal system. When Wagner-Chazalon in *Muskoka Traditions* probed more deeply, "it became clear that those traditions remain alive and provide the roots that support so much of life in Muskoka." Alongside wild fields, decrepit barns, and abandoned farm machinery silently rusting in high grass, he portrays a pioneer's smiling great-great-grandson making maple syrup on a homestead farm he still works today. By contrasting "then" and "now," what emerges is a picture of *both* change and continuity.

Evolution of Justices of the Peace

Justices of the peace in Ontario are themselves a perfect example of such continuity and change. The seven-hundred-year evolution of justices of the peace, from England through colonial days and into late 1800s in Ontario as highlighted in Chapter 2 of Part II, underscores the centrality of JPs to the justice system. Given the weight of centuries of tradition, subsequent decades have not altered the fundamentals of this judicial officer, although significant changes do reflect contemporary realities. Ontario JPs are today governed by a revamped Justices of the Peace Act, enacted in 1989 by Ontario's legislature (and since carried into the Revised Statutes of Ontario 1990 as chapter J.4, and amended) a statute that frames how JPs are appointed, hold office, and perform their duties.

While Ontario's justices of the peace long ago lost their administrative powers in local government, their judicial responsibilities remain largely unchanged. Two statutes conferring most powers on JPs are the Criminal Code of Canada and Ontario's Provincial Offences Act. The Code gives jurisdiction in a number of criminal law matters, while the Provincial Offences Act authorizes JPs to additionally adjudicate "regulatory offence" cases. This provides a hefty workload for Ontario's justices of the peace, since it requires them to handle the majority of provincial offences and municipal bylaw prosecutions, ranging from trespassing, liquor violations, traffic offences, and workplace safety, to environmental protection, dog owner's liability, education matters, and parking and noise bylaw violations. Beyond the Provincial Offences Act, other specific Ontario statutes further top up the JPs' workload.

A JP remains the first point of contact for many citizens interacting with the criminal justice system. JPs may assist a member of the public on the requirements to formulate an information in relation to an offence, an "information" being the written document in which a person describes something that has happened so that a criminal proceeding may commence. Apart from ensuring they are done right, the JP also receives informations. JPs preside in bail release hearings, and in most other pre-trial court appearances, such as for remands. They also have authority to issue search warrants.

Whereas JPs in James Boyer's day were appointed for a territory or district within the province, today's justices of the peace have jurisdiction throughout all Ontario. The province has been subdivided into seven regions (Toronto, East, West, Centre East, Centre West, Northeast, Northwest), to which the JPs have been individually assigned, but their jurisdiction itself remains province-wide. A further grouping of "per diem" JPs are assigned specific judicial work. For example, a JP may be designated to exclusively hear cases arising under the Provincial Offences Act, or even just offences under a specific Ontario statute, or only cases arising under a particular act of Parliament. This focus allows for specialization and familiarity with recurring issues, and contributes to efficiency in the administration of justice.

By 2012 approximately 335 justices of the peace are working in Ontario, and knowing such a number is a major change from the late 1800s, when the Attorney General's Office had no idea how many existed. Back then, there was no viable central system for maintaining such a record. Today there is, and its details are widely available on the internet.

Another contrast is found in today's explicit qualifications for those appointed a justice of the peace, and provision for their training. The Justices of the Peace Act stipulates that an Ontario JP, who may be either male or female and should be bilingual, must have a university degree or post-secondary diploma. No minimum age is specified, but the Act artfully says a candidate must have performed paid or volunteer work equivalent to at least ten years full-time experience. There is a maximum age, however. Initially it was seventy-five, the same as for judges, but that was lowered in 2011 to sixty-five, no doubt encouraging for the couple of thousand applicants waiting in line to be appointed.

Reform of the appointments process is a hallmark of the past forty years across Canada, and in the case of Ontario JPs, the drill today begins with an aspirant ensuring he or she is not disqualified. For instance, no one can apply who is a bankrupt, in arrears on family support, or involved in serious, unresolved professional complaints, claims, civil actions, or financial claims.

Once past that hurdle, an aspirant fills out an application form. After the applicant is checked for criminal convictions and security issues, and comes up clean, the application is then reviewed by an independent Appointments Advisory Committee.

This committee's selection criteria offer insight into how JPs are seen today, a sharp contrast to the late 1800s when no such formality existed. For openers, skills and abilities should include sound practical judgment, strong listening skills, computer skills, experience that is relevant and transferable to the work of a JP, high levels of achievement in paid or volunteer work, ability to analyze and make decisions, proficiency in writing and speaking English and French, capacity to work hard without supervision, and knowledge of how to manage time and workload.

Beyond that, criteria also include an understanding of the role of a JP, ability to keep an open mind while hearing all sides of an argument, capacity to handle stress and the isolation and pressures of the judicial role, and the talent of interacting with people in a strong and dignified way. What is more, the advisory committee looks for such personal characteristics in the applicant as politeness, compassion, and empathy and respect for the essential dignity of all persons. Then the candidate is run through a further screen, to select for moral courage, high ethics, patience, punctuality, good regular work habits, ability to wash the family car, a reputation for integrity and fairness, courtesy, and "an absence of pomposity and authoritarian tendencies."

By this point, it may seem this selection-by-committee list covered everything, but not so. "Community awareness" is yet another criterion. This quality includes keen interest in people and humanity, a demonstrated commitment to community service, and "interest in regional and social issues that give rise to cases coming before the courts." The Justices of the Peace Act additionally directs the advisory committee to "recognize the importance of reflecting the diversity of Ontario's population in appointments of justices of the peace."

Despite the difficulty in becoming a JP, there are many who wish to be considered as candidates. Indeed, at one point the advisory committee was receiving many hundreds of applications every time it advertised in its annual, province-wide recruitment process, to the point where in August 2011 some two thousand candidates were in the system. Each application required thorough review, and if the applicant seemed strong, then he or she proceeded to an interview with a panel of four members of the advisory committee. Clearly this was a formula for make-work on a vast scale. It also meant that, even if a candidate was considered highly qualified, he or she would not be appointed until there was an opening. The queue of waiting aspirants was growing very long. A 2011 reform of this over-the-top process now sanely provides that the advisory committee will advertise on its website for applicants only when there is a vacancy to fill.

At the end of its process, the Appointments Advisory Committee classifies each candidate as "highly qualified," "qualified," or "not qualified." Its recommended appointments are provided to Ontario's Attorney General, who then makes the final choices, and the appointment is implemented by order-in-council.

In James Boyer's day, no lawyer could be appointed a justice of the peace. Today's justice of the peace system continues to be "a lay bench," meaning there is no requirement a candidate have legal training or experience in the justice system, although being a lawyer is not expressly a prohibition. Apart from that limitation, JPs in 1800s Ontario were selected by the powers-that-be according to three qualities that likewise influenced appointment of judges in that era: prominence in the community, availability, and being a friend of the government politically. In the 1800s a newly appointed justice of the peace was given no orientation or training program, except what might informally be provided by old hands. Today all new JPs go through a rigorous training and mentoring program before they can preside on their own. Moreover, JPs receive continuing education to enhance their social awareness. They cannot be politically active.

The standards of conduct expected from Ontario justices of the peace today are independence, dedication to the high quality of the justice system, efficiency in the administration of justice, commitment to equality, and a sense of inclusiveness in the judicial system. Any person may make a complaint about an Ontario justice of the peace, which is dealt with by a Review Council established under the Justices of the Peace Act. The Review Council is also mandated to consider questions relating to a JP who has become disabled.

In the 1890s some justices were appointed as stipendiary magistrates, meaning the Department of the Attorney General paid them. Most, however, were remunerated only under an arcane system patched together with (a) some fees from the court fines they levied; (b) possible contributions from the municipality in which they served; (c) the policy that those serving as JPs *ex officio* were already being remunerated in their public positions as mayors, reeves, and game wardens, and (d) who knows what else? Full-time presiding justices of the peace in Ontario in 2011 are paid $116,123 a year. They also get pension and comprehensive benefits, and three weeks of vacation. A JP may not have any other remunerative work.

Conflicts of interest that would jar people's sensibilities today were incomprehensible to James Boyer and the other JPs who served alongside him at the end of the 1800s. They performed numerous entwining roles while giving the rule of law its meaning. Game warden J.H. Willmott sat as a JP with James in a case involving unlawful deer hunting. He himself heard a couple cases in which Boyer family members were witnesses and one in which his nephew stood accused before him. Perhaps they were better qualified to judge such matters, knowing the realities of deer hunting or their own family's particular attributes.

In any event, practical considerations dictated that JPs be in the community and of the community, rather than detached from it. Having part-time JPs was of a piece with elected representatives being engaged only intermittently in their role. Even the first librarians in Bracebridge were part-timers — men like Josiah Pratt, who simultaneously operated a bookstore and jewellery business as well as serving as a JP; and Moses J. Dickie, who at the same time he was librarian dealt in hay and operated an insurance agency. These men knew the communities they represented because that is where they lived, worked, and interacted with others most of the time, making them directly and continuously aware of their community's problems and possibilities.

Twin factors produced this overlap in roles that today would constitute conflicts of interest: many tasks did not require the time they would later consume; and small communities like Bracebridge did not have surplus talent, so people had to double- and triple-up on functions.

Contemporary Canadians, who prize the "arms-length" separation of political and judicial functions, look askance at the American practice of *electing* judges, on the grounds they could be tempted to do what is popular with majority opinion rather than what is just, the two often being mutually exclusive, in order to get re-elected. Yet in Muskoka men sat on the bench in Magistrate's Court who were elected and who would be standing for election again. Although they were running for mayor or reeve, not campaigning to be justice of the peace, the JP role went with the territory and was as inseparable from how their fellow citizens viewed these men as all the other functions they performed in the small community.

All this has changed today. As the rules described above governing contemporary Ontario JPs make clear, they are to have no other remunerative work, nor any partisan involvement. As well, the Municipal Conflict of Interest Act, and other statutes and promulgated rules dealing with ethical conduct of public office holders, show that over the past 120 years we have turned 180 degrees.

Today's justices of the peace, together with provincial court judges, compose the Ontario Court of Justice, one of the province's two trial court systems. At the courthouses where they preside, JPs are gowned. They are distinguished from judges by a green sash over their robes — green being the colour of the commons, which is why green carpets the House of Commons, occupied by the elected representatives of the people, in contrast to the red-carpeted upper chamber whose appointed members lack that representative connection with the people, and whose Senate chamber emerges from an undemocratic tradition of aristocracy. Wearing a green sash is a particular badge of honour in a democratic society.

Specific Crimes and Infractions

Having first reviewed the enlarged and altered legal framework, and then the revamped role of full-time professional JPs, a third lens through which to now see whether new players are merely re-enacting old scripts is the comparison of specific issues over time.

This starts with understanding the dynamic of how laws dealing with public morality draw a line between prohibited and permissible activity. On one side, public morality is codified in the criminal law and upheld by law enforcers, while on the other side, people push beyond the law's stated limits of toleration. The debate between the two factions is about in which direction, and how far, to move the line. Police prosecute practices that challenge the appropriateness of this dividing line, while courts, legislatures, and civil libertarians seek to hold the line or relocate it according to the moral values and political imperatives of the era.

How that line has been held, or shifted, since the 1890s is easily highlighted by specific examples of infractions and crimes. No more stunning contrast could be imagined than between the "blue laws" that kept Ontario closed tight as a drum on the Lord's Day with sports banned, shops closed, and entertainment prohibited, and today's wide-open Sundays.

Almost as significant a change as the recent secularization of Sunday is the dramatic relocation of the contentious dividing line between permitted and prohibited sexual expression. The contrast between puritanical late-Victorian Canada and today's anything-goes attitudes about sex and sexuality dramatizes just how far that line can shift: compare, for example, the Bracebridge bylaws that prohibited swimming without a bathing costume with the current legal right of females to go topless in public in Ontario — a right extended after a court case resulted in a change in the law in 1997. Same-sex marriages are now lawful in the province, while offences pertaining to homosexual relations between consenting adults have been removed from the Criminal Code. The operation of the sex-workers' trade is today in flux, thanks both to court rulings and changes to the Code over the past century. However far it may have been moved, though, the line has not vanished: sexual abuse of children or one's patients remains a crime.

More than a century ago, as now, people charged with infractions pertaining to the sex trade tended to plead guilty, pay their fine, and go quietly back into the night. Practitioners of the illicit arts knew it was better for them to arouse as little public controversy or community ire as possible. Their fine could more quickly be recouped if things settled down quickly and a prostitute could get back to "business as usual." Such fines are tacitly seen as equivalent to the cost of a licence to continue operation, albeit more discreetly, until normalcy returns. At the same time, members of the community's more high-minded and morally uplifted segments, today as in the past, can persuade themselves that reports of such convictions mean law and morality have been upheld. In short, social hypocrisy continues.

When it comes to hunting and fishing, not much appears to have changed: those in law enforcement continue to come down hard on

Canadians who violate ordinances governing sportsmen's catches, although two differences do stand out. No longer are individual citizens able to prosecute such cases and collect part of the fine for their efforts. Removal of the availability of moieties has professionalized law enforcement, but with the cash incentive to privately prosecute violators gone, the number of eyes in the bush has been reduced. The second difference is a product of the advance of technology. Present-day methods for hunting game out of season, or fishing above the legal limit, have accelerated with air-borne hunting, high-velocity firearms, sonar devices, and other electronic tracking equipment, and detection mechanisms to alert sportsmen of the stealthy approach of law-enforcement officers. These significant advantages in technology have helped humans push many species into extinction during the past century. Of course, conservation officers and game wardens have also benifitted from the advance of science and technology. For today's hunters and anglers and those charged with regulating their activities, a larger legal framework for protecting wildlife, from the Convention on Migratory Birds to the Convention on the International Trade in Endangered Species, has altered the juridical and conservation context as the stakes have grown higher. Yet central features of the relationship between people and wild animals displayed in these 1890s cases — the need for food, the thrill of making a kill or a catch, and the desire for a trophy — remain as real today as they were then.

Lack of support payments for mothers raising children in poverty, unpaid wages for workers who toiled in rightful expectation of earning money, operating a business without a proper licence from the government: all of these were issues of the 1890s, and all persist today, despite the presence of more rules and public officers intended to eradicate such issues.

Gambling, which was illegal then, has now been embraced by the state, with government-run gambling such as lotteries and government-licensed casinos, but there are still rules and enforceable restrictions. Offences involving environmental contamination, and dangers to public health from unsafe food, continue as challenges despite the passage of more laws.

Laws governing alcohol have been modified in many ways since the prohibitionist tides reached their greatest heights from the 1890s through the 1920s. Even so, an enforced legal regime remains in place today to govern intoxicating drink as well as mind-altering drugs.

Road rage is a recent term, one that awaited the arrival of fast automobiles and crowded expressways, but the behaviour that underlies it seems to have been around a while. The main difference is that today's road warriors have moved from horse-drawn wagons and sleighs into air-conditioned, tinted-windowed, wrap-around sound, high-speed motor vehicles. Some drivers today shout and scream at other drivers who they must be drunk to act the way they do, giving a middle-finger salute, shaking a clenched fist, blaring a horn, or even using firearms against them. It's hard to see, though, how today's angry drivers are essentially any meaner or more brazen than the Muskoka driver in the 1890s climbing down from his horse-drawn wagon to attack another teamster with a pitchfork in a fight about who should rightfully have yielded road space to the other.

The crime of "vagrancy" still has some faint echoes today, a half-century after the act of being in public without means of support was decriminalized. In the 1890s constables brought indigent drifters before the JP in Bracebridge because they had "no visible means of support." It was additionally part of this Criminal Code offence that the vagrant be without employment and have no abode. Seventy-five years after that, advocates for civil liberties in Canada achieved enough focused public outcry over these draconian vagrancy provisions that Parliament repealed that section of the Code. In the 1960s those seeking to change the law built a case that it infringed civil liberties, pointing to social agencies that did not exist when the vagrancy law was first created and arguing that those agencies now assisted indigent, unemployed, and homeless people.

Even so, the continuing presence of homeless people, despite the far-reaching embrace of Canada's welfare state, is testament to an enduring problem. The country has not become free of drifters, homeless people, and former residents of rashly closed mental institutions. The vagrancy cases have only dried up because "vagrancy" is no longer punishable by law. In fact, an attribute of contemporary Canada is the widespread prevalence of homeless individuals or "street people," and not only in big cities. Some citizens, lacking shelter, perish by exposure in winter. A friend who has survived as a homeless man in Toronto seems resourceful in the same rudimentary way as those earlier Canadians who fended for themselves against nature – his resourcefulness including an attitude that wraps him and his protective cardboard in a cocoon of ironic humour against cold and scorn alike. He describes himself as "independently wealthy." My friend, a learned man in hard times, also employs Albert Camus's words to describe himself as "possessing nothing but serving no one, poverty-stricken but the free lord of a strange kingdom."

Since the 1890s, the welfare state in Canada has come of age, hostels have replaced jails, and the "free lords" have acquired a different legal status. The continued prevalence of down-and-out individuals has led some to ask, "If someone is on the street with no visible means of support in a country with Canada's extensive welfare system, is the individual to blame, or those who designed and operate the benefits and support programs?" By the 1990s, the provincial government in Ontario answered this question by making it an offence under law for someone to panhandle in the streets or to squeegee-wash car windows at intersections in the hope of extracting money from drivers temporarily pinned down by a red light and guilt. The "problem" had not gone away, and those engineering the legal regime have not yet been able to make it fit properly into the proffered solutions. In the longer view of Canadian history, it appears that the legal context may change, but social realities and human characteristics persist.

Spousal abuse is clearly not a new phenomenon. The plight of abused family members, a black eye on contemporary Canadian society, is a disfigurement we've been wearing a long time: the flying frying pans, broken limbs, hungry children, put-upon wives, absence of money, and lack of love were all part of raw life in late nineteenth century Bracebridge and its outlying rural areas. In terms of social outcomes, it is hard to conclude that the rudimentary responses in Magistrate's Court in the 1890s to issues of domestic violence, spousal support, and care of children have improved much over a century. Of course more is being done, from school counselling services and family support programs, to new laws for spousal support and child welfare, and the much-debated registers of sexual offenders. These and other measures today form a truly vast system to deal with the many dimensions of dysfunctional families. Although the methods and venues have changed, the social problems themselves abide. A difference is that the injustices are often less visible because today's landscape of rival and duplicated social welfare agencies and the plethora of administrative structures and government support programs cover them over in a wrap of bureaucratic gauze. Institutionalized responses to such problems in the human community often fail to resolve them and, in significant new respects, sometimes exacerbate them.

On the health front, these 1890s Muskoka cases highlight concern about diseases arising from contamination, especially as a result of the slaughter of animals, but also from humans: a quarantine was imposed on new arrivals carrying a deadly communicable disease to a community. The family quarantined because of its infection with diphtheria, and the death of two children in that family, are a reminder of similar public health risks today. Public health officials, news media, and citizens remain preoccupied with quarantines, as evidenced with the outbreak of SARS in 2003, the mass slaughter of chickens in British Columbia to stop the spread of avian flu in 2004, and the regular recurrence of similar public safety measures in some part of the world every few months. Public disease and epidemics continue to be in the news, usually wrapped in alarmist sensationalism to keep listeners panicked and tuned in to breaking news.

Kids in trouble with the law is a phenomena that continues in Canada today. Although juvenile offenders were plentiful in Bracebridge a century ago, it would be naïve to suggest that "boys will be boys" regardless of their age or the age in which they live. Throwing stones at a sign or riding horses wildly through the main street are light years away from dealing drugs, knifing or shooting someone at school, or invading homes and killing their peaceful occupants. A big shift since the 1890s has occurred in the culture of crime, with the emergence of organized gangs, and in the ways of trying to deal with youthful offenders.

Canadian law has always recognized the twilight zone of responsibility when a child moves along a continuum from the early years of total dependency in infancy toward increasing acceptance of personal responsibility and self-control as an adult. Because law must apply equally to all, the solution was to draw an arbitrary demarcation line between juveniles and adults at such ages as sixteen, eighteen, or twenty-one years. Overnight, just by crossing these legal lines on a birthday, a child became a juvenile, a juvenile an adult. Despite problems of imposing compartmentalized rules and treatment on individuals who in reality mature at different rates, their enforcement became the unhappy lot of magistrates who found young offenders arraigned before them. The Juvenile Delinquents Act, in place for seventy-five years, became increasingly controversial because it came to be seen as too harsh, with youngsters being held for years on indefinite sentences for broadly defined crimes like "sexual immorality." It was repealed and replaced with the Young

Offenders Act, a more tolerant regime that became increasingly controversial because it was seen by many as too lenient in sentencing. Young offenders could not be named by the news media. Issues arose over whether their "adult" crimes warranted trial in adult rather than juvenile court. Under the Young Offenders Act, young murderers were not tried adult court, but still treated as children, or at least not as adults, occupants of a juridicial twilight zone. Many urged that streetwise juveniles needed to encounter a more severe system of justice because of the "adult" nature and seriousness of their crimes.

Redrawing "the line" in the right place had proven hard, especially because the ground itself was shifting. Recent decades spawned gangs of young offenders, female as well as male, and have seen them use new communications technologies to achieve coordination and focus in carrying out criminal acts, all of this evolving within a culture that no longer condemns criminality as it once did, and in many respects even celebrates it. Amidst heated political controversy and social outcry to again change the location of the line, the Juvenile Offenders Act has now replaced the Young Offenders Act. It seeks anew to embrace appropriate sanctions for young criminals, justice for their victims, and protection for society.

In Muskoka District, where James Boyer heard the heart-wrenching stories of families locked in harmful dependence in the 1890s, a Juvenile and Family Court began in the 1950s, the first court of its kind in the province. Gordon H. Aiken, a lawyer in Bracebridge and Gravenhurst, was appointed its first judge in 1954, and rendered innovative service to young people in Muskoka in and out of the Juvenile and Family Court, before himself going on to become Member of Parliament for Parry Sound–Muskoka District. Some of those appearing before Gordon Aiken in the new Juvenile and Family Court were descendants of those who, a couple of generations earlier, had been in James Boyer's Magistrate's Court just a few doors along the same street.

Turning finally to workers, Canada has experienced a huge shift in labour relations over the century since wage-payment cases came before James Boyer. In 1915 introduction of a statutory program for compensation of injured Ontario workers shifted the issue away from the courts, as employees no longer had to sue for damages but instead could submit their claims to the Workmen's Compensation Board. With the growing strength of labour unions in the twentieth century came new laws for safer working conditions and minimum levels of pay, below which no employer could hire. Creation of tribunals such as Labour Relations Boards to adjudicate issues central to the well-being of wage earners was another step forward.

Men who refused to provide "statute labour" in building and maintaining the roads of pioneer Muskoka were given stiff penalties by James Boyer, which was ironic because in his newspaper writings he railed against statute labour as "this antiquated and draconian measure." He believed government should not extract unpaid labour, but should pay road builders under a government contract for doing the work.

Yet despite these and other advances on the labour front, the long-standing plight of workers in a wage economy continues. Goods are kept scarcer than the demand for them, while advertising heightens demand and drives up the cost of items. As well, trend lines give cause for concern. Wage earners unprotected by unions are more numerous in Canada today, in proportion to the overall workforce, than in the 1950s and 1960s. In addition, many problems that once faced low-paid Canadian workers have not gone away, but have merely been exported by large companies that relocate production to low-wage workers in other parts of the world. Some problems have not been resolved, just transferred to new realms.

Such episodes from the lower echelons of the justice system are a small slice of Canadian heritage, a timeless and universal expression of the raw edges found in all human societies. They sketch ways that members of a vital and dynamic community conducted themselves in trying to resolve, or at least contain, economic, social, and cultural conflicts. These shards of lives in turmoil pierced the limits and strained the meanings of "law and order" in sometimes painful, sometimes amusing, and often trite, ways.

Looking from the twenty-first century to the final decade of the nineteenth, one may find in the commonplace something enduring about the nature of humanity, be surprised by certain unchanging elements of society, and discern how uncomfortable facts are often concealed by imprecise or glib references to the past. Even more, one may realize that for all the talk about change in society, there is more continuity than we sometimes acknowledge.

Chapter Two

ADDING UP THE SMALL CHANGE OF HISTORY

In the long view of history, those 1890s Muskokans in trouble with the law were small change. Their dramas no doubt loomed large to those directly involved. But beyond that, most conflicts and misdeeds ventilated in Magistrate's Court were peripheral skirmishes, played out on the tiny stage of a remote Canadian town.

Yet the commonplace can be uncommonly instructive. If merely taken one by one, it is true these small-town episodes were just cameo appearances by bit players, often the downtrodden members of society, *les misérables*. The composite of these individual scenarios, however, presents a revealing montage of Canada's justice system working in the lives of ordinary people during the final decade of the nineteenth century.

Some were hapless victims beset by tribulations and terrors, others robust characters tearing through civilization's thinly painted stage sets. Whoever they were, this unified tableau of their cases presents a view of society not seen by anyone at the time, except, perhaps to some degree, the magistrate who adjudicated and recorded them all.

The troubled souls who appeared in James Boyer's courtroom seldom found themselves in the comfort of an established church. Their recreational sports were frowned upon by society's "better" members and the Criminal Code alike. Many of their wars were fought, not in military uniform or upon foreign lands, but as private battles on home turf against spouses, non-paying employers, game wardens, hygiene inspectors, or fellow down-and-outers in muddy streets around the local taverns.

Many who faced their day of reckoning before the JP were day labourers and scratch farmers from an economic underclass whose lives obeyed Muskoka's hard code of necessity. Muskoka was as harsh in its conditions as it was hardened in its culture. By 1891 two-thirds of the people were dwelling in rural areas, many destitute. No programs of public support helped the indigent or homeless, the abused or abandoned. The era's governing outlook was, rather, that those in poverty were the creators of their own fate, and responsible for it. This Old Testament morality especially influenced the outcomes in cases of individuals charged as vagrants and prostitutes.

If people were forced to be self-reliant, it was because there was no other choice: Canada's welfare state had yet to emerge. It was no aberration that the one quality most abundant in 1890s Muskoka was tough love.

Helpless, impoverished, conniving, frustrated, and exploited members of society encountered enforcement of law and the face of justice in Magistrate's Court, the front line in the battle to establish and maintain the rule of law. "On a daily basis," wrote local historian Grace Barker, people in the late 1800s "suffered discomfort and took risks to a degree this generation can scarcely imagine." In the main, these Muskokans were stern, resolute, plainspoken, and gritty folk, who bore their hardships with dignity and took their pleasures where they could find them.

The resilient qualities of many of these accused persons, which is what, on their bad days, put them in court facing a day of reckoning, also contributed to the pioneer settlement's exhilarating qualities and dangerous vitality. As well, not every case entailed hardscrabble life or unalloyed gloom. Some were so trivial as to be comic. Others portray small human impulses and practices that charm by being ageless. Prankish fun cropped up in the form of an old-fashioned "charivari" — a late-night remonstration by young men outside the home of a newly wed couple — which left most townsfolk smirking, the few prudes who called for prosecution of this "disturbance of the peace" tisk-tisking, and the bemused magistrate trying to maintain appropriate solemnity. The raw life could also be a robust one.

A universal quality appears in the particulars of these people's stories and the role of the local Magistrate's Court, in much the same way that municipal councils around the world face similar issues whatever the country and regardless of whatever political superstructure operates above them. Human society in its local dimension everywhere must come to grips with realities of daily living, from water supply and sewage, to traffic in the streets and products in the shops. Local authorities around the globe must deal with the errant and exuberant behaviours of the individuals who shape their community's contours and push the limits of the law in their streets.

The same tempests and tribulations of humans scrounging to get by in Bracebridge and rural Muskoka in the late 1800s could be found most anywhere in North America during that era, from the drunk evicted at the train station late in the night to the frightened woman pursued by a stalker in Washington who moved to Toronto for safety, only to find that the man she'd hoped to evade had trailed her there, forcing her to relocate to Huntsville in northern Muskoka, where he continued to harass her with alternating proposals of marriage and threats of death. These cases, though fixed in 1890s Muskoka, transcend time and place as universal stories.

A justice of the peace in Canada does not get the momentous state trials that settle, or at least confront, deep divisions in the constitutional order or fundamental values of the state. Magistrate's Court does not decide sensational high crimes like espionage, treason, or political corruption, nor even rape, arson, or murder. As a result of their *gravitas,* such cases are destined for higher courts. Those "big" cases qualify for front-page coverage in the newspaper because editors see them as historic turning points for society, recognize their entertainment value as sensational news, and may even appreciate their educational value as morality plays. Galvanizing cases of that calibre give rise to movies and books. Bracebridge had its share of topside crimes such as murder, financial scandal, arson, and breach of public office. But those full-blown, Shakespearian-like productions were grand affairs compared to the low-life procession enacting its skits across the small stage of Magistrate's Court.

Pressure to "obey the law" arises, in part, from the force for social conformity exerted by those controlling the legislature, municipal councils, police, and courts. Law-abiding citizens play a big role, too. Once a particular value becomes enshrined in law, public institutions uphold and enforce it, or attempt to, even against individuals who do not share the general consensus. For an individual who does not "fit in," the rule of law and its expected norms of conformity in behaviour can feel like a prison, whether or not he or she is actually incarcerated.

For a free and democratic society to enjoy civic equality, to rationally resolve conflict through the rule of law, and to impose predominant public virtues, even the seemingly peripheral Magistrate's Court is as central a forum as the floor of the legislature. It is here that non-conformity must be dealt with, social and economic chaos tempered. Here "the rule of law" becomes the anvil of a working democracy, as blacksmiths of justice hammer errant lives into the desired shape, absorbing the heat as sparks fly.

Sometimes the accused individuals who embody an independent spirit can be re-molded into reassuring compliance. Other times they resist such pressure and do not bend. Usually, it is not even as simple as that. In all cases, however, this effort to dispense "justice" by fitting human behaviour together with the law requires wise discernment on the part of a magistrate. One reason is that rebellion against the established order may be more the product of human emotion than criminal intent, and we give greater leeway to crimes of passion and the ineluctable instincts that propel them than we do to premeditated acts of crime. Another reason is that the rebel may be a reformer.

Front-line justices of the peace do not so much "apply" the rule of law, as if it were some pre-existing pattern, as knit justice together from whatever strands appear before them, different each time in every case. How the JP does this carries implications beyond the fate of those on trial because each case emerges from and reflects Canada's larger society. Magistrate's Court is, as a result, an important place for *all* citizens, not just for those facing charges.

Historian Donald Creighton understood history as "the interaction of character and circumstance," but these 1890s cases from Bracebridge Magistrate's Court on their own give neither character portraits nor allow sustained analysis of their social or economic circumstances. There are just the details, lots and lots of details.

Information about the shadowy lives of many of these Muskokans in Magistrate's Court in 1890s Bracebridge is little known, although some of the surnames continue to be carried by families into the present. The names of some accused, and the places they lived, are distinctive enough to cause one to make the ancestral connection, but it should not be surprising that more than a century later some who lacked even a proper grave-marker in their day should be utterly unknown now. Even one or two JPs who sat with James Boyer in judgment on these people have faded into oblivion: no photo exists, no obituary survives; nothing more than minor facts in census reports and death records.

Yet, taken as a composite, these cases do show how men, women, and youngsters in the late 1800s were more than the stiff people whose stultified expressions and studied poses formally face us from darkly framed photographs against wallpapered walls, staring at the camera about to explode its puff of gunpowder light with the same apprehensive sombreness one might display looking at the rifles of a firing squad. In posing for a photograph, Hannah Boyer chose, for instance, to dress so formally as to be almost comedic, making no effort to capture the vivacious and determined woman she was, or certainly had been in younger years; instead, presenting herself in a portrait of studied respectability and outward stiffness typical of Victorian times. Who knew that her forced effort to look the part expected by polite society masked her secret that she had never married her "husband," who now occupied a pivotal position in the community maintaining governmental order and the rule of law? Although everyone's ancestors of that era are long since reduced to limp dust, with perhaps only photographs remaining to hint at who they were, today we may at least rediscover something of their passions and plights, and glimpse some essentials about the character and circumstance of a few of them, through Magistrate Boyer carefully recorded evidence when they appeared before him.

To be sure, *Raw Life* is not "local history," in the sense it is untypical of the genre that charts the beneficent deeds of steadfast congregations in the many churches of our country's small towns, the erstwhile municipal councils who governed them, or the sports teams that brought home glory by winning regional and provincial championships. Local history texts, if tempted in the direction of grim exposé, often undergo some censorship because writers portraying their community prefer to "put the best foot forward," especially if writing municipally commissioned books for milestone anniversaries, the genesis of much local history writing. Some writers, even if independently creating books on their own, may feel constrained to present the past through rose-coloured lenses. George W. Boyer, James and Hannah's son, writing *Early Days in Muskoka*, which covers the same period as this book, discreetly cut stories that revealed much about earlier conditions but which, he charitably intoned in 1969 as he and I corrected the page proofs together, "might upset some descendants of those families still living in the district." Civic pride and Chamber of Commerce boosterism not only propel a town to greater heights, but can also engineer a four-lane bypass around "unpleasantness best forgotten."

The quest to uphold virtue, aspire to noble purposes, and lead the good life in peaceful relationship with others need not lead one to be sanctimonious about the adventure nor selective in viewing reality. Even so, many accounts record the lives of businessmen and farmers who succeeded, in preference to cataloguing the plight of those who failed. They chronicle events with the same spirit that triumphantly notes the winning hockey teams' pennants displayed in the local arena, but ignores the years of their losses, a community's shame only silently hinted at by missing pennants. The instinct to celebrate heroic accomplishment inspires a stone cenotaph in the centre of town with chiselled names to honour soldiers dead from war, though no counterpart list publicly displays the names of local boys who conscientiously refused to fight in Britain's foreign wars, or who, if they did, spent the rest of their lives as human wrecks in the veterans' wing of Toronto's Sunnybrook Hospital or similar institutions.

Selective histories and the hubris of ungrounded optimism contribute to a frame of mind that denies reality. Stories that are real become eclipsed or eradicated altogether from history. People whose attention is directed only to the stars will miss what is happening in the streets.

High-minded interest in history's larger currents can sometimes even lead to dismissing the minor human details and the trivial nature of commonplace lives, as indeed, the small change of the justice system. In such a larger view, events central to a poor Bracebridge man whose unpaid wages or unfaithful wife had set him on a destructive course, are seen as marginal. Episodes now appearing safely on the printed pages of this book are a sanitary distance from the awkward, smelly, loud, rough encounters with ill-fitting individuals whose behaviour, if it were in the here and now, might instinctively cause one to hurriedly cross to safety on the other side of the street.

History may be led by the "greats," but where the story resides is in the lives and events of ordinary people. This insight has caused a shift over the last forty years in the approach to writing history. Canada's principal traditional themes of constitutional and political history have been upstaged by accounts of social history and personal experience. The plight of minority groups has been given as much prominence as the performance of majority governments. Writers of engaging Canadian history have emerged as much from our nation's newsrooms as from campus cloisters, presenting dramas about what made us who we are, and doing so in accessibly written and compelling narratives of human choices and individual consequences, connecting us *emotionally* to those who went before by bringing *their experience* to life. In recent decades many older Canadians have discovered that our history is not "dull," and lament, "I sure wish history was presented like this when I was in school."

This more humanistic approach taps a deeper thirst, or at least stronger human interest, by rendering our national story to more closely portray life as people really live it. Over a decade ago, television producer Mark Starowicz, in the popular CBC series *Canada: A People's History,* helped Canadians see, hear, and feel the country's story. The series, Starowicz explained, not only described "the great and the famous, apparently in control of their destinies," but equally portrayed the dramatic narratives of "the people who bobbed like corks in the great seas of history, in control of very little." Of course the risk is that so-called "people's history" inverts traditional history telling by excluding a grand thesis, or even a context, for the stories. Patrick Watson, an even more renowned CBC television producer and on-air personality, criticized Starowicz's television series, and the book based on it, for failing to give "the people" a version of the past that was not just impressive, but *comprehensible*. Despite the use of prominent scholarly consultants for the CBC's big-budget project, contended Watson, the series failed to provide any grounding context, or even maps, into which someone could sensibly place the colourful string of daring and shocking developments as experienced by the individual "bobbing corks" in their times.

When academically trained scholars pore through the archives, even when social historians or criminologists have genuine interest in society's underclass, the authentic story could still escape, for the most elementary reason that many people whose brief episodes give glimpses into conditions of their era did not write letters or diaries. They left neither record nor remnant for latter-day scholars to sift and synthesize into a report for wider audiences. As Edward Greenspan touchingly points out, the surviving accounts of these cases kept by Magistrate James Boyer "may be the only remaining written record of the participants' very existence."

Sometimes the thread connecting back to such people is so slender that only the most diligent of curious persons can hope to discern it.

When social worker Phyllis Harrison, working in Ottawa as an information officer for the Children's Aid Society in 1968, first came across references in their files to "home children," she was puzzled. The experiences of these thousands of British orphans, gathered up from the slums of East London and Liverpool and transported as child workers to Canada, was still an untold story. Harrison spent the next ten years tracing it, placing an advertisement of inquiry in forty Canadian newspapers as well as *Legion* magazine. When she began getting response letters in 1969 and 1970, it was clear that for many this was the very first time anyone had even asked, "What was it like to be a 'home child' in Canada?"

A Muskoka farmer and team of plough-horses prepare for spring planting. The lad just behind the horses is perhaps one of the "Barnardo Boys," brought as indentured labourers to Muskoka's remote farms from the 1870s until the 1930s under a generally unsupervised resettlement program to clear Britain's slums and orphanages of impoverished children. Muskoka received the highest number of any place in Canada.

Harrison's effort to document the story produced hundreds of unvarnished letters from many "home children," then in the final years of their lives, and led to publication in 1979 of *The Home Children: Their Personal Stories.* This now-popular record of Canadian social history only exists today because of one woman's intelligent curiosity and persistence. Her efforts uniquely preserved a remarkable saga in British and Canadian history that was about to slip into silent oblivion, an inappropriate fate for a huge program that, from 1870 to 1930, sponged up more than one hundred thousand orphans from England's slums and wrung most out over the empty farmlands of Canada, especially the township farms of Muskoka.

The next year, in 1980, Kenneth Bagnell wrote a further account about this "untold odyssey" in *The Little Immigrants.* In 1997, two British authors returned to update the account in *The Empire's Lost Children,* describing this practice of solving English problems by exporting them to the colonies as "the untold tale." A dozen other books have appeared since. In 2010, Britain's Prime Minister Gordon Brown formally apologized, on behalf of the government, to descendants of the families. In 2011, Ontario's legislature passed a resolution to acknowledge the reality of the province's home children.

Recovering people's place in history also requires what University of Toronto history professor Carl Berger described in 1976 as "a self-conscious effort to establish the meaning of experience for the present."

Berger believed the writing of history is not only "subtly and unpredictably coloured by the milieu in which the historian lives," but "reveals a good deal about the intellectual climate in which it was composed." Berger thus attempted "to extricate himself to some extent from the body of literature from which he had learned about the past, and to see it with the same detachment he would bring to an analysis of the transactions of a remote age."

So, in getting at the historic record and gaining a sense of our past, we face a tall order. We must traverse the intellectual framework in which an earlier storyteller approached the subject, overcome the absence of material to work with, resolve uncertainty about the proper subject matter of an historic account, and settle disagreements over what perspective its author should take.

In extricating ourselves from the literate and literal interpretation of our history, in order to see it more clearly and dispassionately, it can help to directly encounter the record itself. A number of valuable books consist of reprints of early documents, and poring over them is as different as reading scripture instead of commentaries by others on the scriptures, or as seeing one of Shakespeare's plays performed instead of reading scholarly books interpreting that play. Rather than selective passages and interpretive layers of meaning that scholars bequeath us, we can achieve that "detachment he would bring to an analysis of the transactions of a remote age," in Berger's phrase, just by getting a direct dose of unvarnished reality as it was explicitly written down at the time.

By short-circuiting "the intellectual setting" of others and facilitating one's own "self-conscious effort to establish the meaning of experience for the present," to again employ Berger's formulation, Part II of *Raw Life* has presented the sort of thing historians encounter when they pore over original documents in the archives.

Not by abstract reasoning, but by seeing directly how the good, the bad, and the unfortunate are invariably interwoven aspects of the same thing, this book offers that unmediated version for "an analysis of the transactions of a remote age." Because these cases authentically get closer to the human pulse than abstract histories or distilled accounts, they offer a rare look at local conditions and the rawness of individual lives in the nineteenth century's final decade.

In doing so, this lowly Magistrate's Court record from 1890s Bracebridge provides more than a catalogue of grievances. It also gives the news about a town's character and people's challenges in that era. James Boyer's bench book, an emotionally moving record of humanity's struggles, reveals, one episode at a time, that these are not "local" stories so much as renditions of universal experience come to ground in a particular place and time; not the substance of great history, but its telling particulars.

Through the perfect drama of imperfect lives, we can see more sharply a time and place in our country's past. To appreciate light, after all, we need shadow. The accomplishments of well-known actors in a community's principal dramas at centre stage are thrown into sharper relief by the bit-part players who acted at the outer edges of society where they encountered "the justice system," or, more prosaically, the town constable and the justice of the peace. How much greater the good works of the valiant appear, after all, when set starkly in the arid fields where they toiled.

ACKNOWLEDGEMENTS

Peter N. Oliver, historian, author, and editor-in-chief of The Osgoode Society for Legal History, offered advice and research tips about this book. We'd shared work on the Ontario Oral History Project when I was a law student. We'd shared with Roy McMurtry when he was Ontario's attorney general the start of the Osgoode Society. We'd shared teaching his class in Ontario history at York University once illness prevented Peter from continuing. Publication of this book is yet another enduring legacy of Peter Oliver's most worthy and all-too-brief life.

The Osgoode Society itself voted three thousand dollars toward the costs of transcribing the five hundred handwritten pages my great-grandfather James Boyer recorded of his 1890s cases in Bracebridge Magistrate's Court. Juliette M. Cooper then deployed some of her many talents in transposing his pen-and-ink technology from the nineteenth century into contemporary, electronically formatted text.

Johnson Billingsley, great-great-grandson of James Isaac Boyer, pursued the evidentiary trail of our ancestor with the resourceful patience and persistence that made him a successful trial lawyer in Alberta before he took early retirement to devote even more time to the well-being of his family. His researches, culminating in a thick, three-ring binder with forty-one tabs of records on Isaac Jelfs, James Boyer, and Hannah Boyer, their origins, travels, abodes, ancestors, siblings, descendants, land holdings, census data, vital statistics records, published accounts, letters, certificates, grave locations, offices held, and organizations joined, outdo even the ardent researches of other family members who have tried to understand the mystery of James Boyer. Johnson, my nephew and friend, has been a leader and a partner in this detective work. Others on the case included my sisters Victoria Billingsley and Alison Boyer, niece Martha Billingsley, and cousins Keitha Boyer and Beth Rimmer. The fuller story of how Isaac Jelfs became James Boyer, entwined with his love for Hannah Boyer and his many other adventures, will be published separately in a book entitled *Another Country, Another Life.*

Behind the publication of *Raw Life* stands my longstanding friendship with Kirk Howard, president and publisher of Dundurn, whose four decades of success in the challenging world of Canadian book publishing bear testimony to his determination that Canadians know more about our country. I am likewise grateful to Dundurn's vice-president, Beth Bruder; associate publisher and editorial director, Michael Carroll; editor and friend Dominic Farrell, with whom I've worked closely on this book and many others; and director of design and production, Jennifer Scott.

Two leaders in the Canadian and international legal community dedicated to justice, Honourable R. Roy McMurtry and Edward L. Greenspan, pored over these cases from the annals of our country's earlier justice system, then graced this book with their insights and evaluations in, respectively, a message to readers and a foreword. I thank both men for their resilient friendship and support over the years.

I am grateful to two Muskoka men: Honourable D.C. Thomas, an esteemed Muskoka District judge, who provided encouraging words about this book; and Kenneth Veitch, who, like James Boyer, was a long-serving clerk of the Town of Bracebridge, and who assisted with information about the town's early jails. Douglas W. Jemmett, Ontario land surveyor in Bracebridge, volunteered valuable research and maps of Macaulay Township to pinpoint the free-grant Muskoka lots claimed in the 1890s by James Boyer.

A friend since law school days together, Honourable Randall Scott Echlin, judge of the Superior Court of Justice (Ontario) and exceptional baseball enthusiast, kept urging me to finish this book. He'd read it in draft and even wrote these words to be published with it as an endorsement:

> Patrick Boyer's latest "labour of love" gives real insights into the role of magistrates in nineteenth-century Ontario. Another bonus, the book is a rich source document: I found *Raw Life* truly useful when researching early Ontario employment law. In creating this unique opportunity to browse through a magistrate's rare 1890s "bench book" of the cases he tried, Boyer also makes an important contribution to understanding society and justice — and just how little some things have changed over the decades!

A man of irrepressible good cheer, Randy believed this book could be like a baseball diamond in a cornfield; if he blurbed it, I would write. Had I got it done before August 2011, he would have seen it in his lifetime.

ABOUT THE AUTHOR

J. Patrick Boyer, Q.C., holds a master's degree in Canadian history from the University of Toronto, a doctor of laws degree from the same university's Faculty of Law, and an honours degree in economics and political science from Carleton University. He studied French-Canadian literature at Université de Montréal, has a diploma in international law from the Academy of the International Court of Justice in The Hague, and an honorary doctorate from the University of Ottawa granted in recognition of his contributions to democratic development in Canada and abroad.

Boyer has worked as a print journalist in Ontario, Saskatchewan, and Quebec; has written regular newspaper columns, hosted television shows; and as a member of the Writers' Union of Canada served on its National Council. *Raw Life* is his twentieth book. His other titles in the legal field include *A Passion for Justice*, a biography of Canada's legendary law reformer James C. McRuer; a comprehensive six-volume work on Canadian election law; and *Boyer's Ontario Election Law.*

Before election to the House of Commons in 1984, Boyer was a partner of the Toronto law firm Fraser & Beatty, today's Fraser Milner Casgrain LLP. Active in both the Ontario and Northwest Territories bars, he dealt nationwide with communications law, land claims issues, and electoral law matters.

As MP for Etobicoke-Lakeshore, he chaired parliamentary committees on equality rights, the status of disabled persons, and electoral reform. Boyer sponsored a private member's bill, the *Canada Referendum and Plebiscite Act*, that paved the way for the government's national referendum on the Charlottetown Accord constitutional amendments in 1992. Boyer was parliamentary secretary for External Affairs, and later for National Defence, through the tumultuous end of the Cold War, the fall of apartheid in South Africa, and the first Gulf War with Iraq.

On faculty at the University of Guelph, Boyer taught courses on democracy, leadership, accountability, and political ethics. He has also taught Canadian constitutional law, democratic law, and Ontario history at Wilfrid Laurier University, the University of Toronto, and York University. He has worked overseas in democratic development projects in Thailand, Cambodia, Vietnam, Bulgaria, Ukraine, and Iraq.

Boyer's continuing deep interest in his native Muskoka is reflected today in frequent articles and speeches about the district's history, his role as president of Muskoka Books, and his membership in Muskoka Heritage Foundation. He lives in Muskoka and Toronto.

BIBLIOGRAPHY

Aitchison, James H. "The Development of Local Government in Upper Canada, 1783–1850." Ph.D. dissertation, University of Toronto, 1953.

Armstrong, Frederick H. "The Oligarchy of the Western District of Upper Canada 1788–1841." *Historical Papers* 12(1) (1977): 86–102.

____. *Upper Canada Justices of the Peace and Association: 1788–1841*. Toronto, ON: Ontario Genealogical Society, 2007.

Armstrong, F.H., H.A. Stevenson, and J.D. Wilson, eds. *Aspects of Nineteenth-Century Ontario: Essays Presented to James J. Talman*. Toronto, ON: University of Toronto Press, in association with the University of Western Ontario, 1974.

Banks, Margaret A. "Evolution of the Ontario Courts, 1788–1981." In *Essays in the History of Canadian Law*, vol. 2., edited by David H. Flaherty. Toronto, ON: Osgoode Society, 1983.

Berger, Benjamin L., Hamar Foster, and A.R. Buck. "Does Law Matter? The New Colonial Legal History." In *The Grand Experiment: Law and Legal Culture in British Settler Societies*, edited by Hamar Foster, A.R. Buck, and Benjamin L. Berger. Toronto and Vancouver: The Osgoode Society and UBC Press, 2008.

Berger, Carl. *The Writing of Canadian History: Aspects of English-Canadian Historical Writing, 1900–1970.* Toronto, ON: Oxford University Press, 1976.

Bettmann, Otto L. *The Good Old Days — They Were Terrible!* New York: Random House, 1974.

Boyer, George W. *Early Days in Muskoka.* Bracebridge, ON: Herald-Gazette Press, 1970.

Boyer, Henry. Diary, 1868–1933. Boyer Family Archives, Bracebridge.

Boyer, J. Patrick. *A Passion for Justice: How "Vinegar Jim" McRuer Became Canada's Greatest Law Reformer.* Toronto, ON: Blue Butterfly Books, 2008.

_____. *Local Library, Global Passport: The Evolution of a Carnegie Library.* Toronto, ON: Blue Butterfly Books, 2008.

Boyer, Robert J. *Early Exploration and Surveying of Muskoka District.* Bracebridge, ON: Herald-Gazette Press, 1979.

_____. *A Good Town Grew Here: The Story of Bracebridge.* 2nd ed. Bracebridge, ON: Oxbow Press, 2002.

Brown, Desmond H. *The Genesis of the Canadian Criminal Code of 1892.* Toronto, ON: University of Toronto Press for the Osgoode Society, 1989.

Careless, J.M.S. *The Union of the Canadas: The Growth of Canadian Institutions, 1841–1857.* Toronto, ON: McClelland & Stewart, 1967.

Clarence Smith, J.A., and Jean Kerby. General Introduction to *Private Law in Canada: A Comparative Study.* Ottawa, ON: University of Ottawa Press, 1975.

Clarke, John. *Land, Power, and Economics on the Frontier of Upper Canada.* Carleton Library Series. Montreal, QC: McGill-Queen's University Press, 2001.

Cotton, Larry D. *Whiskey and Wickedness, Volume 3: Muskoka and Parry Sound Districts, Ontario, 1850 to 1900.* Barrie, ON: Larry D. Cotton Associates, 2004.

Craig, Gerald M. *Upper Canada: The Formative Years, 1784–1841.* Canadian Centenary Series. Toronto, ON: McClelland & Stewart, 1963.

De Brou, Dave, and Bill Waiser, eds. *Documenting Canada: A History of Modern Canada in Documents.* Saskatoon, SK: Fifth House, 1992.

de la Fosse, Frederick. *English Bloods: In the Backwoods of Muskoka, 1878.* Ed. Scott D. Shipman. Toronto, ON: Dundurn Press, 2004.

Denison, George T. *Recollections of a Police Magistrate.* Toronto, ON: Mussen Book Company, 1920.

Denniss, Gary. *Macaulay Township in Days Gone By.* Bracebridge, ON: Herald-Gazette Press, 1970.

Echlin, Randall Scott. "From Master and Servant to *Bardal* and Beyond: 200 Years of Employment Law in Ontario, 1807 to 2007." In *Special Lectures 2007: Employment Law,* edited by Randall Scott Echlin and Chris G. Paliare. Toronto, ON: Law Society of Upper Canada, 2007.

Flaherty, David H. ed. *Essays in the History of Canadian Law.* Vol. 1. Toronto, ON: University of Toronto for the Osgoode Society, 1983.

Foster, Hamar, Benjamin L. Berger, and A.R. Buck, eds. *The Grand Experiment: Law and Legal Culture in British Settler Societies*. Toronto and Vancouver: The Osgoode Society and UBC Press, 2008.

Francis, R. Douglas, and Donald B. Smith. *Readings in Canadian History, Post-Confederation*. Toronto, ON: Harcourt Brace & Company, 1994.

Fyson, Donald. *Magistrates, Police, and People: Everyday Criminal Justice in Quebec and Lower Canada, 1764–1837*. Toronto, ON: University of Toronto Press for the Osgoode Society, 2006.

Glazebrook, G.P. de T. *Life in Ontario: A Social History*. Toronto, ON: University of Toronto Press, 1968.

Greenspan, Edward L., and Marc Rosenburg. *Martin's Annual Criminal Code*. Aurora, ON: Canada Law Book, annual.

Hamilton, W.E. *Guide Book and Atlas of Muskoka and Parry Sound Districts, 1879*. Toronto, ON: H.R. Page & Co., 1879. Limited edition offset reprint. Ed. Ross Cumming. Port Elgin, ON: Richardson, Bond & Wright Ltd., 1971.

"James Boyer." In *The Canadian album: men of Canada; or Success by example, in religion, patriotism, business, law, medicine, education and agriculture; containing portraits of some of Canada's chief business men, statesmen, farmers, men of the learned professions, and others; also, an authentic sketch of their lives; object lessons for the present generation and examples to posterity*. 5 vols. Edited by William Cochrane. Bradford, ON: Bradley, Garretson & Co., 1891, V:348.

Johnson, George H. *Port Sydney Past*. Cheltenham, ON: Boston Mills Press, 1980.

Keele, W.C. *The Provincial Justice, or Magistrate's Manual, Being a Complete Digest of the Criminal Law of Canada, and a Compendious and General View of the Provincial Law of Upper Canada: with Practical Forms, for the Use of the Magistracy*. 2nd ed. Toronto, ON: H. & W. Rowsell, King Street, 1843.

Lewthwaite, Susan. "Law and Authority in Upper Canada: The Justices of the Peace in the Newcastle District, 1805–1840." Ph.D. dissertation, University of Toronto, 2001.

Loukidelis, S.D. "Some Aspects of the Development of the County Courts of Ontario and the Evolution of the Office of County Court Judge, 1792–1881." Master's thesis, Laurentian University, 1978.

MacRae, Marion, and Anthony Adamson. *Cornerstones of Order: Courthouses and Town Halls of Ontario, 1784–1914*. Toronto, ON: Clarke Irwin for the Osgoode Society, 1983.

McEwen, Ann Alexandra. "Crime in the Niagara District, 1827–1850." Master's thesis, University of Guelph, 1991.

McRuer, James C. *Royal Commission Inquiry into Civil Rights*. Toronto, ON: Queen's Printer, 1968.

Murray, David. *Colonial Justice: Justice, Morality and Crime in the Niagara District,*

1791–1849. Toronto, ON: Osgoode Society, 2002.

Murray, Florence B. *Muskoka and Haliburton, 1615–1875: A Collection of Documents.* Toronto, ON: The Champlain Society, 1963.

Neatby, Hilda. *The Administration of Justice Under the Quebec Act.* Minneapolis, MN: University of Minnesota Press, 1937.

Oliver, Peter N. "The Place of the Judiciary in the Historiography of Upper Canada." In *Essays in the History of Canadian Law in Honour of R.C.B. Risk*, edited by G. Blaine Baker and Jim Phillips, 443–468. Toronto, ON: University of Toronto Press for the Osgoode Society, 1999.

Osborne, Bertram. *Justices of the Peace 1361–1848: A History of the Justices of the Peace for the Counties of England.* Dorset, UK: Sedgehill Press, 1960.

Philips, David. "The Black County Magistracy 1835–60: A Changing Elite and the Exercise of Its Power." *Midland History* 3(3) (Spring 1976): 161–190.

Riddell, William Renwick. *The Legal Profession in Upper Canada in Its Early Periods.* Toronto, ON: Law Society of Upper Canada, 1916.

Saywell, John T. "The 1890s." In *The Canadians 1867–1967*, Vol. 1, edited by J.M.S. Careless and R. Craig Brown. Toronto, ON: Macmillan, 1967.

Splane, Richard B. *Social Welfare in Ontario, 1791–1893: A Study of Public Welfare Administration.* Toronto, ON: University of Toronto Press, 1965.

Thomas, Redmond. Bracebridge, Muskoka: *Reminiscences.* Bracebridge, ON: Herald-Gazette Press, 1969.

Waite, P.B. *Canada 1874–1896: Arduous Destiny.* Toronto, ON: McClelland & Stewart, 1971.

Wilson, James K. "The Court of General Quarter Sessions of the Peace: Local Administration in Pre-Municipal Upper Canada." Master's thesis, McMaster University, 1991.

INDEX

MIX
Paper from
responsible sources
FSC® C004071

FSC
www.fsc.org